Racialized Protest and the State

Bringing together leading scholars of social movements and protest, this volume offers an up-to-date overview of several of the key ethnic and racial movements in the contemporary United States. The organizations, strategies, and challenges of the Black Lives movement, mainstream Black organizations, the Mexican-American Dreamer groups, immigrant-rights mobilizations, Arab-American resistance, and White nationalism are all examined by situating them in a rapidly evolving and—in many ways—increasingly unfavorable state context. With empirical studies linked by their dialogue with theories of social movement and protest, and, in particular, recent trends that emphasize the dynamic relations among social movement groups and organizations, *Racialized Protest and the State* also considers the multiciplicity of state players and the roles of hostile civic actors who oppose the movements' challenges. A cutting-edge analysis of an increasingly important dimension of contentious politics in complex and diverse Western societies, this book will appeal to scholars of sociology and politics with interests in social movements, nonviolent resistance, protest campaigns, and ethnic mobilization.

Hank Johnston is Professor of Sociology and Hansen Chair of Peace and Nonviolence Studies at San Diego State University, USA. His recent books include *Social Movements, Nonviolent Resistance, and the State*, *What is a Social Movement?*, and *States and Social Movements*.

Pamela Oliver was the Conway-Bascom Professor of Sociology at the University of Wisconsin-Madison, USA, and is now Professor Emerita of Sociology at the University of Wisconsin-Madison. She is an internationally recognized scholar of social movements and protest, and author of numerous research articles in sociology's leading journals.

The *Mobilization* Series on Social Movements, Protest, and Culture

Series editor: Professor Hank Johnston, San Diego State University, USA.

Published in conjunction with *Mobilization: An International Quarterly*, the premier research journal in the field, this series publishes a broad range of research in social movements, protest and contentious politics. This is a growing field of social science research that spans sociology and political science as well as anthropology, geography, communications and social psychology. Enjoying a broad remit, the series welcome works on the following topics: social movement networks; social movements in the global South; social movements, protest, and culture; personalist politics, such as living environmentalism, guerrilla gardens, anticonsumerist communities, anarchist-punk collectives; and emergent repertoires of contention.

When Citizens Talk About Politics
Edited by Clare Saunders and Bert Klandermans

Social Stratification and Social Movements
Theoretical and Empirical Perspectives on an Ambivalent Relationship
Edited by Sabrina Zajak and Sebastian Haunss

Protesting Gender
The LGBTIQ Movement and its Opponents in Italy
Anna Lavizzari

Nationalist Movements Explained
Comparisons from Canada, Belgium, Spain, and Switzerland
Maurice Pinard

Racialized Protest and the State
Resistance and Repression in a Divided America
Edited by Hank Johnston and Pamela Oliver

For more information about this series, please visit: https://www.routledge.com/The-Mobilization-Series-on-Social-Movements-Protest-and-Culture/book-series/ASHSER1345

Racialized Protest and the State
Resistance and Repression in a Divided America

Edited by
Hank Johnston and Pamela Oliver

LONDON AND NEW YORK

First published 2021
by Routledge
2 Park Square, Milton Park, Abingdon, Oxon OX14 4RN

and by Routledge
605 Third Avenue, New York, NY 10017

First issued in paperback 2022

Routledge is an imprint of the Taylor & Francis Group, an informa business

© 2021 selection and editorial matter, Hank Johnston and Pamela Oliver; individual chapters, the contributors

The right of Hank Johnston and Pamela Oliver to be identified as the authors of the editorial material, and of the authors for their individual chapters, has been asserted in accordance with sections 77 and 78 of the Copyright, Designs and Patents Act 1988.

All rights reserved. No part of this book may be reprinted or reproduced or utilised in any form or by any electronic, mechanical, or other means, now known or hereafter invented, including photocopying and recording, or in any information storage or retrieval system, without permission in writing from the publishers.

Trademark notice: Product or corporate names may be trademarks or registered trademarks, and are used only for identification and explanation without intent to infringe.

Publisher's Note
The publisher has gone to great lengths to ensure the quality of this reprint but points out that some imperfections in the original copies may be apparent.

British Library Cataloguing-in-Publication Data
A catalogue record for this book is available from the British Library

Library of Congress Cataloging-in-Publication Data
Names: Johnston, Hank, 1947- editor. | Oliver, Pamela, editor.
Title: Racialized protest and the state : resistance and repression in a divided America / edited by Hank Johnston and Pamela Oliver.
Other titles: Resistance and repression in a divided America
Description: London, UK ; New York, NY : Routledge/Taylor & Francis Group, 2020. | Series: The mobilization series on social movements, protest, and culture | Includes bibliographical references and index.
Identifiers: LCCN 2020008051 (print) | LCCN 2020008052 (ebook) | ISBN 9780367263539 (hbk) | ISBN 9780429292866 (ebk)
Subjects: LCSH: Minorities--Political activity--United States. | United States--Race relations. | United States--Ethnic relations. | Social movements--United States. | Protest movements--United States. | White nationalism--United States.
Classification: LCC E184.A1 R3237 2020 (print) | LCC E184.A1 (ebook) | DDC 305.800973--dc23
LC record available at https://lccn.loc.gov/2020008051
LC ebook record available at https://lccn.loc.gov/2020008052

ISBN: 978-0-367-51452-5 (pbk)
ISBN: 978-0-367-26353-9 (hbk)
ISBN: 978-0-429-29286-6 (ebk)

DOI: 10.4324/9780429292866

Typeset in Times New Roman
by Taylor & Francis Books

THE HANSEN COLLECTION ON PEACE AND NONVIOLENCE RESEARCH

Racialized Protest and the State is the second title in a special collection that is part of the *Mobilization*-Routledge Book Series on Social Movements, Protest, and Culture. The study of nonviolent strategies for social change is a subfield in the broader study of social movements, protest and contentious politics. Funded by the Hansen Chair for Peace and Nonviolence Studies at the College of Arts and Letters, San Diego State University, this collection aims to contribute to the social science of nonviolent social change and peaceful reform.

The Hansen Collection on Peace and Nonviolence Research

No. 1. *Social Movements, Nonviolent Resistance, and the State*
Hank Johnston, ed.

No. 2. *Racialized Protest and the State: Resistance and Repression in a Divided America*
Hank Johnston and Pamela Oliver, eds.

Contents

List of illustrations   ix
List of contributors   x
Foreword from the series editor   xiii

1 Pacification and resistance in racialized states: a comparative view   1
   HANK JOHNSTON AND PAMELA OLIVER

2 Defensive adaptations: NAACP responses to the U.S. post-racial project 1970–1990   26
   BELINDA ROBNETT

3 Resisting repression: The Black Lives movement in context   63
   PAMELA OLIVER

4 Racist policing, practical resonance, and frame alignment in Ferguson   89
   JOSHUA BLOOM AND ZACHARY DAVID FRAMPTON

5 Active abeyance, political opportunity, and the "new" white supremacy   112
   PETE SIMI AND ROBERT FUTRELL

6 The biographical consequences of repression: Arab Americans in post-9/11 America   140
   WAYNE A. SANTORO AND MARIAN AZAB

7 Localized political contexts: undocumented youth mobilization during hostile times   164
   EDELINA M. BURCIAGA AND LISA M. MARTINEZ

8 Gaining a voice: storytelling and undocumented youth activism in Chicago 186
THOMAS SWERTS

9 Racial, ethnic, and immigration protest during year one of the Trump presidency 208
KENNETH T. ANDREWS, NEAL CAREN AND TODD LU

Index 227

Illustrations

Figures

6.1	Percentage of Arab Americans who report repression two years after 9/11	147
6.2	Number of victims of anti-Islamic hate crimes, 1995 to 2016	148
6.3	The biographical consequences of repression	149
6.4	Comparing the biographical consequences of repression across outcomes	158
9.1	Monthly count of protest events by issue focus, 2017	211

Tables

4.1	Main insurgent and police actions on Canfield Drive in Ferguson, MO, on August 9, 2014	96
6.1	Biographical consequences of repression among Arab Americans after 9/11: bivariate results	154
6.2	Weighted logistic regressions of impact of repression on biographical outcomes among Arab Americans after 9/11	156
8.1	Storytelling as a social movement practice	192
9.1	Regression analysis of cumulative county anti-Trump protests attendance, 2017	220

Contributors

Kenneth T. Andrews is Mason Distinguished Professor and Chair of the Department of Sociology at University of North Carolina, Chapel Hill. His research focuses on the civil rights struggle in the U.S. South and the contemporary environmental movement. He has published numerous widely cited research articles in *American Sociological Review, American Journal of Sociology,* and *Mobilization: An International Quarterly,* among many others. His book *Freedom Is a Constant Struggle* won the CBSM Section Distinguished book award.

Marian Azab is a Ph.D. candidate in Sociology at the University of New Mexico. Her main research interests center on race, gender, repression, and emotions as they apply to political participation among marginalized populations. Her published work has examined how racialization and repression, as well as the emotions they generate, affect differential recruitment into social movement activity among Arab Americans in the post-9/11 era. Her current work investigates how online political networks and patriarchy shaped participation in the 18-day Egyptian uprising of 2011.

Joshua Bloom is Assistant Professor of Sociology at the University of Pittsburgh and winner of the American Book Award. He is principal author (with Waldo Martin) of *Black against Empire: the History and Politics of the Black Panther Party* (University of California Press, 2013), and co-editor of *Working for Justice: the LA Model of Organizing and Advocacy* (Cornell University Press, 2010). His studies of the dynamics of insurgent practice and social transformation have been published in the *American Sociological Review* and other venues.

Edelina M. Burciaga is an Assistant Professor in the Department of Sociology at the University of Colorado, Denver. Her research examines the educational, social, and activist experiences of undocumented young adults. The findings of this research have appeared in *Mobilization: An International Quarterly, Ethnicities, Law and Policy* as well as various edited books and volumes.

Neal Caren is an Associate Professor in Sociology at the University of North Carolina, Chapel Hill. His current research is on contemporary social movements and the uses of media data in the U.S. His research has appeared in journals such as *American Sociological Review, Social Forces, Social Problems*, and the *Annual Review of Sociology*. Currently he serves as the editor of the interdisciplinary social movements journal *Mobilization: An International Quarterly*, the premier journal of research in the field. He is Director of Graduate Studies and Admissions and teaches graduate courses in computational social science, with a focus on collecting and analyzing text data with Python.

Zachary David Frampton received his B.A., with honors, in Sociology at the University of Pittsburgh, where he also won the Avery Award for best undergraduate researcher. He intends to pursue a Ph.D. in the social sciences to further investigate social movements and systems of state organization.

Robert Futrell is Professor and Department Chair of Sociology at University of Nevada, Las Vegas. His primary research specialties include social movements and social change, environmental sociology, and urban sustainability. His current social movement scholarship focuses on the cultural and organizational dynamics of social movement persistence and political extremism.

Hank Johnston is Professor of Sociology and Hansen Chair of Nonviolence and Peace Studies at San Diego State University. His research focuses on nonviolent protests and cultures of resistance in repressive states. He is founding editor of *Mobilization: An International Quarterly*, and edits the *Mobilization* Monograph Series on Protest and Social Movements with Routledge Books. His recent books are *Social Movements, Nonviolent Resistance, and the State* (Routledge, 2019), *What is a Social Movement?* (Polity, 2014), and *States and Social Movements* (Polity, 2012).

Todd Lu is a graduate student in the Ph.D. sociology program at University of North Carolina. His areas of interest are social movements/collective behavior, political sociology, race and ethnicity, mass media, stratification, and inequality.

Lisa M. Martinez is Professor of Sociology at the University of Denver. Her areas of expertise are immigration, racial/ethnic politics, Latina/o sociology, and social inequality. She is currently working on a book manuscript to be published by NYU Press examining the social, economic, and political incorporation of undocumented youth and young adults following the enactment of federal and sub-federal immigration reforms.

Pamela Oliver has recently become Professor Emerita of Sociology at the University of Wisconsin. She is working on an NSF-funded project to compile information on Black protests between the 1990s and the 2010s using electronic archives of Black newspapers and mainstream sources; the project involves an innovative redesign of data collection and storage. She continues to analyze, write, and speak publicly about racial patterns in criminal justice.

xii *List of contributors*

Belinda Robnett is Professor of Sociology at the University of California, Irvine. Her research interests include racial and ethnic inequality, gender relations, political participation, and social movements. Professor Robnett's research has appeared in the *American Journal of Sociology* and *Social Forces*. She is the author of *How Long? How Long? African-American Women in the Struggle for Civil Rights* (Oxford University Press, 1997), and co-editor of *Social Movements: Identity, Culture, and the State* (Oxford University Press, 2002). In 2012 she was awarded with Katherine Tate a National Science Foundation grant to develop a national probability panel survey, *Outlook on Life and Political Engagement*, with an oversampling of African Americans. In 2013–2014 she was a fellow at the Russell Sage Foundation. She is completing her current book, tentatively titled *Surviving Success: Black Political Organizations and the Politics of Post-Racial Illusions*, which examines the NAACP's and Southern Christian Leadership Conference's quest for racial equality and justice in the aftermath of the U.S. civil rights movement.

Wayne A. Santoro is an Associate Professor of Sociology at the University of Maryland. His research interest lies in the intersection of social movements and race. Key lines of work examine the conditions under which governments become responsive to Latino and African American social movements, investigate why racialized populations like Mexican Americans and Arab Americans join protest events, assess processes of institutionalization and radicalization during the decline of the modern civil rights movement, and apply movement scholarship to help understand how city political contexts affect the fate of immigrant and Black neighborhoods. His current work focuses on slave revolts in the antebellum United States.

Pete Simi is an Associate Professor in the Department of Sociology at Chapman University. He has published widely on the issues of political violence, social movements, street gangs, and juvenile delinquency. His co-authored book with Robert Futrell, *American Swastika: Inside the White Power Movement's Hidden Spaces of Hate* (Rowman & Littlefield, 2010), received a 2010 CHOICE Outstanding Academic Book Award.

Thomas Swerts is an Assistant Professor in Sociology at the Department of Public Administration and Sociology of the Faculty of Social Sciences of the Erasmus University Rotterdam. He received his Ph.D. in Sociology from the University of Chicago, where his dissertation comparatively analyzed undocumented activism in Chicago and Brussels. Funded by SSRC, NSF, and the Mellon Foundation, his current research focuses on the dynamics of civil society organizations in deprived neighborhoods. His work has been published in *Mobilization: An International Quarterly* and several edited volumes on citizenship studies, migration politics, and relational poverty politics.

Foreword from the series editor

THE HANSEN COLLECTION ON PEACE AND NONVIOLENCE RESEARCH

This volume is the second in the Hansen Collection of Peace and Nonviolence Research. It is my honor to serve as San Diego State University's Hansen Chair of Peace and Nonviolence Studies and organize this collection. The appointment generously provides resources to address contemporary topics about peace and nonviolent social change—in democracies and non-democracies. Supporting a collection of research monographs on these topics is one way to accomplish that. I am grateful to the Fred J. Hansen Foundation and its trustee, Anton Dimitroff, for the opportunities the Hansen Chair opens. The social science of these themes has been the focus of my scholarship for years, and this second volume in the collection addresses some of the most destabilizing forces to civil peace in the world today: ethnic and racial conflict, the various forms of collective action taken to redress racial and ethnic grievances, and the forces that oppose racial and ethnic justice.

The first volume in the Hansen collection was entitled *Social Movements, Nonviolent Resistance, and the State*. It was published in 2019 by Routledge, the leading academic publisher in the humanities and social sciences. A felicitous partnership has developed between Routledge and *Mobilization: An International Quarterly*, the premier journal of scholarly research on protest, social movements, and contentious politics, published at San Diego State University. Out of that partnership, I have been privileged to edit the *Mobilization*-Routledge Monograph Series on Social Movements and Protest, which now is a decade old, has almost thirty titles in its list, and is where this new Hansen Collection has found a home.[1] I am grateful to the social science editorial team at Routledge for their foresight in providing a base for the collection, and their exceptional professionalism in bringing the first two volumes to fruition. Together, we look forward to offering several more Hansen volumes.

For this second volume, it has been an honor to share the editorial work with Pamela Oliver, Conway-Bascom Professor of Sociology at the University of Wisconsin while we were working on this and now Professor Emerita there. Professor Oliver is a distinguished researcher and award-winning scholar of protest and collective action[2] whose research recently has focused on dimensions of state social control, police and criminal justice-based repression, and its effects on the contentious politics of African-American communities

(Oliver 2008, 2009, 2017). Her chapter in this volume is an excellent example of her approach to these issues and will contribute significantly to contemporary academic and activist discourse about race in the United States.

Professor Oliver brings important and critical perspectives to the study of these topics, and complements in significant ways my own approach, which is more internationally focused and engages the configuration of factors characteristic of autocratic and repressive state regimes. The repression of minority and ethnic rights in non-democracies abroad has broadly shaped my outlook, especially regarding restrictions on cultural expression, civic organization, and discourse. Professor Oliver is also an activist for racial justice in Madison, Wisconsin, which she alludes to in Chapter 3. Her work there complements my own activism in California on immigrant rights and border issues. California is different from Wisconsin, and Mexican-American grievances—as well as those of the Latino population generally—and their relation to U.S. policies and social control agencies are historically and structurally distinct from those of African Americans. Our work together has enriched my own thinking on these topics, and, personally—as in our collaborations in the past—I have learned a lot. I have pursued fieldwork about movements seeking separatist political solutions in autocratic contexts—state regimes where open discussion about race and ethnic differences is constrained and differs from the U.S. Our dialogue develops in the introductory chapter where comparisons with China's closed system and often heavy-handed ethnic-racial, linguistic, and religious policies in minority regions are discussed in the context of ethnic and racial relations the U.S. The comparison enables us to explore the complex and, over time, variable forces of repression and social control by state regimes, their historical legacies and structural patterns, and the extra-institutional forces they control and/or encourage.

By comparing the United States and China in the introduction, we also consider how the construction of ethnicity and race are intertwined with the formation of national states (Johnston 2018; Olzak 2004; Wimmer 2013. The U.S. is a country with different ethnic and racial patterns and logics than China's, and their juxtaposition brings important features of both state regimes into relief. Both are strong high-capacity states that govern large populations that are ethnically and racially diverse. Population patterns differ by proportions, geography, and long-term racial and ethnic histories. China has many ethnic minority groups, but it is fair to say that race is not a compelling concept for most Chinese citizens and does not run through contemporary public discourse there as it does in the U.S.—although Kazakhs and Uyghurs in western regions of China are Turkic peoples, considered Caucasian not Oriental.[3] Tibetan culture differs significantly from the Confucian cultural norms of China, and many Tibetans view the Chinese state as an oppressor rather than liberator.[4] Boundaries between different population groups there are sharpened by histories of geographical isolation, conquest, and cultural and political repression.

Among China's population of 1.4 billion, the majority Han ethnic group constitutes 94% of the total. Diverse and relatively small compared to 1.3-plus billion Han, ethnic minorities in the People's Republic of China add up to approximately 84,000,000 citizens. In the U.S., 130,000,000 non-European-heritage citizens make up about 38% of the population today. By 2045, non-Whites in the U.S. will be a 51% majority. Laws of both states call for equal treatment of all citizens, regardless of racial and ethnic background while recognizing differences. But especially relevant to this volume is that China and the U.S. treat protest mobilization and civil society organization by, and open discourse among, ethnic-racial communities in different ways. Indeed, in Tibetan and Uyghur regions, it is fair to say that separate identities and deep ethnic grievances are perceived as threats to the territorial integrity of China, and the state broaches no challenges to existing political structures, characteristic of the internal colonial template of ethno-national subordination. We argue that dominant racial-ethnic logics of states in their formation affect the ways states both incorporate and control populations, and how minority populations react.[5]

The chapters that follow the introductory essay weave the common thread of the complexity of state contexts in the fabric of their arguments. The volume presents chapters of original and engaging research by leading scholars, such as Belinda Robnett, Kenneth Andrews, Neal Caren, Peter Simi, Robert Futrell, and Wayne Santoro, just to name a few of the most distinguished senior contributors. Nonviolent movements face not only the violent and (more subtle) nonviolent social control actions of the state, but also violent and nonviolent opposition from other groups. In racialized contexts, it is incumbent on social scientists not only to "bring the state back in" but also to consider the complex array of counter forces opposing racial and ethnic justice in democracies. A key goal of assembling these chapters is to examine collective action and responses to Black and Brown populations—concretely, African Americans, Latino Americans, and Arab Americans, who, in the current political context of Trumpism and resurgent White nationalism, are three populations whose choice is compelling. In the background, the social scientist encounters the question: how and why can minority populations remain nonviolent in the face of threats and violence against them? In a state regime that claims democratic principles, how can we come to terms with it all? To ponder these questions is part of the intention of this volume of research.

In general, the story this collection tells is of activists involved in the cascade of protest and resistance that draw on past mobilizations and seek to innovate new and proactive strategies for change. The other side of the narrative is that of the state and its various players. With a diversity of stratagems, deep resources, and privileged positions of offense and defense, state opposition exerts strong demobilization pressures on movements, and elicits assistance from allies such as majority counter-movements and their agents, legal and extralegal. This book seeks to place these cascading events in the context of social movement and ethnic mobilization research

Reactions against a Black president, the Black Lives movement, and immigrant-rights movements contributed to the unexpected election of Donald Trump as president in 2016. His victory cheered and emboldened White supremacists, leading them to be more public and overt. Trump's victory and his administration's actions to ramp up anti-immigrant policies led to a huge wave of protests. Marches and demonstrations began the day after the election in many cities, often mobilized by groups that had been protesting around Black Lives and immigrant rights. A huge women's march and spin-off protests and marches were organized around Trump's inauguration. The final chapter in this collection finds that 12% of these protests were immigration related and 12% race related. Key peaks of mobilization were the Muslim travel ban in January 2017 and the Unite the Right rally in Charlottesville August 2017.

The chapters in this collection chronicle the ongoing struggles between the majority and minorities in the U.S. One major difference between the U.S. and China lies in how ethnic and racial groups can organize and how their protests occur legally—growing at times to be quite large—something that does not take place in China. Another major difference is how spaces for the organization of civil society in the U.S. lead to engagement with the state and with counter-movements on racial-ethnic issues, while in China civil society space is highly constrained, and there are few forums where the authentic grievances of its minorities can be voiced. Civil society groups and social movement organizations are the mobilizing structures for a vibrant and contentious racial politics in the U.S., but not in China, where collective action tends to take "smaller," less obtrusive, often symbolic weapons-of-the-weak forms of resistance.

A final difference, especially relevant to the chapters in this volume, is the changing racial-ethnic portrait of the U.S.—not something that threatens the Han majority in contemporary China—but a social force that lies behind many recent events in the U.S. The revitalization of White nationalism chronicled by Simi and Futrell's chapter, the protests and resistance analyzed in the other chapters, the increasing occurrence of hate crimes in recent years, and the rise of Trump are all directly linked with anxiety among many Whites over loss of dominance and the shift in power driven by demographics. The list goes on: the lie of birtherism, which gave Trump his initial political traction, the Muslim ban, separating children at the U.S.–Mexican border, rejections of asylum seekers, and even assaults on *Roe v. Wade* reflect racial dimensions. The research studies in this volume are up-to-date chronicles of how social science looks at these the ongoing struggles as we look with trepidation to what lies in the future, both in the U.S. and globally.

Hank Johnston

Notes

1 The *Mobilization* book series was inaugurated by Ashgate Publishing with Johnston (2009), and was acquired by Routledge several years ago. The Hansen series was inaugurated more recently (Johnston 2019).

2 Professor Pamela Oliver received the John McCarthy Award for Career Contributions to the Study of Social Movements in 2014. Her McCarthy lecture presents a good summarization of her research and normative perspectives on racial politics and protest (Oliver 2017).
3 These racial categories are legacies of Western colonialism and racial logics of the past. Insofar as they continue to give political meaning, they remain relevant for the analysis of ethnic and racial conflict.
4 The People's Republic of China occupied Tibet in 1950. There was an uprising against Chinese rule in 1959, at which time the semiautonomous government of Dalai Lama fled into exile. He claims over one million Tibetans have died because of Chinese occupation and rule.
5 The Chinese state has recently instituted programs to stamp out Uighur identity, fueled by fears of Islamic extremism and separatism. In Xinjian Provence, religious Uighurs are detained in walled camps—called "job training centers" by the government. They are subjected to programs of indoctrination, forced to renounce their religious beliefs, study Chinese, pledge loyalty to the party, and sing patriotic songs.

References

Johnston, Hank. 2009. *Culture, Social Movements, and Protest*. Farnham: Ashgate.

Johnston, Hank. 2018. "Nationalism, Nationalist Movements, and Social Movement Theory" Pp. 635–650 in *The Wiley-Blackwell Companion to Social Movements*. New York: Wiley-Blackwell.

Johnston, Hank. 2019. *Social Movements, Nonviolent Protest, and the State*. New York: Routledge.

Oliver, Pamela. 2008. "Repression and Crime Control: Why Social Movement Scholars Should Pay Attention to Mass Incarceration as a Form of Repression." *Mobilization: An International Quarterly* 13(1): 1–24.

Oliver, Pamela. 2009. "Talking About Racial Disparities in Imprisonment: A Reflection on Experiences in Wisconsin." Pp. 281–298 in *Handbook of Public Sociology*, edited by Vincent Jeffries. Lanham, MD: Rowman & Littlefield.

Oliver, Pamela. 2017. "The Ethnic Dimensions in Social Movements." *Mobilization: An International Quarterly* 22(4): 395–416. doi:10.17813/1086-671x-22-4-395.

Olzak, Susan. 2004. "Ethnic and Nationalist Social Movements." Pp. 666–693 in *The Blackwell Companion to Social Movements*, edited by D. A. Snow, S. A. Soule, and H. Kriesi. Malden, MA: Blackwell Publishing.

Wimmer, Andreas. 2013. *Ethnic Boundary Making: Institutions, Power, Networks*. New York: Oxford University Press.

1 Pacification and resistance in racialized states

A comparative view

Hank Johnston and Pamela Oliver

In this chapter, we provide the theoretical and conceptual context for understanding the eight chapters that follow. They discuss contemporary racialized movements and protest in the United States by, for, and against African Americans, Latinx Americans, Arab Americans, immigrant Americans, and White nationalist Americans. Most of these chapters began as papers at a conference on race and social movements that was held at San Diego State University on May 6–7, 2018 and funded by the Hansen Charitable Trust for Peace and Nonviolence. A common thread in all the essays is the way that the racial structure of the United States shapes the interaction between movements and states. Nonviolent movements face the violent and nonviolent social control actions of the state, as well as violent and nonviolent resistance from other groups.

Although the empirical studies in this collection are all about the United States, in this chapter we compare the United States and China as we develop our arguments about how the construction of ethnicity and race are intertwined with the formation of states and nations.

Comparing the US with a country with a different ethnic or racial[1] logic brings important features of the US into stark relief. Both the US and China are strong high-capacity states that govern large, ethnically diverse populations. Both formally treat all citizens as equal regardless of ethnicity while recognizing ethnic differences. We argue that the racial or ethnic logic of states in their formation affects the ways they incorporate and control populations. These logics, in turn, affect the standpoints of social movements as they engage the state and each other.

Race, ethnicity, and states

In line with other social scientists, we treat race, ethnicity, and nationality as social constructions that are linked to state formation (Brubaker 2009; Olzak 2004; Saperstein, Penner, and Light 2013; Winant 2000). Empires have long subordinated some regions and cultural groups to the will of dominant regions and cultural groups. The more recent concept of a nation-state holds that state boundaries should coincide with the boundaries of nations, i.e., people with a common culture or language or identity. Nation-states construct a national identity that typically privileges a dominant ethnic group as the nation but do this in widely different ways. In some cases, the state enacts policies of forced linguistic and cultural assimilation to erase group differences, while in other cases the state maintains group boundaries and differences. These processes of state and nation formation in turn sometimes create ethnic groups that are controlled by the state but not necessarily defined as part of the nation (Brubaker 1995; Oliver 2017; Olzak 2004; Wimmer 2008, 2013a, 2013b).

The official history of a state typically omits the historical struggles of minorities to resist domination or skews them in ways to downplay the violence inherent in state creation. State systems can embody bias and prejudice even when official creation myths, sacred founding documents, guiding ideologies, and current laws deny or even prohibit discrimination and bias.

In the face of overwhelming majority power, minorities may assimilate into the majority, if permitted to, or they may resist assimilation or domination by cultivating group identity, nurturing minority community networks, and trying to acquire resources and political power. States respond to minority actions and often directly or indirectly reinforce majority domination in their responses.

States reveal the imprints of their history in present-day ethnic contention. In some states the institutions of governance are the instruments of domination by the majority over other ethnic groups residing within state boundaries. In others, there are built-in governance protections for minorities. Some states are dominated by a powerful minority that has obtained power, typically by military force. Democratic states tend to be dominated by a majority ethnic group, although in post-colonial democratic states there may be an economically dominant minority. The colonial and postcolonial states throughout the Americas, as well as other settler-colonial states in Southern Africa and Australasia, were constructed around European White supremacy, and continue to show these legacies in racial hierarchies, although in distinct ways and different intensities (Bonilla-Silva 1999; Marx 1995, 1996). States often distribute resources along ethnic lines, fostering inequalities that strengthen minority ethnic identities, fester resistance, and sometimes fuel protests (Alonso 1994; Barkey and Parijkh 1991; Enloe 1978, 1981; Loveman 1999).

Critically, states can be formed in ways that juxtapose ethnic or racial groups in hierarchical or hostile relations and can have structures that either lessen or strengthen the boundaries and antagonisms between them. Many countries contain distinct racial or ethnic or religious groups that have a long history of communal conflicts. Other countries contain racial or ethnic or religious groups that have exerted historic domination over other groups and actively resist challenges to that domination. Many countries are experiencing immigration of people of different nationalities and have active nationalist movements seeking to expel or subordinate immigrants. As populations shift, some ethnic or racial groups in democratic nations may contest voting rights of minorities or newcomers as a way of maintaining political dominance.

United States overview

The United States of America was historically constructed as the European White[2] settler nation that forcibly displaced and subordinated the indigenous inhabitants of America. It also forcibly imported African Americans as enslaved laborers and defined them as chattel. Later it conquered and annexed the territory of Northern Mexico and conquered and ruled islands in the Caribbean and Pacific as subordinate colonies. Indigenous American nations were bargained with, enslaved, battled, and gradually defeated beginning in the nearly two hundred years of the colonial period and then accelerating in westward waves after the founding of the (White) United States, culminating in the final Indian Wars of 1870 to 1890. The American Indian population of what became the continental United States declined from an estimated 5 million in 1492 to 600,000 in 1800 to 250,000 by the 1890s (Thornton 1987).

White European Americans developed an ideology of physical racial difference and inherent cultural superiority around these axes of domination and exclusion which reinforced their belief in White supremacy. The modern national identity of "nation of immigrants" retains the construction of nation as White/European immigrant settlers, even though Americans know that there are people with citizenship rights who are not White. The nation is understood as having begun with the arrival of White settlers in the 1600s. Although often initially met with hostility or prejudice, new groups of European migrants (e.g., Irish, Italians, Slavs) were incorporated into White, while the boundary between White and Black remained strong (Painter 2006, 2010).

The White settlers had a relatively egalitarian ethos among Whites (compared to that in Europe) while simultaneously subordinating or excluding other groups. Whites formed an early democracy, with nearly universal manhood suffrage being adopted by the 1850s, while other racial groups (as well as White women) could not vote. The USA overtly encouraged the migration of Europeans into its territory between 1800 and 1910s, provided an easy pathway to citizenship for White immigrants and even in some cases allowed White non-citizens to vote.

However, Asian immigration was prohibited in a series of laws between 1880 and 1924 and Asian immigrants were permanently barred from citizenship.

In the wake of the Civil War and the abolition of slavery 1861–65, Constitutional amendments guaranteed the rights of citizenship and voting to people of all races, but there was violent White Southern resistance to racial equality, and guarantees of equal rights were effectively overturned by state laws and practices that were supported by federal Supreme Court decisions. In addition to finally defeating the American Indians, the United States also acquired the colonies of Puerto Rico, the Philippines (later granted independence), Hawai'i (later made a state), the Virgin Islands, American Samoa, Guam, the Northern Marianas, and the Marshall Islands (now formally independent in an association with the US). Policies of White supremacy including racial segregation and discrimination, the subordination of American Indians on reservations, and the racial exclusion of Asians via immigration laws and other policies were overt through World War II. These policies were challenged and to some extent altered by the Civil Rights Movement and changes in immigration law in the 1960s that gave primacy to the ideal of colorblind or nonracial policies. These seemingly nonracial policies as they were interpreted and implemented permitted White majority dominance to continue with new ideological justifications (Bonilla-Silva 2002; Bracey 2015; Omi and Winant 1986; see also Robnett's Chapter 2 in this volume).

The United States today is experiencing overt political conflict between those who seek to return to the exclusionary policies of the White supremacist nation and those who embrace a multiracial-multiethnic image of nation, but even those White people who embrace a multicultural and multiracial vision of nation often continue to imagine the "nation of immigrants" in which all people have the same history. In this imaginary, the forcible relocation and enslavement of African people is redefined as immigration, and the US colonies in the Caribbean and Pacific as well as American Indian nations and the annexation of northern Mexico are simply erased.

China overview

China's history is very different. Nearly all Chinese people today are descended from people who were living in China thousands of years ago. The Han majority originated in the Yellow River valley and took over territory through settlement and conquest, incorporating other groups into Han by acculturation and intermarriage, including non-Han conquerors. Han is understood as a civilization that includes people of different phenotypes and regional cultural differences. Some historians argue that the idea of the Han as one ethnicity was itself a social construction of the late 19th century. In the modern People's Republic of China, everyone learns in school that the Chinese nation is made up of 56 ethnic groups, but 92% of the population is Han, over a billion people, and nearly everyone in the core Eastern provinces is Han. Non-Han minorities are more common in the Southern and Western provinces. China's constitution stipulates that minority-ethnic regions should have political autonomy, and that local governance should be in the local tongue. Non-Han minority groups receive special protections or rights as backward people who need assistance; non-Han people experience both pressures to assimilate culturally and take Han names and what are seen in Han areas as advantages in college admissions in the form of extra points on the national college entrance exam. Among Han, there are sharp rural–urban divides maintained by a passport system that ties social benefits to place as well as regional linguistic differences. Written Chinese is one language, but spoken Chinese has mutually unintelligible dialects. The educational system favors Mandarin Chinese, putting those who speak other dialects at some disadvantage.

Although it is centralized and autocratic, the government of the People's Republic of China appears to be broadly legitimate to the Han people. However, the legitimacy of the Chinese government is challenged in the Western autonomous regions of Tibet, where 6 million Tibetans are more than 90% of the population (but only 0.4% of the total Chinese population), and Xinjiang, an ethnically diverse area where Turkic peoples are a majority, including 11 million Uighurs. The modern Chinese government claims these regions based on their forcible incorporation into the Chinese Empire in the Qing dynasty of the 1800s, but both regions resisted incorporation to Han China in the past and there is active resistance to Han Chinese rule in both regions today. These western peripheral Tibetan and Uighur areas were relatively isolated from the Han-Chinese center until recently,[3] so that these areas remained linguistically, culturally, and religiously distinct from the Han majority.

The western region is underdeveloped economically but has important raw materials: Xinjiang has 38% of China's coal reserves and 25% of petroleum and natural gas reserves (Wong 2014). Its economic underdevelopment and Han assumptions of cultural superiority undergird a colonial ideology justifying highly intrusive policies. Han cultural ideology views Uighurs as a backward people in need of education and modernization and Tibetans as simple and superstitious people whose culture needs to be brought into the 21st century by Chinese policies. One argument proffered by the government is that Chinese rule has broken down a barbaric feudal system and brought important everyday benefits and infrastructure to the people, from roads to education. Such views are juxtaposed with a celebration of Tibet's cultural roots, such as folk dancing or singing—much of which, ironically, have been eroded by top-down development (Montefiore 2013). Tibetan, Uighur, and other ethnic-minority cultures are trivialized in song, dance, costumes, and tourist-oriented kitsch performances of smiling ethnics.

In 1950 the Chinese People's Army occupied Tibet, asserting the revolutionary control over a "feudal society" where China had long maintained territorial claims. There was an uprising in 1958 against Chinese occupation, which was brutally defeated. It is estimated that thousands of Tibetans have been killed during military occupations and periods of martial law.[4] A Tibetan government in exile was set up in India by the Dalai Lama in 1959. Most of Tibet's monasteries were destroyed in the 1960s and 1970s during China's Cultural Revolution.

Military action and repression in the provinces of Tibet and Xinjiang increased significantly after violent protests and anti-Chinese rioting in 1988 and 2008 in Tibet, and 2009 in Xinjiang. It is typical that today streets in cities and town in both regions have patrolling squads of the Chinese People's Liberation Army and paramilitary groups. Buddhist monasteries and mosques are monitored, with military units and security personnel stationed on the perimeters (Wong 2009, 2012). Even the traditional festivals and religious celebrations mentioned earlier are accompanied by a military presence (Wong 2015a). Small acts of cultural identification are punished. The local populace is intensely monitored by community and workplace cadre, and outward displays of local traditions (namely, not being sufficiently Chinese) are criminalized, as are outspokenness or misplaced words about ethnic Chinese (Buckley 2018).

Comparing racial construction in China and the United States

The US and China are similar in having an ethnic national identity that overlays an official multi-ethnic or multi-racial definition of nation and similar in the dominant ethnic group seeing itself as culturally superior to others. China's ongoing battle to pacify its western provinces and settle the areas with Han might be compared to the Indian Wars on the US western plains 1870–1890. The western regions of China might also be compared to the southwestern United States, where there are cultural clashes between English-speaking White Anglo-Americans and Mexicans and Central Americans who have indigenous ancestry and speak Spanish. However, they differ in recent immigration patterns. Although people from Central and Southeast Asia migrated to China across its thousands of years of history, in the past two hundred years China has had extensive out-migration and very little in-migration. By contrast, the United States is a nation of (White) immigrants, and immigration policy has been central to its racial construction and maintenance as a White nation. Past immigration policy was explicitly oriented toward maintaining a White nation, as it was in Australia, Canada, and other White settler nations, and fears of loss of racial dominance are central to modern debates about immigration in the US.

China also differs from the United States in not having a large distinctive minority of descendants of enslaved people. Scholars agree that there was chattel slavery in China from ancient times until the modern era, although disagreeing about its extent and structure in different eras (Patterson 1977). Enslaved people in China included people captured in other countries, people forced into slavery for criminal offenses, and people who sold themselves or were sold by family members. Slavery was often hereditary. However, unlike in the US, the state of enslavement was not confined to distinctive ethnic groups and the descendants of slaves do not stand out from the majority. This is in marked contrast to the United States, where people from Africa were captured, enslaved, and forcibly relocated as laborers, a racial definition of eligibility for enslavement was generated during the colonial period, and defining and maintaining boundaries and separation between Blacks and Whites was a central feature of the social organization of the United States through the 1960s, if not still today.

Comparing state capacity in China and the United States

Both the US and China are high-capacity states. China's total internal security budget for 2017 was $197 billion. This does not include money directed at security-related municipal programs and the expanding high-tech network of street cameras and other surveillance systems. One study points out that lower wages in China, especially for local police and the widely disliked municipal security called *chengguan*, give social control agencies there a bigger bang for the buck. Taking purchasing power into consideration, estimates of China's internal spending on social control and security are placed at $349 billion for 2017 (Zenz 2018). The figure for the United States was $165 billion. On a per capita basis, China spends $247.60 per person after adjusting for purchasing power, while the US spends $508.54 per person.

Although allowing localized expressions of grievance about local concerns, China routinely suppresses any dissent that challenges the regime or that threatens to create social turmoil.[5] All Chinese people are subjected to a high level of surveillance and intrusion into daily life through ubiquitous security cameras and *chengguan*, local public order officials that monitor urban areas. Arrest and incarceration of dissenters is common throughout China, and the high level of repression leads to acquiescence. Despite these high expenditures on security and surveillance, most Han Chinese citizens of Shanghai or Guangzhou go about their daily lives without much thought, just like most White Americans living in suburbs. In China, there is overt intrusion into and social control of citizens' daily lives that most White US residents would find shocking. However, White US residents have generally come to accept that private corporations are tracking where they go, what they buy, and even what they say on their phones, and that the US National Security Administration is monitoring all their calls.

The security budgets and consequent surveillance are not evenly distributed across either country. The internal security budget in Xinjiang alone saw a ten-fold growth since 2007 to $8.6 billion in 2017 (Zenz 2018), or about $352.57 per person or, adjusting for purchasing power, the equivalent of $15.2 billion or $624.56 a person, higher even that in the US. We do not have comparable US information about regional variations in expenditures, but the large racial disparities in arrest and imprisonment are important features of the US. There is an extremely high level of overt monitoring and intrusion into the lives of Tibetans in Lhasa and Uighurs in Urumqi and of some low-income Black and Latino areas in the US that involves stopping and detaining people and subjecting them to life-altering punishments.

States differ in their levels of centralization versus decentralization, where decentralization of authority can lead to more points of entry for social movements. The United States has multiple levels of government (federal, state, local) as well as different branches (judicial, legislative, executive) plus a distinction between institutions dominated by elected politicians and those dominated by civil service employees. This leads to frequent instances in which different levels or branches of government support different policies which, in turn, provides different points of entry for minority groups. Chinese government is centralized and hierarchical and controlled by a single party that allows no opposition. Local administrators are allowed relative autonomy and flexibility in addressing conflicts at a local level but are taxed with maintaining order at all costs and punished if they do not do so. Groups seeking reform must never seem to challenge the authority of the Chinese state.

The differences between the US and China in state structures make a difference in the possible checks on social control. In China, the police on the streets of Urumqi are part of a campaign directed from the top of a centralized government and dissent to government rule is suppressed throughout China, so there are no countervailing groups who are available as allies. Tibetan monks cannot be released from detention by Chinese courts for lack of due process or habeas corpus. No entity in China can challenge the central authority. China is also relatively impervious to international pressure. By contrast, in the US there are multiple and competing jurisdictions and principles of law including independent judicial review, due process, legal defense by civil rights agencies, police review boards, elections, and tolerance of peaceful collective action to bring attention to injustices. Although the policing of some populations in the US has been extremely coercive (e.g., in the Jim Crow South), with police and courts concurring in repression, there have also been social movements resisting this coercion and seeking to bring actors from different other of the state to exert pressure to reduce the coercion. The US has many civil society organizations and social movement groups that work to counter the repressive excesses of the state, including the ACLU, minority civic organizations like NAACP or League of Latin American citizens, and many others. It also has competing political parties who can seek to rally voters and seek peacefully to remove government officials from office.

Pacification of populations

Some scholars use the term "pacification" instead of "repression" to refer to contemporary policing and social control strategies, typically linking this to the interests of economic and political elites (Kienscherf 2014; Neocleous 2011; Neocleous, Rigakos, and Wall 2013).

Although the term "pacification" can refer to any process ending a war, a more specific historical meaning refers to the construction of empires and the full range of actions designed to get a civilian population to stop resisting and to submit to rule by an alien other. European colonial powers pacified the countries they conquered. European settlers pacified American Indians by waging war on them. The United States pacified the Philippines (Wirtz 2004) and the US military strategy sought to pacify Vietnamese villages in the 1960s (Wirtz 2004). Dafnos (2013) discusses contemporary Canadian strategies to pacify indigenous resistance in the public-order policing of Ontario Provincial Police in the context of the role of Indian Affairs in a settler state.

Using the term pacification rather than repression emphasizes that it is broader than just punishing acts of dissent or resistance. Arrests of dissenters are just a small part of pacification.

Surveillance and counterintelligence are also important in coercive pacification. Social movement researchers have long recognized that close surveillance and harassment generally disrupts groups, increases distrust, and creates emotional stress (Wilson (1977). Reviewing the literature on the covert effects of social control, Cunningham and Noakes (2008) distinguish surveillance—information gathering—from counterintelligence activities. These later tactics include negative publicity or promoting internal dissent to actively hinder a group's ability to carry out its plans. Their research presents evidence that both strategies work to disrupt movements.

Pacification has often involved relocating and concentrating populations, as in the 19th-century US practices of removing American Indians to reservations or the creation of what were at the time called concentration camps to house Japanese Americans removed from the US Pacific Coast during World War II. It also has often involved relocating members of the dominant group into the colonized space to provide the numbers to counter the resistance of the locals. White settlers were encouraged to move west in North America to help occupy the territory. Ethnic Russians were encouraged to move into non-Russian areas in the Soviet Union. Han people have been given incentives to move into peripheral non-Han regions of China. Israeli Jewish settlers are moving into Palestinian areas of the West Bank. These movements of civilian settlers are part of a colonizing project and the civilian settlers have often been targets of violence from the indigenous local people, who view them as threats.

Pacification is an ongoing process that begins with warfare and conquest and then continues as governance. Pacification involves propaganda and attempts to benefit a population to win their "hearts and minds" so that they will comply out of a positive belief in the legitimacy of the regime. The discursive side of pacification involves rewriting history to portray the pacifiers as agents of civilization and those resisting pacification as barbaric or childlike. Pacification often involves coopting legitimate local leaders and persuading them to serve as intermediaries in indirect governance, providing positive incentives to those who do submit, and promoting of a social order that both maintains control and permits daily life activities. Pacification can include offering job opportunities and funding to people and groups who cooperate with the regime.

The origins of the term pacification in colonialism remind us that different groups may be treated differently. Kienscherf (2011) argues that military dimensions of pacification were incorporated into domestic policing in the US in the late 1960s. He sees community policing as the soft side of militarization, which includes concepts of minimum necessary force and proportionality of force and the selective allocation of coercive and consensual social control (Kienscherf 2011, 2014; Parenti 2000). Consistent with pacification logic, police seek to distinguish between good protesters and bad protesters and focus on pacifying risky communities, populations, individuals, or spaces (Kienscherf 2011). Kienscherf (2014) stresses the importance of liberal social control and efforts to produce non-disruptive collective action as part of pacification.

Democracy for whom? Protection for whom?

Most observers agree that the United States is a representative democracy while China is an autocracy, despite China's formally being governed by an elected assembly. Even in democracies, most countries treat different groups within their borders differently, creating undemocratic pockets within democratic states (Sa'di 2015). At a minimum, they distinguish between citizens and non-citizen residents, giving fewer rights and protections to non-citizens. Majority group movements against immigrants and immigration are common. Additionally, even for groups with formal citizenship, institutional practices grounded in a state's racial or ethnic history often lead to unequal treatment of different groups.

Scholars of race and ethnicity generally agree that the US is dominated by White people although they disagree about the best way to conceptualize this. Omi and Winant (1986) define the United States as a racial state in its institutions and practices and treat it sometimes as a pluralist arena in which Whites have disproportionate power and sometimes as an autonomous actor constructing race for its own purposes. Steinman (2012) describes the legacies of the structures of settler colonialism while recognizing that multiple institutional spheres provide spaces for resistance by the American Indian sovereignty movement. Jung and Kwon (2013) argue that the United States is best understood as an empire state that was constructed by conquering and subordinating other groups into inherently hierarchical structures. Bracey (2015) takes a critical race theory perspective, arguing that the US government is inherently White, although it may sometimes yield concessions and benefits to minorities as part of inter-White struggles. Significantly, it can take rights away from minorities at any time without losing its core legitimacy for Whites.

All these theoretical views recognize the tyranny of the majority as the dark side of democracy. Democratic majorities have often voted to kill, displace, enslave, disenfranchise, or disadvantage ethnic or racial minorities. The very existence of a White majority in the United States is a consequence of explicit immigration policies that encouraged European immigration while banning or limiting immigration from Asia and were intertwined with the construction of racial categories and White fears of Blacks (Calavita 2007). White immigrants gained and used control of local police to improve their own competitive economic position by repressing Blacks (Muller 2012; Olzak and Shanahan 2014). Overt hierarchies and structures of domination by race were embodied in government agencies and practices well into the 1960s so that the interests of the White majority were naturalized as "national interests" and "state interests." Even today, most institutions operate under assumptions and practices that automatically and invisibly privilege the majority, even without the overt discrimination that also occurs. The United States has laws and formal bodies charged with guaranteeing the rights of racial minorities, but White-dominated courts and legislatures have formally decided that "equal treatment" provisions designed to undo racial discrimination should be interpreted as requiring that inherited racial advantages must be allowed to persist (Moore and Bell 2017). Police forces, even those staffed by minorities, are tasked with buffering the majority from the consequences of minority disadvantage. Similarly, China formally recognizes minority group rights and even has designated Tibet and Xinjiang as autonomous regions, but in practice is acting to stamp out separate ethnic identities that challenge the control of the central state.

Ethnic conflict and countermovement dynamics

The discussion so far has focused solely on the relation between states and minority populations, but there are also conflicts between non-state actors. Whether they formed peacefully or by conquest or colonialism, states that incorporate multiple racial or ethnic groups may experience conflict between those groups. These conflicts can take on a movement– countermovement dynamic, where there are social movements that oppose each other. In ongoing countermovement struggles, both sides may have elite allies and may have captured different parts of a complex state. In these cases, victories by one side lead to renewed mobilization by the other side. The KKK and other White supremacist groups formed after the US Civil War to violently resist movements for political rights and economic redress for the former African American slaves, successfully disenfranchising the recently enfranchised and re-creating White dominant political structures. The NAACP and other Black organizations were formed to counter these White movements. After the 1954 Supreme Court decision outlawing racial segregation in schools, the White Citizens Council was formed to resist integration and Ku Klux Klan chapters were reinvigorated. After the Civil Rights laws passed, overt support for White supremacy was replaced by a "colorblind" rhetoric (see Robnett's Chapter 2 in this volume) and White supremacists largely removed themselves from mass media notice while continuing to grow quietly (see Simi and Futrell's Chapter 5 in this volume). The Black movement also changed and grew until reemerging to mass media attention with the Black Lives Matter protests of 2014–16.

The boundary between movement and government can be thin. Repressive governments often support or tolerate extra-institutional means of harassment and intimidation. Chinese officials sometimes employ thugs and off-duty policemen for intimidation of activists, threatening their families, silencing them, and/or "disappearing" them, either in dark jails or, permanently, by death (Johnston 2018; Ong 2015). In the Jim Crow South, White governments supported or tolerated vigilante groups that spread fear and terror among Black citizens.

According to the Equal Justice Initiative, at least 4084 African Americans were lynched between 1877 and 1950 in the South. Many of these events were public; others occurred as anonymous hate crimes. White governments often refused to prosecute the killers or, if they prosecuted, all-White juries refused to convict. Famous examples include Isaac Woodard, a newly discharged solider still in uniform who was beaten and left blind by police in 1946 (Gergel 2019) and Emmett Till, a fourteen-year-old boy brutally murdered in 1955 for the "crime" of speaking to a White woman.

Government agencies can institutionalize movement demands and movement partisans can pursue movement goals from within government agencies. Ward (2018) provides a historical overview of White supremacist policing, including collusion with lynching and White violence, suppression of Black movements, weak responses to White supremacist movements, and downplaying evidence for White supremacist infiltration of police in recent years. Some White nationalists have joined police departments as part of their movement agenda. A 2006 FBI report from its counterterrorism division warned that White supremacist infiltration of law enforcement represented a significant threat and there have been many incidents of overt White supremacist activities by law-enforcement officers (Jones 2015). Public examples of law-enforcement officials overtly supporting White supremacy include Sheriff Joe Arpaio in Arizona and Robert Stamm in Virginia (Hedgpeth and Jackman 2019). There are public debates about the relative danger of White and Black groups. In October 2017, a leaked FBI report by its Domestic Terrorism Analysis Unit said that "Black Identity Extremists" were engaging in retaliatory violence against police (Winter and Weinberger 2017); the leaked document itself refers to previous versions written in 2015 and 2016 and defines "black identity extremist" in very broad terms, although it does also say that it is not illegal to have opinions. The Southern Poverty Law Center lists both White and Black separatist groups as "hate groups."[6]

Resistance and pacification in Tibet and Xinjiang

There has been ongoing resistance to Chinese rule of Tibet and Xinjiang. In the Xinjiang capital of Urumqi, anti-Chinese violence erupted in 2009 that left 140 people dead. In Tibet, a covert, small-scale resistance has been waged for years (French 2007), and occasionally more public protests erupt, especially among Tibetan Buddhist monks (Wong 2015a). China does not permit the standard protest repertoire known in the US and Europe (Tilly 1995, 2008). Instead, the resistance repertoire emphasizes weapons-of-the-weak tactics (Johnston 2015, 2018). In Tibet, traditional festivals, touted by the regime to be touristic examples of contented minorities in the new China, may be sites of resistance. One report noted how Tibetans refuse to wear traditional fur clothing because it was raised to a symbolic political issue when the Dalai Lama proclaimed wearing fur as contrary to Buddhist teachings (French 2007), thus dismaying authorities. Another small act of resistance is hanging pictures in one's home of the Dalai Lama, outlawed by authorities as a "saboteur of harmony." Not all resistance is covert. More than 140 Tibetans have self-immolated in political protest since 2009 (Wong 2012, a rare tactic that has a significant history in India, Vietnam, and Korea has been used in a number of countries, including the US (Biggs 2005, 2008). In the context of resistance, non-Han ethnic identification is viewed as threatening.

Just as European colonists pacified their colonies, modern China is seeking to pacify the Tibet and Xinjian Uighur Autonomous Regions (as well as adjacent borderlands in Qinghui and Sichuan Provinces). Chinese paramilitary units are common sights in the region. After a wave of protests and self-immolations in the late 2000s in Tibet, Buddhist monasteries were raided, placed under lockdown, and surrounded by paramilitary units. Three hundred monks were arrested in the town of Kirti, and forced to attend patriotic re-education sessions. Local festivals in Tibet are typically monitored by large deployments of police and military. Intellectuals, outspoken citizens, and academics may be removed through assassination or incarceration, as in the disappearances of leading Uighur spokespeople (Ramzy 2019: 9).

In Xinjiang, there are official programs to eradicate Uighur identity as a Central Asian Islamic people. These include secret prisons, "black factories," late-night abductions, and capricious imprisonment for ethnic Uighurs who are not Chinese enough in their appearance, or whose outspokenness has been reported by Communist Party neighborhood monitors. Police profiling means that having a beard is enough to warrant one's arrest. Religious observance itself can be punished. In Xinjian Provence, practicing Muslims and Uighur dissidents (and also ethnic Kazakhs) are arrested and interned in concentration camps where official programs of indoctrination seek to "stamp out the virus of superstition and old ways." Internees are forced to renounce their religious convictions, learn Chinese (many Uighurs do not know the language well), pledge fealty to the Communist Party, and sing patriotic songs during the day. Hundreds of Uighur intellectuals have been arrested and jailed for their defense of cultural identity (Ramzy 2019). It is estimated by area scholars that perhaps 1 million people have been interned in these indoctrination camps (Buckley and Ramzy 2018: 9), euphemistically called job training centers by the government. Many detained Uighurs are forced to work in "black factories" as part of their indoctrination and continue there when their full internment has ended. Since 2016, when the program started, the increased police presence and atmosphere of fear has been hard to miss in Xinjian (Ramzy 2019).

Discursively, often there is a mix of both propaganda and cultural domination with military occupation. Tibetans and Uighurs are portrayed as carefree, costume-wearing dancers and singers—happy in their cultures and loyal citizens of China (Montefiore 2013). Some legitimate local leaders are coopted into the regime. There are Tibetans and Uighurs who are complicit members of the Chinese Communist Party and who participate in the governance of their regions as internal-colonial administrators, typically not as executive decision makers but as secondary- and tertiary-level state and party administrators.

Pacification policing in the US

The obvious US parallels to China's attempts to pacify Tibet and Xinjiang are in the 19th- century Indian Wars and the Philippine–American War of 1898–1902 which brought the Philippines under US colonial control.

However, some argue that the logic of pacification is being used to suppress Black and Latino populations. The Black urban rebellions of the late 1960s were viewed as an extreme threat, as were the Black Panthers and others who argued for armed self-defense or armed resistance. Davenport (2012) cites Goldstein (2001) as there being an extremely high level of repression in the United States 1967–71 in response to Vietnam War protests, racial disorders, high crime rates, and a counterculture movement. This repression included surveillance by the CIA, NSA, and US Army as well as the FBI's COINTELPRO, legalized wiretapping and eavesdropping, infiltration, disinformation and propaganda campaigns, entrapment, and even assassinations against the Black Panthers (Bloom and Martin 2013; Davenport 2010), the Republic of New Africa (Davenport 2015), and other militant Black groups (Dello Buono 1992). These are highly intrusive state tactics were essentially counter-insurgency tactics.

Oliver (2008) argues that the mass incarceration of African Americans after 1980 was a way of bringing the Black population back under control (see also Alexander 2009). She cites Gary Marx, who studied the overt and covert repression of Black political movements in the 1960s and early 1970s (Marx 1970, 1974), and later wrote about how these same techniques were being used by the late 1970s in Black communities in anti-crime efforts such as undercover fencing operations and infiltration of criminal gangs (Marx 1980, 1981, 1982). In the 1980s and 1990s, these same surveillance operations were put in the service of the drug war, the most important factor in the rise in the mass incarceration of Black people after the mid-1980s (Oliver 2008). Many critical observers called the 1980s drug war politically motivated and racially targeted, and argued that it was state repression, or at least bordered on it (Chambliss 1995; Gordon 1994; Mauer 1999; Tonry 1994). Wacquant (2001) described the ways in which the prison had become more like the ghetto—and the ghetto more like a prison—as the criminal justice system absorbed the extra-penological function of managing dispossessed and dishonored groups.

Other types of coercive social control in Black and Latino areas have included intensive stop-and-frisk policing and high rates of pretext traffic stops justified either for drug interdiction, immigration control, or revenue generation. There has also been an increase in surveillance and policing within schools, including zero-tolerance policies and higher rates of suspensions (Taylor 2016). Rios (2011, 2006, 2015) uses the phrase "youth control complex" to refer to the whole package of school and community policing of young Black and Latinx people. Matthews (2015) describes the day-to-day repression of "stop and frisk" police stops in San Francisco based on analysis of citizen videos of the encounters and analyzes them as degradation ceremonies in which police degrade those stopped. These are methods that, in different raiment and distinct settings could be found in Lhasa or Urumqi, where high-intensity state penetration of local communities occurred, especially after collective violence in 2008 (Tibet) and 2009 (Xinjiang).

Sa'di (2015) describes parallel tactics of extreme surveillance of Palestinians in Israel, even of children's school essays; limited mobility between small areas without passes and permission; widespread abuses and daily humiliations.

There are other forms of control. Many people are on probation or parole and subject to highly intrusive monitoring of their activities. The conditions of supervision in some cases include staying away from people with criminal records, effectively making collective action by supervised people illegal. On at least two occasions, author Oliver observed cases where a returned prisoner scheduled to speak at a prison reform meeting was incarcerated on a parole hold and, thus, prevented from speaking. Other returned prisoners spoke at other meetings and the PO would not give the reason for the hold to volunteers who had been participating in a "circle of support" for the parolee, so intention versus coincidence remained ambiguous. Other forms of control include child protective custody orders and stay-away orders. King (2012) cites examples of stay-away orders, probation holds, and child protective custody orders being used against Occupy Oakland participants to incapacitate them from political action.

None of these programs of repression explicitly criminalized racial minorities, and many of these policies were supported by a significant fraction of Black people. The racial logic of the US is different from China. The US government does not define ethnic pride or identification among African Americans, Mexican Americans, Arab Americans, or Muslim Americans as a threat in itself, possibly because these groups are intermingled geographically and there are no secessionist movements. The US does not currently arrest people for ethnic deviation and put them into cultural re-education centers, although Native American activists would call attention to past parallels in Indian boarding schools, where children were separated from their families and forcibly acculturated. The ideological justification for repression in the US since the Civil Rights Movement has been that a high proportion of minorities are committing illegal acts so suspecting people of criminality of the basis of race is empirically justified. Although overt ethnic displays of clothing or hairstyles or accents signifying adherence to a minority culture are entirely legal in the US, such displays, and sometimes even one's simple existence as a visible minority, may still trigger employment discrimination, exclusion from school, hate crimes, or hostile encounters with police, even though it is illegal for employers and government agents to discriminate on such bases.

Coercive exclusion and policing of immigrants

Immigrants in the US are also subject to repressive social control. Since the creation of ICE (Immigration and Customs Enforcement) in 2003 as an autonomous agency under the Department of Homeland Security, ICE has defined its mission as 100% removal of "removable aliens" (Office of Detention and Removal 2003) and had a budget that by 2013 was higher than all other federal law enforcement combined, in addition to its collaborations with local police and extreme powers of surveillance. The average daily population of detained immigrants rose from 5000 in 1994 to 19,000 in 2001 and to over 39,000 in 2017, with nearly 400,000 people experiencing detention during the year (Detention Watch Network 2019). Detention facilities are run by private prison firms with contracts that guarantee them detainees and have little oversight on conditions of detention. For comparison, the average daily population of people in federal, state, and local corrections facilities in 2016 was 2.16 million (Kaeble and Cowhig 2018). In 2016, about 10.6 million people were admitted to US jails, often for short stays of a few days (Zeng 2018).

Immigration raids, detentions, deportations, and oppressive conditions of confinement were serious threats to immigrants throughout the Obama administration, as were debates about the treatment of refugee children from Central America. These policies were escalated along with overt anti-immigrant rhetoric by President Trump. Administration rhetoric portrays several hundred members (at best) of the youth gang MS-13 as a national security crisis warranting a declaration of emergency, while those defending Central American migrants argue that the source of the MS-13 gangs in Central America is US deportees and that gang violence is one of the reasons people are fleeing the area. Administration policy has spurred ICE agents entering high schools and detaining minors in high-security federal facilities far away from family members. In the summer of 2017 ICE began a major operation on Long Island (Nir and Dollinger 2017). A press conference was called with a photo-op of military vehicles and equipment in the background, and armed police clothed in riot gear aligned in the front. "Operation Matador," as it was called, led to sixty minors being removed from just one high school in Huntington, Long Island, and sent to detention facilities, mostly on the basis of rumors and interpretation of gang signs and gang colors by school resource officers (Dreier 2018). For these young detainees, the immigration detention system and courts are a labyrinthine parallel legal system where, as undocumented minors, their basic rights are mostly ignored (Robbins 2018). For family members and their lawyers, often from immigration aid agencies and the ACLU, it is a system that is often difficult to penetrate. Under Attorney General Jeff Sessions, over 500 young men were arrested, and seventy deported, no questions asked, separated from family members in the US. Accounts of horrific conditions in detention camps are in the news as we write (Dreier 2018).

Racial and ethnic movements in a racialized US

In the US and other societies divided by race or ethnicity, racial or ethnic movements form countermovement pairs. The actions of one group to improve their position relative to other groups triggers a countermovement. Although the riots in Xinjiang and Tibet appear to involve repressed minorities rebelling against the regime or attacking members of the dominant ethnic group, and the 1960s Black urban riots were insurrections by minorities who felt oppressed, the United States today and much of Europe is experiencing mobilization by members of the majority who feel threatened by minorities. A common brand of populism links anti-elite politics of the majority to anti-minority and anti-immigrant politics, generally with the claim that the elites are supporting minorities to the disadvantage of the majority. White movements against minorities have ebbed and flowed throughout US history since 1865. The chapters in this volume about recent movements in the US all show evidence of this movement–countermovement dynamic. At the same time, these countermovements are interwoven with state power.

Several chapters in this volume address the movement–countermovement dynamics in the wake of the victories of the Black Civil Rights Movement. Overt defenses of White supremacy were abandoned, and a new discursive era began.

Belinda Robnett's Chapter 2, "Defensive Adaptations: NAACP Responses to the U.S. Post- Racial Project 1970–1990," traces the evolution of a "post-racial" discourse that altered and coopted the meanings of racism, discrimination, justice, and civil rights. This countermovement discourse against the Civil Rights Movement was advanced by White politicians and White judges who quickly declared that the Civil Rights Movement had "won" and that any attempts to redress the consequences of discrimination against Blacks were unfair discrimination against Whites. Robnett shows how this post-racial discourse forced the NAACP out of the proactive stance of the Civil Rights era and onto the defensive. As each step of the countermovement discourse unfolded and overt Black claims for benefits were redefined as racism and discrimination by powerful state actors, the NAACP engaged in what Robnett calls a defensive strategic adaptation and shifted to new issues and tactics to try to find a ground for action, in the process coming to accept the premises of the hegemonic post-racial discourse.

Pamela Oliver's Chapter 3 "Resisting Repression: The Black Lives Movement in Context" similarly addresses the ways the Black movement evolved after the Civil Rights Movement, with an emphasis on the movements that resisted pacification, discriminatory policing, and mass incarceration. She finds connections between the movements of the 1990s and the issues and forms of Black Lives Matter fifteen years later. She also shows how the Black Lives mobilization built on community organizations that had been operating for years and how these groups sought to shift from the defensive "don't shoot us" mode to a proactive policy agenda.

She also addresses funding patterns and raises questions about the "carrot" side of pacification in foundation funding for Black Lives Movement organizations and calls attention to countermovement dynamics as the Black Lives Movement also inspired White supremacist organizations.

Joshua Bloom and Zachary Frampton's Chapter 4, "Racist Policing, Practical Resonance, and Frame Alignment in Ferguson," focuses on one of the key events in the Black Lives Movement, the 2014 protests in Ferguson after the killing of Michael Brown. With a close-grained analysis of the first nine hours after the killing, they show how Black twitter users were discussing whether this particular killing was an instance of unjust police violence while simultaneously assuming that policing in general was racist. Then, as the police brought in massive force against the small and entirely nonviolent protests at the site, images of the police themselves became critical to the "racist policing frame." Bloom and Frampton emphasize the two-way process of framing as people at the scene defined their situation and then sought allies from a broader movement.

The new post-racial discourse also put overt White supremacists on the defensive, as their rhetoric was also ruled out of bounds. Pete Simi and Robert Futrell's Chapter 5, "Active Abeyance, Political Opportunity, and the 'New' White Supremacy," shows that, instead of changing their ideology to fit in with the new dominant discourse, White supremacists intentionally went into abeyance. They hid their groups from public scrutiny and disguised themselves as social clubs, so they could recruit with little backlash, made extensive use of social media, developed White nationalist music as a cultural space, and then reemerged when the political climate became favorable. As White nationalism spread in response to the threat posed by having a Black president, and then became more open in the Trump campaign, the White supremacists came out from the shadows and emerged as a stronger presence than many had recognized.

Racialization affects other minorities besides African Americans. As Wayne Santoro and Marian Azab emphasize in their Chapter 6, "The Biographical Consequences of Repression: Arab Americans in Post-9/11 America," Arab Americans have been subjected to racialization and discrimination since the 1970s. Initial national news reports blamed Muslim Arabs for what proved to be White anti-government terrorist Timothy McVeigh's bombing of a federal building in Oklahoma in 1995 that killed 168 people and injured 680. These negative portrayals escalated after the terrorist attacks on September 11, 2001. Survey data from Arab Americans show that Arab Americans experienced repression both from state agents who arrested and detained people on suspicion, infiltrated mosques, and surveilled immigrant communities, and also from civilians in the form of hate crimes, threats, employment discrimination, and the small acts of everyday snubs, avoidance, and sotto-voce (or shouted) epithets. Both state repression and repression from White civilians engendered fear. Arab Americans responded by distrusting government more, protesting less, and engaging in electoral politics more. The effects of experiencing repression were especially strong for Arabs who had previously felt more integrated and accepted.

The movement–countermovement dynamic also appears with anti-immigrant movements aimed primarily at Latinx Americans. Again, there are state actors supporting each side, but the anti-immigrant policies have stronger institutionalization in the state. Immigration policies essentially create illegal or undocumented immigration by refusing to sanction migration across borders. One consequence of the 1965 changes in US immigration law and then the increased border enforcement of the 1990s was to make it harder for

Mexicans to migrate legally to the US. This paradoxically led to more Mexican people living without authorization in the US who might otherwise have crossed back and forth as temporary workers. There are movements against immigrants that have succeeded in passing bills that restrict legal immigrants (including the 1996 welfare reform bill that made legal immigrants ineligible for welfare benefits) as well as increasing penalties and removing protections for undocumented immigrants. A 2006 federal bill would have made it a felony to be an undocumented immigrant or aid an undocumented immigrant in any way. This bill provoked huge marches by immigrants and fostered Latino solidarity among people in different statuses. One issue has been young people brought to the US as children who have grown up in the US but lack legal status. Although most people in the US favor a road to citizenship for this group, the movements against immigrants have blocked attempts at restorative legislation.

Chapter 7 by Edelina Burciaga and Lisa Martinez, "Localized Political Contexts: Undocumented Youth Mobilization during Hostile Times," compares movements by undocumented youth in three communities, paying attention to local governments and the ways in which they differ from each other. They compare three cities that vary in their level of support for undocumented immigrants, ranging from Los Angeles with a welcoming context, Denver with a moderate context, and Atlanta with a hostile context, showing how the movements differed in each case. In all cases, the undocumented youth are against racialized exclusion and demanding inclusion in the nation. But they chose more open tactics in places with weaker anti-immigrant movements and more favorable social and legal climate. Los Angeles, for example, as a city with a large and established Mexican-American and Central American population, posed fewer threats and offered greater opportunities for mobilization through a vibrant civil society of immigration associations and more receptive public discourse. In contrast, Atlanta, Georgia, a city that had not been a magnet for immigration prior to the 1990s, but which has seen a rapid increase in immigration from Mexico, posed a more hostile context. Georgia legislators set roadblocks for new immigrants and attempted to limit the access of undocumented arrivals to housing, healthcare, and education. A 2011 law required police to ask for immigration documents and criminalized attending college and using medical services for undocumented residents. Many provisions of this law were eventually reversed by the US Supreme Court, again revealing the way the complex and decentralized US state offers many avenues for pursuing group interests.

Thomas Swerts's Chapter 8, "Gaining a Voice: Storytelling and Undocumented Youth Activism in Chicago," is another look at immigrant youth movements that shows how young Mexican-American activists build community and articulate grievances through narratives, the talk that is the adhesive of social bonds. His research reveals how an especially marginalized and at-risk population draws upon larger discursive resources available in the US. Consistent with Burciaga and Martinez, their ability to speak openly about their stories is tied to a supportive local context and a decentralized state. These are resources not available where patterns of internal-colonial pacification prevail, as in contemporary China. Indeed, we have chronicled how the perversion of public discourse is a common effect of high-intensity, high-capacity pacification of populations (Johnston 2011). On the other hand, the ability to speak publicly and openly derives from the small free spaces that variable and segmented pacification policies allow activists in the US to claim. Creative agents occupying these free spaces, organizing despite fear, and laying stake to public arenas to voice dissent, are the narratives that the authors in this collection of research tell.

The White counter-movements reacting against a Black president and Black Lives Matter and immigrant rights movements contributed to the unexpected victory of Donald Trump for president in 2016. That victory cheered and emboldened White supremacists, leading them to be more public and overt. This electoral victory and the actions that followed to ramp up anti- immigrant policies and increase the visibility of White supremacists led in their turn to a huge wave of protests. There were protests the day after the election in many cities, often mobilized by groups that had been protesting around Black Lives and immigrant rights. A huge women's march and spin-off protests and marches were organized around Trump's inauguration. Chapter 9 by Kenneth Andrews, Neal Caren, and Todd Lu, "Racial and Ethnic Protest During Year One of the Trump Presidency," uses crowdsourced data to map the patterns of protests against the Trump administration in its first year. They find that 12% of the protests were immigration related and 12% race related. Key peaks are the Muslim travel ban in January 2017 and the Unite the Right rally in Charlottesville August 2017. Most of the evidence points to the importance of movement infrastructures as explaining variation between places in the level of protesting, although the size of the immigrant community affects the volume of pro-immigrant protests.

Taken together, the chapters in this book paint a picture of the ongoing struggles between the majority and minorities in the US to define the character of the nation and determine who will be its beneficiaries.

Notes

1 The U.S. is organized around racial divisions and China is organized around ethnic divisions. We treat these concepts as parallel for the purpose of our comparison even as we recognize that there is a long history of debates about these terms.
2 We capitalize White for the sake of consistency in capitalizing the names of all racial/ethnic groups and use it as a synonym for European in the racial sense. We use Black and African American interchangeably, as members of this group prefer both terms and generally find neither offensive. We capitalize Black because this is the preference of most Black people and is consistent with the capitalization of all other names for racial groups. The issues at stake are explained in the essay "Race Names" (Oliver 2017)
3 A rail link between China and Tibet was completed in 2007. By the next year, Chinese tourism to the region had increased by 67%, fomenting concerns among Tibetans that the rail link had the strategic intent of diluting the region's unique character.

4 The Dalai Lama claims over one million Tibetans have been killed by Chinese rule, a figure the Chinese state rejects.
5 Repression is not hermetically sealed in China. Spaces for collective action do sometimes open, not from different jurisdictions or variable interpretations of law, as in segmented pacification, but rather from the interstices that invariably appear in coordinating a broad and uniform policies of regional pacification. The key point is that the state is not a monolithic of social control. When security forces are so expansive, competition among levels of police and security agencies, redundancies, and corruption often open small spaces for resistance. Research in other repressive states has shown that failures of enforcement and the corruption that arises from a lack of independent public scrutiny provide pockets of fresh air for activists can breathe freely in repressive settings (Johnston 2012).
6 https://www.splcenter.org/issues/hate-and-extremism

References

Alexander, Michelle. 2009. *The New Jim Crow: Mass Incarceration in the Age of Colorblindness.* New York: New Press.

Alonso, Ana Maria. 1994. "The Politics of Space, Time and Substance: State Formation, Nationalism, and Ethnicity." *Annual Review of Anthropology* 23(1): 379–405.

Barkey, Karen, and Sunita Parikh. 1991. "Comparative Perspectives on the State." *Annual Review of Sociology* 17: 523–549.

Biggs, Michael. 2005. "Dying without Killing: Self-immolations, 1963–2002." Pp. 173–208 in *Making Sense of Suicide Missions*, edited by Diego Gambetta. Oxford: Oxford University Press.

Biggs, Michael. 2008. "Dying for a Cause—Alone?" *Contexts* 7(1): 22–27.

Bloom, Joshua, and Waldo E. Martin. 2013. *Black Against Empire: The History and Politics of the Black Panther Party.* Berkeley: University of California Press.

Bonilla-Silva, Eduardo. 1999. "The Essential Social Fact of Race." *American Sociological Review* 64(6): 899–906.

Bonilla-Silva, Eduardo. 2002. "The Linguistics of Color Blind Racism: How to Talk Nasty about Blacks without Sounding 'Racist'." *Critical Sociology* 28(1/2): 41–64.

Bracey, Glenn E. 2015. "Toward a Critical Race Theory of State." *Critical Sociology* 41 (3): 553–572.

Brubaker, Rogers. 1995. "Aftermaths of Empire and the Unmixing of People: Historical and Comparative Perspectives." *Ethnic & Racial Studies* 18(2): 189–218.

Brubaker, Rogers. 2009. "Ethnicity, Race, and Nationalism." *Annual Review of Sociology* 35(1): 21–42.

Buckley, Chris. 2018. "China is Detaining Muslims in Vast Numbers. The Goal: Transformation." *New York Times*. September 8. https://www.nytimes.com/2018/09/08/world/asia/china-uighur-muslim-detention-camp.html?module=inline.

Buckley, Chris, and Austin Ramzy. 2018. "In China 'Reeducation' Leads to Forced Labor." *New York Times*, December 17, A1.

Calavita, Kitty. 2007. "Immigration Law, Race, and Identity." *Annual Review of Law and Social Science* 3(1): 1–20.

Chambliss, William J. 1995. "Crime Control and Ethnic Minorities: Legitimizing Racial Oppression by Creating Moral Panics." Pp. 235–258 in *Ethnicity, Race, and Crime: Perspectives across Time and Place*, edited by Darnell F. Hawkins. Albany: State University of New York Press.

Cunningham, David, and John Noakes. 2008. "'What if She's from the FBI?' The Effects of Covert Forms of Social Control on Social Movements." *Sociology of Crime, Law & Deviance* 10: 175–197.

Dafnos, Tia. 2013. "Pacification and Indigenous Struggles in Canada." *Socialist Studies* 9 (2): 57–77.

Davenport, Christian. 2010. *Media Bias, Perspective, and State Repression: The Black Panther Party.* Cambridge: Cambridge University Press.

Davenport, Christian. 2012. "When Democracies Kill: Reflections from the US, India, and Northern Ireland." *International Area Studies Review* 15(1): 3–20.

Davenport, Christian. 2015. *How Social Movements Die: Repression and Demobilization of the Republic of New Africa.* New York: Cambridge University Press.

Dello Buono, Richard Alan. 1992. "Criminalization of Black Radical/Nationalist Struggles: From the African Blood Brotherhood to MOVE." Paper presented at annual meeting of the *American Sociological Association, Pittsburgh, PA*.

Detention Watch Network. 2019. "Immigration Detention 101." https://www.detentionwatchnetwork.org/issues/detention-101.

Dreier, Hannah. 2018. "How Crackdown on MS-13 Caught Up Innocent High School Students." *New York Times Magazine.* December 27: 32.

Enloe, Cynthia H. 1978. "Ethnicity, Bureaucracy and State-Building in Africa and Latin America." *Ethnic & Racial Studies* 1(3): 336–351.

Enloe, Cynthia H. 1981. "The Growth of the State and Ethnic Mobilization: The American Experience." *Ethnic & Racial Studies* 4(2): 123–136.

French, Howard. 2007. "Tibetans Turn Festival into Mute Protest Against China." *New York Times*, August 16, A6.

Gergel, Richard. 2019. *Unexampled Courage.* New York: Farrar, Straus and Giroux.

Goldstein, Robert Justin. 2001. *Political Repression in Modern America from 1870 to 1976.* Urbana: University of Illinois Press.

González, Roberto J. 2009. "Going 'Tribal': Notes on Pacification in the 21st Century." *Anthropology Today* 25(2): 15–19.

Gordon, Diana R. 1994. *The Return of the Dangerous Classes: Drug Prohibition and Policy Politics.* New York: W.W. Norton.

Hedgpeth, Dana, and Tom Jackman. 2019. "Virginia Police Sergeant on Leave after He Shows Symbols Linked to White Supremacist Groups." *Washington Post*, February 7.

Johnston, Hank. 2011. *States and Social Movements.* Cambridge, UK: Polity Press.

Johnston, Hank. 2012. "State Violence and Oppositional Protest in High-Capacity Authoritarian Regimes." *International Journal of Collective Violence* 6(1): 55–74.

Johnston, Hank. 2015. "'The Game's Afoot': Social Movements in Authoritarian States." Pp. 619–632 in Mario Diani and Donatella della Porta, eds. *The Oxford Handbook of Social Movements.* New York: Oxford University Press.

Johnston, Hank. 2018. "Repertoires of Resistance and Repression: The Authoritarian Governance Arena." *Zeitschrift für Menschenrechte/Journal for Human Rights* 12(1): 20–45.

Jones, Samuel Vincent. 2015. "Law Enforcement and White Power: An FBI Report Unraveled." *Thurgood Marshall Law Review* 41(1): 103–108.

Jung, Moon-Kie, and Yaejoon Kwon. 2013. "Theorizing the US Racial State: Sociology Since Racial Formation." *Sociology Compass* 7(11): 927–940.

Kaeble, Danielle, and Mary Cowhig. 2018. "Correctional Populations in the United States, 2016." Bureau of Justice Statistics.

Kienscherf, Markus. 2011. "A Programme of Global Pacification: US Counterinsurgency Doctrine and the Biopolitics of Human (In)security." *Security Dialogue* 42(6): 517–535.

Kienscherf, Markus. 2014. "Beyond Militarization and Repression: Liberal Social Control as Pacification." *Critical Sociology* 42(7–8):1179–1194.

King, Mike. 2012. "Entrapment, Snatch Squads and Probation Holds." Counterpunch.org: https://www.counterpunch.org/2012/05/03/entrapment-snatch-squads-and-probation- holds/.

Loveman, Mara. 1999. "Making 'Race' and Nation in the United States, South Africa, and Brazil: Taking Making Seriously." *Theory & Society* 28(6): 903–927.

Marx, Anthony W. 1995. "Contested Citizenship: The Dynamics of Racial Identity and Social Movements." *International Review of Social History* 40: 159–183.

Marx, Anthony W. 1996. "Race-Making and the Nation-State." *World Politics 48*(2): 180–208.

Marx, Gary T. 1970. "Civil Disorder and the Agents of Social Control." *The Journal of Social Issues* 26(1): 19–57.

Marx, Gary T. 1974. "Thoughts on a Neglected Category of Social Movement Participant: The Agent Provocateur and the Informant." *American Journal of Sociology* 80 (2): 402–442.

Marx, Gary T. 1980. "The New Police Undercover Work." *Urban Life* 8(4): 399–446.

Marx, Gary T. 1981. "Ironies of Social Control: Authorities as Contributors to Deviance through Escalation, Nonenforcement and Covert Facilitation." *Social Problems* 28(3): 221–246.

Marx, Gary T. 1982. "Who Really Gets Stung? Some Issues Raised by the New Police Undercover Work." *Crime and Delinquency* 28(2): 165–193.

Matthews, Katherine D. 2015. "'*Ask Him If You're Being Detained*': Bystander Resistance in Street Police Encounters." Unpublished master's thesis, Department of Sociology, University of California, Santa Barbara. Available through ProQuest Dissertations ProQuest Number: 1600217

Mauer, Marc. 1999. *Race to Incarcerate*. New York: The Free Press.

Montefiore, Clarissa. 2013. "How China Distorts Its Minorities through Propaganda." *BBC*. http://www.bbc.com/culture/story/20131215-how-china-portrays-its-minorities

Moore, Wendy Leo, and Joyce M. Bell. 2017. "The Right to Be Racist in College: Racist Speech, White Institutional Space, and the First Amendment." *Law & Policy* 39(2): 99–120.

Muller, Christopher. 2012. "Northward Migration and the Rise of Racial Disparity in American Incarceration, 1880–1950." *American Journal of Sociology* 118(2): 281–326.

Neocleous, Mark. 2011. "'A Brighter and Nicer New Life': Security as Pacification." *Social & Legal Studies* 20(2): 191–208.

Neocleous, Mark, George Rigakos, and Tyler Wall. 2013. "On Pacification: Introduction to the Special Issue." *On Pacification. Special Issue of Socialist Studies* 9(2): 1–6.

Nir, Sarah Maslin, and Arielle Dollinger. 2017. "U.S. Arrests 39 Members of MS-13, Gang Blamed for Long Island Killings." *New York Times*. June 15: A23.

Office of Detention and Removal. 2003. "ENDGAME. Office of Detention and Removal Strategic Plan, 2003–2012. Detention and Removal Strategy for a Secure Homeland." U.S. Department of Homeland Security Bureau of Immigration and Customs Enforcement.

Oliver, Pamela. 2008. "Repression and Crime Control: Why Social Movement Scholars Should Pay Attention to Mass Incarceration as a Form of Repression." *Mobilization: An International Quarterly* 13(1): 1–24.

Oliver, Pamela. 2017a. "The Ethnic Dimensions in Social Movements." *Mobilization: An International Quarterly* 22(4): 395–416.

Oliver, Pamela. 2017b. "Race Names." *SocArXiv*, November 11. doi:10.31235/osf.io/7wys2.

Olzak, Susan. 2004. "Ethnic and Nationalist Social Movements." Pp. 666–693 in *The Blackwell Companion to Social Movements*, edited by David A. Snow, Sarah A. Soule, and Hanspeter Kriesi. Malden, MA: Blackwell.

Olzak, Susan, and Suzanne Shanahan. 2014. "Prisoners and Paupers: The Impact of Group Threat on Incarceration in Nineteenth-Century US Cities." *American Sociological Review* 79(3): 392–411.

Omi, Michael, and Howard Winant. 1986. *Racial Formation in the United States: From the 1960s to the 1980s*. New York: Routledge & Kegan Paul.

Ong, Lynette. 2015. "Thugs for Hire: State Coercion and Everyday Repression in China." Paper presented for the workshop Collective Protest and State Governance in China's Xi Jinping. Harvard-Yenching Institute, Harvard University, May 18, 2015.

Painter, Nell Irvin. 2006. *Creating Black Americans: African-American History and Its Meanings, 1619 to the Present*. New York: Oxford University Press.

Painter, Nell Irvin. 2010. *The History of White People*. New York: W.W. Norton.

Parenti, Christian. 2000. *Lockdown America: Police and Prisons in the Age of Crisis*. London: Verso.

Patterson, Orlando. 1977. "Slavery." *Annual Review of Sociology* 3: 407–449.

Ramzy, Austin. 2019. "China's New Campaign against Uighurs Has New Target: Their Top Thinkers." *New York Times*. January 6: A9.

Rios, Victor M. 2011. *Punished: Policing the Lives of Black and Latino Boys*. New York: NYU Press.

Rios, Victor M. 2015. "Policed, Punished, Dehumanized." Pp. 59–80 in *Deadly Injustice: Trayvon Martin, Race, and the Criminal Justice System*, edited by Devon Johnson, Patricia Y.Warrne, and Amy Farrekkm. New York: NYU Press.

Rios, Victor M. 2006. "The Hyper-Criminalization of Black and Latino Male Youth in the Era of Mass Incarceration." *Souls: A Critical Journal of Black Politics, Culture, and Society* 8(2): 40–54.

Robbins, Liz. 2018. "Prolonged Detention of Young Immigrants is Illegal, Lawsuit Claims" *New York Times*. February 21: A21.

Sa'di, Ahmad H. 2015. "Social Protest under Authoritarianism: A Critique of Regime Type and Instrumental Rationality-based Explanations." *Sociology – the Journal of the British Sociological Association* 49(3): 455–470.

Saperstein, Aliya, Andrew M. Penner, and Ryan Light. 2013. "Racial Formation in Perspective: Connecting Individuals, Institutions, and Power Relations." *Annual Review of Sociology* 39(1): 359–378.

Shalhoub-Kevorkian, Nadera. 2017. "Settler Colonialism, Surveillance, and Fear." Pp. 336–367 in *Israel and Its Palestinian Citizens: Ethnic Privileges in the Jewish State*, edited by Nadim N. Rouhana and Sahar S. Huneidi. Cambridge: Cambridge University Press.

Sojoyner, Damien M. 2013. "Black Radicals Make for Bad Citizens: Undoing the Myth of the School to Prison Pipeline." *Berkeley Review of Education* 4(2): 241–263.

Steinman, Erich. 2012. "Settler Colonial Power and the American Indian Sovereignty Movement: Forms of Domination, Strategies of Transformation." *American Journal of Sociology* 117(4): 1073–1130.
Taylor, Keeanga-Yamahtta. 2016. *From #BlackLivesMatter to Black liberation*. Chicago: Haymarket Books.
Thornton, Russell. 1987. *American Indian Holocaust and Survival: A Population History since 1492*. Norman: University of Oklahoma Press.
Tilly, Charles. 1995. *Popular Contention in Great Britain 1758–1834*. Cambridge, MA: Harvard University Press.
Tilly, Charles. 2008. *Contentious Performances*. New York: Cambridge University Press.
Tonry, Michael. 1994. "Racial Politics, Racial Disparities, and the War on Crime." *Crime & Delinquency* 40(4): 475–494.
Wacquant, Loic. 2001. "Deadly Symbiosis: When Ghetto and Prison Meet and Mesh." *Punishment Society* 3(1): 95–133.
Ward, Geoff. 2018. "Living Histories of White Supremacist Policing: Towards Transformative Justice." *Du Bois Review: Social Science Research on Race* 15(1): 167–184.
Wilson, John. 1977. "Social Protest and Social Control." *Social Problems* 24(4): 469–481.
Wimmer, Andreas. 2008. "The Making and Unmaking of Ethnic Boundaries: A Multilevel Process Theory." *American Journal of Sociology* 113(4): 970–1022.
Wimmer, Andreas. 2013a. *Ethnic Boundary Making: Institutions, Power, Networks*. New York: Oxford University Press.
Wimmer, Andreas. 2013b. *Waves of War: Nationalism, State Formation, and Ethnic Exclusion in the Modern World*. Cambridge, UK: Cambridge University Press.
Winant, Howard. 2000. "Race and Race Theory." *Annual Review of Sociology* 26(1): 169–185.
Winter, Jana, and Sharon Weinberger. 2017. "The FBI's New U.S. Terrorist Threat: 'Black Identity Extremists'." foreignpolicy.com: https://foreignpolicy.com/2017/10/06/the-fbi-has-identified-a-new-domestic-terrorist-threat-and-its-black-identity-extremists/.
Wirtz, James J. 2004. "Pacification." in *The Oxford Companion to American Military History*, edited by John Whiteclay Chambers. Oxford: Oxford University Press. DOI: doi:10.1093/acref/9780195071986.013.067.
Wong, Edward. 2009. "China Tightens Security in Tibet." *New York Times*, March 9: A6.
Wong, Edward. 2012. "In Occupied Tibetan Monastery, Fiery Deaths." *New York Times*. June 2: A4.
Wong, Edward. 2014. "China Invests in Region Rich in Coal, Oil, Also Strife." *New York Times*, December 20. https://www.nytimes.com/2014/12/21/world/asia/china-invests-in-xinjiang-region-rich-in-oil-coal-and-also-strife.html.
Wong, Edward. 2015a. "A Showcase of Tibetan Culture Serves Chinese Political Goals." *New York Times*. December 19: A6.
Wong, Edward. 2015b. "Tibetans Fight to Salvage Fading Culture in China." *New York Times*, November 29: A4.
Zeng, Zhen. 2018. "Jail Inmates in 2016." Bureau of Justice Statistics.
Zenz, Adrian. 2018. "China's Domestic Security Spending: An Analysis of the Available Data." *China Brief* 18(4). https://jamestown.org/program/chinas-domestic-security-spending-analysis-available-data/.

2 Defensive adaptations
NAACP responses to the U.S. post-racial project 1970–1990

Belinda Robnett

> This blame shifting and role reversing, where victims become perpetrators, where minorities become the majority, has occurred as a result of an organized campaign which continues until this day. It's led by a curious mix of whites and some Blacks, academics, journalists and policymakers. Its supporters say they support civil rights while they oppose everything designed to achieve equity.
> (As quoted in the *New Pittsburgh Courier*, "'Blacks have no one to blame but themselves': Bond cites failures of post-civil rights movement at NAACP banquet," by Sonya M. Toler, November 4, 1998, p. A1)

After the peak of the U.S. African-American civil rights movement, White political elites promoted post-racial discourses to undercut the enforcement of civil rights legislation and argued that advocates like the National Association for the Advancement of Colored People (NAACP) were now obsolete and unnecessary. Black political opportunities expanded considerably after the mid-1960s with a significant increase in Black political representation and even the formation of the Congressional Black Caucus in 1971. Yet, the discursive field began to shift as powerful elites converged in support of a discursive countermovement in the form of a national post-racial project that altered and coopted the meanings of racism, discrimination, justice, and civil rights. Pointing to the success of Black incorporation in the political process and the growth of the Black middle class, the Nixon, Carter, Ford, and Reagan presidencies constructed a powerful narrative that resonated among most Whites and sought to constrain the NAACP's goals of ending discrimination and racism. Faced with overwhelming discursive tactics that undercut the message and threatened the survival of the NAACP, the organization responded with defensive adaptations. In tracing these movement–countermovement dynamics between 1970 and 1990, this chapter extends the literature on strategic adaptations. This discussion is of ongoing significance as civil rights movement organizations including the NAACP continue to press for civil rights enforcement and to counter the re-articulations of race as manifested through code words, accusations of reverse discrimination, and the promotion of colorblind ideals employed by presidents, media, and intellectuals.

Defensive adaptations

Recently there has been a burgeoning literature on strategic adaptation, on how social movement actors adapt to the changing political and cultural terrain. Studies show that social movement actors are successful in gaining concessions when they strategically adapt to the changing political and cultural terrain are most successful. For example, McCammon's (2012: 19) comparative analysis of women's jury movements finds that social movement organizations must recognize changes in the broader political and cultural environment, reflect on whether or not tactical change is needed to adapt, shift tactics in response to the changed environment and implement the new tactics for a successful political outcome. Through an analysis of the discursive field, or "discursive terrain (s) in which meaning contests occur" (Spillman 1995: 140–141; Steinberg 1999: 748), in which these adaptations take place, this chapter argues that such adaptations may not always produce a successful or intended outcome.

Movement victories are not always final. Countermovement strategies and tactics can undercut or undo the successes of social movements. States can be powerful actors in this process (Pena and Davies 2017). "When governments and their policies are regarded as legitimate, extrainstitutional challenges are perceived as superfluous or counterproductive" (Maney, Woehrle, and Coy 2005). *Defensive adaptations* are a subtype of strategic adaptations employed by social movement groups that are under attack. Defensive adaptations may entail alterations to the movement's frames, but also programmatic and organizational changes that respond to the specific *types* of political and cultural opportunity challenges that activists face, particularly following social movement successes.

A racial project

Drawing on Omi and Winant (2015) the state-elite sponsored countermovement to the civil rights movement is conceptualized as a *racial project* that drew upon White racism and served to sustain the U.S. racial hierarchy. The authors provide a definition of racial projects as follows:

> We conceive of racial formation processes as occurring through a linkage between structure and signification. *Racial projects* do both the ideological and the practical "work" of making these links and articulating the connection between them. *A racial project is simultaneously an interpretation, representation, or explanation of racial identities and meanings, and an effort to organize and distribute resources (economic, political, cultural) along particular racial lines.* Racial projects connect what race means in a particular discursive or ideological practice and ways in which both social structures and everyday experiences are racially *organized*, based upon that meaning. Racial projects are attempts both to shape the ways in which social structures are racially signified and the ways that racial meanings are embedded in social structures.
>
> (2015: 125)

Omi and Winant point to the stages through which the meanings of race shifted beginning in 1970. This chapter extends their work. It provides detailed historical specificity and examines contestation processes that result in defensive adaptations on the part of social movement organizations, a topic not examined in Omi's and Winant's analysis. The state's post-racial project was and is at odds with that of civil rights organizations and had a tremendous negative effect on the capacity of the NAACP to influence social change on behalf of African Americans. As Omi and Winant stress, "Racial formation, therefore, is a synthesis, a constantly reiterated outcome, of the interaction of racial projects on a society-wide level" (Omi and Winant 2015: 127). Outcomes are shaped by the *interactions* of multiple racial projects that are not static but evolve over time. Racial projects may emanate from the state, media, intellectuals, public understandings, and social movement actors. This chapter focuses on the interactions between state-promoted meanings of race in the form of counterframes that challenged civil rights frames. These framing battles shaped public policy, and led to defensive adaptations of social movement actors as they struggled to gain control over their message.

Framing contests

Framing contests take place within the discursive field, or "discursive terrain (s) in which meaning contests occur" (Spillman 1995: 140–141; Steinberg 1999: 748). Various sets of factors engage in the discursive field or discursive opportunity structure (Ferree, Gamson, Gerhards, and Rucht 2002: 62; Gamson and Meyer 1996; Koopmans and Statham 1999; Noakes and Johnston 2005) that may include civil rights movement leaders, the media, state actors, and the larger public. They "rebut, undermine, or neutralize a person's or group's myths, version of reality, or interpretive framework" (Benford 1987: 75). The idea that state actions determine social movement outcomes is not new, but few studies (for an exception see Pena and Davies 2017) systematically examine the ways in which government discourses outside of repression and concessions can impact the capacity of social movements to effectuate change (Tilly and Goldstone 2001). As Noakes and Johnston (2005: 18) point out, "The state also engages in the struggle for cultural supremacy—albeit at a considerable advantage—by promoting frames that, if accepted, increase its legitimacy and expand its domain." Government has greater access to media and can undercut the legitimacy of movements. Thus, state actors are in an optimal position to "shape the cognitions of large numbers of people ... create their beliefs about what is proper; [and] their perceptions about what is fact" (Edelman (1971: 7). For example, Marx's (1979: 95) analysis of U.S. repression of the left in the 1960s shows that, "Actions of government ... can damage or facilitate a movement ... by creating an unfavorable public image or destroying leadership." Many of the tactics employed by the U.S. government had a negative impact on several left movements, including the civil rights movement, but Marx does not focus on the contestation process between the government and the organizations. Similarly, Staggenborg's (1991) seminal book on the pro-choice movement provides an insightful theoretical analysis and discussion of the multiple attacks by anti-abortion foes, and of the structural and institutional attempts by the Reagan administration to undercut *Roe v. Wade*, but little attention is devoted to its discursive contestation of women's right to choose.

In an effort to address this gap in the literature, Pena and Davies (2017) compare government counterframing strategies on two democratic regimes, Argentina and Brazil. Two models are offered to capture the distinctions in government responses to protest, centrifugal (responses that push government and protesters apart) and centripetal (responses that bring government and protesters together). The former emphasizes an us–them oppositional counterframe, while the latter seeks to blur this boundary. The authors state, "In the inclusive approach the commonalities between the government and the movement are emphasized" (Pena and Davies 2017: 7). This typology and the concept of centripetal responses helps to explain the post-racial discursive counterframing strategy employed by most of the presidential administrations that will be discussed. It builds on the conceptualizations of the processes of centripetal responses. Pena and Davies suggest that this approach is unlikely in government responses to racial-ethnic demands.

They state:

> The form of protest to which the counterframing response is directed is assumed to be broad-based and promoting general demands for reform, rather than drawing from a particular ethnic or social group in relation to which there may already be powerful in-group/out-group distinction from the governing party, or concerned with the promotion of a particular sectoral demand in relation to which boundary distinction and blurring may not be viable approaches to counterframing.
>
> (Pena and Davies 2017: 8)

However, this centripetal approach was taken by most presidential administrations between 1970 and 1989. There are factors that explain this choice. First, the post-racial counterframing directly challenged the meaning of the civil rights central frame of equal rights and opportunities for all. As Snow and Benford (1992) argued, the civil rights master frame was persuasive because of its "punctuation and accentuation of the idea of equal rights and opportunities amplified a fundamental American value that resonated with diverse elements of American society and thus lent itself to extensive elaboration" (p. 148). The co-optation of civil rights movement framing undercut the capacity of the NAACP to make claims on behalf of Black Americans. As will be discussed, the federal government—with powerful discursive resources at its disposal—largely won the framing contest.

Methods

To trace these framing battles a number of qualitative data sources are used, including archival materials from the Library of Congress NAACP Papers; the NAACP's *The Crisis* magazine, 1970–1989, and secondary sources including newspaper articles from the *Los Angeles Times* (1970–1989), the *New York Times* (1970–1989), and a variety of Black newspapers (1970–1989). Relevant newspaper articles were obtained using key words input into the ProQuest database. Archival materials as well as newspaper articles and magazines providing NAACP leaders' public speeches or announcements were hand coded for prevailing themes and patterns according to the methods of grounded theory (Glaser and Strauss 1967). My first task was to code the frames directed at the broader public. Second, I coded prevailing NAACP frames directed at politicians found in correspondence, reports, and speeches presented before Congress and other political representative gatherings. Frames were coded by year, and changes in frames were coded.[1] This analysis clustered the framing war between the federal government and the NAACP according to four stages between 1970 and 1990.

Stage one: 1970–1973

The countermovement's rise

Although there was strong support for principles of racial equality among Whites in the 1970s, support for government implementation of policies designed to enforce those principles were met with significant opposition.[2] In 1970, 75% of Whites agreed in principle that "white students and (Negro/black) students should go to the same schools," and that figure increased to 86% in 1972, and held steady through the latter part of the 1970s (Schuman et al. 1997: 104–105). Identical attitudinal patterns are found "toward principles of equal treatment in employment, in public accommodations, and in seating on public transportation" (Schuman et al. 1997: 111). This upward trend in support of principles of equality has been generally stronger than White support for the implementation of programs and policies to support equal rights. For example, in 1972, 54% of White Americans agreed that Washington should not enforce racial integration in schools, 35% felt government should intervene, and 12% expressed no interest (Schuman 1997: 123).

Nixon's approach to the civil rights question was rather straightforward. On the issue of busing to achieve school desegregation, for example, Nixon stated:

> My own position is well known: I am opposed to busing for the purpose of achieving racial balance in our schools. ... But what we need now is not just speaking out against more busing, we need action to stop it. First, I shall propose legislation that would call an immediate halt to all new busing orders by Federal Courts – a moratorium on new busing. And, next I shall propose a companion measure – the Equal Educational Opportunities

Act of 1972. This act would require that every state or locality grant equal educational opportunities to every person regardless of race, color or nation origin. For the first time in our history, the cherished American ideal of equality of educational opportunity would be affirmed in the law of the land by the elected representative of the people in Congress.

(*New York Times*, Transcript of Nixon's Statement on School Busing, March 17, 1972)

Nowhere in the speech is a reference to "forced busing," as would become a symbolic phrase under President Ford. Nixon's approach was more direct and referenced framings employed during the civil rights movement. Nixon, of course, sought to appeal to Whites, even liberals. In the following statement, he addressed the implied meaning behind anti-busing sentiments:

One emotional undercurrent that has done much to make this issue so difficult is the feeling that some people have that to oppose busing is to be anti-black. This is dangerous nonsense. There's no escaping the fact that some people do oppose busing because of racial prejudice. But to go on from this to conclude that antibusing is simply a code word for prejudice is a vicious libel on millions of concerned-parents who oppose busing— not because they are against desegregation, but because they are for better education for their children.

(*New York Times*, Transcript of Nixon's Statement on School Busing, March 17, 1972)

Nixon provides a rationale for the lack of support for busing that moves the debate away from racial prejudice to quality of education. He continued:

Many have invested their life savings in a home in a neighborhood they choose because it had good schools. They do not want their children bused across the city to an inferior school just to meet some social planner's concept of what is considered to be the correct racial balance or, what is called progressive social policy. And most people, including a large and increasing number of blacks, oppose it for reasons that have little or nothing to do with race.

(*New York Times*, Transcript of Nixon's Statement on School Busing, March 17, 1972)

Thus, he situates the problem away from racist beliefs and practices.

Opinions on race directly impacted voting patterns. A 1972 Illinois study of the presidential vote found that race influenced which candidate, Nixon or George McGovern, was supported. "'73% of white voters who believed that America had done enough to help blacks voted for Nixon. The majority of Illinois' voters felt that Nixon's stance on black rights mirrored their own'" (*Tri-State Defender*,

May 5, 1973, 22(18): 6, "Being Frank: Poll Says U.S. Has Done Enough on Civil Rights," by Stanley L. Frank quoting Oliver Quayle's Poll).

By 1972, attuned to White public opinion, erstwhile political allies backed away from their previous support of the NAACP because it championed federal government enforcement of school desegregation, anti-discrimination housing laws, and equal opportunity in employment and college admissions. This occurred although Democrats controlled both the House and the Senate. As Morsell, Associate Director of the NAACP pointed out,

> From one end of the country to the other, men and women of all political persuasions who have been counted in the ranks of civil rights fighters have scurried to cover in the face of a popular anti-busing mood based on ignorance of the facts.
> (NAACP Roy Wilkins Papers, Box 18, Statement of John A. Morsell, Associate Director, NAACP, On Behalf of the Leadership Conference on Civil Rights, Before the Platform Committee of the Republican National Convention, Miami Beach, Florida, August 16, 1972, 3:30 P.M.)

That President Nixon and his administration capitalized on anti-busing public opinion is clear.

Stage one NAACP defensive adaptation: in the best interests of Whites and Blacks

Morris (1999: 522) reflected, in the cold war period, "Racism and democracy were opposing ideologies." NAACP President Wilkins continued to emphasize the common fate of Whites and Blacks. He stressed that "regardless of the opinions of many whites, some in key political positions, civil rights for minorities are bound up with the general welfare of all Americans" (as quoted in the *Los Angeles Times*, February 22, 1973, p. C7, "Civil Rights for Minorities Are Tied to the Welfare of All," Roy Wilkins, ProQuest). Wilkins warned, "Race discrimination, especially that which is tied ... to some federal policy, hurts more than one-tenth of Americans and damages to a far greater extent the nation's world image" (ibid.).

Later that year, when the Watergate scandal emerged which ultimately led to Nixon's resignation, Wilkins once again reframed the need for Whites to support Black civil rights because it was in their own interest to do so. Without referring to the 1972 break-in at National Democratic Headquarters in the Watergate Hotel, which was authorized by the Committee to Re-Elect the President, he stated, "Most white people, like people everywhere, brush aside the talk about Negro constitutional rights until their own personal rights are endangered" (*Los Angeles Times*, October 30, 1973, p. A7, "Out of the Sickness, Perhaps a Cure for the Denial of Rights," Roy Wilkins, ProQuest). Thus, in many ways, the NAACP continued its 1960s master frame of equal rights and opportunities.

Stage two: 1974–1976

Framing a "post-racial America": the racial project of the (racial) state

The year 1974 was to mark the beginning of a state-supported countermovement that actively employed frame co-optation in its political discourse. This new countermovement strategy precipitated a restriction of ideological opportunities and began the process of the delegitimization of the NAACP. The appropriation of 1960s civil rights framing that in no small part led to 1960s legislative and legal victories now became the foundation of "post-racial" U.S. discourse.

According to this emerging perspective, one that tapped into long-held U.S. cultural identities of whiteness (Roediger 1991), Black civil rights had been achieved, and while discrimination persisted, most U.S. citizens (Whites) were no longer racists. Any remaining barriers could be overcome by hard work and a motivation to achieve the American Dream. While Nixon restricted the enforcement of civil rights legislation, he had not created a counterframe that coopted and distorted the message of the civil rights movement. Now the NAACP's master frame that rested on moral imperatives and appealed to the longstanding U.S. narrative of "liberty and justice for all" was undercut by political and intellectual elites.

Gerald Ford became president after Nixon's resignation on August 4, 1974. His speech that year before the National Urban League strongly suggests that Blacks had achieved civil rights and that the primary obstacles to Black mobility were a lack of skills and an insufficient education. He stated:

> This Nation has raised the last generation of American citizens that will see some of its members denied opportunity to find and hold decent jobs ... Minorities and women are not standing on the outside trying to get Civil Rights laws on the books. The laws are on the books and significant numbers are now on the inside helping to enforce them ... Minorities are no longer marching and staging sit-ins to gain access to lunch counters and other public accommodations. The thrust of the 70s is to own some of those lunch counters and other business enterprises ...
>
> Even with the progress which has been made, minorities and women continue to occupy the lowest-paying, least desirable jobs—when they have jobs at all. Non-discrimination laws cannot alone change these gross disparities. Because of this, the National Urban League, Opportunities Industrialization Centers and others will become more important than ever. Through your involvement and your close working relationship with industry and government you have developed the expertise, the know-how that renders you an essential national resource. I have no doubt that you will fulfill that role.
> (As quoted in the *Sun Reporter*, August 17, 1974, XXXI(33), p. 6, "Ford's Speech to the National Urban League," ProQuest)

Similarly, Ford, in his 1975 address before the NAACP Convention, suggested that Black advancement was now in the hands of the organization. Successful Blacks must uplift those left behind. He stated:

> I have come here not to offer a checklist of specific programs and promises for blacks. I come as President of all the people to talk with you about common problems and common- sense approaches … Today, laws ensure the rights of all Americans. The end of racial discrimination by law has paved the way to the beginning of full participation. But the progress you have made has been threatened by a troubled economy. It is not rich against poor, black against white. Instead, there is mutual recognition that any of us may be the next victim of unemployment and that all of us will most certainly be the next victims of inflation …
> (NAACP Papers, Administrative File VIII: Box 11, Office of the White House Press Secretary, The White House, Text of Remarks by the President to be Delivered to the 66th Annual Convention of the National Association for the Advancement of Colored People, Sheraton Park Hotel, July 1, 1975)

The Ford Administration was promoting a post-racial discourse that framed the civil rights struggle as having been won, thus insisting that Black progress depends largely on the groups' ability to pull itself up by the bootstraps. At a Black Baptist National Convention in St. Louis, Missouri, he more clearly articulated his post-racial discourse. Emphasizing that Americans constitute a family with a common destiny and the need to "appeal to higher aspirations than the law," he stated:

> The American experience has been that competition in all walks of our national life strengthens our country. As a people we believe in competition. Today, as never before, Blacks are competing in our society and America is better for it. This is the American dream being fulfilled. Many of our problems of modern living cannot be dealt with through legislation, through government money. They can only be solved from within the home, within the community, and within the private enterprise system of competition.
> (As quoted in the *Oakland Post,* October 12, 1975, 11(98), p. 3, Text of President Ford's Remarks to National Baptist Convention, AP)

Ford was not alone in his viewpoint, and his articulation of a post-racial discourse resonated with the general White public.

Stage two defensive adaptations to the "post-racial" frame

Expanding the focus

Although the NAACP remained steadfastly focused on discrimination against Blacks, it considerably expanded its attention beyond the confines of racial desegregation. Some of their new programs overlapped with the concerns of the poor and other oppressed groups. In addition to supporting affirmative action policies, the organization attacked conventional measures of evaluating academic and employment qualifications. The 1971 Supreme Court ruling in the *Griggs v. Duke Power Company* case, declared it illegal to employ tests that did not directly measure the probability of job success in hiring and promotion. The NAACP argued that this precedent should be applied to the use of the Scholastic Aptitude Test in assessing the suitability of applicants to the Reserve Officer Training Corps and military academies. They also resolved that standardized tests unfairly place children in special education classes, label "black children as uneducable, and serve to discriminate against them in admissions to college, graduate, and professional programs" (NAACP Papers, Administrative File, VIII, Box 8, NAACP 65th Annual Convention Resolutions, July 1–July 5, 1974, New Orleans, Louisiana, Resolution VI, 11. Testing, *The Crisis*, April 1975, p. 129).

While these issues served as extensions of their previous concerns, the organization branched out even further, addressing police brutality for the first time in their 1970s annually published resolutions (NAACP Papers, Administrative File, VIII, Box 8, NAACP 65th Annual Convention Resolutions, July 1–July 5, 1974, New Orleans, Louisiana, Resolution IV. Civil Rights). 1. The Vice of Over-Reaction; 2. Police Brutality, *The Crisis* April 1975, pg. 124) They also focused attention on discrimination in the prosecution and sentencing of Blacks by increasing prison chapters and creating Project Rebound, a New York pilot program designed to "rehabilitate, ex-offenders through counseling, job placement, education and other services… to reduce recidivism" (*Sacramento Observer*, Apr. 3, 1974. Vol. 11, Iss. 7; pg. B-3, Crime Is Nation's No. 1 Problem by Roy Wilkins, ProQuest).

Organizational restructuring

Despite the expanded focus, members of the NAACP Board were dissatisfied with Wilkins' leadership and in a publicly nasty fight ousted him from the organization. On January 10, 1976, they hired McKinsey & Company Inc., a consulting firm. The latter's report noted several problems with the administration and strategic approach of the NAACP with an emphasis on funding and public relations (Roy Wilkins Papers, Box 18, Meeting the Challenge, NAACP 1976, January 10, 1976 by McKinsey & Co., Inc. p.8)

> In part, they urged the NAACP to hire professionals who could solicit corporate and institutional grants; to increase the racial composition of its membership; and, to improve public relations to "change majority attitudes towards civil rights" (Roy Wilkins Papers, Box 18, Meeting the Challenge, NAACP 1976, January 10, 1976 by McKinsey & Co., Inc. p.19). Thus, by the mid- 1970s the organization was acutely aware of the need to better convey its message to the masses.

Stage three: 1977–1978

The racial project's "class not race" frame

While President Jimmy Carter did not engage in promoting post-racial discourse, the wheels continued to turn in Congress and in the public arena. Determined to oust Ford, the NAACP and other Black organizations mobilized support for the election of President Jimmy Carter, bringing him approximately 94% of the Black vote. After the election there were over 3000 Blacks holding public office most of whom were from the South (Roy Wilkins Papers, Box 13, NAACP 1976 Voter Education Report Summary, Political Action, by W. C. Patton, Recapitulation).

Congress passed two anti-desegregation measures in the Housing, Education, and Welfare (HEW) appropriations bill. The first "limited HEW's authority to conduct school desegregation surveys" and the second strengthened the Byrd amendment "that bars the government from requiring busing for school desegregation if the bus takes a pupil beyond the school nearest his or her home. The measure bars busing coupled with pairing and clustering of schools for the purpose of desegregation" (*Los Angeles Times*, July 28, 1977, Aim at Congress, Rights Leaders Told, ProQuest). The Carter Administration fended off support for a measure that "would have prevented the government from imposing quotas, ratios or other numerical criteria in student admissions and employment discrimination cases" (ibid.).

The thrust of an increasingly accepted U.S. post-racial discourse emphasized class divisions among African-Americans with the success of the Black middle class touted as proof of a post-racial society, and emblematic of the decline in racism and discrimination. An article in *Time* magazine serves as a perfect example of the contradictions in American racial discourse in 1977 that simultaneously blamed the victim (and the victim's culture), while acknowledging institutional racism and discrimination. Upwardly mobile Blacks and Latinxs are compared to the Black underclass "stuck at the bottom [and] removed from the American dream (p. 14)." As *Time* reported in its August 29, 1977 issue, "[The underclass] are more intractable, more socially alien and more hostile than almost anyone had imagined ... Though its members come from all races and live in many places, the underclass is made up mostly of impoverished urban blacks, who still suffer from the heritage of slavery and discrimination" (NAACP General Office File, VIII: 391.2, *Time*, August 29, 1977, "The American Underclass: Destitute and Desperate in the Land of Plenty," p. 14).

While the article acknowledges "the flight of manufacturing firms—many requiring only semi-skilled or even unskilled labor—to the suburbs and the Sunbelt ..." (p. 18) and, "the overly strict and exclusionary union apprenticeship rules" (p. 21) that contribute to high rates of Black unemployment and poverty, the Black subculture is also blamed. The article suggests that juxtaposed against a subculture characterized as "psychological[ly] and material[ly] destitute" that condones and supports "looters or arsonists or violent criminals" is "one of America's great success sagas. The rise of many blacks to the secure middle class" (p.15). Acknowledging the persistence of "some discrimination," the article states that "more and more nonwhites are seen in at least the junior management ranks of banks and corporations and government, where they are moving up" (p. 15). Harvard University sociologist David Riesman is quoted as saying, "'The awareness that many blacks have been successful means that the underclass is more resentful and more defiant because its alibi isn't there'" (p. 15). The implication is that while traces of racism linger, Blacks have only themselves to blame for their impoverished conditions. Poor Whites and Hispanics, the article suggests, are able to stay the course and advance because they lack the pathologies of the Black underclass who suffer from "the weakness of family structure, the presence of competing street values, and the lack of hope amidst affluence" (p. 16). For the Black underclass, income and jobs are unrelated, and "for many women in the underclass, welfare has turned illegitimate pregnancy into a virtual career" (p. 18). The article concludes that "there is no all-embracing solution, at any price" (p. 18), and the "underclass must help itself out of its morass" (p. 27). Post-racial discourse, then, continued to shift away from blaming racist practices and acts of discrimination for continuing racial inequality that must be offset by government enforcement of civil rights legislation and racial integration.

The liberal intellectual forum in support of Black civil rights was increasingly replaced by White liberal arguments steeped in the new racial ideology. Nathan Glazer's book *Affirmative Discrimination* argued that racial discrimination was no longer a significant factor in the new post-civil rights society. Articles appearing in the liberal *New Republic* touting meritocracy were nearly indistinguishable from George Will's conservative position on affirmative action policy that appeared in the *Washington Post*. Black leaders found themselves fighting against what Whites believed was the myth of continued racial discrimination because the civil rights movement battle was over and Blacks now enjoyed racial equality (*Black Enterprise*, January 1978, 8(6), p. 41, "New Racism," by Joel Dreyfuss). As Joel Dreyfuss wrote in a *Black Enterprise* article, Black "demands for equality are viewed as a danger to the high standards of society. The implication is that the white male domination of American institutions is the result of a merit system that ... simply rewarded the most able" (ibid., p. 42). And he points out that Whites do not view Blacks as the most able.

Stage three defensive adaptations: school quality, voiceless minorities, Black coalitions, school quality

There was a detectable shift in the NAACP's framing of concerns regarding educational opportunity. Previously, the organization focused almost exclusively on racial integration as a means of obtaining racial equality in education. Now, the organization extended the educational equality concern to all citizens.

Recently appointed NAACP Executive Director Benjamin Hooks stated, "Our nation can no longer ignore the fact that the quality of education in our schools is steadily deteriorating. Johnny, irrespective of race, is being graduated from high school without having achieved the basic survival skills of reading, writing and arithmetic" (NAACP Administration File VIII 53: 1, "Excerpts from the Remarks of Mr. Benjamin L. Hooks, Executive Director/Chief Executive Officer of the National Association for the Advancement of Colored People," 1977 p. 6).

The tide of non-support of school busing continued even among liberal Democrats. On December 9, 1977, a legislative anti-busing bill co-authored by Senators Thomas F. Eagleton (D- Mo) and Joseph Biden (D- Del), was approved by the Senate. The Department of Health, Education and Welfare could no longer use federal funds "to require, directly or indirectly, the transportation of any student to a school other than the school which is nearest the student's home, except for a student requiring special education" (as quoted in *Los Angeles Times*, March 29, 1978, p. A2, "Law on Busing Aims to Hurt Integration, HEW Charges"). Carter signed the bill in December 1977 (Halpern (1995: 157), and the Justice Department would not challenge its passage (ibid., 1978, p. A2).

The writing was on the wall, and although the NAACP continued its pursuit of desegregation, litigating 27 school desegregation cases, there was a discernable shift towards an emphasis on the quality of all children's education. Shifting the focus on quality did not preclude a continued interest in school desegregation, but it signaled a growing acknowledgment that full integration was likely unachievable. A less controversial approach was a focus on increasing the quality of schools for both Blacks and Whites. With a full commitment, segregated Black schools could be improved.

Voiceless minorities

Although Hooks did not abandon advocacy on behalf of African Americans, by September of 1977, he emphasized policy changes designed to help the poor, women, and all minorities. In meeting with President Carter, Hooks described the NAACP mission:

> We were there on behalf of more than 500,000 NAACP members, and in a larger sense, the broad mass of voiceless minorities and women throughout the country who have little access to the decision-making power centers of our country. Our laundry list included: Unemployment, welfare reform, minimum wage, health, age discrimination and employment act, tax reform, energy, criminal justice, the Humphrey-Hawkins full employment bill, urban policy, housing, education, electoral college reform, Africa and consumer protection.
> (*Tri-State Defender*, November 5, 1977, 26(45), p. 5, "New day begun: the NAACP's success with President Jimmy Carter," by Benjamin L. Hooks)

Regarding employment and economic development, the NAACP advocated for "the right to a job; [and] the right to earn a living for one's family; and the right to escape the welfare rolls" (NAACP Administration File VIII 53:1, Excerpts from the Remarks of Mr. Benjamin L. Hooks, Executive Director/ Chief Executive Officer of the National Association for the Advancement of Colored People, p. 2a, 1977).

Black-organization coalitions

Frustration with Carter's slow and inadequate response to the increasing Black crisis led the NAACP and other Black organizations to adopt a new "collective" strategy. For the first time since the 1964 March on Washington, led by Dr. Martin Luther King Jr., all the major Black organizations met to discuss priorities and to set an agenda for Carter. The meeting of what would later be known as the Black Leadership Forum was held at the National Urban League's headquarters in New York.

The myriad interests focused on three priorities that included

> Ample financing for the ambattled [sic] urban policy being developed under the leadership of the Department of Housing and Urban development; substantially increased commitments of money to combat unemployment, particularly among black youth, and a plan developed in the Office of management and Budget for the reorganization of the equal employment enforcement functions of the Federal Government.
> (*New York Times*, December 19, 1977, p. 15, "Black Leaders: A New Approach at White House," by Roger Wilkins)

The Black leadership's hour-long meeting on December 14, 1977 in the Roosevelt Room of the White House with President Carter, Patricia Roberts Harris, the Secretary of Housing and Urban Development, and other Administration officials was marginally successful (*New York Times*, December 15, 1977, p. 25, "Black Leaders Find Carter Ready to Aid: But after Meeting at White House, They Express Doubt that He Will Obtain Enough Money," by David E. Rosenbaum). Carter agreed to support a revised and considerably watered-down version of the Humphrey–Hawkins bill. The 1977 version did not include a provision for new jobs, omitted "any requirement for the Federal Government to be the 'employer of last resort' for the chronically unemployed," and deleted "the provision barring the President from sacrificing his low unemployment goal for the sake of fighting inflation. The bill also extend[ed] the timetable for attaining the four percent unemployment goal by two years to 1983" (as quoted in *The Skanner*, December 15, 1977. Vol. III(9), p. 2, "Jobs for the Poor: NAACP Executive Director," by Benjamin L. Hooks, ProQuest). He also pledged to support an urban renewal program that would require an expansion of several government programs at a cost of $8 billion to $12 billion dollars (*New York Times*, December 15, 1977, p. 25, "Black Leaders Find Carter Ready to AID:

But After Meeting at White House, They Express Doubt that He Will Obtain Enough Money," by David E. Rosenbaum). The leaders doubted that Congress would approve the substantial increase but pledged to continue pressing for funding to address the needs of the urban poor.

Programmatic and goal adaptations to post-racial frame

Hooks gradually expanded the organization's programmatic and goal foci. For example at the January 7, 1978 NAACP Policy and Planning Committee meeting in New York City, the group outlined several new priorities including the "development of an economic package addressing problems of joblessness; teenage unemployment; energy; taxation; establishment of NAACP Communications Department; launching of ACT-SO (Afro-American, Academic, Cultural and Technological Olympics); and carrying out of sustained voter registration drive, particularly in urban centers" (NAACP Administration File VIII 53:2, Strictly Confidential, Minutes, NAACP Policy and Plans Committee, Hotel Sheraton, New York City, Saturday, January 7, 1978 p. 6). Longtime staffer Nathaniel Jones was concerned that these "subject areas" be incorporated into the NAACP's older ongoing programs (NAACP Administration File VIII 53:2, Strictly Confidential, Minutes, NAACP Policy and Plans Committee, Hotel Sheraton, New York City, Saturday, January 7, 1978, p. 7). There was some concern that the public might perceive the expansion of programs and goals as a shift in priorities. Longtime staffer Gloster Current cautioned that the NAACP not appear to abandon its commitment to school desegregation or to the "traditional civil rights thrusts" (ibid., p. 9). In the end, the committee agreed that the economic focus should hold the highest priority and, "requested staff to develop strategies and resources necessary, without abandoning or lessening [the] thrust on other fronts" (NAACP Administration File VIII 53:2, Strictly Confidential, Minutes, NAACP Policy and Plans Committee, Hotel Sheraton, New York City, Saturday, January 7, 1978 p. 10).

Although integrating the new programs into existing ones, it was clear that the NAACP was expanding its agenda and reshaping its image to address issues beyond the equal rights and opportunities frame. Later they discussed the Electoral College, undocumented workers, and abortion rights. Another significant shift focused on energy policy. The NAACP hosted an NAACP National Energy Conference and released The NAACP National Energy Report (NAACP Board of Directors VIII 66:2, December 1, 1978, Report of the NAACP National Energy Conference). Additionally, Hooks expanded the organization's network by meeting with Black and Latinx leaders in Washington, D.C. to plan a policy presentation to the White House and Justice Department officials (NAACP Administration File VIII 53:4, Minutes: NAACP Policy & Plans Committee, November 15, 1978, New York). The NAACP's expansion of its framing, goals and policies to include issues that extended beyond Black-centered civil rights, initially proved more difficult than anticipated. A media frenzy ensued that questioned the suitability of the organization's new foci, particularly on energy.

Stage four: the racial project intensifies 1978–1989

The racial project's four powerful counterframes

Reverse discrimination

In late June of 1978, the U.S. Supreme Court, with a 5–4 ruling, supported Allan Bakke's claim that the UC Davis medical school's admission policy that considered race was illegal and constituted reverse discrimination against White applicants. Bakke was admitted to the program. However, the State Supreme Court's ruling that race cannot be used in affirmative action policies was overturned. Of the ruling, Nathaniel Jones, NAACP General Counsel, stated, "'It was untenable. It had to be reversed. Otherwise it would have changed the 14th amendment from a shield protecting our rights into a sword that could be used to decapitate us'" (as quoted in *Sun Reporter*, June 29, 1978, Vol. XXXV(26), p. 3, "Affirmative Action Threatened: Blacks React to the Bakke Decision," by Peter Magnani). Jones believed that the Bakke case was representative of a growing "'climate of intense hostility' against minorities in the United States. 'We're under siege'" (ibid.).

Ironically, the Supreme Court's decision rested on its belief that the UC Davis policy violated Section 601 of the Civil Rights Act of 1964. The Act was designed to protect Blacks and other racial minorities from discrimination. Now, it was applied to the rights of Allan Bakke.

Section 601 states, "No person in the United States shall on the ground of race, color, or national origin, be excluded from participation in, be denied the benefits of, or be subjected to discrimination under any program or activity receiving Federal financial assistance" (as quoted in *Bay State Banner*, July 6, 1978, 13(39), p. 4, "A Giant Step Backwards"). The majority opinion, written by Justice Powell, also stated that Blacks were not entitled to special protections under the Fourteenth Amendment (ibid.) but that race conscious remedies are permissible if the State employs them to remedy or eliminate the effects of discrimination (NAACP Board of Directors VIII 66:3, Annual Report Introduction, p. 2). They did not believe that UC Davis' desire to increase minority representation justified discrimination against non-minorities. Supreme Court Justice Thurgood Marshall stated in his dissenting opinion:

> While I applaud the judgment of the court that a university may consider race in its admissions process, it is more than a little ironic that, after several hundred years of class-based discrimination against Negroes, the court is unwilling to hold that a class-based remedy for that discrimination is

permissible. The experience of Negroes in America has been different in kind, not just in degree, from that of other ethnic groups. It is not merely the history of slavery alone but also that a whole people were marked as inferior by the law. And that mark has endured.
(As quoted in *Sun Reporter,* July 6, 1978, Vol. XXXV(27), p. 4, "Only Black on the Court: The Text of Marshall's Dissent")

The only Black on the Supreme Court, Marshall succinctly argued his case for Black exceptionalism—the uniqueness of racism against Black Americans. Implicit in his argument is a belief in the persistence of racial discrimination. The majority opinion, in contrast, equated the races, and outlawed the use of racial quotas and set-asides that treat Blacks and other minorities as a special class deserving greater protection under the Fourteenth Amendment. This ruling set the stage for the further cooptation of the meaning of discrimination and racism. The frame would flip such that Whites were now the victims of discrimination. The meaning of discrimination and civil rights victories would change.

In 1984, the Justice Department's Civil Rights Division was at odds with the NAACP in that it stood staunchly against support for affirmative action programs and became a champion of its demise. Hooks, appearing on CBS's *Face the Nation*, castigated William Bradford Reynolds, chief of the Justice Department's Civil Rights Division. The latter had praised a recent Supreme Court decision upholding seniority systems in a Memphis, Tennessee case, *Firefighters v. Stotts*, in which three senior White firefighters had been laid off instead of recently hired Blacks. The fire department claimed it was compelled to retain the Black firefighters to comply with their affirmative action plan. The court held that affirmative action plans, compliant with federal anti-discrimination laws, must be designed to aid individuals not groups. Reynolds celebrated the decision calling it a "'monumental triumph for civil rights'" (as quoted in *Los Angeles Times*, June 18, 1984, p. B9, "NAACP Chief Says Official's Hiring Stand Will Stir Racial Tension," by Don Irvin). Reynolds proclaimed his intent to examine "all court ordered affirmative action plans involving the federal government to rid them of 'race-conscious' provisions" (ibid.). The Justice Department's quest was met with support from several in Congress, including Senator Orrin G. Hatch (R-Utah), and chair of the Senate Labor and Human Resources Committee, who argued that the firefighters had been victims of a system that was "'used to discriminate against them, [and that] you don't end discrimination by discriminating against others. Civil rights today has become a quest for civil rights privileges that leads to preferential treatment of certain people over other people, and thus reverse discrimination'" (ibid.). Hatch further argued that the decision was a "'victory for blacks. It means that blacks who were in that seniority pipeline are not going to lose their jobs because of prejudice'" (ibid.). Thus, civil rights victories, that had in the past reflected the greater inclusion of Blacks, now stood to defend the privileges of Whites. The language places Whites as victims of discrimination and Blacks as recipients of preferential treatment in an otherwise color-blind system.

Code words

Candidate Ronald Reagan was a master at the use of code words during his presidential campaign. On August 3, 1980, he made a reference to "states' rights" in a speech before a predominantly White audience in Philadelphia, Mississippi. The term has had a long history that was exacerbated during the civil rights movement and most Southern states resented federal government enforcement of Black rights. When three civil rights activists, Andrew Goodman, James E. Chaney, and Michael H. Schwerner, disappeared in Mississippi, the FBI discovered the activists had been murdered and buried with local law-enforcement assistance. After the passage of the 1965 voting rights act, White Southern politicians seeking the Black vote steered clear of the term. Thus, when Reagan stated his support for states' rights and his commitment to, "'restore to state and local governments the power that properly belongs to them'," either wittingly or unwittingly, to Blacks, he conveyed a message of support for a return to Jim Crow laws. President Carter capitalized on Reagan's remarks. During his appearance at Atlanta's Ebenezer Baptist Church, where Martin Luther King, Jr., previously presided as its minister, Carter stated, "'you have seen in this campaign the stirrings of hate and the rebirth of code words like 'states' rights' in Mississippi and in a campaign reference to the Ku Klux Klan relating to the South'" (as quoted in *New York Times*, September 27. 1980, p. 8, "Race Issue in Campaign: A Chain Reaction," by John Herbers).

On December 11, 1980, leaders of several Black organizations including the NAACP, the National Urban League, the Southern Christian Leadership Conference, and the National Urban Coalition, met with President-elect Ronald Reagan at Blair House across the street from the White House. Benjamin Hooks was there as chairman of the Black Leadership Forum. Reagan persisted in his belief in states' rights such that each state could protect Blacks' rights. He was unsupportive of busing for the purposes of school desegregation, and was reluctant to make a specific commitment to appointing Blacks to his Cabinet. In fact, announced on the day of his meeting with the Black leaders, were eight nominees for cabinet positions. All were White men (*New York Times*, December 12, 1980, p. A31, "Black Leaders Declare Differences Remain After a Talk with Reagan," by David E. Rosenbaum).

The color-blind frame

The Reagan Administration ushered in seemingly race neutral terminology that directly challenged Black demands. For example, Assistant Attorney General William Bradford Reynolds spoke before the Black National Bar Association in support of the administration's stand against quotas and affirmative action programs. He also asserted a color-blind position stating:

> We are not a special interest law firm, and we cannot tailor either our legal interpretations or our enforcement policies to serve any particular

group, whether its membership is defined by economic circumstances, political affiliation, race, sex or any other simply irrelevant criteria.
> (As quoted in *Los Angeles Times*, August 9, 1983, p. A1, "Justice Dept. Not Just for Minorities, Blacks Are Told," From Reuters)

The Reagan Administration was successfully outmaneuvering the NAACP by hijacking the latter's arguments. Vice President George Bush's speech at the 1983 NAACP convention acknowledged the Reagan Administration's disagreement with the organization's position on affirmative action programs stating:

> We differ on quotas. Our position is that we just don't think the way to fight racism is by setting up race as a criterion. Our approach is to fight racism and discrimination not by seeking quotas but by seeking justice—and that's the principle on which the NAACP itself was formed.
> (NAACP Papers, Administration File VIII: 32, Excerpts from Remarks by Vice President George Bush at the National Convention of the National Association for the Advancement of Colored People Rivergate Convention Center New Orleans, Louisiana Friday, July 15, 1983)

Of his recent appointments, Reagan in a speech before the American Bar Association commented, "'I don't believe you can remedy past discrimination by mandating new discrimination. They are committed activists for genuine civil and human rights'" (As quoted in *Los Angeles Times*, August 8, 1983, p. C5, "Reagan Not Racist, but Policies Seem to Be," by David S. Broader). Reagan employed the term "mandatory quotas" to show his contempt for and to further stigmatize affirmative action programs (ibid.). Regarding his appointments to the U.S. Commission on Civil Rights, including his choice of conservative Linda Chavez to be staff director, Reagan explained:

> We do not, and we will never, just because they are men or women, whites or blacks, Jews, Catholics or whatever. I don't look at people as members of groups, I look at them as individuals and as Americans. I believe you rob people of their dignity and confidence when you impose quotas. The implicit and false message of quotas is that some people can't make it under the same rules that apply to everyone else.
> (As quoted in *Los Angeles Times*, August 2, 1983, p. B1, "Reagan Calls Criticism of Nominees 'Hogwash': Defends Civil Rights Appointees in ABA Speech while seeking to Rebut Charges of Unfairness," by Robert Shogan)

The Administration stated its clear position as a champion against discrimination and injustice, and as no less committed to it than the NAACP. They differed only in method. Bush implied that while the NAACP was willing to fight inequality employing reverse racism with quotas, the administration was not.

Thus, the administration enjoyed the higher moral ground. Newly appointed Chair on the Commission for Civil Rights Pendleton believed that Black civil rights leaders were practicing a "'new racism'" by supporting preferential treatment for minority groups. The new racists were, he suggested, "typically supporters of civil rights. Many of them are the media-designate Black leaders." He continued, "Our so-called black leaders are spending every moment peddling pain, complaining about budget cuts ..." but not trying to work with President Reagan to forge a color-blind society (*Los Angeles Times*, March 5, 1985, p. A1, "Black Leaders Draw Charge of 'New Racism'," AP).

Class not race frame amplification

In the widely publicized debate between a White former civil rights activist, Carl Gershman, and Kenneth Clark, a prominent Black psychologist, the former strongly suggests that racism is no longer a significant impediment to Black upward mobility (*New York Times*, October 5, 1980, p. SM6, "A Matter of Class," by Carl Gershman). In contrast, Clark argued that a new form of racism was impeding Black progress and contributing to the conditions of the Black underclass. Clark stated, "I find it difficult to understand how it is possible to comprehend the cycle of pathology that characterizes the ghettos except in terms of racial oppression. Race, not class, must be the answer" (*New York Times*, October 5, 1980, p. SM6, "A Matter of Class: Kenneth B. Clark Responds," by Kenneth B. Clark). Gershman criticized Black leaders and scholars for their failure to acknowledge and address Black pathologies, and concluded that the Black middle class must face the intraracial class divide. Citing the work of Wilson, who argued that class is a more significant predictor of life chances than race, and Sowell, who suggested that affirmative action programs stigmatize Blacks and undermine their motivation to acquire better skills, Gershman emphasized the closing economic gap between similarly educated Blacks and Whites. Driven by the maintenance of their class, Gershman contended that Black leaders' support of affirmative action programs served to benefit the middle class rather than the poor. The ideological myth that White racism disadvantages Blacks, he asserted, was propagated to selfishly sustain the positions of civil rights organizations and Black leaders. Quoting Clark, who was also critical of the Black middle class albeit for deserting the underclass and for failing to adequately address their plight, Gershman accused the Black bourgeoisie of ignoring the cultural pathology of the poor that suffered from "'low aspirations, poor education, family instability, illegitimacy, unemployment, crime, drug addiction, and alcoholism'" (as quoted in *New York Times*, October 5, 1980, p. SM6, "A Matter of Class," by Carl Gershman).

Not only was the nation and Congress increasingly hostile towards federal programs to enforce racial equality, but racial discourse had shifted away from racial discrimination to "the tangle of pathologies" that purportedly served to sustain and worsen Black poverty in what was now coined the "ghetto underclass." A series of scholarly books written from the mid-1960s to the late 1970s by African Americans, including Kenneth Clark's *Dark Ghetto*, Thomas Sowell's *Race and Economics*, and William Julius Wilson's *The Declining Significance of Race*, were employed by conservatives and White liberal intellectuals to support the view that poor Blacks were "culturally" different than middle-class Blacks.

As *Chicago Tribune* journalists Timothy J. McNulty and Hanke Gratteau describe in their December 1, 1985 article, "The black underclass is a group of undetermined number in the central cities joined by ignorance, crime [either as criminal or victim] and poverty. The common characteristics are joblessness, teenage pregnancy, illegitimate births, female-headed families, serious crime and welfare dependency" (NAACP Papers, General Office Fund VIII 391: 3, *Chicago Tribune*, "In a Nation of Riches, A Permanent Underclass," 12/1/85, by Timothy J. McNulty and Hanke Gratteau, Patrick Reardon also contributed to this story, p. 3). They summarize the mood of many regarding government entitlements targeted towards the black underclass as follows:

> It has absorbed billions of dollars and persisted through all Great Society programs. Now it has helped create a backlash at the failure of some of those programs. And angry resentment exists throughout the nation today, and there is accepted scorn for notions of liberalism and social legislation aimed at the disadvantaged.
>
> (Ibid.)

In the late 1980s, headlines from the *Chicago Tribune* alone included titles such as "City Worker Among 47 Charged with Illegally Receiving Welfare," "Cards Fight Welfare Fraud," "23 People Charged with Welfare Fraud," "Woman Gets Jail for Welfare Fraud," and "25 Indicted and Welfare Fraud Probe" (http://articles.chicagotribune.com/keyword/welfare-fraud/featured/3). Ronald Reagan and other conservatives believed that welfare and the Great Society programs created an incentive that discouraged Blacks from seeking work and encouraged them to live off of government entitlements. In Reagan's radio addresses and his State of the Union Message, he characterized Black poverty as a "'national tragedy'" and blamed it on "'misguided welfare programs'" that have encouraged illegitimacy and single female-headed households. Welfare, he stated, was a "'spider's web'" that did not release its victims (as quoted in *New York Times*, March 3, 1986, "Letters: Poverty is Thriving Under Reagan," by Ronald Takaki, Professor of Ethnic Studies University of California Berkeley, February 16, 1986).

Laissez-faire liberalism

There was an increasing divide among liberals that reflected a significant departure from the coalition that formed in support of Black civil rights during the 1960s. As John Brown Childs, a professor of anthropology and

Afro-American studies at Yale, so aptly described in his 1980 *N.Y. Times* article "Liberals vs. Liberals," laissez-faire liberals, or those "who believed that individual success depended simply on the willingness to work," increasingly dominated government policy.

The split with social liberals, "who believed that a deep and pernicious racism prevented the advancement of black people" was brought to a head by the economic crisis (*New York Times*, August 22, 1980, p. A 23, "Liberals vs. Liberals," by John Brown Childs). Accordingly, Black organizations now faced a new ideological reality. Brown suggested:

> The tactics and strategies of black organizations must now be tied to the reality of the revival of American laissez-faire liberalism. Rather than calling upon an old coalition that has been abandoned by the laissez-faire liberals as an alternative to the isolation of blacks and social liberals, a turn toward more congenial socialist programs that offer solutions to fundamental national problems may be necessary.
> (*New York Times*, August 22, 1980, p. A 23, "Liberals vs. Liberals," by John Brown Childs)

In other words, in the post-racial era, organizations such as the NAACP needed to focus their attention on the class rather than racial divide.

There was increasing pressure on Black leaders to abandon government remedies as the primary solution for Black American problems, in favor of a focus on fixing Black dysfunctional families, culture, and communities. High-profile academics such as Glenn C. Loury, an African American and a Professor of Public Policy at Harvard's Kennedy School of Government, were highly critical of Black leadership. In Loury's article in the December 1984 issue of the *New Republic*, he castigated the NAACP for its failure to criticize black criminal behavior, but instead to blame the effects of racism (NAACP Papers, Administration File 108: 9, "Racial Politics, Black And White: A New American Dilemma," by Glenn C. Loury, *The New Republic*, December 31, 1984, p. 16). The problem was that the vast majority of Whites, "'see the poverty of these communities as substantially due to the behavior of the people living there. They are unconvinced by the tortured rationalizations offered by black and (some) liberal white spokesman'" (ibid., p. 15). Loury suggested that this ideological split served to alienate Black leadership from the political mainstream. He implored Black leaders to adapt to the ideological shift regarding race in America. Loury argued:

> Those leaders must find the courage and wisdom to heed growing signs of racial political isolation, and to seek accommodation and compromise. What is required is that black leaders, from a mature and varied set of ideological positions, adopt strategies consonant with the shifting political realities.
> (Ibid., p. 18)

Stage four defensive adaptations: desperate measures and frame capitulation

Recognition of the "new racism"

The rise of discourse associated with the Moral Majority further strained the capacity of the NAACP to define its goals in explicitly racial terms. NAACP Assistant National Director Michael Meyers' report was particularly concerned about the ways in which current post-racial discourse was undermining the image and interests of the organization. He stated:

> What is significant is that language has a role in the way we are perceived in the way we behave. The way we talk about ourselves and how others talk about us. For example, it is no accident that the vanguard of right-wing ideology have described themselves as members of the "Moral Majority." Language played a crucial role during the political fight on the Administration's budget proposals in painting civil rights lobbyists as representing "special interest" groups. The media—without hesitation or apology—adopt the language of our adversaries—i.e. the use of such phrases as "forced busing" and "reverse discrimination." The persistence of the use of such language by the brokers of power and media can no longer, if we ever did, be viewed as coincidently the circumstance of ignorance.
> (Administrative File VIII 53:8, NAACP Internal Management Staging Guide 1981: "Meeting the Challenge, Fulfilling Unkept Promises—Preliminary Draft of an Advocacy Program for the NAACP," p. 7, by Michael Meyers)

Meyers noted the way in which welfare had become "a powerfully negative code-word in America" that "connotes waste, [and] fraud" but "the American public has not yet reviewed the large-scale subsidy programs for the wealthy as an equivalent if not larger tax burden" (ibid.). At the NAACP 1981 Annual Convention in Denver, Colorado, the Board of Directors formulated an emergency resolution, "The New Right," to address the problem of the Moral Majority rhetoric stating:

> The 72nd Annual Convention of the NAACP denounces the ever-growing cult of so-called "new conservatism" and old-fashioned racism in the United States ... by its Orwellian use of language and disingenuous use of code-words such as "forced busing," "racial quotas," "reverse discrimination," and "getting government off the backs of the people" in an attempt to pander to the anxieties of whites and with the effect of perpetuating odious barriers to equal opportunities for all Americans.
>
> Therefore, the delegates to this 72nd Annual NAACP Convention go on record as repudiating this *ideological movement* as injurious to the interests of all Americans in general and black people in particular

precisely because it represents the undertow of a rising tide of anti-poor and anti-black behavior by public officials, politicians, major institutions and private citizens, and creates an unwholesome climate of divisiveness in a nation that subscribes to the motto "From Many One."
(NAACP Papers Administration File VIII, 30, Memorandum, To: Senior Staff, From: Michael Meyers, RE: Resolutions Adopted by 72nd Annual Convention, November 10, 1981, Emergency Resolution 4, The New Right (Adopted), p. 4)

The NAACP had reason for concern over the power of Moral Majority discourse as it spilled over into the political arena. Despite the 1980 Supreme Court decision in *Fullilove v. Klutznick*, that upheld a "congressionally-enacted percent set-aside of federal funds for state and local public works" (The Leadership Conference, Civil Rights 101, Affirmative Action & The Courts, http//www.civilrights.org/resources/civilrights101/affirmaction.html 10/18/2011), Reagan Administration advisers were submitting proposals to the president that would effectively dismantle government's role in enforcement of civil rights and substantially undermine the implementation of affirmative action programs. At the convention, the Board also adopted a resolution that castigated Reagan Administration advisors for having "submitted a report to the president of the United States alleging that implementation of Title VII has been improper and [for claiming] that EEO enforcement efforts have 'created a New Racism' in America" (NAACP Papers Administration File VIII, 30, Memorandum, To: Senior Staff, From: Michael Meyers, RE: Resolutions Adopted by 72nd Annual Convention, November 10, 1981, Civil Rights Resolution 3, Affirmative Action (Adopted), pp. 13–14).

Molding public opinion

To shift the prevailing discourses and ideology, Michael Meyers suggested a new programmatic overhaul of the NAACP and stated, "NAACP must, to achieve the most modest of goals, better structure its efforts at molding public opinion" (Administrative File VIII 53: 8, NAACP Internal Management Staging Guide 1981: "Meeting the Challenge, Fulfilling Unkept Promises—Preliminary Draft of an Advocacy Program for the NAACP," p. 14, by Michael Meyers). To do so, Meyers urged the organization to develop a unit for investigative research that would publish position papers in the organization's magazine, *The Crisis*. Providing investigative journalistic pieces to be distributed broadly would help the organization to frame its message and goals based on facts. Moreover, the NAACP would monitor the *New York Times* "to respond to inappropriately written articles, and inaccurate stories and misinformed opinion pieces" pertinent to civil rights objectives" (p. 14).

An April 1981 meeting with Vice President George Bush at the White House was historic in that, for the first time, the organization presented a 130-page document entitled *Alternative Policies in the Public Interest for*

Economic Growth, "a carefully crafted alternative budget plan. The plan was also sent to the 535 members of Congress (previous White House–NAACP meetings almost always dealt with basic and general civil rights problems without the presentation of detailed economics initiative designed to help in their correction)" (*The Crisis,* "The Dual Society is an Unequal Society," June 1981, In This Issue, p. 1 by Chester A. Higgins, Sr.). The NAACP further released national policy recommendations for economic growth and to combat inflation. The specific policy positions were unprecedented and spoke to the organization's formation of a research unit designed to combat rhetoric and misinformation with facts and alternative social change solutions.

Given the general belief that the battle for racial equality was won, the NAACP was no longer a central focus in the media. Hooks' report elaborated, "The NAACP is fighting an image battle. It receives less media coverage for its activities than organizations which exist mostly on rhetoric. The NAACP must devise an effective public relations strategy if the Association is to make a significant impact on society" (Administrative File VIII 53: 6, Meeting the Challenge: NAACP: Thrust for the 80s: Report to the National Board of Directors: Submitted by Benjamin L. Hooks, Executive Director, April, 1980).

To this end, Hooks proposed a more systematic approach to manage the organization's visibility. The organization made significant progress in gaining media visibility and conveying its identity, policies, and programs to the general public. At the 1980 Annual Convention there were

> over 416 members of the press, including representatives of six different countries, seventeen networks, four wire services and eight national magazines present. The 1-hour daily public television offerings, and the half hour nightly shows, reached an estimated 10 million people. The 1-hour Saturday 'wrap-up' show reached an estimated 30 million people.
> (NAACP Papers, Administration File VIII 53: 6 NAACP Annual Report 1980, Public Information, by Paul H. Brock, Director, p. 41)

Additionally, following the convention, Hooks was the featured guest on several prime time television shows, the presidential debates, and both the Republican and Democratic national conventions.

Targeting corporate America

Another proposed strategic shift was the development of anti-discrimination campaigns that could garner short-term victories for the organization. Meyers suggested targeting corporations or companies that produced negative depictions of Blacks. For example Quaker Oats had long shown "Aunt Jemima," a Black mammy, on its products. A boycott would bring positive visibility to the organization and highlight the organization's activism (NAACP Papers, Administration File VIII, 53: 8, Summary Minutes, Policy and Plans Committee, Saturday, October 25, 1981, O'Hare Hotel, p. 4). Hooks worked with corporations to elicit voluntary agreements to increase Black employment, promotions, and board members (*The Crisis*, March 1982, 89(3), pp. 93–128, Whole Number 790, "We Demand Our Fair Share! ... From America's Wealth, Operation Fair Share Points the Way," by Curtis E. Rodgers, pp. 6–10). The movie industry was an additional sight of engagement with the NAACP demanding not only more and better representations of Blacks in films, but also increased jobs. Noting that few to no Blacks were in front or behind the cameras, the organization threatened a boycott of Hollywood films (*Los Angeles Times*, July 1, 1982, p. B21, "NAACP Adopts Plan for Movie Boycott," by David Treadwell).

Expanding coalitions

In addition to advertising their successes, and gaining greater visibility, they expanded their networks and coalitions with non-Black groups. For example, they supported the National Coalition Against the Death Penalty, and began initiating actions such as contacting the media, and sending wires to governors and pardon boards, to block executions of those on Death Row. They also cultivated ties to the United Nations Association, the International League for Human Rights, and the ACLU. Meyers became chair of the Zimand Award Committee of the National Child Labor Committee. The coalition approach was not without its difficulties, however. For example, Benjamin Hooks served as a board trustee of the National Conference of Christians and Jews (NCCJ). This organization decided to present its highest award for leadership in civic and humanitarian affairs to President Ronald Reagan. Although the award was given to him, the NAACP encouraged a massive letter-writing and phone-call protest. On the day Reagan received the award, 30,000 protesters lined up outside the New York Hilton Hotel. (NAACP Papers, Administration File, VIII, 54: 1, 1982 Annual Report, The Office of Research, Policy & Plans, NAACP Executive Department, Michael Meyers, Director p. 6).

Direct action

When addressing the needs of the poor, the NAACP's tactics shifted to activism. Hooks led a march on Washington on August 27, 1983, and acknowledged the 1941 March on Washington that was planned by A. Philip Randolph, founder of the Brotherhood of Sleeping Car Porters, to demand fair employment practices. 1,800 NAACP branches participated as well as 615 additional national organizations, and civic and religious leaders. Co-chairing the coalition were Coretta Scott King, and Southern Christian Leadership Conference president, Joseph Lowery. During the march, Hooks professed, "One out of every three blacks in this country is officially listed below the poverty line. One out of five adults is unemployed. One out of two can't find jobs." The NAACP, he asserted, will continue to protest the "disgraceful economic disparity blacks are experiencing today. We will present a list of demands to Congress and continue to put pressure on government officials until the purposes of this market are fulfilled" (NAACP Washington Bureau Papers, IX 564: 6, July 29, 1983, "Hooks to Lead March on Washington on August 27 in 20th Commemoration). Hooks' speech specifically attacked President Reagan and his economic approach. He stated:

> We have come to declare war—political war if you please—on the present policies of the Reagan Administration. Policies that punish the poor and reward the rich ... We serve notice on President Reagan that we are not here to live in the past and leave here simply singing "We Shall Overcome." We're here because we are committed to the elimination of Reaganism in 1984. We have come to declare war on unemployment.

Hooks used the march to articulate the organization's purpose. He continued:

> America, we are marching today—20 years later—for much more than we marched for in 1963. The dream is bigger because the problems are more complex. The enemy is more subtle, racism is more sinister. 20 years ago we were marching for political freedom. Today we march for economic equity and total parity.
> (NAACP Board of Directors Papers VIII 71: 15, August 27, 1983, Remarks of Benjamin L. Hooks Executive Director, NAACP, Twentieth Anniversary Mobilization, Jobs, Peace, and Freedom, Washington, D.C., pp. 2–4)

The executive director's speech articulated the NAACP's evolved foci by juxtaposing the goals of the 1960s Black civil rights movement to the current needs of Black Americans.

Strategically, Hooks' words signaled an organizational transition beyond a civil rights movement focus to explicitly include social and economic parity.

Self-help

1983 also marked the beginning of a significant shift in the NAACP's agenda to include a focus on internal social factors impacting the Black community. While the organization had celebrated the tenth anniversary of its prison program in 1982, this was the first time that it developed programs specifically focused on social change within the Black community (NAACP 1982 Annual Report, The NAACP Prison Program, p. 48, E185.5 N275). On September 12, 1983, Executive Director Hooks announced plans for an NAACP summit meeting on the Black family. His announcement stated:

> In recent years we have been bombarded with frightening facts and figures regarding the rapid deterioration of the black family. The precipitous

growth of female- headed households can be traced almost directly to systemic racism in America. We also believe that it is beyond debate that government assistance programs for poor mothers need to be completely reconceptualized and redesigned. While a program or a summit meeting designed to find ways to extract us from this vicious cycle may not appear to be sexy or have any bearing on civil rights advocacy, it is my contention that finding ways to end the precipitous slide of the black family is one of the most important items on the civil rights agenda today.
(NAACP Administrative File, VIII, 107, statement by Benjamin L. Hooks, NAACP Executive Director, announcing plans for an NAACP Summit meeting on the Black Family. The statement was made at a news conference at the Vista Hotel in New York on September 12, 1983, pp. 1–2)

The Association was developing a comprehensive program to address the presumed deterioration of the Black family. Hooks further asserted that all of the struggle for school integration would be futile if the Black family did not provide the child with discipline and a nurturing environment. He further stated:

We can fight to have the Fair Housing Law extended, but unless the black family is strengthened and our younger blacks receive the motivation, inspiration and education necessary, a fair housing ordinance will be [meaningless].... unless we do something about the problem with the black family, until the work ethic is taught in the household, all of our work is for naught.
(NAACP Administrative File, VIII, 107, statement by Benjamin L. Hooks, NAACP executive director, announcing plans for an NAACP Summit meeting on the Black Family. The statement was made at a news conference at the Vista Hotel in New York on September 12, 1983, p. 2)

Although many media reports suggested that a consensus formed that Blacks must become less reliant on the government and more reliant on Black institutions (NAACP Administrative File, VIII, 107: 5, *New York Times,* May 7, 1984, p. A14, "Blacks See Blacks Saving the Family," by Dorothy J. Gaither), the recommendations suggest a continued commitment to press for legislative and government involvement. It was not abandoning its emphasis on the role of the President's Administration or Congress in helping to ameliorate the crisis.

Incorporating the hegemonic master frame

If the viewpoint of the Reagan Administration, conservatives, and laissez-faire liberals was correct, then what was the purpose of the NAACP? Its opponents viewed the organization as racist. In their view, the organization demonstrated support for reverse discrimination and disregard for the civil rights of Whites. While refusing to completely abandon their struggle for the implementation of civil rights policies to enforce fair housing, equal employment opportunities, and desegregated schools, the NAACP implemented several programs in the 1980s to address what Blacks could do to improve community conditions, in part, to address the critics. The identity and purpose of the organization was at stake. They did not want to become a community service organization. The core of the organization's mission could not be strategically adapted to fit the changing cultural and political context. At the same time, the organization's survival was threatened by their dogged adherence to the goals. Hooks became increasingly aware of its cost. At the 1986 Annual Convention, the Director addressed the problem head on stating:

> In a real sense the NAACP has had to make adjustments along the way to make sure that we are indeed fighting the right battle and not off somewhere fighting needless scrimmages in order to satisfy a few of our critics. Those who cry: "self-help, self-help, self-help", as if this were a new concept which they themselves discovered this morning, would be surprised to know that self-help was the hallmark of black progress throughout our journey from slavery till now and has been a part of the NAACP's advocacy for all of its 77 years of existence. To the theoreticians, wordsmiths, academic nitpickers, Harvard-trained but who lack brains—men and women whose only experience with self-help has been helping themselves at the expense of those who they purport to want to help. We will not be dissuaded; we will not be deterred and we shall be heard.
> (NAACP Papers, Administrative File VIII 36: 5, Address to be Delivered By Benjamin L. Hooks Executive Director of the NAACP To the National Convention of the NAACP Baltimore, Maryland, Sunday, June 29, 1986, pp. 26–27)

Hooks, once again, articulated the goals of the NAACP, stating:

> There are three basic things that confront us now: 1. Implementation and enforcement of rights previously won; 2. Maintaining the gains we have already made, even as we attempt to press forward; 3. Seeking the elimination of a dual economic system–achieving economic parity.
> (NAACP Papers, Administrative File VIII 36: 5, Address to be Delivered By Benjamin L. Hooks Executive Director of the NAACP To the National Convention of the NAACP Baltimore, Maryland, Sunday, June 29, 1986 pp. 23–24)

Addressing the nuances of racism, Hooks acknowledged the end of obvious racist acts but emphasized the difficulties of fighting "subtle forms of discrimination" as well as the lack of media attention that once covered protests but no longer reported on less sensational NAACP activities.

Despite the NAACP's decade's long adaptations to the varied iterations of the post-racial project and the organization's massive expansion of self-help programs, it was not enough. Thus, they began to pivot towards an inclusion of the hegemonic discourse. In Hooks' speech at the 78th annual convention in New York on July 5, 1987, he stated:

> Even though we have won tremendous victories in the struggle for equality, there are many of our brothers and sisters whom progress has passed by. Scholars and the members of the press speak of these unfortunate men and women and their children glibly as "the Black underclass." We may find the term "underclass" too abrasive for our taste; we may reject it because of all its negative images and connotations. But we cannot reject the reality that there are men and women, boys and girls, who tonight, are devoid of hope, who have no faith in themselves or in their tomorrow's. Theirs is the poverty of hope, of ambition, even of dreams. Today, many are condemned to the debilitations of the welfare system, the opium of dependence. Others turn to prostitution and to crime. All too many seek relief in crack and cocaine. Too many of our children are bored with and uninspired by school, so they drop out—taking their places among the legions of unemployed and unemployable.
>
> Too many of our young women—girls, really—are bearing children without benefit of marriage. This dreadful cycle of babies having babies is repeated...
>
> The NAACP is neither blind to the plight of our less fortunate brothers and sisters, nor deaf to their cries. [We have] a long-range planning document, which is intended to point the Association's direction into the 21st century, addresses the troubling concerns of crime and violence in the Black community, of drug and substance abuse, of teenage pregnancy, of school dropouts and youth unemployment. We are working to enhance and implement our Back-to-School/Stay-in-School program; to stimulate the work ethic.
>
> We cannot do the job alone. We call upon the more fortunate segments of Black America to enlist in this fight—or to re-enlist.... We know that Black America must do much of this work itself, for it is our future we must save. If we are not prepared to work for our salvation, our race will be doomed. We will never stop insisting that the total American society accept its clear responsibility to banish racism, which is the fertile soil of so much misery. Just as we fight against the KKK, we will fight against cocaine and crack. Just as we fight the raping and destruction of the virtues of our black women by men of the white race, we shall stand up and struggle against mistreatment of black women by a few Black men who do not want to respect Black womanhood. Just as we struggled for the maintenance of family ties during the long history of slavery and its aftermath, we shall fight for the continued existence of the strong Black family.
>
> (NAACP Papers Administration File VIII 37: 13, Address Delivered By Benjamin L. Hooks, Executive Director National Association for the Advancement of Colored People to the 78th Annual Convention New York Hilton Hotel New York City Sunday, July 5, 1987)

What was abundantly clear from the director's speech was that he had come to, at least publicly, embrace much of the framing so prevalent in the media, among conservative and liberal laissez-faire intellectuals, and by presidential administrations.

A year later, in his annual report, Hooks clearly stated the perspective that funding would not ameliorate the increase in teen pregnancies, drug addiction, and violence. He declared.

> The church and other moral foundations of the community must be unafraid and unyielding to every vestige of amorality which permeates our community. If President Bush ordered out the Navy, the Army, the Air Force and the Marines, and assigned them the responsibility of preventing unwanted pregnancies in our community ... even with a $100 billion defense budget, the resource will be inadequate. Rather, it will take an unprecedented effort on our part to address this problem. I am convinced that no amount of money can solve this problem.
> (NAACP Papers, Board of Directors VIII 76: 5, Annual Report, National Association for the Advancement of Colored People, 1988, February 11, 1989, New York, NY, Benjamin L. Hooks Executive Director, p. 18)

The NAACP had in many ways capitulated to the pressure to assign blame for the lack of Black progress onto the values and cultural practices of poor Blacks, especially poor Black single mothers and their so-called illegitimate children. The resolution, therefore, rested on the backs of the Black middle class who purportedly embraced mainstream American values of morality. Hooks' report continued:

> There are those who get upset with me and others in the movement for constant reminders that blacks who have made it, those who are one step removed from poverty... Those who are one paycheck removed from disaster, should reach back and help those institutions and bridges that have been responsible for the limited progress we've made over the years. Too many who live the good life largely because of the blood, sweat, and tears of those who did not shrink from the call to sacrifice, spit on the graves of those who gave their all in order that we might have the degree of freedom that we now enjoy. Today, I do not retract one word.
> (NAACP Papers, Board of Directors VIII 76: 5, Annual Report, National Association for The Advancement of Colored People, 1988, February 11, 1989, New York, NY, Benjamin L. Hooks Executive Director, p. 19)

Absent from the discourse was a discussion of the role of government in supporting the independence of these women and protecting and bringing about equality for their children. The fact that gender equality in the workforce continued to impact the life chances of all women, was not a part of mainstream discussions regarding the solution to Black poverty. Although the NAACP lobbied for job training programs and child care subsidies, Hooks did not connect these issues to the plight of poor single-female-headed households. The fact of the matter was that even if Black women were not single parents, and Black men worked in low-wage jobs, this would not be sufficient to lift them out of poverty. In earlier years, the NAACP had taken strong stances in support of a living wage. This now gave way to a focus on the morality of Black women and the lack of a work ethic on the part of Black men.

Their 1987 Resolutions differed markedly from those of previous years in that there was considerably more focus on self-help initiatives. For example, regarding education, not a single resolution focused on issues of racial integration or school busing to achieve that goal. Instead, resolutions called for greater access to quality early childhood education programs; the formation of a program to oversee the academic progress of Black athletes; and, the development of a program to inform and educate youth, especially Black athletes, about the use of illegal drugs. A resolution called on Black parents to teach sex education to their teenage girls and boys (NAACP Papers, Washington Bureau IX 533: 1, Resolutions adopted by the 78th Annual National Convention of the NAACP July 5–9, 1987 New York Hilton Hotel New York, New York, p. 13).

It was not that the organization had abandoned its resolutions regarding government assistance, only that there was a much greater emphasis on Black community self-help. Indeed, they implored Congress and the Reagan Administration to support laws to fund larger societal problems. Their resolution on welfare reform acknowledged that many of the unemployed youth had not completed high school, but asked Congress to support job-training programs to "ensure job placement and meaningful employment rather than menial tasks" (NAACP Papers, Washington Bureau IX 533: 1, Resolutions adopted by the 78th Annual National Convention of the NAACP July 5–9, 1987 New York Hilton Hotel New York, New York, p. 10). Demands for government assistance, however, were often wedded to self-help resolutions. The NAACP was employing a dual strategy of appeasing critics by creating a self-help community-based frame while maintaining demands for government assistance.

Conclusion

Pena and Davies's (2017) analysis of Brazil's response to protests through boundary blurring showed the appropriation of protesters' frames, the weakening of the opposition's stance against the government, and the separation of moderates from radicals. While not entirely optimal, the government made concessions and gained the public support for its efforts. The centripetal approach served to "widen ... the political debate and consolidate calls for institutional reform" (Pena and Davies 2017: 29). This was not the outcome for the demands made by the NAACP. The cases differ in significant ways, of course. First the NAACP was no longer staging protests or direct action, the radical flank was annihilated through repressive efforts, and there was no opposition party in support of civil rights movement enforcement. Instead, the centripetal counterframing approach served to delegitimize the NAACP; to shrink the political debate; and to diminish calls for institutional reform.

Centripetal tactics, as manifested through post-racial discourse employed during the Ford and Reagan Administrations and inherited by the Carter Administration, sought to blur racial distinctions and deny the reality of continuing racism in the U.S. While appearing to embrace the master frame that served to win 1960s civil rights legislation, the latter was now a weapon promoted to undermine the gains and to block concrete government enforcement measures to promote equitable racial-ethnic outcomes. It provided a perfect template of the ways in which "ideologies can 'mask' or 'obfuscate' the issues" (Snow 2004: 402). The capacity of the NAACP was undercut by a state-promoted U.S. post-racial project that spanned decades and continues today. Despite its attempts to defensively adapt, each iteration was met by a continuing escalation of counterframes that reshaped common understandings of race, racism, discrimination, equality and justice. In many respects, this is an incredible feat, and speaks to the power of the state to promote an ideological countermovement with material consequences. It was forged through a de facto countermovement, an unacknowledged coalition of state leaders, elites, intellectuals, the media, and the majority of the White public. Indeed, it has no official label or organizational boundaries, and is difficult to name. I have identified it in this study as a concerted White racial project to roll back the civil rights gains of the previous decades. This project was and continues as a decades-long, sustained state-promoted post-racial project and demonstrates a form of soft repression or "the collective mobilization of power, albeit in non-violent forms and often highly informal ways to limit and exclude ideas and identities from the public forum" (Ferree 2004: 141).

Post-racial counterframes not only moved through stages over time (see Omi and Winant 2015), but did so in a fashion that, first, countered each defensive adaptation employed by the NAACP, and second, progressively undercut any claims to continued widespread racial discrimination and restrained acknowledgement of Black exceptionalism (i.e. Lee and Bean 2007, 2010). With Ford's self-help prescriptions and focus on economic uplift for all, to Reagan's four-stage escalation of post-racial counterframes, by the late 1980s the NAACP had little choice but to publicly and defensively adapt much of the post-racial hegemonic frame. In conjunction with public intellectuals and the media, the Reagan Administration promoted the post-racial ideology by championing accusations of reverse discrimination to undercut support for affirmative action programs; implementing code words such as "states' rights" to weaken federal-level enforcement of the Civil Rights and Voting Rights Acts; promoting colorblind discourse that fails to acknowledge discriminatory practices; and amplifying class inequality to replace the reality of continued racial discrimination while emphasizing the notion of a Black "underclass" whose culture purportedly leads to entrenched poverty and unemployment.

Recent research shows that countermovements often engage in frame appropriation (Lio, Melzer and Reese 2008) by "adopt[ing] and reconstruct[ing] elements of their opponent's language and ideologies for their own use" (Lio, Melzer, and Reese 2008: 10) "while subverting its intent" (Burke and Bernstein 2014; see also Gallo-Cruz 2012; Marshall 1985, 1986). Also, described as frame transformation (Snow 2004: 395), the process has been implemented by White supremacists who view themselves as victims of discrimination and as a minority group (Berbrier 1998: 439, 2002; Ferber 1998). Similarly, the state-promoted counterframes culminated in the cooptation of the meaning of discrimination (Whites were now the victims) and civil rights success (a weakening both legally and legislatively of civil rights laws to protect Black rights).

The NAACP's continuous efforts to maintain its master frame of equal rights and opportunities through the enforcement of school desegregation, equal opportunity employment, and desegregated housing coupled with its embrace of affirmative action programs that considered race in the evaluation process, placed the organization at ideological odds with presidential administrations, the general White public, and even liberal allies. The ideological contradictions upon which the reluctance and ultimately the failure to enforce the 1964 Civil Rights Act rested, served to sustain the status quo and to cement institutionalized racism in the U.S. Positioning forced implementation as antithetical to U.S. American values, glossed over the many ways in which those values were daily violated without complaint. As long as such implementations favored Whites, they remained consistent with U.S. American ideology. As Vernon Jordan, Executive Director of the National Urban League, described in his article, the daily practices of preferring Whites over Blacks is built into the presumptions of the U.S. American meritocracy that devises arbitrary measures of competence that ultimately favor Whites (*The Crisis*, October 1974, 81(8), pp. 282–283, Together! By Vernon E. Jordan, Jr.). Even nepotism in the form of preferential college admissions for children of financial contributors or the well-connected never reached the level of legal challenges aimed at affirmative action policies or school busing.

The NAACP believed that the alternative to school busing for racial integration and affirmative action programs was the persistence of inherently unequal schools and the underrepresentation of minorities in all professions. Indeed, as a 2017 *New York Times* analysis of data from sources including the National Center for Education Statistics concluded, "The share of black freshmen at elite schools is virtually unchanged since 1980. Black students are just 6 percent of freshmen but 15 percent of college-age Americans" (Jeremy Ashkenas, Haeyoun Park and Adam Pearce, August 24, *NYT* 2017). A Harvard University, civil rights project paper by Orfield and Lee (2005) stated:

> More than 60% of Black and Latino students attend high poverty schools, compared with 30% of Asians and 18% of Whites. Gains achieved by black students in the south are gone. In the wake of the Brown decision, the percentage of black students in majority white

southern schools went from zero to a peak of 43.5 percent in 1988. But those changes have reversed in recent years, with data from Harvard's Civil Rights Project showing that by 2011 that figure was back to 23.2 percent, just below where it stood in 1968.

Yet, "The south today is still the most integrated region in the nation for black students, but the trend has increasingly been away from integration" (Orfield and Lee 2005).

Thus, the NAACP's focus had been correct. For them, the ideological dilemma posed by many was less about a dissonance between U.S. American values and civil rights enforcement, than it was about the acceptability of value violations for some groups over others. Couching the issue of civil rights enforcement in a U.S. American value-laden discourse provided the perfect subterfuge upon which to maintain business as usual that favors White privilege and mobility.

Notes

1 This study also relies on several polling data sources for public attitudes and discourses. Schuman, Steeh, Bobo, and Krysan (1997) employ multiple surveys, including those from Gallup, the National Opinion Research Center (NORC), and the Institute for Social Research, to tracked changes in racial attitudes from 1942 to 1995. The questions that assess viewpoints on the implementation of equal treatment include those that address school desegregation, busing, open housing laws, and affirmative action-government expenditures. Secondary sources are also employed to assess public opinion and public discourse shifts on race, including newspaper and magazine articles that discuss such issues, summarize public opinion poll data, provide text of speeches by organization leaders or public officials, and summarize the public mood.
2 As Schuman et al. (1997) point out, White support for racial equality and Black civil rights had increased steadily since 1942, the year that survey data became available. Support for principles of equality appeared to increase irrespective of specific political events including landmark legal decisions, political unrest, or presidential party. For example, White support for Black and White students attending the same schools increased steadily throughout both the Nixon and Reagan years. Schuman et al. (1997) attribute these changes to generation replacement. At least in principle, younger cohorts are more supportive of racial equality.

References

Benford, Robert D. 1987. "Framing Activity, Meaning, and Social Movement Participation: The Nuclear Disarmament Movement." Ph.D. dissertation, Department of Sociology, University of Texas, Austin.

Berbrier, Mitch. 1998. "'Half the Battle': Cultural Resonance, Framing Processes, and Ethnic Affectations in Contemporary White Separatist Rhetoric." *Social Problems*, 45: 431–450.

Berbrier, Mitch. 2002. "Making Minorities: Cultural Space, Stigma Transformation Frames, and the Categorical Claims of Deaf, Gay and White Supremacist Activist in Late Twentieth Century America." *Sociological Forum* 17(4): 553–591.

Burke, Mary C. and Mary Bernstein. 2014. "How the Right Usurped the Queer Agenda: Frame Co-optation in Political Discourse." *Sociological Forum*, 29(4): 830–850.

Clark, Kenneth. 1965. *Dark Ghetto: Dilemmas of Social Power*. Middleton, CT: Wesleyan University Press.

Edelman, Murray. 1971. *Politics as Symbolic Action*. Chicago: Markham.

Ferber, Abby L. 1998. *White Man Falling: Race, Gender, and White Supremacy*. Lanham, MD: Rowman & Littlefield.

Ferree, Myra Marx. 2004. "Soft Repression: Ridicule, Stigma, and Silencing in Gender-Based Movements." In *Repression and Mobilization*, edited by Christian Davenport, Hank Johnston, and Carol Mueller, pp. 138–155. Minneapolis: University of Minnesota Press.

Ferree, Myra Marx, William Anthony Gamson, Jurgen Gerhards, and Dieter Rucht. 2002. *Shaping Abortion Discourse: Democracy and the Public Sphere in Germany and the United States*. New York: Cambridge University Press.

Gallo-Cruz, Selina. 2012. "Negotiating the Lines of Contention: Counterframing and Boundary Work in the School of the Americas Debate." *Sociological Forum* 27(1): 21–45.

Gamson, William A. and David S. Meyer. 1996. "Framing Political Opportunity." In *Comparative Perspectives on Social Movements*, edited by Doug McAdam, John D. McCarthy, and Mayer N. Zald, pp. 275–290. New York: Cambridge University Press.

Glaser, Barney, and Anselm Strauss. 1967. *The Discovery of Grounded Theory*. New York: Aldine Transaction.

Halpern, Stephen C. 1995. *On the Limits of the Law: The Ironic Legacy of Title VI of the 1964 Civil Rights Act*. Baltimore, MD: John Hopkins University Press.

Koopmans, Ruud, and Paul Statham. 1999. "Ethnic and Civic Conceptions of Nationhood and the Differential Success of the Extreme Right in Germany and Italy." In *How Social Movements Matter*, edited by Marco Giugni, Doug McAdam, and Charles Tilly, pp. 225–251. Minneapolis: University of Minnesota Press.

Lee, Jennifer and Frank Bean. 2007. "Reinventing the Color Line: Immigration and American's New Racial/Ethnic Divide." *Social Forces* 86(2), 561–586.

Lee, Jennifer and Frank Bean. 2010. *The Diversity Paradox: Immigration and the Color Line in Twenty-First Century America*. New York: Russell Sage Foundation.

Lio, Shoon, Scott Melzer, and Ellen Reese. 2008. "Constructing Threat and Appropriating 'Civil Rights': Rhetorical Strategies of Gun Rights and English Only Leaders." *Symbolic Interactionism*, 31(1), pp. 5–31.

Maney, Gregory M., Lynne M. Woehrle, and Patrick G. Coy. 2005. "Harnessing and Challenging Hegemony: The U.S. Peace Movement after 9/11." *Sociological Perspectives* 48: 357–381.

Marshall, Susan. 1985. "Ladies against Women: Mobilization Dilemmas of Antifeminist Movements." *Social Problems* 32(4): 348–362.

Marshall, Susan. 1986. "In Defense of Separate Spheres: Class and Status Politics in the Antisuffrage Movement." *Social Forces* 65(2): 327–351.

Marx, Gary T. 1979. "External Efforts to Damage or Facilitate Social Movements: Some Patterns, Explanations, Outcomes, and Complications." In *The Dynamics of Social Movements*, pp. 94–125. Cambridge, MA: Winthrop Publishers, Inc.

McCammon, Holly J. 2012. *The U.S. Women's Jury Movements and Strategic Adaptation: A More Just Verdict*. New York: Cambridge University Press.

Morris, Aldon D. 1999. "A Retrospective on the Civil Rights Movement: Political and Intellectual Landmarks." *Annual Review of Sociology*, 25: 517–539.

Noakes, John A. and Hank Johnston. 2005. "Frames of Protest: A Road Map to a Perspective." In *Frames of Protest: Social Movements and the Framing Perspective*, edited by Hank Johnston and John A. Noakes, pp. 1–29. Lanham, MD: Rowman & Littlefield.

Omi, Michael and Howard Winant. 2015. *Racial Formation in the United States*. New York: Routledge.

Orfield, Gary and Chungmei Lee. 2005. "Why Segregation Matters: Poverty and Educational Inequality." *The Civil Rights Project*, Cambridge, MA: Harvard University.

Pena, A.M. and T.R. Davies. 2017. Responding to the Street: Government Responses to Mass Protests in Democracies. *Mobilization: An International Quarterly* 22(2): 177–200.

Roediger, David. R. 1991. *The Wages of Whiteness: Race and the Making of the American Working Class*. New York: Verso.

Sawyers, Traci M. and David S. Meyer. 1999. "Missed Opportunities: social Movement Abeyance and Public Policy". *Social Problems*, 46(2): 187–206.

Schuman, Howard, Charlotte Steeh, Lawrence Bobo, and Maria Krysan. 1997. *Racial Attitudes in America: Trends and Interpretations Revised Edition*. Cambridge: President and Fellow of Harvard College.

Snow, David. 2004. "Framing Processes, Ideology, and Discursive Fields." In *The Blackwell Companion to Social Movements*, edited by David A. Snow, Sarah A. Soule, and Hanspeter Kriesi, pp. 380–412.

Snow, David A. and Robert D. Benford. 1992. "Master Frames and Cycles of Protest." In *Frontiers in Social Movement Theory*, edited by Aldon D. Morris and Carol McClurg Mueller, pp. 133–155. New Haven: Yale University Press.

Sowell, Thomas. 1975. Race and Economics. New York: David McKay Publications.

Spillman, Lyn. 1995. "Culture, Social Structures and Discursive Fields." *Current Perspectives in Social Theory*, 15: 129–154.

Staggenborg, Suzanne. 1991. *The Pro-Choice Movement: Organization and Activism in the Abortion Conflict*. New York: Oxford University Press.

Steinberg, Marc W. 1999. "The Talk and Backtalk of Collective Action: A Dialogic Analysis of Repertoires of Discourse among Nineteenth-Century English Cotton-Spinners." *American Journal of Sociology*, 105: 736–780.

Tilly, Charles, and Jack Goldstone. 2001. Threat (and Opportunity): Popular Action and State Response in the Dynamics of Contentious Action. In *Silence and Voice in the Study of Contentious Politics*, edited by R. Aminzade, 179–194. Cambridge: Cambridge University Press.

Wilson, William Julius. 1978. *The Declining Significance of Race*. Chicago: University of Chicago Press.

3 Resisting repression
The Black Lives movement in context

Pamela Oliver

The Black Lives movement and protest wave of 2012–2016 built upon a long history of prior mobilizations about racially biased social control in the United States. Racial domination and racially organized violence were inherent features of the construction of the nation and central to maintaining its White supremacist character for at least the first 150 years of its existence. Non-Whites were not even imagined as full citizens by the White[1] majority until after the Civil Rights Movement of the 1960s. Movements by African Americans for equal treatment and access to resources were often met by aggressive and violent repression from both official police agents and White civilians. White mobs resisted racial integration in Chicago in 1966 and in Boston and Louisville in 1974–1976. The Black urban rebellions of the 1960s were countered by militarized force and militant movements were subjected to an extremely high level of repression (Davenport 2012; Goldstein 2001) including surveillance by the CIA, NSA, US Army, and the FBI's COINTELPRO; legalized wiretapping and eavesdropping; infiltration, disinformation, and propaganda campaigns; entrapment and even assassinations against the Black Panthers (Bloom and Martin 2013; Davenport 2010), the Republic of New Afrika (Davenport 2015), and other militant Black groups (Dello Buono 1992; Marx 1970, 1974). These tactics were then used in the 1980s and after to counter crime and illegal drug sales in Black communities in a manner that many observers argued effectively criminalized entire populations and put them under intense police surveillance (Chambliss 1995; Gordon 1994; King 2017; Marx 1980, 1981, 1982; Mauer 1999; Oliver 2008; Tonry 1994; Wacquant 2001; Kristian Williams 2011). Although Michelle Alexander (2009) calls the system of mass incarceration the "new Jim Crow," many other observers highlight the way that "stop and frisk" policing after 2000 (Fagan, Davies, and Carlis 2012; Lerman and Weaver 2014; Vitale and Jefferson 2016) even more resembles the Jim Crow practices of everyday humiliation and degradation as people are expected to submit, without resistance, to suddenly being stopped and patted and groped (Jones 2018; Matthews 2015; Rios 2015). Byfield (2019) argues that the new predictive policing models are allowing for racialized surveillance.

This chapter sketches the history of reformist and radical Black and non-Black movements against state violence and mass incarceration, emphasizing the continuities between earlier efforts and the Black Lives protests of 2014–2016. It shows how Black Lives activists sought to convert the energy and attention of the protests into a sustained and proactive movement for Black progress. My observations in one city are used to illustrate the continuities and the ways local actions both had their own trajectories and interacted with national events.

Resistance to repression before Black Lives Matter

Black movements against repression

There were many Black activist campaigns against unequal justice prior to the Civil Rights era. The campaign against lynching was led initially by Ida B. Wells-Barnett (Wells-Barnett and Douglass 2005; Wells-Barnett 1895; Wells-Barnett 1969) and continued as the NAACP campaigned for a federal anti-lynching bill in the 1930s (Zangrando 1965). The Communist Party's International Defense League took up the cases of many Black people unfairly accused of crimes, most famously the 1930s Scottsboro Boys campaign which had broad support and also attracted NAACP involvement (Niven 2006), including Rosa and Raymond Parks (Theoharis 2013). Besides engaging in proactive litigation against segregation, NAACP lawyers defended Black people unfairly charged with crimes and Black victims seeking justice (Meier and Rudwick 1976; Theoharis 2013). Black protests about White mob violence and lynching pressured President Truman to support Civil Rights in 1946 (Bloom 2015). The Civil Rights Congress (CRC) 1951 We Charge Genocide campaign documented hundreds of incidents of lynching and police violence in all parts of the US in a petition to the United Nations (Civil Rights Congress 1951).The CRC also protested the death penalty and supported prisoners. An extended CRC campaign in the 1950s for clemency for Wesley Robert Wells gained wide support and Wells himself became a participant, writing from inside prison (Hamm 2000). This is reminiscent of the campaign since 1982 against the death sentence for Mumia Abu-Jamal (freemumia.com 2019; mumiaabujamal.com 2019; Timothy Williams 2011) and other extended campaigns on behalf of people believed to be unjustly incarcerated.

In the 1960s, violent police repressed nonviolent Civil Rights protests and police violence was the precipitant to most Black urban riots (Kerner, Lindsay, and Harris 1968). Taylor (2016, Chapter 4) cites a 1968 *New York Times* poll that found that 52 percent of Blacks blamed "police brutality" as a "major cause of disorder" compared to only 13 percent of whites, while 63 percent of everyone polled believed that "until there is justice for minorities there will not be law and order." Unpunished police violence was also the precipitant for the major riots/insurrections in Miami in 1980 and Los Angeles in 1992. About a third of the Black protest events described in news wire stories concerned unfair policing, including widely covered protests about police killings in New York in the 1990s and again in 2006, and protests and riots after police killings in Cincinnati in 2001 and Oakland 2009 (Oliver, Hanna, and Lim 2019).

In the late 1960s, the Black Panther Party openly carried weapons and called for armed self-defense against police violence, in addition to organizing self-help programs such as free breakfasts and schools (Bloom and Martin 2013), a strategy that was met with extensive state violence. There were local Black Panther chapters in dozens of cities that each had their own mix of self-help and self-defense programs (Jeffries 2007, 2010, 2018). The Black Guerrilla Family was formed in 1970 as a political organization of California prisoners with ties to the larger Black Power movement as a response to the overt targeting of Black Muslims and Black militants in California prisons and the alliance of prison guards with the White Aryan Brotherhood prison gang (Friedman 2018). The Attica New York prisoner uprising in 1971 was tied to Black Power and brutally suppressed when police forces stormed the prison and killed 33 inmates and 10 hostages. Resistance by prisoners continued. In 2018, prisoners in a number of facilities around the country went on a two-week strike for better conditions (McFarland 2018) with demands including prevailing wages for work, opportunity for parole, rehabilitation and education services, ending racially disparate sentencing policies, and the right to vote for incarcerated people (Incarcerated Workers Organizing Committee 2018).

After the massive violent repression of the Black Panthers and other militant Black Power groups, the Black Power movement of the 1970s shifted toward more institutional strategies focused on entering the professions (Bell 2014) and on gaining political and electoral power, including Black political conventions in the 1970s (Johnson 2007), which fed into Jesse Jackson's Rainbow Coalition campaigns of the 1980s (Pierce 1988, 2003). The 1978 Supreme Court Bakke decision weakening affirmative action put the movement on the defensive and portended the continuing erosion of Black gains after the election of Ronald Reagan as president in 1980 (Robnett, Chapter 2 of this volume).

Black mobilization around policing issues rose in the 1990s. The 1992 not guilty verdict for the police who beat Rodney King led to a major insurrection in Los Angeles and a rise in Black political consciousness and mobilization in the 1990s. Louis Farrakhan of the Nation of Islam called for Black men to repent and take responsibility in the Million Man March of October 1995, an event that drew extensive discussion and publicity among African Americans and had somewhere between 400,000 and a million attendees. The build-up to the Million Man March overlapped with extensive television coverage of the trial of Black football star O.J. Simpson charged with murdering his White ex-wife and her boyfriend; polls showed most Whites thought Simpson was guilty while most Blacks thought he was not guilty and that police had planted evidence.

In 1997, Black activist scholars Angela Davis and Ruth Wilson Gilmore along with Rose Braz founded Critical Resistance (Critical Resistance 2018), a mixed-race prison abolitionist organization that popularized the phrase "prison industrial complex" and held a 1998 conference with 3500 people in attendance. The organization is still active and the phrase "prison industrial complex" has wide currency in activist circles and is now used to refer broadly to the whole continuum of criminal justice institutions.

The Radical Black Congress was formed by 3000 people who came to a convening in 1998 in the wake of continuing attacks on Black gains and the enthusiasm generated by the Million Man March (Brewer 2003; Ransby 2018). In a retrospective, RBC leaders Will Fletcher and Jamala Rogers (2014) say it was ideologically diverse and encompassed experienced activists who were members of various left-wing and nationalist groups, as well as individuals, and made "education, not incarceration" its primary focus in 2001. The RBC became fragmented in the wake of the attacks of September 11, failed to integrate its younger members, and eventually folded in 2008 (Fletcher and Rogers 2014).

In the late 1990s, campaigns against racial profiling in traffic stops and the phrase "Driving While Black" were launched by the NAACP, the ACLU and other organizations that conducted empirical studies, wrote reports, and drew attention to the issue (Browne 1999). Al Sharpton led a protest against racial profiling that blocked I-95 in New Jersey (Taylor 2016).[2] Taylor cites data from 1999 that reported that 59 percent of Americans said the police engaged in racial profiling and 81 percent of those said it was wrong (i.e. about 48 percent of the total). Camp and Heatherton (2016) and the activists they interview describe activist mobilizations in New York and other cities against stop-and-frisk policing and racial profiling in the 1990s and the connections between these mobilizations and the later community mobilizations.

Black feminists began in the 1970s to developed an intersectional analysis that critiqued the racism of the (White) women's movement and the sexism of the (male) Black movement and, as part of its larger agenda, theorized a continuum of intimate, community, and state violence toward Black women expressed in a 1980 conference of the National Conference on Third World Women and Violence (Richie 2012; Thuma 2015). Black feminists argued that as the domestic violence movement went mainstream and gained external funding, it failed to prioritize services for poor Black women and supported a rise in punitive social control that both increased state violence against Black women and worsened issues of intimate and community violence (Ransby 2015). Incite! was founded in 2000 by women of color who attended the Color of Violence Conference and addressed the integration of intimate partner violence, police abuse, prison abuse, and healthcare abuse (Ransby 2015; Richie 2012). It is still active as an organization of women, trans people, and gender nonconforming people with chapters in a dozen cities. Its activities now center on confronting the state as the main organizer of violence, focusing on both violence against minority communities and within them. Incite! supports broad coalitions with other oppressed groups, is critical of the "non-profit industrial complex," and partners with other groups, including Critical Resistance, with whom it issued a joint statement in 2001 (Incite! 2018). Ransby (2015) also stresses the activism of Black gay and lesbian people in the 1990s, especially around HIV/AIDS, as a precursor of the later prominence of queer people in the Black Lives movement, and Green (2019) similarly lifts up several decades of mobilizing by queer Black people as background to the prominence of queer people in the Black Lives movement.

The energy of the mobilizations against discriminatory policing dissipated after the terrorist attack of September 11, 2001. Taylor (2016) and Fletcher and Rogers (2014) explicitly state that the attack dissipated the Radical Black Congress and Taylor stresses that poll data showed that Blacks had even higher support for profiling Arabs than Whites. Protest event data shows a steep drop in Black protests after 9/11 (Oliver, Hanna, and Lim 2019).

Black protests rose again in the latter half of the 2000s. Black Americans saw racial injustice in the mismanagement of the flooding in New Orleans after Hurricane Katrina in 2005 and in the failure to rebuild housing in Black areas of the city. Disruptive protests received extensive news coverage about a police killing in New York in 2006 (Oliver, Hanna, and Lim 2019). In 2007 there was an extensive online mobilization organized by ColorOfChange.org over an incident in Jena, Louisiana. Six black high school students were overcharged for beating up a White student whom they believed had hung a noose on a tree at the high school. The noose apparently was in retaliation for the Black students sitting in an area traditionally reserved for Whites. The online campaign culminated in a march of 20,000 in Jena with numerous coordinated sympathy rallies around the country and a wave of follow-up protests calling for more punishment of noose-hanging and other hate crimes (Oliver, Hanna, and Lim 2019).

In short, the revived "Black Lives" movement that emerged after 2012 appears to have strong continuities with these earlier mobilizations of the 1990s, especially in their focus on aggressive street policing and police violence, and in the strong leadership roles of Black women and queer people and the emphasis on criminal justice issues, as well as the revived mobilizations after 2005.

Criminal justice reform groups

Not all the resistance to escalated and disparate repression through the criminal justice system comes from social movement organizations, and not all of is radical or critical. Even as there was substantial support given to the rise in mass incarceration and intensive surveillance through academic works on "broken windows," "nothing works," "incapacitation," and "super- predators" (among other buzz words that supported the rise in the punitive state) there were other academics who critiqued these policies (Oliver 2008). As I have described elsewhere (Oliver 2009), in 1999 I entered the arena of local discussions of criminal justice policy in Madison, Wisconsin, as a volunteer and then public sociologist. I found an array of different kinds of reformers: a faith-based advocacy group; partially overlapping Black and White networks of long-time activists; mostly Black criminal justice and social service professionals (e.g., police, judges, prosecutors, court commissioners, juvenile justice workers, school administrators, social workers) who promoted reform from within institutions; a variety of primarily White foundation-funded advocacy groups; a few professors; and Black activists based in Black churches or Black organizations. As in other places (e.g., Owens 2014), a small organization of ex-prisoners was also visible. As Taylor (2016) and Bell (2014) remind us, Black college educated people often entered public employment, with especially high concentrations in criminal justice and social service institutions, and often took their concerns about social justice with them. While varying in the details, there is reason to believe that most larger communities have similar fields of organizations and activists.

The Wisconsin reform network was in contact with national organizations and networks. Cadora (2014) lists national policy groups working to reduce imprisonment rates including multi-issue groups (ACLU, The Urban Institute, Community Resources for Justice, the Brennan Center for Justice, the Council of State Governments, and the Pew Center on the States) and issue-specific advocacy groups (The Sentencing Project, Families Against Mandatory Minimums, the Drug Policy Alliance, the Justice Policy Institute, the Center for Effective Public Policy, Justice Strategies, the Safer Foundation, the JFA Institute, the Vera Institute of Justice).

Recommendations from these national policy groups affected Wisconsin policy initiatives and discussions. Cadora says the most effective policy proposal was the Justice Reinvestment initiative focused on saving states money by reducing incarceration by providing community services; Wisconsin initially participated but pulled out when the state legislature refused to fund it. The Milwaukee district attorney participated in a Vera Institute initiative to reduce disparities in prosecution through focused data analysis. Cadora also discusses underwriting from private foundations and the support of the report by the National Research Council (2014). Dagan and Teles (2014) emphasize that since 2008 there have also been conservative advocacy groups opposing high incarceration, generally from concerns about fiscal crises and a shift of attention to terrorism. Michelle Alexander's *The New Jim Crow* (2009) brought much wider public discussion to the issues of mass incarceration, both nationally (Ransby 2015) and locally. New activists were energized and a new group was formed in Madison, the local chapter of a predominantly White faith-based community organizing network that had already been active elsewhere in Wisconsin around a race-blind "treatment instead of prisons" campaign. After 2010, both the local chapter and the state organization became much more race-focused. The local chapter attracted substantial mixed-race participation that included both older and younger people, ex-prisoners as well as professionals, and a range of ideological positions, including people articulating prison abolitionism. An active ex-prisoner's group was spun off from and supported by the state organization. Although I went to a few meetings and stayed on the mailing list, I was not an active participant in this group as it has evolved and went through some organizational conflicts, so my impressions of its politics are superficial, but it does seem to have portended the coming wave of mobilization.

Through 2010, the reformers I worked with were committed to reducing racial disparities in the system and saw both mass incarceration and racial discrimination as real problems, along with systems that penalized poverty and problematic behavior arising from unequal life conditions. Some reformers were connected to more radical networks. Reformers disagreed about how to weigh system bias versus consequences of poverty versus systemic racism versus capitalism as the main factors in incarceration, and there were tensions among groups with different positions. Nevertheless, regardless of ideology, the main activities of all groups in the field involved persuasion and report-writing and collaborative rather than conflictual relations between state and non-state actors. This changed with the coming of the Black Lives movement.

Black Lives Matter and reinvigorated resistance

Neither police violence nor disorderly resistance to police violence nor organized advocacy about criminal justice were new in the 2010s. What changed after 2012 was the way that protests about police violence built on each other and cascaded into a larger movement. The protest wave was a product of the larger political context and built upon substantial pre-existing community organizing and social movement networks. Taylor (2016) emphasizes the context of disillusionment with the Obama presidency, including his failure to stay the execution of Troy Davis, and the Occupy protests of 2011–12, especially in New York, Oakland, and Atlanta where there were large numbers of Black protesters. In addition, Black people and other minorities dissatisfied with the White-dominated Occupy movement created Occupy the Hood (Grainger 2013; Morrow 2011; Paye 2012; Taylor 2016). Substantial mobilization and media attention built around the killing of Trayvon Martin by George Zimmerman in 2012 and Zimmerman's not guilty verdict 2013 (Ransby 2015). National activist mobilization was well underway in 2012 and 2013, before the protest wave of 2014. Of the 20 organizations identified as part of Black Lives Matter on the partial and non-random list compiled by Alisa Robinson (2017), seven (35 percent) were founded before 2012, six (30 percent) were founded in 2012 or 2013; only seven (35 percent) were founded in 2014 or 2015.

Most visible to outsiders was the phrase "Black Lives Matter," created as a Twitter hashtag on the day of the Zimmerman verdict in 2013 by Alicia Garza, Patrisse Cullors, and Opel Tometi. These three were experienced community organizers who had met through Black Organizing for Leadership and Dignity (BOLD 2018), a national organization based in Washington, DC that trains community organizers. When the Ferguson protests started in August of 2014, Black Twitter was an important conduit of information about the protests (Bonilla and Rosa 2015; Ray, et al. 2017; Ray, Brown, and Laybourn 2017). Johnetta Elzie, DeRay McKesson, and Brittany Packnett were especially prominent for frequent tweeting and producing a newsletter *The Movement Today* (Randle 2016; Thrasher 2015). Black Twitter used the hashtag #Ferguson in the initial protests, but the power of the #BlackLivesMatter hashtag and message caught on and was used much more often after November 22–24 when Tamir Rice was killed and, two days later, the grand jury declined to prosecute Darren Wilson, the officer who killed Michael Brown (Anderson and Hitlin 2016).

Although the initial protesters in Ferguson after the killing of Michael Brown in August of 2014 were neighborhood residents, the massive police response in the context of heightened media attention, including the death of Eric Garner in New York two weeks previously, drew in other protesters. Most initial protesters came from the surrounding St. Louis area, but activists quickly converged from all around the country (Taylor 2016; Rogers 2015; Weddington 2018a; Ransby 2018). A "Black Lives Matter Freedom Ride" of 500 people from 18 cities organized by Garza, Cullors and Tometi came to Ferguson on Labor Day weekend (Solomon 2014).

Weddington (2018a) stresses that the initial protests around the deaths of Eric Garner and Michael Brown were by local activists, not national movement organizations nor Black Lives Matter. He discusses the criticisms community organizations have of the "official" Black Lives Matter organization, and emphasizes the importance of studying local Black activism, not just large national-level named organizations. Ransby (2018) and Taylor (2016) similarly give detailed attention to the wide range of local organizations in many cities that undergird the Black Lives movement.

Protests using the phrase "Black Lives Matter" spread around the country in the fall of 2014. Weddington (2018b) analyzes 29 generally small and legal protests in 2014–2017 of a local Albany, NY SMO founded in 2013, finding that most protests focused on local issues, while some were solidarity protests tied to national events. Analyzing crowd-sourced data on police killings and Black Lives Matter protests in 2014–2015, Williamson, Trump, and Einstein (2018) find more Black Lives Matter protests where there had been more people killed by police, even after subtracting those who had been unarmed.

Black Lives Matter in Madison, Wisconsin

Madison events intertwined with national events and built upon existing organizations and networks. Local discussions of racial disparities in criminal justice had been going on for at least 15 years. On October 2, 2013 a local NGO published and received extensive local publicity for a report that had been in preparation for at least a year titled "Race to Equity" (Wisconsin Council on Children and Families 2013) documenting Madison's racial disparities in criminal justice, education, and economic well-being. In December 2013, Rev. Alex Gee, a Black activist minister whose church had a longstanding community development arm (Nehemiah 2018), published a local newspaper editorial titled "Justified Anger" that cited this report and personal experiences (Gee 2013). A local foundation and the newspaper funded several public meetings in 2014, both mixed-race meetings to promote discussion and Black-only meetings led by Rev. Gee to form a broad coalition called Justified Anger to demand change.

Younger Black Madison activists who had traveled to Ferguson in the fall of 2014 became impatient with what they saw as a glacial pace of change and negotiation in the Justified Anger meetings, as well as the emphasis on older professionals, and formed a coalition of three younger activist groups that began protesting in Madison after the Ferguson non-prosecution in November 2014, initially under the name Ferguson to Madison and then under the name Young, Gifted and Black (YGB) Coalition. The initial demands referenced ongoing local issues: (1) no new jail, (2) community led resources, (3) release those incarcerated for crimes of poverty. Two of the YGB groups were small and had been recently formed around local issues, including the police killing of a White man a few years before. The third, Freedom, Inc. (Freedom Inc. 2018) is a community service and advocacy group with paid staff founded in 2003 by a Hmong woman who believed in culturally specific programming, hired Asian staff to ran programs for Hmong and other Southeast Asians, and hired Black staff to create and run programs for African Americans. M. Adams, the Black co-director of Freedom, Inc., originally hired as an intern, emerged as one of the most visible leaders of YGB. YGB was a Black-only group but it sponsored and worked closely with a non-Black ally group and did a great deal of outreach to the White community. YGB itself has no staff, but most of its leaders are employed by local nonprofit organizations or the university.

The YGB Coalition in Madison had already held several protests in opposition to a new jail and about police violence in general when an unarmed young man, Tony Robinson, was killed by a Madison police officer on March 6, 2015. Street protests ramped up after that and drew in more widespread participation of people of all races. Freddie Gray was killed in Baltimore in April 2015, an event that led to protests and then riots in Baltimore and gained massive national media attention (Ransby 2018). In May 2015, Justified Anger presented a document called *Our Madison Plan* calling for significant financial investment in developing the Black community in Madison and held a large roll-out meeting with a buffet dinner provided by the funders that was attended by several hundred people of all races. The campaign to stop the jail, a coalition of several groups including YGB and several non-Black groups that had previously been involved in criminal justice issues, won a temporary victory in May 2015 that called for three task forces over the summer to develop alternatives to a new jail.

In July 2015, the national network of the Movement for Black Lives held a national conference in Cleveland attended by over 1000 people and drafting the Vision for Black Lives that would be rolled out in August of 2016. Freedom, Inc., represented by its Co-Director M. Adams, participated in this meeting and the 2016 roll-out.

The Black Lives movement elsewhere

A similar pattern of new mobilizations building on and expanding existing networks appears elsewhere. Taylor (2016) discusses three of them: (1) a broad Cleveland coalition, Cleveland Action, that formed in response to the Tamir Rice killing and included clergy, academics, and the Council on American–Islamic relations; (2) a Philadelphia group called the Philly Coalition for REAL Justice 2014–15 that organized against police brutality; and (3) Dallas Mothers Against Police Brutality organized solidarity between the anti-police brutality and immigrant rights movements. Other national groups that predated Black Lives Matter but were founded amidst the broader mobilizations after 2010 are also mentioned by Taylor (2016).

These include Dream Defenders (Dream Defenders 2018), a Florida organization of Black, immigrant, and poor people founded in 2012 and currently being sued by GEO for saying it cages children; and Million Hoodies (MillionHoodies 2018), a chapter-based organization founded in 2012 a month after the death of Trayvon Martin that initially focused on tracking police violence and now has 11 paid staff. Ransby (2015) discusses many of these same organizations and also devotes attention to the organizations in Baltimore and Chicago. In Chicago, the Black Lives Matter organization web site (Black Lives Matter Chicago 2018) says that it is entirely volunteer run and is active in policing and other issues. Among other activities, it links to a campaign led by Mariame Kaba that began in 2010 for reparations for the actions of Chicago police officer John Burge who tortured over 100 people into confessing crimes they did not commit between 1972 and 1991 (Chicago Torture Justice Memorials 2018). Mariame Kaba also led a grassroots Chicago campaign in 2014–2016 called We Charge Genocide (We Charge Genocide 2018) using the slogan and tactic of the 1951 campaign by the Civil Rights Congress: they collected reports of oppressive policing in Chicago, prepared a report, and sent a delegation of young people to Geneva to present it to the UN. The group's "about" says that it is entirely volunteer and avoids the "nonprofit industrial complex." The organization Assata Daughters (Assata's Daughters 2018) is a Black women's organization founded in 2015 that identifies with the radical tradition of Assata Shakur and defines itself as part of the larger Black Lives Matter movement. Its web site says it is volunteer run and solicits donations for expenses.

Another key organization, BYP100 (BYP100 2018a), grew from a conference of 100 young Black activists convened in 2013 by University of Chicago professor Cathy Cohen's Black Youth Project (an information hub founded in 2004). Attendees, led by Charlene Carruthers, a Black queer feminist community organizer, decided to create the organization when the Zimmerman verdict was announced at the time of the conference. It organized in Chicago and elsewhere around police violence issues but quickly established itself as a multi-issue organization (BYP100 2018b) and now has 11 paid staff members and chapters in nine cities. Its history is also described by Ransby (2015). Ransby (2015) also stresses the actions of MXGM (Malcolm X Grassroot Movement), an organization founded in 1990 that grew out of the Republic of New Afrika and has chapters in New York, Atlanta, Washington, DC, Dallas-Fort Worth, New Orleans, Oakland, Detroit, and Jackson, Mississippi, where it promotes cooperative economic development, self-sufficiency, and sustainability.[3] In Jackson, Mississippi, the organization successfully contested for political power (Florini 2014; Spence 2015). After the killing of Trayvon Martin, it also published Operation Ghetto Storm (Eisen 2012) documenting police killings which inspired subsequent efforts by others, including the *Washington Post*.

The founders of the national Black Lives Matter organization encouraged the formation of chapters and sought to control the use of the "Black Lives Matter" name. Many of the groups that affiliated with Black Lives Matter had existed under other names prior to affiliating with Black Lives Matter, or created a Black Lives Matter chapter as a front or coalition of activists already involved in other groups. Many groups in many cities that were part of the larger Black Lives mobilization never took the Black Lives Matter name. The national Black Lives Matter organization still exists. It has been criticized by some other organizations that are part of the broader Black Lives movement for seeking to portray itself as "the" movement and monopolize resources, for failing to acknowledge other grassroots groups, and for its move toward electoral politics and a liberal agenda.[4]

The Black Lives movement seeks a proactive agenda

As the protests ramped up, longtime Black activists expressed interest and enthusiasm but also concern about keeping the movement nonviolent and channeling it into sustained mobilization. Taylor (2016) describes these conflicts as being primarily between the Black masses and the Black elites. While that is certainly one axis of contention, the conflicts appear multi-dimensional. Newly mobilized people with no clear ideology beyond a generalized Black consciousness worked with activists with a wide variety of specific ideologies. Those ideologies included Black nationalism, various types of race-conscious socialism/Marxism, liberal Democrat, various religious or communitarian traditions, and race-conscious conservativism.

Tactically, there were splits between those favoring electoral strategies, those favoring community organizing, those favoring disruptive direct action, and those favoring separatism and self-help.

The network of community organizations from which the movement grew quickly sought to seize the momentum and broaden its agenda beyond "don't kill us." A Movement for Black Lives agenda meeting that included 1200 people met in Cleveland in late July 2015. The *New York Times* apparently did not cover the event at all. An Associated Press article reported some of the speeches from the opening session and the goal of creating a movement (Gillispie 2015). A Cleveland news source covered the event itself (Blackwell 2015a; Morice 2015) and published multiple stories giving competing accounts of an incident in which conference participants confronted an officer arresting a Black boy and were pepper sprayed by the officer (e.g., Blackwell 2015b; Naymik 2015). *Essence* reported that attendees would include Cleveland Action, Ferguson Action, and Million Hoodies Movement for Justice (Lewis 2015). NPR (Florido 2015) featured an interview with conference organizers Maurice Mitchell and Waltrina Middleton along with Nat Williams, director of the Hill-Snowdon Foundation. Williams stated that Hill-Snowdon stressed the importance of founding conventions, comparing the Cleveland meeting to the 1909 Niagara Falls conference called by W.E.B. DuBois, and said his organization had committed nearly a million dollars in grants over three years to the group. Coverage of the conference by Socialist Alternative called attention to the meeting's importance as the first major event since the 1998 Black Radical Conference, but also expressed concerns about funding from George Soros and the Ford Foundation grants that support the groups organizing against police violence, worrying that this leads movements into safe channels that do not challenge capitalism (Hawkins 2015).

On August 1, 2016, the Movement for Black Lives (M4BL) rolled out its comprehensive proactive agenda "A Vision for Black Lives" posted at https://m4bl.net/ in a well-organized social and mass media campaign timed to follow the Democratic and Republican conventions.

The preamble states that the agenda is rooted in Black communities but also recognizes the shared struggle with all oppressed people. Additionally, it stresses that it is intentional amplification of the "particular experience of state and gendered violence that Black queer, trans, gender nonconforming, women and intersex people face." The agenda lists six major policy areas: "End the War on Black People," "Reparations," "Invest-Divest," "Economic Justice," "Community Control," "Political Power." Each policy area includes a series of more specific demands and each of these is backed up by a longer policy paper. The platform received coverage from many left-liberal blogs and news sources, and serious mainstream news media coverage from the *St. Louis Dispatch*, two articles in the *Christian Science Monitor* and several in the *Atlantic*, as well as on the NBC news web site. The *New York Times* gave only vague coverage of the platform in an article that did not list the details of the proposals or link to them (Alcindor 2016); two *New York Times* articles in September discussed the cancellation of a benefit for M4BL because of the small part of the platform that condemned Israel's treatment of Palestine, and two other articles in August mentioned that it, in addition to the NAACP, opposed charter schools.

Debates about funding

Sustainable movements require activists who have sources of food and shelter and can provide for dependents. Who is paying or supporting activists become important elements of movements (Oliver and Marwell 1992). By 2015, the Black Lives movement was drawing in White progressive donor and foundation support (Taylor 2016), as the NPR and Socialist Alternative coverage of the 2015 Cleveland meeting made clear. Several meetings were held and articles written in the summer of 2015 encouraging progressive donors to give money to the Black Lives movement (Schlegel 2015), and there was some news coverage of this (Vega 2015; Vogel and Wheaton 2015). As mentioned above, the Hill-Snowdon Foundation launched the Making Black Lives Matter Initiative in May 2015, committing $900,000 over three years to support Black-led organizing, leadership development, and strategic convenings (Hill-Snowdon Foundation 2018). Cordery (2016) describes other funding: Solidaire, founded in 2012 in response to the Occupy movement, gave $300,000 in rapid response support to Movement for Black Lives groups in Ferguson, Baltimore, Minneapolis, and Chicago; Resource Generation, an organization of young wealthy people, gave $1 million to various groups; the North Start Fund quickly gave $280,000 to New York Groups, and the Women Donors Network pledged to raise more than $1 million for racial justice. Cordery advocates that funders seek to be more flexible for rapid-response funding and says that most of the funding for the 2015 Cleveland meeting was raised within a few weeks from individual donors. Writing for *Politico*, Vogel and Wheaton (2015) emphasize the role of the Democracy Alliance, a major liberal funding club close to the Democratic Party, whose members were funding St. Louis's Organization for Black Struggle, and less disruptive groups that have provided support for the Black Lives movement, including Black Youth Project 100, Center for Popular Democracy, Black Civic Engagement Fund, ColorOfChange.org, and Advancement Project. In July of 2016, the Ford Foundation announced that it would make six-year investments in organizations that are part of the Movement for Black Lives in partnership with other donor groups with a stated goal of channeling $100 million into Black Lives movement groups (Kelly-Green and Yasui 2016; McGirt 2016). In short, Black Lives movement organizations are on many donor lists.

There are longstanding debates about the role of funders in movements. Taylor quotes Aldon Morris (1984) on how foundations funding SNCC sought to channel it into voter registration efforts and away from more disruptive tactics. Francis (2015) describes how the Garland Fund moved the NAACP away from its focus on racial violence in the 1950s to a focus on education. Many writers have criticized the political agenda of the Ford Foundation. Marquez (2003) describes how external funding shaped the agendas of key Mexican American organizations, including the National Council of La Raza, the Southwest Voter registration Education Project, and the Mexican American Legal Defense and Educational Fund, as well as the Texas Industrial Areas Foundation network of grassroots organizations. Ferguson (2013, 2015) examined Ford Foundation funding of Black Power and argues that Ford funded inward-looking segregated programs that treated Black people as a problem to be kept separate.

Incite! published a collection entitled *The Revolution Will Not Be Funded* over a decade ago (2007) whose writers discussed the ways in which programs were distorted by funding issues, and many activists since have debated the NGO-ization of reform or the "nonprofit industrial complex." In the introduction to *The Revolution Will Not Be Funded*, Smith (2007) argues that funding is a cover for White supremacy by providing relief that does not challenge hierarchies, and in the same volume Rodríguez (2007) argues that funding moderate groups provides a cover for violent repression of radicals. Kohl-Arenas (2015) studied negotiations between funders and groups addressing migrant poverty in California and argues that funders operate as consensus brokers that exclude challenges to power relations, Oyakawa (2017) discusses the conflict in the Ohio Organizing Collaborative between funders' priorities and the populist logic of the organization. Frantz and Fernandes (2018) also found that funders pulled workers' centers away from confrontational politics.

Black Lives movement funders associated with the Democratic Alliance doubtless have a partisan agenda, and other funders doubtless also have a channeling agenda. At the same time, there is a wide diversity of arrangements between funders and the groups they fund, and some donor money supports groups that are contentious and challenge the system. Cordery (2016) discusses the importance of movement building and relationships of trust between philanthropists and the groups they fund, so that they do not need to ask for accountability reports, and stresses that many local groups self-fund, including crowdfunding to raise bail money or expenses for activists. The alternatives to donor funds are to do what can be done on a volunteer-only basis, charge dues, sell products such as T-shirts or newspapers, write and sell books, get a job with a non-profit or university, or become a paid public speaker. All these options have been pursued by some organizations and activists.

Surviving the White counter-revolt

Even as the Movement for Black Lives was attracting substantial White ally support and rolling out its proactive agenda in the summer of 2016, the White counter-revolt was in full swing. In the campaign of Donald Trump, White supremacy moved from covert "dog whistle" language to overt attacks on immigrants and rejection of Black movement demands. Although the Black Lives movement had attracted substantial White support, it (along with the Obama presidency) had also heightened White racial threat. Ironically, the peak in "Black Lives Matter" as a phrase in Google trends occurred in mid-July. On July 7, as activists and news media were gearing up for the second anniversary of Michael Brown's killing and the Vision for Black Lives was being prepared for its August 1 rollout, a Black sniper shot 12 police officers, killing five of them, at a peaceful Black Lives Matter march in Dallas that was protesting police killings in Minnesota and Louisiana. Police killed the sniper with a robot at the scene after a standoff where he told police negotiators that he was upset about police shootings and wanted to kill White people, especially police officers. His Facebook page showed support for the New Black Panther Party (Fernandez, Pérez-Peña, and Bromwich 2016). Within 24 hours, news articles were characterizing this as the end of the Black Lives Matter movement and police and other officials were blaming Black Lives Matter protests for police killings. Although there had been sprinklings of "All Lives Matter" and "Blue Lives Matter" in Google Trends before, there is a strong peak in those terms as well at the same time, although they never eclipse Black Lives Matter.

After the surprise election of Donald Trump in November, national (White) media attention turned from the Black Lives movement to the mass protests against his election and then the ongoing dance of presidential announcements of yet another anti-immigrant action or Republican Congressional attacks on the Affordable Care Act or passage of massive tax cuts, or news about Russian hacking of the US election, or pecuniary and sexual scandals of public officials. Although I do not have confirmation of time or place, I saw statements by Black Lives activists that movement activists were already planning in September and October for a possible Trump victory.

The Black Lives movement has left center stage, but it has not gone away. Alisa Robinson's compilation[5] of Black Lives Matter protests or demonstrations lists 2638 events as of April 6, 2019, including 429 demonstrations in at least 168 locations that occurred in 2017 (per a report) and at this writing in the spring of 2019 is still reporting one or two dozen events a month.[6]

Most of the organizations that existed before the wave of mobilization that began in 2012 are still operating, as are many of the newer organizations. Ransby (2018) describes the ongoing work of the Movement for Black Lives (M4BL) coalition, including a 2017 electoral justice project that obtained funding and trained leaders, including Madison's M. Adams. Anspach (2018) reviews the state of the movement in the fall of 2018, arguing that it is moving forward on many of the campaigns outlined in the 2016 Agenda, including campaigns to restore voting rights to felons and to build Black voting power generally, strategies of shifting funding from criminal justice to other programs, a campaign against cash bail, and a campaign against GEO, the firm that contracts for immigrant detention centers and gives money to political candidates.

Other groups continue to address criminal justice issues. The Million Hoodies Movement for Justice (MillionHoodies 2018) was co-founded in 2012 by Daniel Maree, a social media strategist who initiated a "Million Hoodies" online campaign around the Travyon Martin case (Ehrlich 2013), and Dante Barry, who had previously worked for the Roosevelt Institute, a liberal think tank. It initially focused on collecting incidents of police misconduct and now focuses on developing a new generation of human rights leaders among students and young people of color. Johnetta Elzie and DeRay McKesson, who became well known for frequent tweeting of Ferguson protests and producing a newsletter *The Movement Today* (Randle 2016; Thrasher 2015) went on win a Howard Zinn

Freedom to Write award and collaborated with data scientist Samuel Sinyangwe and fellow Ferguson Tweeter Brittany Packnett, who was on President Obama's Task Force on 21st Century Policing, to create "Mapping Police Violence" and a larger Campaign Zero (Campaign Zero 2018) that is focused on criminal justice issues, including ending broken windows policing, cutting school to prison pipeline, and seeking alternatives to incarceration.

Conclusion

This chapter has put the Black Lives movement into context, to show how this movement focusing on resisting police violence was not new but arose from the fundamental divisions of US society and built on prior movement activism. After the gains of the Civil Rights era and the intensive repression of the Black Power movement at the end of the 1960s and the early 1970s, the Black movement shifted into a more institutional and self-help phase. A series of Black conventions sought to build Black political power. Black organizations like the NAACP, the SCLC, and the Urban League continued to pursue reforms in an increasingly hostile climate.

Black electoral politics expanded along with Black Power cultural organizations. But, as Robnett's Chapter 2 in this volume explains, the Black movement lost the proactive initiative in the 1970s and was increasingly in a defensive mode against attacks on Affirmative Action in the context of a political emphasis on attracting White voters. The massive repression of Black urban rioters and Black militants morphed into intensive policing of Black neighborhoods and mass incarceration.

Regardless of their political ideology, be it radical or reformist, most of the resistance to this repression took the form of advocacy: collecting data, writing reports, giving speeches, advocating legislation, and filing lawsuits. Across the decades since 1970, this has been punctuated by periodic eruptions of relatively spontaneous mass protest to egregious acts of police violence. Some of these eruptions included property damage or assaults on persons and became riots or insurrections. In other cases, particularly in New York, activists helped convert the protest energy into sustained disciplined peaceful disruptive protests around specific incidents.

Despite the lack of consistent attention from mainstream White news sources or academics, African American groups developed the ideologies and networks that undergird the more recent Black Lives mobilization. Local activist networks or what Aldon D. Morris (1984) calls local movement centers built on those established in the Civil Rights and Black Power (Jeffries 2007, 2010, 2018) eras and continued to do what they could. There was a mobilization wave in the 1990s that probably was sparked by the widely publicized video of Los Angeles police beating Rodney King in 1991 and the not guilty verdict for the police who beat him followed by the Los Angeles riot in 1992. There was a growth of Afro-Centric celebrations and bookstores in the 1990s, the massive mobilization around the 1995 Million Man March, and the extensive publicity around the O.J. Simpson trial. There was a great deal of Black political action in the latter half of the 1990s to resist repression. The NAACP and other reformist Black organizations, in alliance with some White organizations including the ACLU, developed the "driving while black" and "racial profiling" campaigns, and there were at least some disruptive protests that were part of these campaigns, although they got little attention in the White press. Incite!, a woman of color organization addressing issues of violence and incorporating queer voices, was formed in the late 1990s, and Black queer people were mobilizing in other organizations as well. The Black Radical Congress adopted "education not incarceration" as its central focus, and Black radicals along with White radicals founded Critical Resistance. Protests and "riots" about police violence were regular occurrences in Black communities, and a few of them received national news coverage, including several cascading protest waves in New York City in the 1990s, as well as the 2001 Cincinnati riot. In the broader social movement scene, widespread mobilization in the anti-globalization movement and the role of the anarchists led to the Battle of Seattle in 2000 and an overall increase in disruptive politics.

Then the attacks of 9/11 happened and largely stalled all that mobilization for about five years. Protests were centered in the movement against the Iraq War and, in 2006, in defense of immigrants against harsh proposed anti-immigrant legislation. In the second half of the 2000s, there were Black protests about police killings and the online organizing for the "Jena 6" protests about discrimination in criminal justice and failure to prosecute hate crimes. The most recent protest wave began with the right-wing anti-Obama Tea Party mobilization of 2009–2010 and then, after the Republican victories in 2010, with left-wing opposition to austerity programs in the Occupy movement of 2011. Black people were important parts of Occupy protests in several cities and in spin-off Occupy the Hood movements in many other cities. Protests calling for the prosecution of George Zimmerman for the killing of Trayvon Martin in 2012 and about Zimmerman's not guilty verdict in 2013 heightened attention to police violence and set the stage for the mass mobilization to come. The police killings of Eric Garner in New York and then Michael Brown in Ferguson in August 2014 launched a protest wave that peaked in 2016. Many of the organizations fostering these protests and the broader advocacy campaign around repression had been formed before 2014 and many received substantial outside funding. The prominence of women and queer people in the Black Lives movement connects directly to the development of Black feminist intersectional politics and their analysis of the intertwining effects of state violence and personal violence, along with their call to attend to women and queer and trans people, not only men, as victims of state violence. Continuities with the themes and rhetoric of Black Power are also evident in the recent mobilizations.

Within a year, these activists were holding meetings seeking to shift all that energy around resisting police violence into a proactive agenda for social change that would address the underlying conditions creating subordination as well as the system of repression that reinforced subordination. By 2016, the movement was attracting widespread White support and elite allies and financial support, even as it was also threatening many White civilians and many police agencies. The unexpected election of Donald Trump in November 2016 shifted media and activist attention toward anti-Trump protests, anti-immigrant policies and pro-immigrant protests, and overt White supremacists. The Black movement did not demobilize but shifted ground as the political environment shifted. From the standpoint of mainstream news media coverage, the Black Lives movement appears to be in abeyance. This does not mean that it has gone away, but that it is shifting strategies to survive for the long haul in a hostile environment.

At this writing, in the spring of 2019, the Black Lives movement still exists and gives evidence of still having elite support, quite possibly as part of the partisan struggle among elites for control of government. At the same time, White civilians have become bolder in their harassment of Blacks and other minorities and overt White supremacists have been demanding attention. The intensive policing practices in poor Black communities show no sign of having been eased and have probably been reinstated in many places with federal support. Policing, internment, and deportation of immigrants is a focus of attention. Given the configuration of external support that was documented in 2016 and obvious political realities, one substantial line of action is electoral, including both mobilizing Black voters and resisting efforts by Republicans to weaken Black voting rights. Another is continuing pressure on local criminal justice systems where local conditions are favorable. The movement against mass incarceration has gone mainstream, as conservatives as well as liberals are seeking to reduce prison and jail populations, and the more radical "prison abolitionism" movement continues to challenge the ideological underpinnings of the entire system. There are also growing efforts to highlight the treatment of Black immigrants and form stronger alliances between immigrant rights and Black groups, building on efforts that began in the mid-2000s. Traditional Black Civil Rights organizations are forming alliances with other groups seeking to resist conservative and racist policies and movements.

Predictions about where all these efforts will go in the coming years or decades are iffy at best. Both the physical and political environment are becoming more and more volatile and there are growing strains on both majority and minority populations. Movement actors cannot control outcomes and must make strategic guesses about how to respond to the actions of others in a complex and increasingly chaotic system.

Movements around major social cleavages do not have final conclusions, neither complete victories nor complete defeats. The only thing we can know for sure is that the actors on both sides are still there and there will be another round in an ongoing struggle.

Notes

1 I capitalize White for the sake of consistency in capitalizing the names of all racial/ethnic groups and use it as a synonym for European in the racial sense. I use Black and African American interchangeably, as members of this group are roughly balanced in their preferences for each term and generally find neither offensive. I capitalize Black because this is the preference of most Black people and is consistent with the capitalization of all other names for racial groups. I have explained the issues at stake in my 2017 essay "Race Names." SocArXiv.com, no. doi:10.31235/osf.io/7wys2 (November 11, 2017). https://osf.io/preprints/socarxiv/7wys2/.
2 This was also reported in a May 26, 1998 article in the *Philadelphia Tribune*.
3 The organization's current web presence is low on content, with archived pages containing much more material.
4 See, for example, http://blacklivescincy.com/home/2018/03/28/why-black-lives-matter-cincinnati-is-changing-its-name/
5 Alisa Robinson has collected news accounts of Black Lives Matter protests and organizations and policy statements and made them available through a creative commons license at https://elephrame.com/textbook/BLM/chart. She has also maintained an archive of organizations and policy statements: list of BLM orgs: https://elephrame.com/textbook/BLMOrganizations/chart; list of BLM policy platforms: https://elephrame.com/textbook/BLMPlatforms/chart; summary of BLM published November 1, 2016: https://elephrame.com/textbook/What-is-the-Black-Lives-Matter-movement/article; report about BLM published in 2016: https://elephrame.com/textbook/2017-Report-on-the-Black-Lives-Matter-movement/article.
6 I counted 23 events recorded for March 2019 and 12 for September 2018, each time counting for the most recent month.

References

Alcindor, Yamiche. 2016. "Black Lives Matter Coalition Makes Demands as Campaign Heats Up." *New York Times*, August 2. http://www.nytimes.com/2016/08/02/us/politics/black-lives-matter-campaign.html.
Alexander, Michelle. 2009. *The New Jim Crow: Mass Incarceration in the Age of Colorblindness*. New York: New Press.
Anderson, Monica, and Paul Hitlin. 2016. "Social Media Conversations about Race; How Social Media Users See, Share and Discuss Race and the Rise of Hashtags Like #Blacklivesmatter." Last modified August 2016. http://www.pewinternet.org/2016/08/15/social-media-conversations-about-race/.
Anspach, Rachel. 2018. "The Movement for Black Lives Sharpens Focus in Trump Era." Rewire.news, https://rewire.news/article/2018/09/13/the-movement-for-black-lives-sharpens-focus-in-trump-era/.
Assata's Daughters. 2018. "Assata's Daughters Home Page." Retrieved October 21, 2018. https://www.assatasdaughters.org/.
Bell, Joyce M. 2014. *The Black Power Movement and American Social Work*. New York: Columbia University Press.
Black Lives Matter Chicago. 2018. "Black Lives Matter Chicago." Retrieved October 21, 2018.https://www.blacklivesmatterchicago.com/.
Blackwell, Brandon. 2015a. "Black Lives Matter, Other Activist Groups to Convene in Cleveland for National Conference." Cleveland.com, June 11. https://www.cleveland.com/metro/index.ssf/2015/06/black_lives_matter_other_activ.html.

Blackwell, Brandon. 2015b. "Cleveland RTA Video Shows Movement for Black Lives Activists Surround Police Before Officer Uses Pepper Spray (Raw Video)." Cleveland.com, https://www.cleveland.com/metro/2015/07/cleveland_rta_video_shows_move.html.

Bloom, Joshua. 2015. "The Dynamics of Opportunity and Insurgent Practice: How Black Anti- Colonialists Compelled Truman to Advocate Civil Rights." *American Sociological Review* 80(2): 391–415. https://dx.doi.org/10.1177/0003122415574329.

Bloom, Joshua, and Waldo E. Martin. 2013. *Black Against Empire: The History and Politics of the Black Panther Party.* Berkeley, CA: University of California Press.

BOLD (Black Organizing for Leadership and Dignity). 2018. "Bold Black Organizing for Leadership and Dignity." https://boldorganizing.org/.

Bonilla, Yarimar, and Jonathan Rosa. 2015. "#Ferguson: Digital Protest, Hashtag Ethnography, and the Racial Politics of Social Media in the United States." *American Ethnologist* 42, no. 1: 4–17. https://dx.doi.org/doi:10.1111/amet.12112.

Brewer, Rose M. 2003. "Black Radical Theory and Practice: Gender, Race, and Class." *Socialism and Democracy* 17(1) (January 1, 2003): 109–122. https://dx.doi.org/10.1080/08854300308428344.

Browne, J. Zamgba. 1999. "NAACP Releases New Report on Profiling." *New York Amsterdam News* 90(24): 3.

Byfield, Natalie P. 2019. "Race Science and Surveillance: Police as the New Race Scientists." *Social Identities* 25(1) (January 2, 2019): 91–106. https://dx.doi.org/10.1080/13504630.2017.1418599.

BYP100. 2018a. "About BYP 100." Retrieved October 21, 2018. https://byp100.org/about- byp100/.

BYP100. 2018b. "Agenda to Build Black Futures." Retrieved October 21, 2018. https://agendatobuildblackfutures.org/our-agenda/.

Cadora, Eric. 2014. "Civics Lessons: How Certain Schemes to End Mass Incarceration Can Fail." *The Annals of the American Academy of Political and Social Science* 651: 277–285. https://www.jstor.org/stable/24541707.

Camp, Jordan T., and Christina Heatherton, eds. 2016. *Policing the Planet: Why the Policing Crisis Led to Black Lives Matter.* New York: Verso.

Campaign Zero. 2018. "Campaign Zero." Retrieved October 21, 2018. https://www.joincampaignzero.org/.

Chambliss, William J. 1995. "Crime Control and Ethnic Minorities: Legitimizing Racial Oppression by Creating Moral Panics." Pp. 235–258 in *Ethnicity, Race, and Crime: Perspectives across Time and Place*, edited by Darnell F. Hawkins. Suny Series in New Directions in Crime and Justice Studies, ed. Austin T. Turk. Albany, NY: State University of New York Press.

Chicago Torture Justice Memorials. 2018. "Chicago Torture Justice Memorials Home Page." Retrieved October 21, 2018. https://www.chicagotorture.org/.

Civil Rights Congress. 1951. *We Charge Genocide: The Historic Petition to the United Nations for Relief from a Crime of the United States Government Against the Negro People.* New York: Civil Rights Congress.

Cordery, William. 2016. "Resourcing the Movement for Black Lives." Grassroots Institute for Fundraising Training (blog), March 17, 2016. https://www.grassrootsfundraising.org/2016/03/resourcing-the-movement-for-black-lives/.

Critical Resistance. 2018. "Critical Resistance Home Page." Retrieved October 21, 2018. https://criticalresistance.org/.

Dagan, David, and Steven M. Teles. 2014. "Locked in? Conservative Reform and the Future of Mass Incarceration." *The Annals of the American Academy of Political and Social Science* 651: 266–276. https://www.jstor.org/stable/24541706.

Davenport, Christian. 2010. *Media Bias, Perspective, and State Repression: The Black Panther Party*, Cambridge Studies in Contentious Politics. Cambridge: Cambridge University Press.

Davenport, Christian. 2012. "When Democracies Kill: Reflections from the US, India, and Northern Ireland." *International Area Studies Review* 15(1): 3–20. https://dx.doi.org/10.1177/2233865912437149.

Davenport, Christian. 2015. *How Social Movements Die: Repression and Demobilization of the Republic of New Africa*, Cambridge Studies in Contentious Politics. New York: Cambridge University Press.

Dello Buono, Richard Allan. 1992. "Criminalization of Black Radical/Nationalist Struggles: From the African Blood Brotherhood to Move." Paper presented at the Annual Meeting of American Sociological Association, 1992, Pittsburgh, PA.

Dream Defenders. 2018. "Dream Defenders Home Page." https://www.dreamdefenders.org/.

Ehrlich, Brenna. 2013. "Million Hoodies for Trayvon Martin Founder: The Fight Isn't Over. Daniel Maree Urges Celebs and Supporters to Keep Fighting for Justice." MTV News. Last modified July 16, 2013. https://www.mtv.com/news/1710634/trayvon-martin-million-hoodies-org/.

Eisen, Arlene. 2012. Operation Ghetto Storm: 2012 Annual Report on the Extrajudicial Killing of Black People (Updated Edition November 2014). https://www.operationghettostorm.org/.

Fagan, Jeffrey, Garth Davies, and Adam Carlis. 2012. "Race and Selective Enforcement in Public Housing." *Journal of Empirical Legal Studies* 9(4): 697–728. https://dx.doi.org/10.1111/j.1740-1461.2012.01272.x.

Ferguson, Karen. 2013. *Top Down the Ford Foundation, Black Power, and the Reinvention of Racial Liberalism*. 1st ed., Politics and Culture in Modern America. Philadelphia: University of Pennsylvania Press.

Ferguson, Karen. 2015. "How Have Black Lives Mattered to American Philanthropy?" HistPhil (blog), https://histphil.org/2015/08/03/how-have-black-lives-mattered-to-american-philanthropy/.

Fernandez, Manny, Richard Pérez-Peña, and Jonah Engel Bromwich. 2016. "Five Officers Killed as Payback, Chief Says." *The New York Times*, July 9, 2016.

Fletcher, Jr., Bill, and Jamala Rogers. 2014. "No One Said That It Would Be Easy." *Black Scholar* 44(1) (Spring): 86–112. https://dx.doi.org/10.5816/blackscholar.44.1.0086.

Florido, Adrian, host. 2015. "'Black Lives Matter' Activists Meet in Cleveland to Plot Movement's Future (Transcript of Radio Broadcast)." All Things Considered. July 23, 2015. https://www.npr.org/2015/07/23/425654428/black-lives-matter-activists-meet-in-cleveland-to-plot-movements-future.

Florini, Sarah. 2014. "Recontextualizing the Racial Present: Intertextuality and the Politics of Online Remembering." *Critical Studies in Media Communication* 31(4) (August 8): 314–326. https://dx.doi.org/10.1080/15295036.2013.878028.

Francis, Megan. 2015. "Do Foundations Co-Opt Civil Rights Organizations?" HistPhil (blog), https://histphil.org/2015/08/17/do-foundations-co-opt-civil-rights-organizations/.

Frantz, Courtney, and Sujatha Fernandes. 2018. "Whose Movement Is It? Strategic Philanthropy and Worker Centers." *Critical Sociology* 44(4–5): 645–660. https://dx.doi.org/10.1177/0896920516661857.

Freedom Inc. 2018. "Freedom, Inc. Home Page." https://www.freedom-inc.org/.
freemumia.com. 2019. "Who Is Mumia Abu-Jamal?" Retrieved April 6, 2019. https://www.freemumia.com/who-is-mumia-abu-jamal/.
Friedman, Brittany. 2018. "Guerrilla: Racial Coercion, White Supremacy, and the Rise of the Black Guerilla Family." PhD thesis. Department of Sociology. Northwestern University.
Gee, Alex. 2013. "Justified Anger; Rev. Alex Gee says Madison Is Failing Its African-American Community." *Capital Times*, December 18, 2013.
Gillispie, Mark. 2015. "Conference Aims to Unite Efforts of Black Activist Groups." *US News Online*, July 24.
Goldstein, Robert Justin. 2001. *Political Repression in Modern America from 1870 to 1976*. First Illinois edition. Urbana, IL: University of Illinois Press.
Gordon, Diana R. 1994. *The Return of the Dangerous Classes: Drug Prohibition and Policy Politics*. New York: W.W. Norton.
Grainger, Garrett L. 2013. "The Struggle within the Struggle: Neoliberalism and Group Schism within a Multiracial Social Movement Organization." Master's Thesis. Department of Sociology. University of Wisconsin-Madison. https://search.library.wisc.edu/catalog/9910162018402121.
Green, David B. 2019. "Hearing the Queer Roots of Black Lives Matter." https://medium.com/national-center-for-institutional-diversity/hearing-the-queer-roots-of-black-lives-matter-2e69834a65cd.
Hamm, Theodore. 2000. "Wesley Robert Wells and the Civil Rights Congress Campaign." *Souls* 2(1) (January 1): 22–33. https://dx.doi.org/10.1080/10999940009362196.
Hawkins, Eljeer. 2015. "Reflections on the Movement for Black Lives Convening in Cleveland." *Socialist Alternative*, August 9.
Hill-Snowdon Foundation. 2018. "Making Black Lives Matter Initiative." Retrieved October 20, 2018. https://www.hillsnowdon.org/mblm-initiative.
Incarcerated Workers Organizing Committee. 2018. "Prison Strike 2018." https://incarceratedworkers.org/campaigns/prison-strike-2018.
Incite! 2018. "Incite! Home Page." Retrieved October 21, 2018. https://incite-national.org/.
Incite! Women of Color Against Violence. 2007. *The Revolution Will Not Be Funded: Beyond the Non-Profit Industrial Complex*. Cambridge, MA: South End Press.
Jeffries, Judson L., ed. 2007. *Comrades: A Local History of the Black Panther Party*. Bloomington: Indiana University Press.
Jeffries, Judson L., ed. 2010. *On the Ground: The Black Panther Party in Communities across America*. Jackson, MI: University Press of Mississippi.
Jeffries, Judson L., ed. 2018. *The Black Panther Party in a City Near You*. Athens, GA: University of Georgia Press.
Johnson, Cedric. 2007. *Revolutionaries to Race Leaders: Black Power and the Making of African American Politics*. Minneapolis, MN: University of Minnesota Press.
Jones, Nikki. 2018. *The Chosen Ones: Black Men and the Politics of Redemption, Gender and Justice*. Oakland, CA: University of California Press.
Kelly-Green, Brook, and Luna Yasui. 2016. "Why Black Lives Matter to Philanthropy." Ford Foundation Equals Change Blog. https://www.fordfoundation.org/idea/equals-change-blog/posts/why-black-lives-matter-to-philanthropy/.
Kerner, Otto, John V. Lindsay, and F.R. Harris. 1968. Report of the National Advisory Commission on Civil Disorders. US Government Printing Office Washington, DC.
King, Mike. 2017. *When Riot Cops Are Not Enough: The Policing and Repression of Occupy Oakland*. New Brunswick, NJ: Rutgers University Press.

Kohl-Arenas, Erica. 2015. "The Self-Help Myth: Towards a Theory of Philanthropy as Consensus Broker." *American Journal of Economics and Sociology* 74, no. 4: 796–825. https://dx.doi.org/doi:10.1111/ajes.12114.

Lerman, Amy E., and Vesla M. Weaver. 2014. "Staying Out of Sight? Concentrated Policing and Local Political Action." *The Annals of the American Academy of Political and Social Science* 651: 202–219. https://www.jstor.org/stable/24541702.

Lewis, Taylor. 2015. "Hundreds of Activists Travel to Cleveland for Black Lives Matter Convention." *Essence*, July 24.

Marquez, Benjamin. 2003. "Mexican-American Political Organizations and Philanthropy: Bankrolling a Social Movement." *Social Service Review* 77(3): 329–346.

Marx, Gary T. 1970. "Civil Disorder and the Agents of Social Control." *The Journal of Social Issues* 26(1) (Winter): 19–57.

Marx, Gary T. 1974. "Thoughts on a Neglected Category of Social Movement Participant: The Agent Provocateur and the Informant." *American Journal of Sociology* 80(2) (September): 402–442.

Marx, Gary T. 1980. "The New Police Undercover Work." *Urban Life* 8(4) (January): 399–446.

Marx, Gary T. 1981. "Ironies of Social Control: Authorities as Contributors to Deviance Through Escalation, Nonenforcement and Covert Facilitation." *Social Problems* 28, no. 3 (February): 221–246.

Marx, Gary T. 1982. "Who Really Gets Stung? Some Issues Raised by the New Police Undercover Work." *Crime and Delinquency* 28(2) (April): 165–193.

Matthews, Katherine D. 2015. "'Ask Him If You're Being Detained': Bystander Resistance in Street Police Encounters." M.A., unpublished Master's thesis: Department of Sociology. University of California, Santa Barbara. Available through ProQuest. ProQuest dissertations & Theses Global.

Mauer, Marc. 1999. *Race to Incarcerate*. New York: The Free Press.

McFarland, Susan. 2018. "U.S. Inmates Start National Prison Strike to Protest 'Modern-Day Slavery'." UPI. August 21, 2018. https://www.upi.com/Top_News/US/2018/08/21/US-inmates-start-national-prison-strike-to-protest-modern-day-slavery/1981534860390/.

McGirt, Ellen. 2016. "Who Is Funding Black Lives Matter." *Fortune*. August 8, 2016. https://fortune.com/2016/08/08/funding-black-lives-matter-ford/.

Meier, August, and Elliott Rudwick. 1976. "Attorneys Black and White: A Case Study of Race Relations within the NAACP." *The Journal of American History* 62(4): 913–946. https://dx.doi.org/10.2307/1903844.

MillionHoodies. 2018. "Million Hoodies Movement for Justice." https://www.millionhoodies.net/.

Morice, Jane. 2015. "Thousands of 'Freedom Fighters' in Cleveland for First National Black Lives Matter Conference." Cleveland.com. https://www.cleveland.com/metro/2015/07/thousands_of_freedom_fighters.html.

Morris, Aldon. 1984. *The Origins of the Civil Rights Movement: Black Communities Organizing for Change*. New York: Free Press.

Morris, Aldon D. 1984. *The Origins of the Civil Rights Movement: Black Communities Organizing for Change*. New York: Free Press; Collier Macmillan.

Morrow, Christian. 2011. "'Occupy the Hood' Expanding." *New Pittsburgh Courier*, November 9–November 15. City Edition.

mumiaabujamal.com. 2019. "About Mumia." Retrieved April 6, 2019. https://www.freemumia.com/who-is-mumia-abu-jamal/.

National Research Council. 2014. *The Growth of Incarceration in the United States: Exploring Causes and Consequences*, edited by Jeremy Travis, Bruce Western, and Steve Redburn. Washington, DC: The National Academies Press.

Naymik, Mark. 2015. "Police and Movement for Black Lives Need to Stop Overreacting (Video): Mark Naymik." Cleveland.com. https://www.cleveland.com/naymik/2015/07/police_and_movement_for_black.html.

Nehemiah. 2018. "Nehemiah Center for Urban Leadership Development." https://nehemiah.org/.

Niven, Steven J. 2006. *Scottsboro Boys*. New York: Oxford University Press.

Oliver, Pamela. 2008. "Repression and Crime Control: Why Social Movement Scholars Should Pay Attention to Mass Incarceration as a Form of Repression." *Mobilization: An International Quarterly* 13(1): 1–24. https://www.metapress.com/content/v264hx580h486641.

Oliver, Pamela. 2017. "Race Names." *SocArXiv.com*. doi:10.31235/osf.io/7wys2 (November 11). https://osf.io/preprints/socarxiv/7wys2/.

Oliver, Pamela E. 2009. "Talking About Racial Disparities in Imprisonment: A Reflection on Experiences in Wisconsin." Pp. 281–298 in *Handbook of Public Sociology*, edited by Vincent Jeffries. Lanham, MD: Rowman & Littlefield.

Oliver, Pamela E., and Gerald Marwell. 1992. "Mobilizing Technologies for Collective Action." Pp. 251–271 in *Frontiers in Social Movement Theory*, edited by Aldon Morris and Carol McClurg Mueller. New Haven, CT: Yale University Press.

Oliver, Pamela E., Alex Hanna, and Chaeyoon Lim. 2019. Black Protest Events in the US 1994–2010: Issues, Campaigns and Trends. https://osf.io/preprints/socarxiv/aq5xj.

Owens, Michael Leo. 2014. "Ex-Felons' Organization-Based Political Work for Carceral Reforms." *The Annals of the American Academy of Political and Social Science* 651: 256–265. https://www.jstor.org/stable/24541705.

Oyakawa, Michelle. 2017. "Building a Movement in the Non-Profit Industrial Complex." PhD dissertation, Department of Sociology, Ohio State University. Available through ProQuest. ProQuest Dissertations & Theses Global.

Paye, Amity. 2012. "Occupy the Hood Makes Big Plans During Hood Week Atlanta." *New York Amsterdam News*, July 26–August 1.

Pierce, Paulette. 1988. "The Roots of the Rainbow Coalition." *The Black Scholar* 19, no. 2: 2–16. https://www.jstor.org.ezproxy.library.wisc.edu/stable/41067448.

Pierce, Paulette. 2003. "Neglected Legacy: The Black Power Movement and Jesse Jackson's Presidential Campaigns." *Humanity & Society* 27(4): 481-97. https://journals.sagepub.com/doi/abs/10.1177/016059760302700406

Randle, Aaron. 2016. "Now You See Me: A Look at the World of Activist Johnetta Elzie." Complex.com. March 8.

Ransby, Barbara. 2015. "The Class Politics of Black Lives Matter." *Dissent* 62(4) (Fall 2015): 31–34. https://dx.doi.org/10.1353/dss.2015.0071.

Ransby, Barbara. 2018. *Making All Black Lives Matter: Reimagining Freedom in the Twenty-First Century*. Oakland, CA: University of California Press.

Ray, Rashawn, et al. 2017. "Ferguson and the Death of Michael Brown on Twitter: #Blacklivesmatter, #TCOT, and the Evolution of Collective Identities." *Ethnic and Racial Studies* 40(11) (September 2): 1797–1813. https://dx.doi.org/10.1080/01419870.2017.1335422.

Ray, Rashawn, Melissa Brown, and Wendy Laybourn. 2017. "The Evolution of #Blacklivesmatter on Twitter: Social Movements, Big Data, and Race." *Ethnic and Racial*

Studies 40(11) (September 2): 1795–1796. https://dx.doi.org/10.1080/01419870.2017.1335423.

Richie, Beth. 2012. *Arrested Justice: Black Women, Violence, and America's Prison Nation*. New York: New York University Press.

Rios, Victor M. 2015. "Policed, Punished, Dehumanized." Pp. 59–80 in *Deadly Injustice: Trayvon Martin, Race, and the Criminal Justice System*, edited by Devon Johnson, Patricia Y. Warne, and Amy Farrekkm. New York: NYU Press.

Robinson, Alisa. 2017. "List of 27 Black Lives Matter and Ally Organizations." Retrieved October 21, 2018. https://elephrame.com/textbook/BLMOrganizations/chart.

Rodriquez, Dylan. 2007. "The Political Logic of the Non-Profit Industrial Complex." Pp. 21–40 in *The Revolution Will Not Be Funded: Beyond the Non-Profit Industrial Complex*, edited by Incite! Women of Color Against Violence. Cambridge, MA: South End Press.

Rogers, Jamala. 2015. *Ferguson Is America: Roots of Rebellion*. St. Louis, MO: Mira Digital Publishing.

Schlegel, Ryan. 2015. "Why Foundations Should Support July's Movement for Black Lives Convening." NCRP: National Committee for Responsive Philanthropy, June 9. https://www.ncrp.org/2015/06/movement-for-black-lives-convening.html.

Smith, Andrea. 2007. "Introduction: The Revolution Will Not Be Funded." Pp. 1–18 in *The Revolution Will Not Be Funded: Beyond the Non-Profit Complex*, edited by Incite! Women of Color Against Violence. Cambridge, MA: South End Press.

Solomon, Akiba. 2014. "Get on the Bus: Inside the Black Life Matters 'Freedom Ride' to Ferguson." Colorlines (blog). September 5. https://www.colorlines.com/articles/get-bus-inside-black-life-matters-freedom-ride-ferguson.

Spence, Lester K. 2015. *Knocking the Hustle: Against the Neoliberal Turn in Black Politics*. Brooklyn, NY: Punctum Books.

Taylor, Keeanga-Yamahtta. 2016. *From #Blacklivesmatter to Black Liberation*. Chicago: Haymarket Books.

Theoharis, Jeanne. 2013. *The Rebellious Life of Mrs. Rosa Parks*. Boston: Beacon Press.

Thrasher, Steven W. 2015. "What Next for Black Lives Matter in Ferguson After City's Police Shooting?" *The Guardian (US Edition)*. March 13.

Thuma, Emily. 2015. "Lessons in Self-Defense: Gender Violence, Racial Criminalization, and Anticarceral Feminism." *Women's Studies Quarterly* 43(3/4): 52–71. https://www.jstor.org.ezproxy.library.wisc.edu/stable/43958549.

Tonry, Michael. 1994. "Racial Politics, Racial Disparities, and the War on Crime." *Crime & Delinquency* 40(4): 475.

Vega, Tanzina. 2015. "How to Fund #Blacklivesmatter." CNN Politics. June 5. https://www.cnn.com/2015/06/05/politics/funding-civil-rights-movement/index.html.

Vitale, Alex S., and Brian Jordan Jefferson. 2016. "The Emergence of Command and Control Policing in Neoliberal New York." Pp. 157–172 in *Policing the Planet: Why the Policing Crisis Led to Black Lives Matter*, edited by Jordan T. Camp and Christina Heatherton. New York: Verso.

Vogel, Kenneth P., and Sara Wheaton. 2015. "Major Donors Consider Funding Black Lives Matter." *Politico*. November 13.

Wacquant, Loic. 2001. "Deadly Symbiosis: When Ghetto and Prison Meet and Mesh." *Punishment Society* 3(1) (January 1): 95–133. https://dx.doi.org/10.1177/14624740122228276.

We Charge Genocide. 2018. "We Charge Genocide Home Page." https://wechargegenocide.org/.

Weddington, George. 2018a. "The Fall of 2014: Recovering the Roots of the Black Lives Movement." Race, Politics, Justice (blog). September 1. https://www.ssc.wisc.edu/soc/racepoliticsjustice/2018/09/01/the-fall-of-2014-recovering-the-roots-of-the-black-lives-movement/.

Weddington, George. 2018b. "Organizing Against Incarceration: Foucault's 'Carceral Continuum'." Paper presented at the Association of Black Sociologists, Philadelphia, PA.

Wells-Barnett, Ida B. 1895. *A Red Record: Tabulated Statistics and Alleged Causes of Lynchings in the United States, 1892–1893–1894 Black Though and Culture*. Chicago: Donohue and Henneberry, Electronic reproduction. Alexandria, VA: Alexander Street Press, 2003. https://www.aspresolver.com/aspresolver.asp?GILD;10000399149.

Wells-Barnett, Ida B. 1969. *On Lynchings: Southern Horrors. A Red Record. Mob Rule in New Orleans*. The American Negro, His History and Literature. New York: Arno Press.

Wells-Barnet, Ida B., and Frederick Douglass. 2005. *The Red Record: [Tabulated Statistics and Alleged Causes of Lynching in the United States]*. Cirencester, England: Echo Library/Paperbackshop Ltd.

Williams, Kristian. 2011. "The Other Side of the Coin: Counterinsurgency and Community Policing." *Interface: A Journal For and About Social Movements* 3(1): 81–117.

Williams, Timothy. 2011. "Execution Case Dropped Against Abu-Jamal." *New York Times*December 7.

Williamson, Vanessa, Kris-Stella Trump, and Katherine Levine Einstein. 2018. "Black Lives Matter: Evidence That Police-Caused Deaths Predict Protest Activity." *Perspectives on Politics* 16(2): 400–415. https://dx.doi.org/10.1017/S1537592717004273.

Wisconsin Council on Children and Families. 2013. Race to Equity: A Baseline Report on the State of Racial Disparities in Dane County. https://racetoequity.net/baseline-report-state-racial-disparities-dane-county/.

Zangrando, Robert L. 1965. "The NAACP And a Federal Antilynching Bill 1934–1940." *The Journal of Negro History* 50(2): 106–117. https://dx.doi.org/10.2307/2715996.

4 Racist policing, practical resonance, and frame alignment in Ferguson

Joshua Bloom and Zachary David Frampton

Michael Brown, a Black teenager, was killed on Canfield Drive in Ferguson, MO, by officer Darren Wilson at about noon on Saturday, August 9, 2014. Local Black activists protested what they charged was a case of racist policing. Soon, hundreds of people in the local Black community (see below), and hundreds of thousands of people globally, were discussing the case on social media (Hitlin and Vogt 2014). Many adopted the activists' framing of the killing as an expression of racist policing. And some offered support. For example, by the next morning, Reverend Al Sharpton—a leading national anti-racist activist—had set a date to travel to Ferguson (AP 2014).

When Michael Brown was killed, it was not at first obvious that a lot of people would adopt the racist policing frame about the killing. At the time, there was not yet a national Black Lives Matter organization, and the phrase "Black Lives Matter" was still unfamiliar to most people. The killing of Eric Garner three weeks earlier and the killing of Trayvon Martin two and a half years earlier had garnered national attention. Michelle Alexander's *New Jim Crow* (2010) got many people talking about racism in criminal justice. Historically, many Black protest organizations sought to challenge racist policing (see, e.g., Bloom and Martin 2016). But in the period preceding August 2014, in contrast to the period that followed, large-scale protests of racist policing in response to police killings of Black people was relatively infrequent and localized.[1] Something changed in Ferguson.

Social movement theorists have devoted a great deal of attention to the question of frame alignment. For people to take collective action, they have to see the issue at hand in a similar way, i.e., share a subjective framing of it. Frame theorists originally focused on activists' linguistic activities of frame bridging, amplification, extension, and transformation as they seek to bring others into alignment with them (see Snow et al. 2019 for review). This line of theorizing would suggest that previously mobilized activists were important for creating frame alignment in Ferguson and that detailed research would find social movement organizations at the core of the initial mobilization, linguistically engineering frame alignment. However, several lines of recent theorizing emphasize that framing is not static but develops dynamically in reference to interactions between activists and authorities as ordinary people seek to make meaning of the situation (Benford 1997; Ellingson 1995; Koopmans and Olzak 2004; McDonnell, Bail, and Tavory 2017; Snow and Moss 2014; Steinberg 1999).[2] Frames and framing are never just about ideas; they are always tied to and mutually constitutive of practices. Frame resonance is a practical matter—it depends on whether the framing, as part of a broader set of potential practices, and given the conditions in which they are enacted, offer a practical means for addressing a situation. Sometimes frames and practices reaffirm the basic goodness of the society, sometimes they produce submission to authority, sometimes they are the frames and practices of affluent people who see themselves as solving problems. Sometimes frames and practices by oppressed people support insurgency.

We consider Ferguson as a case of frame alignment in the emergence of an insurgency. Insurgent practice theory suggests that those who are oppressed can intentionally trigger frame alignment through engaging in actions that force the authorities to respond. This approach is somewhat distinct from resource mobilization or political process approaches in that it takes a practice-centered view of movements. Rather than comprised by organizations or the members of a social category, insurgent movements are seen as the widespread adoption of a novel set of insurgent practices. In this approach, an insurgent is any individual who participates in practices that disrupt established institutions for transformative social aims. Over time, successful insurgents *do* often build formal movement organizations—like SNCC's formation following the 1960 sit-ins, or the national spread of Black Panther Party offices in 1968–9. But the crux of sustained insurgent mobilization is the often informal development of a powerful and relatively coherent set of insurgent practices (frame, tactics, and target) that can sustain disruption in a given political environment. This is accomplished when an insurgent practice draws third parties, i.e. those who are neither insurgents nor authorities—to support insurgents in the face of repression by authorities. Effective insurgent practices offer potential insurgents a means to influence their situation. While people are trying out all different kinds of framings all the time, and all different kinds of tactics, the emergence of a powerful set of insurgent practices capable of sustaining deep and far-reaching disruption, and thus substantially transforming social power relations, is quite rare (Bloom 2014; Bloom 2015; Bloom and Martin 2016).[3]

The insurgent practice theoretical framework guides this study, and suggests a novel approach to analyzing the frame alignment process in the emergence of insurgency in Ferguson. In particular, we ask how and to what extent did the police response to insurgent practice in Ferguson, on August 9, 2014, lead third parties to adopt a "racist policing" frame?

In the past, it was usually impossible to know exactly how actions and reactions unfolded in an emergent event. But social media allow us to see how people talked to each other in real time about the events in Ferguson as they happened. It is possible to see how the people who were on the street at the time and place of the killing drew in third-party supporters, that is, other Black people who were not themselves initially present at the killing. Rather than the engineered linguistic product of a formal social movement organization, it was through a series of defiant actions that insurgents drove alignment around the framing of Michael Brown's killing as an expression of racist policing. Many local Black people and some observers nationally felt personally threated by the circumstances of the killing of Michael Brown, and sought means of redress. Contrary to theories that focus on the problem of ideological alignment, we find that there was virtually unanimous agreement among local Blacks that the police were in general racist. Instead, initial debate focused on whether this specific incident was an instance of racist police violence, or whether Brown had done something that made his killing just. Then, as the day progressed, those at the site engaged in small-scale nonviolent acts of defiance or protest and the police reactions became increasingly aggressive and militaristic. Twitter discussions increasingly focused on the reactions of the police and developed a consensus that this was a clear instance of racist policing. Widely shared pictures of hundreds of police in riot gear and armored vehicles brought in third-party support from all over the country. Thus, in the nine hours after Michael Brown was killed, through the interactive dynamics of insurgent practice and police response, the initially ambiguous event subject to multiple interpretations took on meaning as an instance of racist policing, and an insurgent movement emerged.

Practical resonance and frame alignment

Frame theory has provided the most influential approach to accounting for the subjective aspects of mobilization.[4] The crux of frame theory is the proposition that collective action requires a shared understanding, i.e., frame alignment. Frame theory thus focuses analysis on the question of how activists come to share such an understanding.

In their foundational work, Snow et al. define "frame alignment" as "the linkage of individual and [Social Movement Organization (SMO)] interpretive orientations, such that some set of individual interests, values and beliefs and SMO activities, goals, and ideology are congruent and complementary." They propose that "by rendering events or occurrences meaningful, frames function to organize experience and guide action, whether individual or collective. So conceptualized, it follows that frame alignment is a necessary condition for movement participation" (1986: 464). Classic frame theory proposes that this frame alignment, in turn, fundamentally depends on the congruence of an activist frame with the underlying ideology of potential adherents so that SMO framings "resonate" with the underlying ideologies, values, and beliefs of potential activists (Snow and Benford 1988; Benford and Snow 2000).

Classically, frame theorists "identified four … basic strategic alignment processes: frame bridging, amplification, extension, and transformation" (Snow et al. 2019).

Although the earliest writings often implied that movement frame alignment was generated primarily by the linguistic activities of formal SMOs and their activists as they sought to advance frames that would resonate with ideologies in target populations, many scholars—including the founders of frame theory—have developed more dynamic approaches. We draw on these works, plus insurgent practice theory, to advance several propositions about how frame alignment dynamically develops in the emergence of insurgency. In short, we propose that frame resonance, and thus frame alignment, is a fundamentally *practical* process. The resonance of insurgent frames with potential supporters depends on the insurgent practices of which they are a part, and authority responses. We develop three propositions concerning practical resonance and frame alignment in insurgent politics that guide our analysis of the emergent insurgency in Ferguson.

McDonnell, Bail, and Tavory (2017) put the frame theoretical concept of resonance on a practice-theoretical foundation. Rather than the product of ideational "credibility," and "salience," they argue that resonance emerges in response to practical situations or challenges. Oliver and Johnston (2000) illuminate the ways that structural conditions shape movement ideational processes. People have deeply rooted ways of understanding the world that are thickly enmeshed in their structured social roles, commitments, and histories. These deeper commitments and understandings often motivate collective action. Steinberg (1999) also emphasizes the historical and institutional grounding of discursive movement practices. He argues that discourse itself is structuring and constraining—tied to social organization—but also "multi-vocal," subject to different interpretations, and contests over them. Opposing the view of frames as independent ideational productions, Steinberg situates contentious discursive practices as "grounded in ongoing contention within institutional histories" (1999: 749). Beyond ideational congruence, frame resonance concerns practical solutions to pressing problems. In insurgent politics, we propose that:

1 Frame resonance emerges in practical response to situational political challenges.

Snow and Moss (2014) show that frames are not always crafted anew for a situation, but may already be available for use when appropriate. Drawing on George Herbert Mead, they argue that constituents may be primed with certain frames of understanding, and as a consequential situation develops, activists can draw on these frames to address the challenges that arise. Relatedly, McDonnell, Bail, and Tavory attribute the resonance of a frame to its practical utility in a given situation. They argue that the resonance of a frame (or other cultural object) for an audience is not static and is not determined by the congruence of that frame with the underlying values and beliefs of the audience, but instead emerges when forward-moving actors encounter cultural objects that help them address a problem. "Cultural objects do not resonate because they are resonant—they are experienced as resonant *because they solve problems better than the cognitive schema afforded by* [familiar] *objects or habituated alternatives*" (McDonnell, Bail, and Tavory 2017: 10) This theorization simultaneously accounts for the depth of people's social positionality and related understandings and the dynamic, strategic, interactive, and situational way that actors align understandings. Frame alignment, in this view, is not determined by the congruence between fixed frames and underlying beliefs and values. "To the extent that resonance is about congruence, we argue that it is about the act of *making* a cultural object congruent as a person works through a situation or problem they face rather than having an already congruent or familiar solution ready at hand" (McDonnell, Bail, and Tavory 2017: 3). Some of the framing activities prompted by resonant objects lead third parties away from activist views. Benford (1997) touches on a similar point. These works resituate framing activities as actively engaged by third parties rather than unilaterally shaped by SMOs. In insurgent politics, we propose that:

2   Third parties actively engage in their own framing activities, using resonant cultural objects to make sense of the situation.

Not only does frame alignment emerge, in this sense, through the practical problem-solving activity of ordinary people. The whole practical situation, especially the interaction between insurgents and authorities in insurgent politics, shapes frame alignment. McAdam (1996) shows that tactics can play an important framing role. Ellingson (1995) argues that, rather than discretely linguistic processes, frame alignment is fundamentally shaped by collective actions themselves. He concludes that

> processes of frame alignment are influenced ... by the course and interpretation of collective action events. Such events intervene in the process of creating frames or discourses, change the value actors assign to collective beliefs, and motivate some groups to abandon a set of arguments and adopt those of a rival or create new ones.
>
> (1995: 136–7)

Bloom's studies of postwar Black Freedom Struggle, and insurgent practice theory, reinforce these points, and suggest further extensions regarding frame resonance and alignment in insurgency (Bloom 2014, 2015; Bloom and Martin 2016). Black insurgent mobilization did not develop continuously through the post-war decades. It developed in waves, and each wave of insurgent mobilization involved a distinct, yet internally consistent, set of insurgent practices, each comprising a unique combination of frames, tactics, and targets. In each wave of Black Freedom Struggle, the framing of the insurgent practice was largely inseparable from the tactics. The efficacy of the overarching set of insurgent practices was specific to the political contours of the moment. In particular, in each wave, the capacity to sustain disruption as a source of power from below depended on the way that a specific set of practices leveraged broader political cleavages to draw third-party support in resistance to repression.[5] Broader social adoption of the frame tended to follow the efficacy of the insurgent movement, rather than the other way around. Thus, framing was not an independent ideational exercise. It was intertwined with the development of a powerful and relatively coherent set of insurgent practices that constituted each wave of the Black movement. Thus, in insurgent politics, we propose that:

3 Situational dynamics—including the practical action of non-activists—drive frame alignment. In particular, the character of repressive action by authorities in response to insurgent practice plays a crucial role in the frame alignment process.

Research design

For the purposes of this analysis, the overarching aim is to explain how and to what extent the character of police action in Ferguson on August 9, 2014, led third parties to embrace a "racist policing" frame. While only a few dozen activists were directly involved in insurgent activities that day in Ferguson, hundreds of thousands of third parties who were not directly involved engaged in discussions online that day trying to make sense of the situation. Many quickly aligned their understanding of the situation with insurgents, framing the situation as an instance of racist policing. We develop our analysis along the lines of three specifying questions concerning each of the three explanatory propositions developed above.

1 First, our preliminary priority is to assess what motivated some locals to engage the framing process. For local third parties to adopt the insurgent "racist policing" frame, they had to first pay attention to the situation and seek to understand it. If frame resonance responds to practical political challenges, what practical concerns were at stake here? Did local third parties not involved in the initial activism attempt to explain the situation, and to the extent they did, what motivated these efforts?
2 Second, is frame alignment statically determined by the congruence between activist frame and constituent ideology, or actively constructed by potential supporters engaged in their own framing efforts? If third parties engage their own framing activities, we ought to see evidence of such framing activities on social media. Was this the case in Ferguson on August 9, 2014? If so, around what kinds of questions did the early framing efforts by local third parties revolve?
3 Third, in the context of such discussions, how was photo and video evidence about the character of police actions in Ferguson that day received? How did it influence both local and national efforts to make sense of the situation? To what extent did such evidence contribute to third party adoption of a "racist policing" frame?

Considering frame alignment as an important aspect of the mobilization process, we are interested especially in local third parties "at risk" of supporting insurgents in the initial mobilization process; i.e., we seek to explain what motivated the interest of third parties who could conceivably challenge repressive action and materially support the insurgents mobilizing in Ferguson that day. To construct a pool of individuals who plausibly could have chosen to support insurgents, we began by identifying as many third parties as possible active on Twitter who decided to come see the insurgency for themselves in person that day. We identified 22 such individuals. These individuals ranged in age from teenagers to senior citizens. Some were elected officials; some were news reporters. There were a few activists. Most just lived nearby and were concerned or curious about what was going on. Except for one White reporter, all these individuals were Black. As far as we know, none of these individuals participated in direct confrontation with the police that day, and only one—State Senator Maria Chappelle-Nadal—participated in a memorial vigil. We then generated a much larger pool of potential third-party supporters by including everyone local these individuals were in Twitter conversation with that day.[6] This comprised a pool of *hundreds of local tweeters* "at risk" of support, representing a range of perspectives and positions on the insurgency.

To consider third-party responses to evidence of police repressive action, we then worked in the other direction. We constructed a comprehensive sequence of insurgent and police actions in Ferguson that day triangulating Twitter and other time-stamped sources (see Bloom and Frampton 2019 for a detailed account and analysis of the interactive dynamics on the street).

Table 4.1, below, provides a timeline of the main insurgent and police actions.

Evidence of police actions on Twitter

There are no prior studies we are aware of that have assembled this kind of detailed data on the perspectives of so many potential supporters and how they changed over the course of the day in response to developing events. It has been hard to study the initial gestation of third-party support for a specific insurgency. Participant observers are rarely present, and when they are, it is usually only one person who is limited in how much of the early mobilization process they can observe. No one observer can be in hundreds of thousands of places at once to observe the range of responses to events as they unfold. News coverage is also spotty at best. Retrospective interviews are especially poor at reconstructing subtle framing processes as such processes are thoroughly re-situated in memory due to subsequent life-changing events.

Movements that have succeeded construct their own frames. Thus, in providing access to rich data on many people's reactions to events as they unfolded, social media has drastically improved the prospects for analyzing subtle and previously obscure early framing processes.

To identify individuals who came to the site to check out the situation in person, we explored the universe of tweets that day through a variety of

Table 4.1 Main insurgent and police actions on Canfield Drive in Ferguson, MO, on August 9, 2014

Insurgent Actions	Police Actions
12 pm. Michael Brown and Dorian Johnson walk down middle of Canfield Drive and defy police order to get out of street.	12 pm. Following confrontation, Michael Brown killed. Police leave body bleeding in street for hours.
12–3 pm. Dozens gather outside police tape where Michael Brown's body lies in street. Minor chants and protests. Report of gunfire in the area.	3 pm. Police respond with canines, assault rifles, and armored vehicles. They force everyone off the street, clear the area, and erect a blockade at Canfield and West Florissant 0.3 miles away.
3–7 pm. Prayer Vigil in intersection at Canfield and West Florissant. Increasingly angry protests at police blockade there.	3–7 pm. Police maintain a militarized blockade. They tape off Canfield Drive, and post a double line of armed officers facing crowd to prevent entrance to the neighborhood. Armored vehicles and police from many jurisdictions stand by.
7 pm. Once the blockade is removed, Michael Brown's mother and supporters create a rose petal memorial blocking Canfield Drive at place Michael Brown was killed. 8:30 pm. Insurgents refuse to allow police car to pass. 8:30–9 pm. Several dozen nonviolent protesters defy police and refuse to clear the street where Michael Brown was killed. They raise their hands in the air chanting "We Are Michael Brown!" Hundreds of angry Black residents on sidewalk appear to support them.	8:30 pm. Hundreds of police storm Canfield Drive armed with assault rifles and canines. Police helicopters above. Police vehicles crush rose petal memorial. Police once again try to clear the area. 9 pm. Police retreat and leave.

sampling schemes until it became very hard to identify additional such individuals. We aspired toward a comprehensivist approach in identifying such individuals, implementing searches on a wide range of Boolean search terms; utilizing geo-coding when available; tracing re-tweeted images to their originators; and following social networks among tweeters. We far exceeded the saturation point, making our analysis robust. The character of Twitter conversations we studied were not significantly changed by identifying additional individuals past about the halfway point in our analysis.

Nonetheless, we did not have the resources to closely read every one of the hundreds of thousands of salient tweets that day. So while the probability is small, it is possible that we missed some Twitter conversations involving local third parties "at risk" of supporting insurgents that were qualitatively different than the ones in our sample.

Conversely, it is likely that some third parties "at risk" of supporting the insurgency but not using Twitter underwent a somewhat different process of deciding whether to support insurgents. For example, those third parties who accessed only mainstream news coverage of the events had access to a very different—and much more limited—set of information concerning developments on Canfield Drive that day. It is worth studying the ways that richness of data access, and different forms of data access, shape the likelihood that third parties will decide to support an insurgency. But those questions are beyond the scope of this study.

Findings

We present the findings from the analysis in three sections along the lines of the three specifications of the central substantive question, related to the three theoretical propositions, above.

1 Practical concerns: assessing the personal threat

If frame resonance responds to practical political challenges, what practical concerns were at stake following the killing of Michael Brown? Local Black people in Ferguson were concerned to understand the threat the situation posed to themselves and their loved ones. To assess the implications of the killing, many locals were especially concerned to make sense of *why* police killed Michael Brown.

Classic frame theory suggests that mobilization depends fundamentally on the congruence between the activist framing and the underlying beliefs and values of potential activists. Insurgents confronting the police in Ferguson on August 9, 2014 almost always implied, and sometimes explicitly claimed, that the killing of Michael Brown was an expression of racist policing. In the discussion among potential third-party supporters that day, we found very little debate concerning whether policing practices generally were racist. Most local Black people appeared to assume they were.

For example, Conrod wrote "Go to traffic court in Ferguson. Everyone w/ a ticket is Black. We don't make up the whole population. They target us. They go where we live" (Conrod 20140809a). Delafro noted: "I've seen kids of color getting harassed by cops for just standing, breathing, existing" (Delafro 20140809a). LoveKhyB wrote: "It's hard to teach these young men to respect the police when all they have ever seen from the police is hate and murder" (LoveKhyB 20140809a). And FLOCKAfierce wrote: "Some white folks honestly cannot comprehend why anybody would run from the police. You can't fault someone for not understanding" (Flocka 20140809b). These kinds of general statements garnered little attention or debate.

The active debates among local Black third parties in Ferguson that day were much more specific. At issue was not a general question about whether policing is racist, but rather the specific and consequential question of whether the killing of Michael Brown constituted an instance of racist policing. In the context of institutionalized racist policing in Ferguson (DoJ 2015)[7], the killing of Michael Brown by police created a consequential practical puzzle for local Black people. With imperfect access to information, local Black third parties had a personal interest in understanding the police killing of Michael Brown, and in assessing whether it was a racist action that had implications for their own treatment and that of their loved ones.

Various eyewitnesses speaking publicly the first day claimed that Brown was walking casually down Canfield Drive when the officer confronted him, and after a brief altercation, Brown fled, was shot in the back, and then killed with his hands up. For example, Piaget Crenshaw, a 19-year-old Black woman, said, "I witnessed the police chase after the guy, full force. He was unarmed. He ran for his life. They shot him. And he fell. He put his arms up to let them know he was compliant and that he was unarmed. And they shot him twice more, and he fell to the ground and died." Piaget specifically made the parallel with Trayvon Martin's killing, and called the incident "brutality from a different race—it is racial profiling" (Fox 20140809a).

Police handling of Michael Brown's body had a strong impact on people at the scene and online. Michael Brown had been shot multiple times and killed at about noon. Police cordoned off the area and left his body lying face down in the middle of the Canfield Drive, bleeding out of his head and back. As Michael Brown's body lay there, local Black people gathered outside the police tape. One man video-recorded a conversation with a friend as he tried to make sense of the situation. He recounted: "They say he had his hands up and everything." Attempting to understand why the police killed Michael Brown, the friend asked, "They trying to get at him?" The man responded "I don't know, I wasn't out here. I just heard the gunshots." The first man, upset, denounced the police as "some lousy mother fuckers ... They've just got him laying in the street, dead as a mother fucker. They've just got him laying here." The friend observed "This is fucking unreal" (TDiddy 20140809a 3:45–)

One young woman shared a photo of Michael Brown's body bleeding in the street with the caption "How in the hell do you shot [sic] an unarmed teenager? Somebody please tell me!" Michael Brown's cousin shared a photo of him vibrant and alive. Toya, a local young woman, tweeted the two photos together with the comment, "My heart so heavy for this young man," and lots of others chimed in, and several hundred re-tweeted it (Toya 20140809a).

Viewing the image of Michael Brown's body left bleeding in the street was the way many people first heard about the case. The police left Michael Brown's body lying in the street for hours, which many local Black people saw as callous and dehumanizing. Shawty tweeted "They had that body laying out in the ground for ... hrs. Like, why?" (Elzie 20140809L). MrRe wrote: "Had that child laid out there like fucking roadkill ..." Liberienne added: "They did not cover his dead body. He lay there, decomposing" (Elzie 20140809m,n).

As local third parties heard about the killing of Michael Brown, many were upset and tried to make sense of why the police had killed him, often in conversation with witnesses or friends on the scene. Chuckey asked "Shot 10 times ... why?" (Chuckey 20140809b). Eman who witnessed the killing, tried to explain: "i have no idea. As far as i know, no reason. He was running. apparently" (Eman 20140809k). Nate wrote: "How [the fuck] you shoot somebody after you told em to put they hands up. 10 times? Not necessary bra" (Nate 20140809b). Ray, who did not live in Canfield apartments, but a couple minutes away, went over to check out what was happening (Ray 20140809a,b). He wrote: "They shot that boy 10 times that shit wasn't even necessary" (Ray 20140809c). "Why shoot somebody that's unarmed" (Ray 20140809d). Johnetta exclaimed: "I'm overwhelmed. Why would you kill an unarmed 17 year old?!?! Who surrendered?!?!" (Elzie 20140809af).

2 Assessing the racism of police action

If third parties engage their own framing activities, we ought to see evidence of such framing activities on social media. Was this the case in Ferguson on August 9, 2014? And, if so, around what kinds of questions did the early framing efforts by local third parties revolve?

At the heart of the frame alignment process were local Black people's own efforts to make sense of the character of Michael Brown's killing. Were the specific actions by police in this situation racist? Some of this early discussion hinged on the question of whether Michael Brown had committed a crime before he was killed.

The rumor circulated that Michael Brown had stolen rellos, a kind of mini-cigar, from the Quick Trip convenience store. Delisha, trying to make sense of the veracity of the story, wrote: "Rellos? I thought all places kept that shit behind the counter. But I could be wrong" (Davis 20140809a). Chucky responded: "They are" (Chuckey 20140809c).

A number of third parties challenged the conclusion that Michael Brown had stolen anything. Poe wrote: "No clear evidence that he actually stole from quick trip" (Poe 20140809n). FLOCKAfierce wrote: "WE DONT EVEN KNOW IF HE STOLE SOMETHING AT ALL." Vandalyzm reported that: "The cashier stated that he stole nothing. Nor did anyone at QT call the police" (Vandalyzm 20140809a). Johnetta reposted a post from Jasmine containing a firsthand account of the shooting that denied Michael Brown had stolen anything: "He did not steal anything from anywhere. He was walking home the police pulled up on him, hit him with the car door. Shot him once, when he fell to his knees the officer stood over him and shot him in the head. I'm here now and was here when it happened" (Elzie 20140809ag). Cash questioned the veracity of the account: "who is that? A news reporter because the report said different ... wait that's a Facebook friend. Ok." And Johnetta responded that it was an eyewitness account (Elzie 20140809ah).

Various local third parties were obviously troubled by the situation and struggled to make sense of what had happened with incomplete information. Tony wrote: "I gotta get more information, man. Something ain't adding up" (Joseph 20140809a). In a quick series of posts, FLOCKAfierce tried to make sense of the killing. "It's soooooo many different stories circulating at once [I don't know] what to think or believe now…. I just read on [Facebook] that he wasn't even running from the police. He was walking home and they ran up on him. Lord I dnt know …. It's breaking my heart man. Seeing this little guy face down in the pavement. We deserve to know what happened … I get that stealing is wrong. Running from the police even is still wrong, BUT you're telling me this was the LAST resort at restraining him … You're tell me this young man was murdered in the street over a misdemeanor theft? Shot TEN times for a MISDEMEANOR if he stole at all … Whatever he stole was less than $500 hell less than $50. NO I'm not justifying stealing. The force doesn't match this crime…. They saying he had his hands up and they shot him once and he fell and the shot him again. I can't man…. Man I couldn't hold back. I'm so hurt … after watching that [Instagram] video i started crying. this is truly heartbreaking" (Flocka 20140809c-j).

As the discussion progressed, a debate ensued with a few local Black people asserting that Michael Brown deserved what he got, and many others pushing back against the idea that it was relevant whether or not Michael Brown had stolen anything. From the start, many framed the killing of Michael Brown as an expression of racist policing.

Bunyan wrote: "These niggas gotta stop giving cops a reason to do dirty shit … I swear I ain't trying to be funny" (Bun 20140809a). GeekNStereo responded: "Wait you have to give cops a reason to harass you?! Please!" (Stereo 20140809a). Bunyan floated the question: "If he had never shoplifted would the police had been after him?" Elzie responded: "No one knows if he even stole anything. Next question" (Elzie 20140809ai). Bunyan responded: "Yall missing the point & right now y'all upset so you won't see it." (Bun 20140809b). Cash took a similar position "Criminal activity waived cuz they killed a guy? We gotta do better on a whole" (Elzie 20140809aj). Sarah countered that the whole question was irrelevant: "Debate now over whether he shoplifted. Irrelevant. NOTHING justifies shooting an unarmed teenager ten times" (Kendzior 20140809a). Rashad agreed with this perspective: "So many stories goin around but all have the same ending: UNARMED BLACK KID KILLED BY POLICE" (Rashad 20140809a).

Pheno wrote: "So are we ignoring the fact that he stole something and ran? Or does that not matter?" Ayo responded "So that means shoot him 10x?" Tory responded: "and what was the rest? The whole thought. Validated death that you agree by asking did he steal? A child did something wrong and he was killed. And yall validating it. If it's okay to you. Stealing = death?" (Toya 20140809b; Russell 20140809b,c).

Conrod recounted a conversation with an older relative, and criticized the idea that Michael Brown's actions might justify his killing. He wrote: "You know what really bothers me? As I relayed what had happened, an elder relative immediately asked 'what did he do? Why was he running?' Racism is so institutionalized that black people can't see how brainwashed we've become. We focus on 'surviving' instead of what's right. Regardless of the details of the situation, no unarmed person should be shot multiple times by a police officer. We side with our oppressors and don't even realize it" (Conrod 20140809d-g).

In some of these conversations, the pushback against the "haters" who justified the killing of Michael Brown became heated. Vernie wrote: "Stop putting yourself in a position to be dealt with by the police." Desire responded "Stop being black in American then?" (Elzie 20140809ak). Emily wrote "Now, so a blk male saying stop appearing guilty to police & you will be a-ok on these streets? That's what I read?" (Emily 20140809a). Beauty_jackson wrote: "You think being a good nigger won't get you fucked up or shot? That's cute" (Dione 20140809a). Yves wrote: "Massuh is always right Uncle fucking Tom ass niggas" (Elzie 20140809am).

Many local Black third parties took the position that the police killing of Michael Brown was fundamentally an expression of racism. Tory wrote: "You forgot to say black. Black teenager killed by police. That's really the key" (Russell 20140809d). TallAndTatted tweeted about Michael Brown: "if he was white he most likely wouldn't be dead." Elzie responded "Absolutely not. He would've gotten a talking to … They killin us everywhere" (Elzie 20140809e,f). Kelsy wrote: "Been hearing about stories similar to this my whole life. but this is breaking my heart because it's so close to home" (Kelsy 20140809a). Peter recalled: "Ferguson PD killed my Grandfather Reginald Hampton 30 years ago. I feel for the family" (Stephen 20140809a). Oz wrote: "They gone keep killing us and telling us we shouldn't have looked so dangerous" (Flocka 20140809k). Toya wrote: "I'm so disgusted right now. I'm angry, sad, heartbroken, everything bad right now. Seems like a black life is worthless nowadays" (Toya 20140809c).

Johnetta concurred: "Not teaching my kids to roll over and play nice so the white people with badges and guns won't hunt, shoot and kill them … [I don't care] how much ass you kiss. Your black ass can get shot and killed to for no got damn reason. Wake up … Murdered him for walking down the fucking street. When has walking down the damn street in YOUR NEIGHBORHOOD ever been illegal?! … They killed this baby for walking down the damn street." (Elzie 20140809an-aq). Rik wrote: "Why was he running? BITCH because he scared to death of cops. And what black youth in low income community isn't?" (Rik 20140809a). Shire responded: "Word is that he didn't even fucking run he stopped, put his hands up and they still shot him." (Shire 20140809a). BookofJonah wrote: "Just being black is reason enough, ANYTHING we do is reason enough to kill us." (Jonah 20140809a).

3 The role of repressive action by police in the frame alignment process

In the context of third-party framing efforts, how was the character of police response to insurgents in Ferguson that day received?

In the context of local Black people's efforts to make sense of whether police were acting racist, photos and videos of callous and threatening action by police, not least repressive action against people nonviolently protesting the killing of Michael Brown, became resonant cultural objects that powerfully influenced people's understanding of the situation and the frame alignment process. The resonance of insurgent frames with local Black third parties was not a fixed question of frame congruence. Instead, local Black third parties viewed police responses to insurgent actions fundamentally in terms of their ongoing interpretive debates about the character of the police killing of Michael Brown. The character of authority responses, often captured in photo and video circulated online, became resonant cultural objects which local Black people—who were already trying to make sense of whether this was an instance of racist policing—took into account.

Michael Brown's body lay bleeding face down in the street for hours. Dozens of people from the neighborhood, almost all Black, gathered outside the police tape. Michael Brown's mother, supported by friends, complained to police. A small group of perhaps a dozen people chanted several protests including "No Justice, No Peace!" Police reported shots fired nearby.

At about 3 pm, hundreds of police moved in with assault rifles, dogs, and armored vehicles to clear the area. They chased people off of the street of the Canfield Green apartment complex where Michael Brown was killed, told residents they had to stay inside, and forcibly removed all observers a third of a mile away to the corner of West Florissant Boulevard where they constructed a blockade to keep people out. These police actions became the focus of online discussion among local Black people. Vandalyzm challenged the haters citing the police action as evidence: "Y'all not getting the fact that they showed up in riot gear with assault rifles and ARE NOT ALLOWING ANYONE TO LEAVE THAT NEIGHBORHOOD" (Vandalyzm 20140809a).

One of the people who heard about the killing after the neighborhood had been cleared and people were locked outside the blockade was Johnetta "Netta" Elzie, a St. Louis local who had a significant presence on local Black Twitter. Elzie lived about fifteen minutes from Canfield Green apartments, but her aunt and cousin lived there (Elzie 20140809a,b). In the discussion among Elzie and her friends, information about the repressive police action resonated and was incorporated into their efforts to make sense of the situation. Elzie tweeted that police were carrying military-style weapons. A friend replied: "Jesus are you serious?" Elzie confirmed, and then elaborated: "SWAT + 200/300 police?! Ferguson not even big enough for all that" (Elzie 20140809g,h). Elzie retweeted a photo of the police armored vehicle near the blockade, and another friend replied in disbelief (Elzie 20140809i). Elzie compared the situation to the war in Gaza (Elzie 20140809j).

As images of the militarized police action spread, local Black people tried to make sense of what they were seeing. Many explained the police actions as expressions of institutional racism, reflective of the customary and racist treatment of Black people. Discussions among Elzie and her friends on Twitter are illustrative. NotBeezy wrote: "I cannot recall ONE incident in my lifetime where i saw a police officer and felt safe or protected." AlexDon responded: "Ever." (Elzie 20140809o). AirIn wrote: "People are literally afraid of us, as if we are animals … It's baffling" (Elzie 20140809p). Elzie pointed out the historical irony of White people being afraid of Black people: it's like we're "the ones to be afraid of, like we're the ones who hung/burned/castrated ppl & took pics smiling next to the bodies … Like we're the ones who raped and mutilated men, women and children … Like we're the ones who kidnapped and stole HUMANS for centuries and sold them … Black people aren't the ones. Be afraid of your got damn selves white folks" (Elzie 20140809q,r,s,t). Civil wrote: "Shit isn't safe out here for us. None of us. Woman, man, child" (Elzie 20140809v). Elzie concurred: "Can't even walk down the street" (Elzie 20140809w). Crown despaired: "As a father of 2 little black boys how am I supposed to sleep at night?" (Elzie 20140809x). Upset about the situation, Elzie and several of her friends eventually drove down to Canfield "for black people" (Elzie 20140809y,z,aa).

Antonio French posted a picture of an armored police vehicle outside the blockade that was retweeted hundreds of times. Responses to Antonio French's tweet of the armored vehicle show how the threatening police response was taken up as part of people's efforts to make sense of the situation. Some commentators strongly identify with the protesters as Black people: "Then they wonder why in the fuck we thugs …", "Because we are enemy combatants." Other commentators suggest that the police actions are expressions of institutional racism: "This is the real danger in the black communities. Where do people go for protection from thug cops?", "Funny how they didn't bring out this hardware when the T-Partiers where protecting the Bundy Ranch.", "Is this Circa South Africa 1982 or is it America 2014?" (representative same-day comments on image of armored vehicle, French 20140809a).

An image of a police armored vehicle caught Kelsy's attention. She retweeted it with the note "omg." Then, she retweeted images of police with dogs and shotguns, and the note "UNBELIEVABLE." And another picture of armored truck. "i wanna cry so bad," she commented … "is this MY city? these pics and photos look like their from the 1960s." After a while her surprise and sadness turned to anger. Addressing police she tweeted: "YOU ARE IN OUR NEIGHBORHOOD STARTING SHIT. GET. OUT" (Kelsy 20140809b–f).

Several hours later after police removed the blockade, a hundred or so mourners and protesters reconvened on Canfield Drive at the spot where Michael Brown was killed. Michael Brown's mother, Lezly McSpadded, constructed a rose-petal memorial at the site. People lit candles. Several young women blocked the street at the memorial site, and would not let police pass.

At about 8 pm police stormed the area, perhaps two hundred officers from multiple jurisdictions, came from behind the protesters, charging up Canfield Drive, sirens wailing. The police pushed through the protesters, and drove over the rose-petal memorial Michael Brown's mother had constructed, crushing it. The crush of police cars remained parked on top of the rose-petal memorial, lights flashing. Police helicopters circled above, shining spotlights on the scene below (French 20140809ah,ai).

In response to photos of the crushed rose-petal memorial, Thespin tweeted: "Can't even have a memorial for this murdered child without #FergusonPolice destroying it. Disgusting" (Thespinster 20140809a). Lisa responded: "Heartless!"(Lisa 20140809a). D asked: "Did his mother not just leave some of those? ... no words" (Macdonald 20140809a). Sara wrote: "Oh Lord have mercy" (Holmes 20140809a). Ashleigh posted a broken heart emoji (Ashleigh 20140809a).

To many, police crushing the rose-petal memorial appeared to demonstrate a lack of respect for Michael Brown's humanity. Tezzy pointedly characterized the police action as "Disrespectful" (Tezzy 20140809a). Mstrmnd agreed: "Blatant DISRESPECT" (Mstrmnd 20140809a). R said "Not OK" (R 20140809a). Marcus called "foul" (Marcus 20140809a). Ant stated: "That's coldblooded" (Allen 20140809a). Cheryl declared "ATROCITY in our own back yard!" (Morin 20140809a). Allen insisted "we putting double out there tomorrow!" (Gates 20140809a). X concluded "fuck the cops man" (X 20140809a).

More people decided to join the protest and stepped into the street to confront the police at the spot where Michael Brown was killed. With their cars parked on top of the rose-petal memorial, the police again responded with the threat of violence, demanding protesters clear the street. As they had earlier, police brandished assault rifles as they confronted nonviolent protesters. Using snarling dogs, police attempted to force protesters out of the street and back onto the sidewalk (SLPD 20140809d,e; French 20140809h). The police helicopter continued to circle overhead shining a spotlight on the crowd (French 20140809L).

Antonio French tweeted video and photos of the police with dogs confronting nonviolent protesters (French 20140809h,m,n,o). Hundreds retweeted them. Elzie, on her way to the scene, retweeted the photos, commenting: "You can't even mourn the loss! Look at the police dogs" (Elzie 20140809ae). Making sense of the situation, Shire proclaimed: "Helicopters, Attack Dogs, Armed Police. We are the victims." (Shire 20140809b) MrRe commented: "First riot gear now dogs? THEYDONTGIVEAFUCKABOUTUS" (Fan 20140809a). Rashad responded: "You would think we did something wrong" (Rashad 20140809b). Les, a Black St. Louis native tweeted "Looking a little like déjà vu for some of our grandparents" (Les 20140809a).

Brenna quickly found a historical photo from the Civil Rights movement that looked a lot like Antonio French's photo of the police with dogs confronting protesters on Canfield Drive, and tweeted the two images side-by-side with the caption "Someone please remind me what year it is again? #ferguson" (Muncy 20140809a). Her tweet was retweeted more than 6,000 times.

While there were no television cameras on site, news spread both locally around the Ferguson area,[8] and globally, with many commenting in real time about the character of the police response. Barbara wrote acerbically: "Response to grieving community. Wow" (Reid 20140809a). Relly wrote: "fucking disgusting" (Relly 20140809a). Ken wrote: "THIS IS SHAMEFUL AND WRONG" (Ken 20140809a). The images of threatening police repressive action amplified the racist policing frame. Tea noted: "Times change police DONT" (Tea 20140809a). Big added: "ain't shit changed" (Big 20140809a). Mia mused that in Ferguson, the year was "1964 apparently" (Mia 20140809a). Slack tweeted "AmeriKKKa" (Slack 20140809a). Zek noted: "Racism is still alive" (Zek 20140809a). Sharee concluded: "don't matter the year. It's up to us" (Sharee 20140809a).

Conclusions

Social media data allowed unpacking of the process of frame alignment in the early phases of mobilization in Ferguson on August 9, 2014. Consideration of how potential local supporters responded to events as they unfolded is revealing. In conclusion, we will summarize the findings in terms of each of the three specifying questions, and their implications for a general understanding of frame alignment processes.

First, the analysis shows that frame resonance was not an independent ideational process.

Instead, it was a situated response to a practical challenge (McDonell, Bail, and Tavory 2017) based on deeper understandings of the world posed by structured social roles (Oliver and Johnston 2000) grounded in institutional histories (Steinberg 1999). Local Black third parties, and to some extent observers around the country, felt personally threatened by the police killing of Michael Brown and their handling of his body. The situation posed a practical political challenge about how this threat would be managed. The resonance of a "racist policing" frame grew out of the broader political situation, rather than an independent ideational process.

Second, in response to the specific practical political challenges posed by the killing of Michael Brown in Ferguson, and as McDonnell, Bail, and Tavory (2017) argue, potential supporters actively engaged in their own framing activities, trying to make sense of the situation. While the insurgent "racist policing" frame was already available (Snow and Moss 2014) and congruent with the general viewpoints of most local Black third parties, general congruence was insufficient to generate frame alignment. Instead, third parties sought to make sense of the specific situation. A central topic of debate was the accusation that Michael Brown had been involved in a petty theft before he was killed. People tried to assess the available evidence as best they could. But many local Black people also challenged the premise that such accusations were relevant. Many saw allegations of petty theft as tantamount to justifying murder. In short, frame alignment, was constructed by observers working through their own interpretations of a pressing situation using the framings, and other cultural resources available.

Third, in particular, evidence of repressive actions by police in Ferguson proved crucial in driving the frame alignment process. Police crushing the rose-petal memorial constructed by Michael Brown's mother seemed callous to many observers. Police wielding assault rifles and police dogs against nonviolent protesters seemed threatening to many local Black people. In the initial phases of mobilization on Canfield Drive, insurgents defying police made few programmatic declarations, and their words rarely reached potential local third-party supporters directly. But photos and videos of the callous and threatening actions by police were widely disseminated on social media. These photos and videos became powerfully resonant cultural objects which local Black people and third-party observers nationally used as important resources in making sense of the practical political challenge posed by the killing of Michael Brown. This footage convinced many to adopt the insurgents' framing of the situation as an instance of "racist policing."

It was not dry ideational congruence that led people to adopt insurgents' frame of "racist policing" in Ferguson on August 9, 2014. Given the documented racist character of policing in Ferguson (DoJ 2015), the idea that policing was generally racist was consistent with the lived experience of local Black people and seemed to fit the facts of the case. But beyond an assessment that the frame fit, it took practical action to make the framing salient (Ellingson 1995; McAdam 1996). When insurgents on the street nonviolently defied the police, the repressive police response exposed the institutionalized racism in local policing for the world to see.

Consistent with insurgent practice theory (Bloom 2014, 2015; Bloom and Martin 2016), the callous and threatening character of repressive action by police did more than the words of activists ever could to characterize the situation as an instance of racist policing.

Much of what people saw on social media and even on the television news that first day in Ferguson—despite news stations largely adopting language provided by police—was a heavy-handed police response to nonviolent defiance. Insurgents' greatest role in shaping the shared subjective understandings that enabled escalating mobilization was not their linguistic spin. The resonance of the insurgent "racist policing" frame was *practical*. Protesting at the police tape, constructing the rose-petal memorial in the middle of the street, and nonviolently defying police orders to disperse—insurgents achieved frame alignment through practical actions that drove interactive political dynamics on the ground.

Notes

1 Thus the "racist policing" frame had been developed, but had not been strongly attached to a coherent set of insurgent practices. Coupling charges of racist policing with blocking traffic, mourning in streets, and defiance of police orders, in the wake of a police killing of a Black person, began to proliferate following the killing of Michael Brown and the large-scale insurgent mobilization in Ferguson. For insightful work on these kinds of non-organizational dynamics of movements, and the way ideas developed earlier are picked up by insurgents when practical situations are conducive, see Oliver (1989).

2 These newer approaches have striking affinities with the theories of Gramsci (1971) and Bourdieu (1990).
3 A range of contemporary texts have explored related theoretical perspectives. See Gaston (2017), Jansen (2016, 2017), and Kay and Evans (2018) for exemplary work.
4 With tens of thousands of cumulative cites to the major theoretical statements (Benford and Snow 2000; Snow and Benford 1988; Snow et al. 1986), Google Scholar March 31, 2019.
5 It is worth noting that core defenders of insurgents often reject the basic premise of insurgent collective action. For example, in 1969, politically moderate Whitney Young, Executive Director of the Urban League, worked as a key ally of the Black Panther Party, calling for a Federal special investigation into the police and FBI orchestrated killing of revolutionary Black Panther leader Fred Hampton. Young did not agree with the Black Panthers' revolutionary politics, yet acted as a key ally to challenge repressive actions taken by authorities against them (Bloom and Martin 2016: 244). This is not just the difference between diagnostic and prognostic framing—Young's moderate diagnosis of the political situation was as different from the Black Panthers' anti-imperialist diagnosis as much as his moderate political prescriptions appeared non-sensical from the vantage of the Panthers' revolutionary prognosis.
6 Not all local accounts are explicitly geocoded as local. We used geocoding as one way of getting into local networks. Once we were in local networks, we found other people who were clearly local, either because they were actually driving down to the local events, or because they were regularly interacting in person with other local individuals. This required looking through not only movement related posts of candidate individuals, but the range of posts from those individuals in the days preceding the protests. "Local" means they live in the greater Ferguson area, including not only Ferguson proper, but Jennings and other parts of North County, and other parts of Saint Louis. Since we were sampling for potential protesters, we worked out from the networks of people who got involved rather than trying to do some kind of random sampling of everyone who lived in the area.
7 DoJ 2015 = United States Department of Justice, Civil Rights Division. 2015. "Investigation of the Ferguson Police Department."
8 See, e.g., retweets FLOCK, and BLV (Flocka 20140809a; Law 20140809a).

References

Alexander, Michelle. 2010. *The new Jim Crow: Mass incarceration in the age of color-blindness.* New York: The New Press.
AP. 2014. "Sharpton plans Mo. visit in deadly shooting's wake." Associated Press State & Local. August 10. https://advance-lexis-com.ezproxy.library.wisc.edu/api/document?collection=news&id=urn:contentItem:5CWC-4KY1-DYN6-W3P4-00000-00&context=1516831.
Benford, Robert D. 1997. "An insider's critique of the social movement framing perspective." *Sociological inquiry* 67. 4: 409–430.
Benford, Robert D., and David A. Snow. 2000. "Framing processes and social movements: An overview and assessment." *Annual review of sociology* 26. 1: 611–639.
Bloom, Joshua. 2014. Pathways of insurgency: black freedom struggle and the second reconstruction, 1945–1975. PhD Dissertation, Department of Sociology, University of California-Los Angeles.
Bloom, Joshua. 2015. "The dynamics of opportunity and insurgent practice: How black anti- colonialists compelled Truman to advocate civil rights." *American sociological review* 80. 2: 391–415.

Bloom, Joshua and Zachary Frampton. 2019. "Nine hours on Canfield Drive: Insurgent mobilization, repression, and 3rd party response in Ferguson." Unpublished manuscript.

Bloom, Joshua, and Waldo E. Martin, Jr. 2016. *Black against empire: The history and politics of the Black Panther Party*. Oakland: University of California Press.

Bourdieu, Pierre. 1990. *The logic of practice*. Stanford: Stanford University Press.

DoJ (United States Department of Justice, Civil Rights Division). 2015. Investigation of the Ferguson Police Department. March 4.

Ellingson, Stephen. 1995. "Understanding the dialectic of discourse and collective action: Public debate and rioting in antebellum Cincinnati." *American journal of sociology* 101. 1: 100–144.

Gastón, Pablo. 2017. "Contention across social fields: Manipulating the boundaries of labor struggle in the workplace, community, and market." *Social problems* 65. 2: 231–250.

Gramsci, Antonio. 1971. *Selections from the prison notebooks*. Edited by Quintin Hoare and Geoffrey Nowell Smith. New York: International Publishers.

Hitlin, Paul, and Nancy Vogt. 2014. "Cable, Twitter picked up Ferguson story at a similar clip." Fact Tank. Pew Research Center. https://www.pewresearch.org/fact-tank/2014/08/20/cable-twitter-picked-up-ferguson-story-at-a-similar-clip/

Jansen, Robert S. 2016. "Situated political innovation: explaining the historical emergence of new modes of political practice." *Theory and society* 45. 4: 319–360.

Jansen, Robert S. 2017. *Revolutionizing repertoires: The rise of populist mobilization in Peru*. Chicago: University of Chicago Press.

Kay, Tamara, and Rhonda Lynn Evans. 2018. *Trade battles: Activism and the politicization of international trade policy*. New York: Oxford University Press.

McAdam, Doug. 1996 "The framing function of movement tactics: strategic dramaturgy in the civil rights movement". In Doug McAdam, John McMarthy, and Mayer Zald, eds., *Comparative perspectives on social movements: Political opportunities, mobilizing structures, and cultural framings*. New York: Cambridge University Press.

McAdam, Doug, John McCarthy, and Meyer Zald, eds. 1996. *Comparative perspectives on social movements: Political opportunities, mobilizing structures, and cultural framings*. New York: Cambridge University Press.

McDonnell, Terence E., Christopher A. Bail, and Iddo Tavory. 2017. "A theory of resonance." *Sociological theory* 35. 1: 1–14.

Oliver, Pamela E. 1989. "Bringing the crowd back in: The nonorganizational elements of social movements." *Research in social movements, conflict and change* 11: 1–30.

Oliver, Pamela, and Hank Johnston. 2000. "What a good idea! Ideologies and frames in social movement research." *Mobilization: An international quarterly* 5. 1: 37–54.

Snow, David A., et al. 1986. "*Frame alignment processes, micromobilization, and movement participation*." *American sociological review* 51. 4: 464–481.

Snow, David A., and Robert D. Benford. 1988. "Ideology, frame resonance, and participant mobilization." *International social movement research* 1. 1: 197–217.

Snow, David A., and Dana M. Moss. 2014. "Protest on the fly: Toward a theory of spontaneity in the dynamics of protest and social movements." *American sociological review* 79. 6: 1122–1143.

Snow, David A., Rens Vliegenthart, and Pauline Ketelaars. 2019. "The framing perspective on social movements: Its conceptual roots and architecture." Pages 392–410 in David O. Snow, Sarah A. Soule, Hanspeter Kriesi, & Holly J. McCammon, eds., *The Wiley Blackwell companion to social movements*. Oxford, UK: Oxford University Press.

Steinberg, Marc W. 1999. "The talk and back talk of collective action: A dialogic analysis of repertoires of discourse among nineteenth-century English cotton spinners." *American Journal of Sociology* 105. 3: 736–780.

Appendix: social medial data

Allen 20140809a. https://twitter.com/aa32808/status/498291431619190785.
Ashleigh 20140809a. https://twitter.com/ashthedancer_/status/498298856170590208.
Big 20140809a. https://twitter.com/Big_Swole90/status/498306448716464128.
Bun 20140809a. https://twitter.com/BayouBun/status/498235907078500353.
Bun 20140809b. https://twitter.com/BayouBun/status/498236961866280960.
Chuckey 20140809b. https://twitter.com/R0zayN0Chazer/status/498272155088347136.
Chuckey 20140809c. https://twitter.com/R0zayN0Chazer/status/498264049088352256.
Conrod, C. Jay. 20140809a. https://twitter.com/cjayconrod/status/498262984095846401.
Conrod 20140809d. https://twitter.com/cjayconrod/status/498269147466194944.
Conrod 20140809e. https://twitter.com/cjayconrod/status/498269597565325313.
Conrod 20140809f. https://twitter.com/cjayconrod/status/498269885579816960.
Conrod 20140809g. https://twitter.com/cjayconrod/status/498270540885262336.
Davis 20140809a. https://twitter.com/DelishaDavis/status/498263227478724608.
Dione 20140809a. https://twitter.com/themelaniedione/status/498242666040397824.
Elzie 20140809a. https://twitter.com/Nettaaaaaaaa/status/498244563757047809.
Elzie 20140809b. https://twitter.com/Nettaaaaaaaa/status/498281426249195520.
Elzie 20140809e. https://twitter.com/Nettaaaaaaaa/status/498233615247867904.
Elzie 20140809f. https://twitter.com/Nettaaaaaaaa/status/498233930596642816.
Elzie 20140809g. https://twitter.com/Nettaaaaaaaa/status/498236831003975680.
Elzie 20140809h. https://twitter.com/Nettaaaaaaaa/status/498248811802677248.
Elzie 20140809i. https://twitter.com/Nettaaaaaaaa/status/498252023381254145.
Elzie 20140809j. https://twitter.com/Nettaaaaaaaa/status/498256033337196544.
Elzie 20140809l. https://twitter.com/Nettaaaaaaaa/status/498270092690325505.
Elzie 20140809m. https://twitter.com/Nettaaaaaaaa/status/498274100419121153.
Elzie 20140809n. https://twitter.com/Nettaaaaaaaa/status/498280077306523648.
Elzie 20140809o. https://twitter.com/Nettaaaaaaaa/status/498234452414177280.
Elzie 20140809p. https://twitter.com/Nettaaaaaaaa/status/498233039797768192.
Elzie 20140809r. https://twitter.com/Nettaaaaaaaa/status/498234846221582336.
Elzie 20140809s. https://twitter.com/Nettaaaaaaaa/status/498234950793965569.
Elzie 20140809t. https://twitter.com/Nettaaaaaaaa/status/498235128347234304.
Elzie 20140809v. https://twitter.com/Nettaaaaaaaa/status/498272072196292609.
Elzie 20140809w. https://twitter.com/Nettaaaaaaaa/status/498274784333934592.
Elzie 20140809x. https://twitter.com/Nettaaaaaaaa/status/498236666722676736.
Elzie 20140809y https://twitter.com/Nettaaaaaaaa/status/498308721622020096.
Elzie 20140809z. https://twitter.com/Nettaaaaaaaa/status/498290278885625857.
Elzie 20140809aa. https://twitter.com/Nettaaaaaaaa/status/498289148868833280.
Elzie 20140809ae. https://twitter.com/Nettaaaaaaaa/status/498292649497878528.
Elzie 20140809af. https://twitter.com/Nettaaaaaaaa/status/498227078227959808.
Elzie 20140809ag. https://twitter.com/Nettaaaaaaaa/status/498237583332093952.
Elzie 20140809ah. https://twitter.com/Nettaaaaaaaa/status/498242421361098753.
Elzie 20140809ai. https://twitter.com/Nettaaaaaaaa/status/498239384332673024.
Elzie 20140809aj. https://twitter.com/Nettaaaaaaaa/status/498240887793541120.

Elzie 20140809ak. https://twitter.com/Nettaaaaaaaa/status/498259833577943040.
Elzie 20140809am. https://twitter.com/Nettaaaaaaaa/status/498243050619928576.
Elzie 20140809an. https://twitter.com/Nettaaaaaaaa/status/498242117794160640.
Elzie 20140809ao. https://twitter.com/Nettaaaaaaaa/status/498247523010502656.
Elzie 20140809ap. https://twitter.com/Nettaaaaaaaa/status/498250931633278976.
Elzie 20140809aq. https://twitter.com/Nettaaaaaaaa/status/498252700207677441.
Eman 20140809k. https://twitter.com/TheePharoah/status/498191842089771008.
Emily 20140809a. https://twitter.com/emilyBOOMBOOM/status/498239214161784832.
Fan 20140809a. https://twitter.com/MrReTweetYoGirl/status/498289865919066112.
Flocka 20140809a. https://twitter.com/FLOCKAfierce/status/498292969280004096.
Flocka 20140809c. https://twitter.com/FLOCKAfierce/status/498237203676274688.
Flocka 20140809d. https://twitter.com/FLOCKAfierce/status/498237420693757952.
Flocka 20140809e. https://twitter.com/FLOCKAfierce/status/498239288526376960.
Flocka 20140809f. https://twitter.com/FLOCKAfierce/status/498240390042894336.
Flocka 20140809g. https://twitter.com/FLOCKAfierce/status/498242733559918592.
Flocka 20140809h. https://twitter.com/FLOCKAfierce/status/498243000787415040.
Flocka 20140809i. https://twitter.com/FLOCKAfierce/status/498243588942090240.
Flocka 20140809j. https://twitter.com/FLOCKAfierce/status/498244857370931200.
Flocka 20140809k. https://twitter.com/FLOCKAfierce/status/498263827452923904.
Fox 20140809a. https://fox2now.com/2014/08/09/man-shot-killed-in-ferguson-apartment-complex/.
French, Antonio. 20140809a. https://twitter.com/AntonioFrench/status/498248648699150336.
French, Antonio. 20140809h. https://twitter.com/AntonioFrench/status/498283038338711552.
French, Antonio. 20140809l. https://twitter.com/AntonioFrench/status/498284334806495233.
French, Antonio. 20140809m,n,o. https://twitter.com/AntonioFrench/status/498285405142540289.
French 20140809ah. https://twitter.com/AntonioFrench/status/498281990396063744.
French 20140809ai. https://twitter.com/AntonioFrench/status/498282243157426176.
Gates 20140809a. https://twitter.com/AllenGatesDope/status/499785439373312000.
Holmes 20140809a. https://twitter.com/saraholmesSTL/status/498288575851397120.
Jonah 20140809a. https://twitter.com/TheBookofJonah/status/498238691018829825.
Joseph 20140809a. https://twitter.com/Tony_Be/status/498255701861335040.
Kelsy 20140809a. https://twitter.com/_kelsology/status/498245730960539648.
Kelsy 20140809b. https://twitter.com/_kelsology/status/498250520838930433.
Kelsy 20140809c. https://twitter.com/_kelsology/status/498285902817280002.
Kelsy 20140809d. https://twitter.com/_kelsology/status/498288929104089089.
Kelsy 20140809e. https://twitter.com/_kelsology/status/498288006151675904.
Kelsy 20140809f. https://twitter.com/_kelsology/status/498300692243562496.
Ken 20140809a https://twitter.com/awickedlaf/status/498308225469390848.
Kendzior 20140809a. https://twitter.com/sarahkendzior/status/498257525767028736.
Law 20140809a. https://twitter.com/RyleighzMom/status/498321266504237056.
Les 20140809a. https://twitter.com/LesIzMore/status/498290352847998976.
Lisa 20140809a. https://twitter.com/_lisaperry/status/498362168463855616.
LoveKhyB 20140809a. https://twitter.com/_LoveKhyB/status/498210510156730368.
Macdonald 20140809a. https://twitter.com/paintedhuman/status/498306751385862144.
Marcus 20140809a. https://twitter.com/marcussalinas_/status/498321766272749569.

Mia 20140809a. https://twitter.com/ambermiaa_/status/498310870058139648.
Morin 20140809a. https://twitter.com/MorinCheryl/status/498316443831009280.
Mstrmnd 20140809a. https://twitter.com/6ftSlay/status/498304982559780865.
Muncy 20140809a. https://twitter.com/brennamuncy/status/498289596463980544/photo/1.
Nate 20140809b. https://twitter.com/LuhhNate/status/498191775794593792.
Poe 20140809n. https://twitter.com/TefPoe/status/498242264704233473.
R 20140809a. https://twitter.com/thegoodvillain/status/498288329381523456.
Rashad 20140809a. https://twitter.com/RashadAintShit/status/498244156758568960.
Rashad 20140809b. https://twitter.com/RashadAintShit/status/498291678612971521.
Ray 20140809a. https://twitter.com/_Ray2Timez/status/498514393815326720.
Ray 20140809b. https://twitter.com/_Ray2Timez/status/498194904837677056.
Ray 20140809c. https://twitter.com/_Ray2Timez/status/498175797069246464.
Ray 20140809d. https://twitter.com/_Ray2Timez/status/498176256236457985.
Reid 20140809a. https://twitter.com/reid_bj/status/498290599305297920.
Relly 20140809a. https://twitter.com/HateTheseFools/status/498294007802646528.
Rik 20140809a. https://twitter.com/Rik_FIair/status/498252209059299329.
Russell 20140809b. https://twitter.com/VanguardTNT/status/498209273260683265.
Russell 20140809c. https://twitter.com/VanguardTNT/status/498210521015787520.
Russell 20140809d. https://twitter.com/VanguardTNT/status/498210883894407170.
Sharee 20140809a. https://twitter.com/shareefkeyes/status/498312392485658624.
Shire 20140809a. https://twitter.com/AsShire/status/498253427344801792.
Shire 20140809b. https://twitter.com/AsShire/status/498290233578774528.
Slack 20140809a. https://twitter.com/CocoaBrownJesus/status/498293571087527937.
SLPD 20140809d. https://bloximages.newyork1.vip.townnews.com/stltoday.com/con
    tent/tncms/assets/v3/editorial/8/0a/80a4d87e-ef80-5741-88d1-d61a4cc375ba/
    53e6e2bb6d660.image.jpg.
SLPD 20140809e. https://bloximages.newyork1.vip.townnews.com/stltoday.com/content/
    tncms/assets/v3/editorial/d/f6/df6b1a76-2ed4-5376-b7dd-5cdcceb68876/54071ee9d0a
    b6.image.jpg.
Stephen 20140809a. https://twitter.com/D1N_PeterPan/status/498200438684938240.
Stereo 20140809a. https://twitter.com/GeekNStereo/status/498237258101559297.
TDiddy 20140809a. https://www.youtube.com/watch?v=X4ioKoqfEnk.
Tea 20140809a. https://twitter.com/tealovely69/status/498294183400976384.
Tezzy 20140809a. https://twitter.com/TezzyWap/status/498290266143342592.
Thespinster 20140809a. https://twitter.com/thespinsterymc/status/498289619226861568.
Toya 20140809a. https://twitter.com/AyoMissDarkSkin/status/498195516425920513.
Toya 20140809b. https://twitter.com/AyoMissDarkSkin/status/498203995169509376.
Toya 20140809c. https://twitter.com/AyoMissDarkSkin/status/498200880391282688.
Vandalyzm 20140809a. https://twitter.com/Vandalyzm/status/498329674440011776.
X 20140809a. https://twitter.com/mathieupandolfo/status/498335627164016640.
Zek 20140809a. https://twitter.com/zekNcashe/status/498324751975469056.

5 Active abeyance, political opportunity, and the "new" white supremacy

Pete Simi and Robert Futrell

This chapter discusses two broad periods in U.S. white supremacism and explains the recent mobilization among various white supremacist factions. We explain that for much of the last three decades, white supremacists pursued "active abeyance," which we define as a strategic withdrawal from traditional public approaches to activism and recruitment. Instead, they engaged in more informal, private forms of activism directed at sustaining and growing the movement.

We see this shift to abeyance as a deliberate response stemming from movement leaders' strategic efforts to maintain adherents' engagement and avoid repression in an increasingly hostile cultural and political climate that pushed "old guard" groups, such as the Ku Klux Klan, National Alliance, Hammerskins, and others, ever farther to the margins of U.S. society.

Recently, white supremacists have partially stepped into the public eye as they responded to new political opportunities tied to Donald Trump's U.S. presidential campaign and election, along with a global increase in fascist politics. In addition to political changes, white supremacists' technological savvy positioned them to take advantage of new opportunities provided by internet platforms, which they use to link individuals and groups, promote messages of hate and violence, target enemies, and recruit new adherents.

One result has been what many observers describe as a "new" landscape of white supremacy. But, in fact, white supremacists' resurgence emanates from networks and ideas that activists have long been nurturing outside the public eye. We end with some observations about this so-called newness, and suggest that the picture, while messy and nuanced, requires that we understand connections between waves of white supremacist activism, to avoid oversimplified explanations of today's political landscape.

White supremacist activism

Observers have long portrayed white supremacist activism as a "fragmented, decentralized, and often sectarian network" of overlapping groups such as Christian Identity sects, neo-Nazis, and white power skinheads, and the Ku Klux Klan (KKK). The KKK, the nation's most notorious symbol of white supremacy, claimed between three and five million members in the mid-1920s. Since then, Klan membership and activities cycled through peaks and valleys, with the most notable actions coming during the 1950s and 1960s civil rights conflicts (Cunningham 2013). Klan support waned in the early 1970s and neo-Nazi skinheads grew during the 1980s. Umbrella groups such as the Aryan Nations led Klan members, skinheads, and others to embrace Nazi symbols and ideology, along with Christian Identity theology, as part of a broader white supremacist worldview (Burris, Smith, and Strahm 2000: 218). Neo-Nazi skinheads combine white power rhetoric and ideology with a youthful aesthetic expressed through music and Nazi symbolism. Like the hooded, white-robed, cross-burning Klan gatherings before them, public displays by neo-Nazi skinheads, brought intense, albeit episodic, media attention that helped to form a new white supremacist stereotype imagined as young wild-eyed, tattoo-laden, belligerent, in-your-face, skinheads.

As authorities and anti-racist groups challenged white power groups, several branches began to withdraw from the most public forms of activism and develop alternatives to maintain members, capture new recruits, nourish movement networks, and sustain their radical ideology. Leaders such as Louis Beam and Tom Metzger advocated for "lone-wolf" tactics to avoid repression directed at white power leaders, organizations, and networks. In this context, conventional movement strategies, such as public marches, rallies, and congresses, gave way to less public forms. Today, right-wing racial extremism persists mostly in underground social networks and on internet forums where participants advocate varied combinations of white supremacist beliefs, anti-government attitudes, and religio-racist fundamentalism. Varying forms and degrees of misogyny are also laced throughout these networks and their rhetoric. Participants include loose collections of people identifying themselves as Identitarians, nationalists, patriots, or the catch-all term alt-right. These groups express conspiratorial anxieties rooted in populist worries about racial and ethnic change, immigration, governmental overreach, and public debt. They share a deep distrust in the government and imagine a shadowy cabal of elites intent on robbing "true" Americans of their freedoms similar to current conspiracy theories that reference the "deep state."

Social movement abeyance

Since Verta Taylor (1989; Rupp and Taylor 1987) introduced the social movement abeyance concept, scholars have embraced the idea as a useful way to explain movement continuity during times when collective action is less visible. Abeyance "depicts a holding process by which movements sustain themselves in non-receptive political environments and provide continuity from one stage of mobilization to another" (Taylor 1989: 761). It refers to a period when committed activists continue movement activities by turning efforts inward to maintain the continuity of activist networks, sustain an ensemble of goals and strategies, and "promot[e] a collective identity that offers participants a sense of mission and moral purpose" (Taylor 1989: 762). Abeyance reveals social movement participants' agency *between* the more visible and dramatic episodes of political contention that most research highlights.

While the abeyance concept provides insight into the connection between separate upsurges in activism over time, several related questions about the nature of abeyance processes remain underdeveloped. First, to what extent is abeyance a conscious strategic choice versus a latent outcome spurred by external threat and repression? Taylor and Crossley (2013) note that abeyance patterns reflect movement responses to both structural and cultural dynamics and that organizational factors, resources and political opportunities shape movement emergence, strength, and decline. Likewise, cultural factors, such as movement narratives, collective identity, and members' emotional investments influence how movements ebb and flow. Johnston (1991) used the related concept, "movement dormancy," to capture how both state repression and persistent identity elements shape movement cycles. But most studies did not fully clarify whether the shift to abeyance is an intentional strategy proposed by movement leaders responding to either an unfavorable social climate or internal movement dynamics, or, alternatively, whether abeyance proceeds independently of or even in opposition to movement leaders' designs.

In her study of women's rights activism, Taylor seems to imply a combination of the two. At times, abeyance appears as a latent effect of closing political opportunities that leads to a decline in participation and recruitment (see also Mooney and Hunt 1996). "As a movement loses support, activists who had been most intensely committed to its aims become increasingly marginal and socially isolated" (Taylor 1989: 762) creating a cadre of activists who find a niche for themselves. More recently, Taylor and Crossley (2013: 64) note that movements "in a hostile political environment ...bereft of opportunities ... [persist in] pockets of movement activity, or free spaces." At other times, abeyance is characterized as a manifest outcome of choices made by movement leaders to withdraw from more visible public actions and rally committed members for later efforts (also see Sawyers and Meyer 1999). Taylor and Crossley (2013: 69) also appear to describe abeyance as a conscious adaptive strategy: "for a movement to survive periods of relative hiatus, activists must alter their goals [and] tactical repertoires."

We consider social movement abeyance as a complex, reflexive process with both reactive and proactive responses to different degrees at different times in a movement's campaigns. Our general task, then, should be to specify abeyance causes, processes, and facilitating mechanisms associated with particular cases. For instance, Taylor and Crossley (2013) demonstrate how structural constraints on feminist mobilizing limited where activists could organize and the types of tactics they used. They also identify various innovative ways feminists responded under these constraints to sustain their networks and modify their tactics.

We will elaborate the abeyance concept by highlighting how abeyance can include active, strategic choices among activists to de-emphasize public forms of action in favor of more covert, private activities not only to sustain the movement, but to increase participation and network connections that leaders can engage when they perceive new opportunities have emerged. We follow Tarrow (1998) and others (Eisinger 1973; Meyer 2004) who conceptualize political opportunities as openings in established political structures that can manifest with changes such as new divisions among political elites, a decline in repression against disenfranchised groups, or increasing political enfranchisement. Political opportunities are "consistent—but not necessarily formal or permanent—dimensions of the political struggle that encourage people to engage in contentious politics" (Tarrow 1998). Opportunities are situationally and temporally dependent and must be perceived (Tarrow 1998). Mobilization, then, rests on collective perceptions that the time is right to act publicly, collectively, and contentiously.

While centralized organizations were once more common in the white supremacist movement, during the 1990s, the movement shifted toward more diffuse, "submerged" networks (Melucci 1989, 1996) where activists interacted and experimented with white power visions. Within these networks, fragmented and transitory relationships among activists coalesced in small, hidden cells rather than more public groups. Aryan leaders encouraged the trend by calling for "leaderless resistance" and "lone wolf" tactics to avoid linking individual activists with organizations.

We attribute the movement's active abeyance strategy, in part, to its marginalized, stigmatized political status as an extremist, anti-democratic movement operating in a liberal democracy. Most studies focus on progressive movements in democratic states (Taylor 1989; Sawyers and Marullo, Pagnucco, and Smith 1996; Meyer 1999; Weigand 2001; Rojas 2007; Klandermans 2010; Rupp 2011) and attribute movement abeyance to a non-receptive political and social environment with few opportunities to cultivate political allies or broadly mobilize members to protest (Tilly 1978; Tarrow 1998 [1994], McAdam 1999 [1982]).[1] But these studies presume that movements represent a reformist "people's politics" that exists alongside routine representative politics, aimed at democratizing society. While progressive movements certainly do face repression, anti-democratic, fascist campaigns, such as white supremacy, seldom see major shifts in political opportunities that signal they have allies to ease repression and advocate for their goals.[2] And, while there are social, political, and economic costs for all social movement actors (McAdam 1986, 1988, 1989; Whalen and Flacks 1989; Whittier 1991; Taylor and Raeburn 1995), the personal consequences for white supremacists can be especially high. They face anti-racist counter-movements, which typically mobilize much larger numbers (Dobratz and Shanks-Meile 1997: 163–210; Daniels 2009). They also face serious and persistent stigmatization, social scrutiny, violent repression, job loss, blacklisting, and the disruption of personal relationships (Simi and Futrell 2009). Active abeyance strategies aim, in part, to shield members from stigma, marginalization, and repression, while they nourish collective identity and transfer cultural capital from seasoned members to new recruits to keep the cause alive.

A prevailing assumption is that abeyance signals movement contraction and member disengagement. As Taylor (1989) observes, abeyance characterizes a movement in retreat in which only a small set of the most committed participants remain active. But active abeyance among white supremacists suggests a much more engaged, strategic effort. Instead of contraction, we see the movement's shift to abeyance as an attempt among members to emphasize more privatized forms of movement involvement, increase participation, and encourage members to infiltrate and secure power in various social institutions such as government, military, and education. Active abeyance signals an intentioned strategic shift to decrease the risk of stigma and repression from public activism. They aim to help the movement grow, albeit slowly, by retaining participants whose commitment may waver in the face of severe stigma, and by recruiting those otherwise hesitant to begin participating for similar reasons.

Recently, white supremacists have embraced more public actions in response to the shifting political, cultural, and technological opportunities. In electoral politics, white supremacists defined Barack Obama's two-term presidency as a deep and tangible threat to white status by an illegitimate leader coming for their guns and signaling "victory" for multicultural values. Donald Trump's subsequent presidential candidacy and election altered the political landscape in ways that legitimated and encouraged white supremacists' views. White supremacists also interpreted global fascism's spread as a signal that their status is rising across international borders. In this context, some factions have sought to rebrand white supremacy under the banners "alt-right" or "white nationalism," to regain footholds in cultural debates about identity and civil rights. And, white supremacists are embracing new technological opportunities provided by the internet and social media platforms to link individuals and groups, promote messages of hate and violence, recruit new adherents, and target enemies. In recent years, group numbers have risen, white supremacists are organizing public protests, canvassing college campuses and other public locations, and analysts are documenting increases in hate crimes across the country (Levin, Nolan, and Reitzel 2018).

This recent resurgence flows from white supremacist networks that sustained an active underground movement, while drawing back from public efforts. Rather than conceptualizing withdrawal from public activism as movement disengagement and contraction, we argue that *active* abeyance better captures white supremacists' efforts to pursue different types of strategic mobilization to retain, and even grow, their ranks, and consciously position themselves to reemerge in a more supportive political culture. While some scholars, journalists, and policy makers regard this recent white supremacist resurgence as something totally "new," we suggest that a more accurate understanding, while messy and nuanced, requires that we recognize connections between waves of white supremacist mobilization, to avoid oversimplified explanations about the nature of contemporary extremism.

Methods/data

We draw from a broad range of data sources that reflect our more than 20 years of observing US white supremacist activism. Data sources include ethnographic fieldwork completed between 1997 and 2004, ongoing intensive life-history interviews with former white supremacists conducted since 2012, primary data derived from websites and social media platforms collected at various points during our period of observations, and various documents such as intelligence reports published by civil rights organizations, investigative journalists, and government agencies including the Federal Bureau of Investigation and Department of Homeland Security.

In terms of ethnographic data, we draw from a wide range of interviews and observations conducted with movement activists in the US. The participant observation includes Christian Identity adherents in the southwest and northwest, and a variety of white supremacists in Southern California. We made twenty-three house visits with groups in Arizona, Nevada, and Utah. These visits lasted from one to three days and gave us access to a variety of social gatherings, such as parties, Bible study sessions, hikes, and campouts. Additionally, we made four separate three- to five-day visits to the Aryan Nations' former headquarter in Hayden Lake, Idaho, to observe and interview participants at Aryan Nations World Congresses and informal gatherings that Aryans organized outside the official congress proceedings. Our fieldwork in Southern California included observations of social gatherings and twenty-two stints in activists' homes ranging from two days to five weeks.

Active abeyance in the WSM

Starting in the 1990s, white supremacists began emphasizing less public protest and recruitment strategies as an effort to adapt and adjust traditional protest modes to sustain and, potentially, grow the movement. As we alluded to above, these strategic and organizational changes emerged in response to the decreasing public support for and increasing repression of the movement. In this context, white supremacist leaders found their older tactics ineffective for retaining members and recruiting new ones. When common strategies are "so often marked by failure and defeat that they ... appear outmoded" (Beckwith 2000: 179), strategic change is likely (Beckwith 2000; Tilly 1984; Tarrow 1994, 1998). Such changes are often much more than just "simple experimentation" at the margins of a movement's existing "repertoire of contention" (Tilly 1978). Rather, they are "concerted efforts" (Beckwith 2000: 181) to adjust to external pressures and prior strategic failures. These efforts become especially salient when members perceive continued reliance on prior strategies as too costly and likely to produce future movement decline (Tilly 1978; Beckwith 2000). Strategic shifts defined their response to various forms of repression, combined with opportunities for new means of networking, which led movement leaders to, quite purposefully, begin incorporating new tactics and strategic elements into the existing repertoire.

We describe these changes as a move toward "active abeyance," which involves the deliberate de-emphasis of public actions and encouragement of privatized forms of movement participation. Various white supremacist pockets consciously advocated abeyance as a strategy to sustain activist networks, goals, and collective identity, and to eventually expand the movement by providing routes into activism less likely to gain the notoriety and stigma that more open, public forms typically do. Leaders called for "lone wolf" tactics which entail activists' absolute detachment from movement networks in order to become immersed in society. Others called for less radical, but nonetheless covert, approaches to activism and movement maintenance. As Blee (2002: 167) noted, this strategic change redefined "those who use overtly racist symbols in public or who adopt an exaggerated racist style [as] movement novices ... [and emphasized that white power] culture, in this sense, is most powerful when it is least obvious."

Private abeyance structures: families and informal gatherings

Taylor (1989) and Whittier (1995) have shown that identity work within small circles of like- minded people is crucial to sustain "abeyance structures." Members of the white supremacist movement (hereafter WSM) define families as providing the earliest opportunities for identity work crucial for recruiting activists and sustaining solidarity and commitment to white-power ideals (Polletta and Jasper 2001). In small group contexts such as the family "collective identities are expressed in cultural materials—names, narratives, symbols, verbal styles, rituals, clothing and so on" (Polletta and Jasper 2001: 285). Family is especially significant when considering the hostile social conditions WSM adherents face. As Couto (1993: 77) explains, "when the conditions of repression are paramount and the possibility of overt resistance is small, narratives are preserved in the most private of free spaces, the family ..." As other strategies seemed less viable, the family became more important than ever among white supremacists for fostering racist ideologies and sustaining their commitment to the cause (Veugelers 2011, 2013).

White-power parents use the family as a site of resistance by creating and displaying movement symbols and paraphernalia in the home. Pictures of Adolf Hitler and many other items such as pictures, posters, cards, newsletters, racist comic and coloring books, and children's "movement uniforms" (e.g., miniature Klan robes, t-shirts, fatigues) commonly decorate their homes. These items help to reinforce political identity and establish more direct connections to the movement. During our research, we saw parents use daily rituals, such as prayers, dinners, and bedtime routines, to instill white power viewpoints through racist and anti-Semitic statements. Likewise, parents often label children, and even pets, with surnames or nicknames tied to Aryan symbolism to make clear linkages between the child's sense of self and white supremacy.[3]

Homeschooling represents white supremacists' most systematic approach to political socialization of their children. Home schooling allows families direct control over the dissemination of white power ideology while masking and delegitimating "mainstream" world views. Movement leaders define homeschooling children as a crucial tactic for white supremacy's survival, since homeschooling protects children from mainstream schools, which white power activists perceive as brainwashing agents who perpetuate myths about the "wonders of race-mixing" and force a "Jewish-liberal ideology" upon children. At-home education provides the opportunity to "re-center" European-American racial consciousness, while simultaneously subverting multicultural values.

Families are not just havens to raise committed white power children. Within these spaces, parenting itself offers parent-activists unique opportunities to reinforce their own movement commitments (Simi, Futrell, and Bubolz 2016). Parenting in ways that reflect movement aims constitutes a form of activism. By expressing their politics through family rituals, rules, stories, and symbolism, white supremacist parents establish their activist identity as relevant and pervasive across myriad daily experiences. Parents see their efforts to infuse Aryan culture in the home as an important, strategic parental socialization process for their children that also reinforces their own activist identity.

Tactics employed in white power families focus on enhancing both parents' and children's movement solidarity in a societal context hostile to those messages. Regarding our argument about active abeyance, white power members use families as private spaces to nourish both individual and collective identities required to sustain the movement. We are not implying that using families as a vehicle for resistance is new, merely that its level of relative importance is heightened during abeyance (Veugelers 2011, 2013). For a movement actively seeking abeyance, the family may become critical to preventing movement collapse.

White power activists also employ a wide range of informal gatherings to continuously engage members. Many racist activists heeded calls by movement leaders to hold and participate in smaller, more casual and much more confidential gatherings. They often hold these under the auspices of, or combined with, more routine social functions such as parties, Bible study groups and other activities which attempt to conceal their white power aspects to outsiders. The informal gatherings typically contain a mixture of intentional political activism and casual interaction. Their mostly private character decreases the chance for notoriety and stigma.

Some followers turned to small independent churches and Bible study meetings in activists' homes for periodic gatherings where participants believe they are provided with "true" biblical insight instead of watered-down "*Jew*deo-Christian" rhetoric. In these contexts, members experience a great deal of autonomy to elaborate and refine white power ideologies with the support of like-minded activists, under the guise of ordinary theological study.

Some factions periodically combined Bible study with retreats to places the movement identified as spiritually sacred and racially pure, such as northern Idaho. White supremacists imbue these spaces with racialized and religious meanings and use their excursions as bonding rituals to reinforce solidarity among activists.

Periodic small parties ranging from backyard patio get-togethers to field parties are also common and serve several functions. Ideological work in these settings is typical, but unlike more formal movement settings where leaders dominate the discourse with a strict party-line, talk explores and experiments with various white power sentiments. These informal gatherings encourage participants to express their white power beliefs and carouse with other activists. In these settings, activists offer each other morality tales that justify white power and detail ways to live white power lifestyles and get by in an "antifascist" world. Activists often repeat their origin stories about their "political enlightenment." They also detail lone-wolf resistance efforts, such as late-night leafleting in neighborhoods or on university campuses to harassing non-white neighbors, and even physical confrontations with "racial enemies," which provide others with ideas and encouragement for their own lone-wolf tactics.

Participants at these gatherings vary from close friends who are staunch and open white power activists to a mix that includes non-adherents and, at times, even non-whites. The activists typically understand the precise makeup at each gathering, and their assessments affect how they express their racial sentiments. At the most private gatherings, the setting remains focused on white power themes without scrutiny from non-committed others. In these spaces, participants can also show off important symbols of movement affiliation such as flight jackets with white power patches, tattoos, military-style boots, confederate flags, and Nazi-salutes, without worry of stigma and repression. In contrast, at gatherings not organized exclusively around white power themes with some non-racist adherents attending, members will consciously "dress-down" to conceal their white power sentiments and are more hesitant to use racialized rhetoric and images to reduce the risk of unwanted confrontations. However, some activists will engage non-members in political conversation to gauge their receptiveness to extremist ideas. When they sense that someone might be a good recruit, they focus on building a friendship and, ultimately, drawing the person into activism (Simi and Futrell 2015).

These informal gatherings illustrate how white supremacists use leisure activities as a means for enacting resistance away from public scrutiny. Parties, crash pads, Bible meetings, and outings with like-minded activists help them anchor white power ideals, induce and maintain solidarity, and discuss activities that might aid the movement. Many members find these gatherings comforting and secure in an otherwise hostile climate toward white power beliefs in other spheres of their lives. Their efforts underscore that we need to pay attention to how movements create interaction sites to sustain participants and the character of those sites, to fully capture how they build collective identity and movement solidarity (Kendrick 2000: 192).

Activists organize their own events and activities in order to attract adherents by purposefully appealing to their sense of identity. And, as Hirsch notes, "successful recruitment to a revolutionary movement is more likely if there are social structural-cultural havens available where radical ideas and tactics can be more easily germinated" (Hirsch 1990: 216). These contexts not only enhance opportunities for retaining existing members but also aid in recruiting new ones.

Semi-publics spaces: music and internet

Growing difficulties with public demonstrations led white supremacists to emphasize more controlled semi-pubic displays of activism. They employed music events and internet spaces to draw members together, build alliances, and communicate movement identity. Music events provide a level of organization and camaraderie that smaller informal gatherings and family-based activism cannot. They bring a wider range of people and networks together to create a sense of vibrancy and continuity for a somewhat fragmented and discontinuous movement.

Internet spaces enabled a wide range of white power groups and activists to create dense inter-organizational connections through which to communicate movement information (Burris, Smith, and Strahm 2000). White supremacists were among the first internet adopters and they quickly learned how to use the space for "virtual activism" (Back, Keith, and Solomos 1998).

Starting in the 1970s, white power music grew into a prominent feature of white supremacist culture. By the mid-1980s, movement leaders and activists were organizing impromptu home concerts, bar shows, and then festivals in the 1990s, which drew members together into powerful contexts for transmitting movement identity and sustaining movement networks (Futrell, Simi, and Gottschalk 2006). By 2000, white supremacist music had evolved into one of the most pervasive means of racist expression among both veteran and newly recruited activists. Many gatherings included Aryan music produced by more than 100 U.S. white supremacist bands and more than 200 bands in 22 countries (Southern Poverty Law Center 2002). At the time, two of the most notorious white supremacist organizations—The National Alliance and Hammerskin Nation—were closely tied to the two most prominent white supremacist recording companies, Resistance Records and Panzerfaust Records.

Music events, from bar concerts to multi-day festivals, offer activists emotionally loaded experiences that nurture collective identity. Participants report feeling dignity, pride, pleasure, love, kinship, and fellowship in these settings; emotions that vitalize and sustain member commitments to movement ideals (Futrell, Simi, and Gottschalk 2006). Typical shows involve four or five bands, with brief speeches from activists and movement leaders (e.g., Tom Metzger) between sets. Audiences are mostly young, male skinheads who fill a bar that organizers stock for the night with movement literature, CDs, and other paraphernalia. Bouncers keep counter-movement activists out in an effort to maintain the event's ideological purity. Festivals increase the size and intensity and offer opportunities for fellowshipping with national and international activists, as well as young members and long-time activists. Both the festivals and bar concerts provide a level of organization and camaraderie that smaller informal gatherings and family-based activism do not. They bring a much wider range of people and networks together in semi-public settings to create a sense of vibrancy and continuity for a somewhat fragmented and discontinuous movement.

Understood in terms of collective identity, these semi-public performances represent a continuous and persistent movement to both the participants and those hearing about them from afar. The events also serve as much more planned and controlled public presentations than marches and rallies more prone to disorganization and counter-movement disruptions. Consequently, they serve as effective ways to retaining existing members and recruit new adherents otherwise hesitant to participate in such high-risk, stigmatized activism.

Among the earliest internet adopters developing the Liberty Net in 1983 (Daniels 2009), white supremacists embraced cyberspace to facilitate communication, organization, and recruitment, which were all pivotal to active abeyance. A number of scholars and watchdog groups have noted white supremacists' savvy at linking members and organizations through list-serves, chat rooms, and bulletin boards that provide space for real-time communication where they create and sustain virtual communities (Burris, Smith, and Strahm 2000; Burghart 1996; Hoffman 1996; Back, Keith, and Solomos 1998. Their early adoption enabled white power groups and activists to create dense inter-organizational connections and spaces for "virtual activism" (Burris, Smith, and Strahm 2000). Early links were especially common between Klan and neo-Nazi skinhead sites, and between Christian and non-Christian white power sites, both nationally and internationally (Burris, Smith, and Strahm 2000), all aimed at providing information about the movement and incentives for involvement. White supremacists also used these virtual networks to market and distribute white power music, books, and movement paraphernalia, and advertise and coordinate music festivals and bar shows.

The internet offers white supremacists critical opportunities for planning and networking on a scale that simply did not exist before the emergence of this technology (Hoffman 1996). As white power websites grow in number and diversity, potential adherents can find their way into the movement with discretion and anonymity through a group most suitable for them (Burris, Smith, and Strahm 2000: 231). As Todd Schroer (2001) explains, these forums help "reduce the perceived risk of contacting these groups. If you have to go to a Klan rally or actually write to [groups] to get involved in hate, that's a big barrier to overcome" in an extremely oppositional climate. Virtual spaces offer degrees of both intimacy and safety not found in other white power movement settings. Consequently, they have played a crucial role in attracting new activists, drawing peripheral members closer to the movement, and maintaining the commitment among those already active.

The abeyance structures we identify here enable activists to enact white power culture and identity within submerged networks (Melucci 1989, 1996), largely out of view of the public eye and embedded in otherwise innocuous everyday practices. They provide "free spaces" (Evans and Boyte 1992; Futrell and Simi 2004)[4] removed from the physical and ideological control of opponents where members nourish solidarity, counter-hegemonic ideas, and oppositional identities that encourage movement participation (Polletta 1999). The networks of recognition (Pizzorno 1986; Emirbayer 1997) they sustain continually validate adherents' commitments and provide covert routes of entry into the movement which help members better avoid the stigma of participating in more public forms of activism. In short, the racist cultural practices enacted in these gatherings help forge a shared racist agenda, internal solidarity, and a sense of efficacy within a wider public context of hostility toward the movement.

White supremacy membership has consistently ebbed and flowed in numbers and across right-wing extremist networks, including anti-government and anti-immigration groups (Zeskind 2009). During the 1990s, many white supremacists tied themselves to militia groups that increased in number, but then mostly fell apart in the aftermath of the 1995 Oklahoma City bombing (Crothers 2003). By the early 2000s, as key national leaders died or were incarcerated, an organized public face became even more difficult to achieve, lending more credence to the need for strategic abeyance. White power networks persisted in the abeyance structures we have described, under the radar of most Americans. Barack Obama's 2008 presidential election and conspiratorial frustrations about the Great Recession re-energized white supremacists. Lone-actor terrorists executed repeated violent massacres, as others lashed out through less publicized, but more consistent, street-level violence (Simi and Futrell 2015). The birther movement provided an opportunity for an amalgam of far-right extremists to rally around a racist cause cloaked under thinly veiled questions about Obama's citizenship and legitimacy to serve as president.

During this time, authorities came to (at least partially) acknowledge right-wing extremism as a serious concern. By 2009, the U.S. Department of Homeland Security identified white supremacist and violent antigovernment groups as important domestic terror threats (U.S. Department of Homeland Security 2009). West Point's Combating Terrorism Center confirmed a dramatic rise in the number of right-wing extremist attacks and violent plots (Perliger 2012).[5] In 2013, the SPLC counted more than 1,000 active "antigovernment patriot groups" in the U.S., with almost 800 active white supremacy hate groups among them.[6] In 2014, U.S. Attorney General Eric Holder reconstituted a committee on domestic terrorism that was first established after the 1995 Oklahoma City bombing but then shelved after 9/11 as the federal government shifted focus to international terrorism. But, overall, the federal response, in particular, has been largely focused on Islamic extremism with much less attention directed toward far-right extremism (Johnson 2012). This type of inattention provided an external condition that synergistically helped to facilitate active abeyance.

Opportunities and reemergence

White supremacists' reluctant, but purposeful withdrawal into abeyance structures helped to sustain, and in some cases, grow activist networks. Racist and anti-Semitic activism did not die but drew back into more privatized forms, lying in wait for new mobilization opportunities.

Recently, some white supremacists have transitioned from active abeyance to embrace more public activism in response to the shifting political opportunities. Specifically, Donald J. Trump's presidential candidacy and election, combined with white supremacy's rebranding under the broader banner of "alt-right" and "white nationalism," helped to draw activists toward more public forms of protest. Internationally, campaign notoriety and electoral successes among right-wing fascist parties in Europe signaled new prospects for U.S. white supremacy.

Simultaneously, white supremacists also took advantage of technological opportunities to use a broad range of virtual spaces, online platforms, and cyber-networks to extend white supremacy's presence in the political landscape.

Political opportunities

The shift from the Obama to the Trump presidency vastly transformed how white supremacists perceived their political power. Obama's presidency symbolized to white supremacists a tangible threat that they could point toward—the first African-American president who was "coming for their guns" and the "victory" of multicultural society (Zeskind 2009).[7] They perceived few powerful allies, even among the persistent and growing bi-partisan divisions, and experienced heightened repression toward explicit white supremacist groups and activities.

In fact, some white supremacists had long criticized any efforts to participate in institutionalized politics as an ineffective waste of time and energy since they saw the state as little more than an arm for the shadowy cabal of "new world order" elites intent on white racial genocide. But as Obama's presidency concluded, Trump's candidacy helped create a receptive political environment for fear mongering and ethnic, racial, and religious scapegoating. As with any movement, white supremacists perceived signals that demonstrated new opportunities for more public actions and movement gains.

These signals emerged before, during, and after Trump's campaign, and included three overlapping types: rhetorical, personnel, and policy. Rhetorical examples include both racist statements and tweets supporting white supremacist ideals. For example, Trump launched his campaign with a speech that called Mexican immigrants "rapists" while promoting his signature policy to "build a great, great wall on our southern border" to hold them at bay (Philips 2016). During the presidential campaign and after the election, Trump retweeted white supremacist Twitter accounts 75 times, including tweets from an account handle "@WhiteGenocideTM," sent out a meme that used the alt-right's Pepe the Frog symbol, vastly overstated "black on white crime" using figures culled from white supremacist sources, and even amplified a virulent, racist (and false) conspiracy theory about white genocide in South Africa (Easley 2016; Williams 2018). White supremacists respond to these statements as nods to the cause by the U.S. president and praise him for it. Regarding the @WhiteGenocideTM retweet, one Stormfront member wrote: "He willingly retweeted the name. The name was chosen to raise awareness of our plight. He helped propagate it. We should be grateful." Andrew Anglin, who edits the notorious white supremacist *Daily Stormer* website, explained to his followers that "[Trump] is giving us the old wink-wink. It could only be deliberate … Today in America the air is cold and it tastes like victory" (Berger 2016; Kharakh and Primack 2016). When Trump was elected, white supremacists celebrated with statements such as, "We finally have one of us in the White House" and "Hail Trump!" (Goldstein 2016). Since the election, President Trump has continued to rely on rhetoric familiar to white supremacists by describing immigrants from Mexico and Central and South America as an "infestation" (Graham 2018). Additionally, when he described Haiti, El Salvador, and African countries as "shithole countries" and compared them unfavorably to nations like Norway, he was quite literally speaking white supremacists' language; they repeatedly refer to the world's "non-white" regions as "shithole countries" and "cesspools," and their immigrants as "infestations." Even more directly, during his mid-term election campaigning, President Trump declared, "You know what? I'm a nationalist" (Sonmez 2018), which white supremacists and others interpreted as his clearest effort to connect to white nationalist aims.[8]

Both during and after the campaign, Trump consistently surrounded himself with key figures who would resonate with white supremacists. Trump began his presidency with Steve Bannon as his chief White House Advisor. Bannon ran Breitbart News, which he infamously described as a "platform for the alt-right" (Posner 2016). He embraces a clash of civilizations vision reflected in the white supremacist French novel *the Camp of the Saints* (Raspail 1973), which describes immigrant waves taking over and destroying Europe in a race war. On at least four occasions, video recordings show Bannon favorably describing the book as an accurate assessment of today's world (Blumenthal and Rieger 2017). More specifically, Bannon's clash of civilizations perspective sees Christianity in a world-historical war with Islam, which helped to justify a host of anti-Islamic policies, including Trump's controversial "Muslim travel ban." Sebastian Gorka, who served as an early deputy assistant to President Trump, also supports virulent anti-Islamic views and was reportedly involved in a Hungarian group tied to neo-Nazis.

Investigative journalists uncovered that during the early 2000s, "he [Gorka] was active in Hungarian politics, had close ties to Hungarian far-right groups and worked with 'openly racist and anti-Semitic groups and public figures'" (Jacobson 2017). Attorney General Jeff Sessions, who some have called a "career racist," is a well-known advocate for voting rights restrictions, fought confederate flag removal, and was unable to be confirmed as a US District

Court in 1986 for being "too racist" (Speri 2016). Among other things, the Attorney General once commented positively about the Ku Klux Klan and called a white civil rights lawyer "a disgrace to his race." During his time as Attorney General, Sessions implemented a zero-tolerance immigration policy, aggressive deportation efforts, and undermined civil rights protections in ways lauded by white supremacists (White 2018; Newkirk 2018). Stephen Miller, a former Sessions aide and Trump's senior advisor, has been tied to avowed white supremacist Richard Spencer, an advocate for a "white ethno-state" who referred to Miller as his "mentee" (Southern Poverty Law Center 2018). Miller has long-held anti-Islamic and anti-globalist views, and has been close to several Breitbart News staffers.

White supremacists look beyond Trump's personnel to his administration's policies and directives for evidence that they have support in the government's highest office. Trump followed his campaign promise to ban all Muslim immigration with efforts to establish a more circumscribed Muslim travel ban and push for a southern border wall with Mexico. These policies tightly align with white supremacists' calls for staving off "the brown invasion" to protect "white civilization." The administration's direction to the Department of Homeland Security to refocus terrorism surveillance away from domestic far-right extremists and only to Islamic jihadist threats also signaled tacit support to white supremacists. Simultaneously, white supremacists interpret the administration's directives to Immigration and Customs Enforcement (ICE) to intensify efforts to locate, incarcerate, and deport undocumented immigrants, as a tactic in a grand operation to "whiten" America.

Segments in the white supremacy movement see Trump's presidency as a political opening to more explicitly and forcefully express "white identity" issues.[9] We see many discernible responses among both organized and unaffiliated white supremacists that indicate emboldened expression of overt racism and anti-Semitism over the past 3 years that has taken a variety of forms. Hate crimes have increased over consecutive years since 2016 and there is some evidence that ties growing hate crime numbers to Trump's Muslim-ban announcement during the presidential campaign (Center for the Study of Hate & Extremism 2018). The Anti-Defamation League also documented a substantial increase in white supremacist activity, such as leafleting, on college campuses from 2016 to 2017 (Anti-Defamation League 2018). The growing number of hate groups reflect trends initially observed following Barack Obama's election (U.S. Department of Homeland Security 2009). And, the resurgence has been global with extreme far-right electoral "successes" in France, Germany, Greece, Poland, and many other European countries along with large increases in right-wing extremist non-governmental organizations such as the Nordic Resistance Movement across Scandinavia. In some instances, these organizations have helped galvanize public marches and rallies with turnouts in the hundreds of thousands in France, Greece, Italy, and Poland.

White supremacists' most emboldened public expression in the U.S. came with the 2017 "Unite the Right" (UTR) rally in Charlottesville, Virginia. Organized as a protest against a confederate statue removal, UTR drew more than 500 white supremacists from more than 39 US states for a two-day demonstration. The first night, a group marched through the University of Virginia campus with tiki torches chanting, "White lives matter!" "Jews will not replace us!" and "Blood and soil!". The next day, wielding shields, clubs, guns, along with swastika and Confederate flags, they marched to protest plans to remove the city's 1924 statue of the Confederate general Robert E. Lee. Violence erupted and a white supremacist drove his car into a crowd of counter- demonstrators, killing one counter-protester and injuring 19 others.

The event's size, coordination, and overt extremism surprised many observers. The rally's scale and planning betrayed a more organized and committed racial and anti-Semitic extremism than many anticipated. Mobilization relied on long-term online and offline communication across movement networks to plan arrivals, march times, and guide participants in the movement's "new optics" that downplay visible neo-Nazi symbolism (Conti 2017; Miller-Idriss 2018). These optics were most evident at the Friday night march with young fascists holding tiki torches and, dressed in "normie" clothing, with little overt racialist symbolism other than their racist and anti-Semitic chants. Saturday's larger march brought more overt white supremacist symbolism, clashes with counter-protesters, nation-wide attention, and widespread condemnation.

White supremacists initially lauded the rally as a forceful return to the public eye. President Trump's response to the racial violence, in which he suggested that both the white supremacists and counter-protesters had "fine people on both sides …," intensified extremists' perceptions that they have an ally in the Oval Office (Thrush and Haberman 2017). Former KKK leader and white supremacist politician David Duke described Trump's response as at least tacit support, if not endorsement, for white supremacists' efforts and claimed that the rally was "the fulfillment of President Donald Trump's vision for America" (Nelson 2017). Neo-Nazi Andrew Anglin praised Trump:

> He didn't attack us. He just said the nation should come together. Nothing specific against us. He said that we need to study why people are so angry, and implied that there was hate on … both sides! … There was virtually no counter signaling of us at all. He loves us all.
>
> (Sutton 2017)

Whether Trump and his advisors explicitly align themselves with the white supremacist movement is secondary to white supremacists' perceptions about them. Many white supremacists believe these officials, their policies, and their practices align with white power ideals and they feel emboldened to act publicly in ways they have been less inclined to pursue in the recent past. They are still cautious, however, about how public they should be in their efforts. UTR drew widespread condemnation, lawsuits, and for many attendees their white-supremacist identities were publicly exposed, leading to disgrace, job loss, and prosecutions in some cases. Counter-protesters continue to mobilize against similar events rendering them less effective as powerful pro-movement spectacles. In response, movement leaders appear divided around questions about whether public displays that provide a context for counter-protesters to mobilize are as valuable for messaging and recruitment compared to other less visible forms of resistance. Since Charlottesville, many white supremacist groups are "opting for unpublicized, unpermitted demonstrations over public rallies that draw hundreds of counter-protesters" (Kelley 2018).

Some white supremacist leaders see Charlottesville and subsequent public demonstrations as a failing strategy. One year after UTR Andrew Anglin pleaded with his followers to avoid public confrontations, assuring them that:

> We cannot win a battle on the streets. We cannot win a protest movement organizational battle. We are currently winning a culture war and were long before … Charlottesville. We need to remain in the realm of hip, cool, sexy, fun. We need to speak to the culture.
>
> (Anglin 2018)

To "speak to the culture" they continue to pursue underground forms of resistance such as private gatherings along with their savvy internet-based activism.

Technological opportunities

In addition to changes in the political environment, white supremacists have taken advantage of innovations in computer-mediated technologies to invigorate and sustain their cause. Their longstanding use of these communication technologies meant they were well positioned to capitalize on new twenty-first-century digital networking platforms in the face of common misconceptions that suggest these groups only attract the unsophisticated and poorly educated. From online chat rooms and blogs to social networking sites such as Twitter, Facebook, Gab.ai, Reddit, and 4 and 8Chan, white supremacists use the internet to articulate, accelerate, and amplify the spread of racist ideas and forge connections among far-flung racists, anti-Semites, nativists, neo-fascists, masculinists, conspiracists, and a host of others. Combined with tech companies' content-neutral approach and America's legal approach to free speech, the U.S. is a haven for online hate (Daniels 2009).

We see three overlapping features that capture how white supremacists utilize the internet's networking capabilities. First, they use these technologies to generate and distribute propaganda. White supremacist propaganda comes in many forms and has been widely accessible on the internet since the technology's earliest days (Daniels 2009). Some propaganda is rudimentary, relying on plain text and opting for explicitly hateful terms and images. Other propaganda uses multifaceted and dynamic visual and auditory components intended to attract and compel viewers with white supremacist style and symbolism, albeit often in coded terms and techniques to avoid direct connections to hatred. For instance, white supremacists strategically deploy racial identity as they advocate for and perform stylized versions of "white nationalism" that includes hip, nostalgic, and respectable dress suits, polos, khakis, and "fashy haircuts," as well as fitted shirts and jackets scrubbed of the most overt insignia (e.g., swastikas) in favor of subtle symbolic codes. Richard Spencer and his National Policy Institute exemplifies what Kelly J. Baker (2016) calls a sanitized "white collar supremacy," while the neo-Nazi National Socialist Movement recently banned swastikas as a cosmetic overhaul intended to rebrand their look and draw in "patriotic White Americans." Such symbolic subterfuge attempts to disguise the worst forms of racial extremism.

Drawing upon the increasing popularity of Mixed Martial Arts (MMA) among white supremacists especially in Europe, newly formed fight-club type groups, such as the Rise Above Movement (RAM) and more recently Revolt Through Tradition, provide another example of how different types of propaganda flow from these organizations (Zidan 2018). These groups posts glossy action-oriented videos designed to appeal to young, white males. The clips show physically fit, well-groomed young men in stylish t-shirts and other athletic gear demonstrating their training regimen interspersed with clips of their violence at public rallies. Racist and anti-Semitic music also remains an important facet of white supremacist propaganda. Online platforms, such as YouTube, support easy access to white power music and videos. Podcasts, such as *the Daily Shoah* (mocking Comedy Central's *The Daily Show* and the Holocaust) and *Fash the Nation* (mocking CBS's *Face the Nation*), offer among the most direct connections to white power perspectives on immigration, race relations, feminism, Zionism, anti-globalization, and political correctness. These shows also provide the audience with a new language and symbolism gaining ascendance across movement networks (e.g., terms such as "cucks," or using triple parentheses around names and ideas to denote Jewishness, etc.).

Internet trolling constitutes another more recent dimension related to propaganda messaging. Internet trolls use racist and anti-Semitic memes as a pithy way to package overt and coded ideological messages to both their followers and broader publics. Some memes are explicit in their connotations, others are more veiled and require a background steeped in white supremacy to accurately interpret.

Second, white supremacists continue to use internet platforms to construct and sustain collective identity. Online white supremacy provides access to a culture where adherents can immerse themselves in a "lived environment" with others committed to preserving racist and anti-Semitic narratives and building virtual social solidarity. White supremacy's internet presence symbolizes a community that the merely curious to the deeply committed can connect to "24–7" and find ideas and representations that fit their preferences. Multi-threaded forum sites, such as Stormfront, have long provided space for virtual networking among white supremacists. As we have documented elsewhere, a web presence symbolizes a broader community that sustains collective sensibilities or, as one user put it, gives "a warm feeling knowing there are other people out there that think like you" (Simi and Futrell 2015). More recently, white supremacists have found 4 and 8Chan, Reddit, GAB.ai, and Telegram especially appealing. A proliferation of informal digital grouping on these platforms demonstrate their attractiveness to some members of techy, gamer subcultures who may gravitate toward the anti-political correctness, racism, and misogyny promoted by white supremacy.

Finally, extremists' online practices also appear to enhance recruitment to the cause. Social media successes can enhance interest in extremism among the merely curious and encourage already committed racists. Between 2012 and 2016, major American white supremacist networks on Twitter added about 22,000 followers, an increase of about 600 percent. The increase was driven, in part, by organized social media activism, organic growth in the adoption of social media by people interested in white supremacy, and, to some extent, organized trolling communities trying to flood social media platforms with negative content. Perhaps most worrisome, white supremacists have effectively mixed extremist ideas into mainstream content on Twitter. This "inter-ideological mingling" as Roderick Graham (2016) calls it, uses Twitter's hashtag function to cluster white supremacist terms with more mainstream conservative and progressive ideas, helping them reach wider audiences and normalize their ideology. Researchers have also demonstrated how groups of users tweeting in concert at high volumes can amplify their effect, causing hashtags and content to trend in numbers significant enough to prompt mainstream media coverage (Graham 2016).

Over the last two decades, white supremacists have established an online presence that ties members into a pervasive, ever-present virtual culture that nourishes racial hate and anti- Semitic vitriol. Of course, not all individuals who follow racist Twitter accounts, participate in 4chan threads, listen to podcasts, or watch racist propaganda will necessarily embrace or act on the ideological prescriptions that racial extremists offer, but some certainly will incorporate the ideas as their own. In some instances, online experiences appear central to personal radicalization that leads white supremacists to lash out in violent ways. One notorious example is Dylann Roof, the white supremacist who murdered nine people at Charleston, South Carolina's Emanuel African Methodist Episcopal Church in June 2015. Roof's terrorism, often mischaracterized as "self-radicalization," required the persistent, multidimensional online white supremacist culture that traffics in violent fantasies to help shape his thinking and provide a basis for him to justify his violence as a necessary defense against "white genocide." And for many others, online white supremacy offers spaces to connect with a persistent movement culture steeped in hatred.

Conclusion

We see active abeyance as a strategic adaptation to a political and cultural climate that marginalizes hardcore explicit white supremacy. For white supremacists, active abeyance emphasizes internal movement efforts to create and sustain solidarity within families, using informal gatherings to maintain local networks, and displaying unity in semi-public face-to-face and internet spaces. These efforts comprise the movement's identity work articulated at three organizational levels—primary groups, online and face-to-face secondary group interactions, and movement-wide networks—which helps individual members and small groups connect with wider movement networks and culture. Moreover, the unobtrusive, covert character of these strategies also attempt to resolve the problems of high-risk activism faced by the movement.[10] As a concerted, tactical effort to emphasize activism outside the public eye, active abeyance helps strengthen solidarity, sustain movement organization, and potentially recruit new adherents until new opportunities emerge to pursue different mobilization strategies.

Our argument raises two broad, interconnected questions about social movement abeyance. The first question concerns the extent to which abeyance may be a purposive, strategic choice made by movement leaders and activists to sustain the movement in a context of hostility and repression. As Freeman (1983) noted, a movement's successes are often determined by their ingenuity in finding less obvious leverage points from which to pressure its targets. The more marginalized a group, the more creative and adaptable it may have to be (also see Scott 1985, 1990; Beckwith 2000), and the strategies chosen usually combine the lowest risk with the highest reward related to a particular pattern of repression the movement faces. This ingenuity, creativity, and adaptability is applicable not only to efforts for influencing targets external to the movement, but just as importantly to recruitment and sustain commitment efforts.

Strategic choices to influence movement activists and potential recruits, and to sustain their ties and initiate new ones, may produce vastly different short-term consequences for activism by reducing the relative costs and probable returns associated with movement involvement. For white supremacists, abeyance appears to be an active strategy. By emphasizing private rather than public forms of activism, they seek to reduce the costs of high-risk activism which typically entail strong stigmatization and threats to person and livelihood. We see active abeyance as more than experimentation. It is a concerted, tactical effort to link members largely outside the public eye to strengthen solidarity and expand their ranks.

The second question asks whether abeyance necessarily entails movement decline. A prevailing assumption is that movement abeyance means contraction and disengagement from activism and recruitment. For instance, Taylor (1989), characterizes such movements as being in a state of retreat where only a small set of the most committed participants remains active.

Movements in abeyance are said to become "insular," exhibiting an inward focus aiming solely at retaining already existing, highly committed activists. Active abeyance in the WSM is certainly a response to social pressures that have led to movement contraction and to efforts at creating contexts within which collective identity can endure. At the same time, we have also observed white supremacist contexts that support recruitment away from the public eye.

Although, recruitment in a repressive climate is doubtlessly more difficult than in a more favorable one (Kendrick 2000), we should not disregard the possibility that active abeyance may produce movement expansion. White supremacists' efforts to reduce the effects of public stigma and repression on participation by creating opportunities for covert involvement led to movement expansion, by retaining participants whose commitment is likely to waver in the face of extreme opprobrium and by recruiting those otherwise hesitant to participate for similar reasons. White supremacist music, and especially their internet presence, diffuses strategic abeyance tactics and provide channels for individuals to build direct relationships with likeminded others.

We understand the recent resurgence in white supremacist activism as flowing from nearly three decades in which leaders have encouraged active abeyance strategies to sustain and nourish racist and anti-Semitic activism. Resurgence does not signal some new and distinct mobilization, it has deep roots in prior movement strategy. As Berbrier (2000, 1999, 1998) documents, white supremacist organizations have been experimenting with various strategies to legitimize their claims, including efforts to reframe racism as "white civil rights" and a "cultural heritage" issue, or to frame "hatred" as "in-group love" and to associate whiteness with victimhood. Today's hashtags and other propaganda slogans such as "#whitegenocide," "It's Ok To Be White" and "Racism is Code Word for Anti-White" extend this long-term strategy to find cultural and political themes that might resonate among a broader swath of the white population. Berbrier's work underscores that, despite myriad claims that a generation of "khaki and Polo-wearing" white supremacists and online racist trolls are surprisingly new, their networks, ideas, strategies, and tactics stretch much farther back into our history.

Indeed, abeyance emphasizes that rather than seeing a movement's resurgence as simply a new and novel development, we should determine what linkages— individuals, organizational networks, and ideas—cut across movement generations. As a concept, abeyance pushes us to see less obvious, but very important, points of continuity. If, as Taylor (1989: 761) argues, "abeyance structures provide organizational and ideological bridges between different upsurges of activism" then we can best understand white supremacy's recent surge as part and parcel of the active abeyance processes we have described here.

Notes

1 See Holland and Cable (2002) for insights on how internal processes and organization cultural shape abeyance processes in grassroots social movement organizations.
2 Of course, white supremacists have gained political strength in the past. Seeking to preserve the United States' white Anglo-Saxon "racial purity," the 1920s second-era KKK drew nearly five million members, sponsored successful senate

candidates in six states, won a governorship, and counted a Supreme Court Justice and two presidents as members. Many more KKK members won state and local positions as well (Trelease 1971; McVeigh 2009).

3   Such names might include those associated with Nordic mythology, such as Valkyries (winged warriors of Nordic mythology), Thor (mythological Nordic warrior), and Valhalla (Nordic heaven in Odinist mythology), or names tied to Gaelic roots, such Alana and Haley, to help link children to white power ideologies. Others create names rooted in the word "Aryan," such as Ariana, use nicknames like "Little Hitler," or use familiar names from white power literature (e.g., Hunter after a fictional character in William Pierce's white power fantasy novel of the same name (Macdonald [Pierce] 1989) to mark children and instill their "racial politics" in their children.

4   Evans and Boyte (1992) intend the notion of "free spaces" to apply to the creation of progressive, democratic communities. But as Polletta (1999: 7) has asked, "is there any reason why free spaces do not play a role in right-wing movements" as well? We think not, for it seems just as reasonable that the concept can usefully be applied to "radical, regressive, right-wing," white-power movement communities. Just as Evans and Boyte (1992) point out that communal associations can become free spaces, breeding grounds for democratic change, they also can be breeding grounds for radical, right-wing, racist activism. We would argue that the importance of "free spaces" should not be assessed on the basis of a movement's political orientations and aims but rather on the radical reach of the goals. The more a movement's goals diverge from mainstream ideologies, the more crucial free spaces become to enable members to develop collective identity and attract participants.

5   Although violent attacks by homegrown right-wing extremists receives substantially less attention than violence by jihadist militants, domestic right-wing extremism is more frequent and more deadly (Bergen and Sterman. 2014; Also, see the New America Foundation's International Security project data at http://securitydata.newamerica.net/extremists/analysis).

6   The SPLC's Hate Map documented "939 active hate groups in the U.S. during 2013." They define hate groups as organizations that advocate "beliefs or practices that attack or malign an entire class of people, typically for the immutable characteristics." From this list, we included neo-Nazis, White Nationalists, Christian Identity, Holocaust Deniers, Racist Skinheads, KKK, Neo-Confederates, General Hate groups, Anti-Immigrant groups, and Anti Muslim groups. We excluded anti-LGBT, Black Separatist, and Radical Traditional Catholic groups. Available at: http://www.splcenter.org/get-informed/hate-map (accessed December 12, 2014).

7   Fear and resentment regarding these changes have been broader than the white supremacist movement. A recent article on status threat in the Proceedings of the National Academy of Sciences explains Trump voters were driven mostly by white fears of dwindling cultural and demographic dominance which Trump's campaign articulated in messages about how the "American way of life is threatened" (Mutz 2018). White supremacists have long been on the frontline of thinking in these terms and represent the strongest, longest, and most clearly articulated aspects of this status anxiety.

8   When asked if he intended his statement as a dog whistle to white nationalists to stoke racist and anti-immigrant sentiments, Trump said that he's just "somebody that loves our country" and that he thought "nationalist" is a word "that should be brought back" (Sonmez 2018).

9   Some white supremacists find Trump's ardent support for Israel, along with his Jewish son-in-law Jared Kushner, disconcerting. But others explain it away as politics supporting "ethno-states" that see the ethno-racial purity that white supremacists envision for the U.S. and around the globe.

10 To be clear, neither our attempt to identify and explain active abeyance nor the specific tactics we describe are intended as a general claim applicable to abeyance processes in all movements. We offer sensitizing claims to help future studies by specifying some grounds for active abeyance and some tactics that may be involved.

References

Anglin, Andrew. 2018. "Official Daily Stormer Position: Don't Go to "Unite the Right 2" – We Disavow," available at: https://dailystormer.name/official-daily-stormer-position-dont-go-to-unite-the-right-2-we-disavow/ (accessed August 10, 2018).

Anti-Defamation League. 2018. "White Supremacist Propaganda on U.S. College Campuses Rises 77 Percent Over Past Nine Months: ADL Report," available at: https://www.adl.org/news/press-releases/white-supremacist-propaganda-on-us-college-campuses-rises-77-percent-over-past (accessed August 23, 2018).

Back, Les, Michael Keith and John Solomos. 1998. "Racism on the Internet: Mapping the Neo- Fascist Subcultures in 'Cyberspace'," in *Nation and Race: The Developing Euro- American Racist Subculture*, ed. Jeffrey Kaplan and Tore Bjorgo, 73–101. Boston: Northeastern University Press.

Baker, Kelly J. "White Collar Supremacy," available at: https://www.nytimes.com/2016/11/25/ opinion/white-collar-supremacy.html (accessed November 26, 2016).

Beckwith, Karen. 2000. "Hinges in Collective Action: Strategic Innovation in the Pittston Coal Strike." *Mobilization*, 5: 179–200.

Belew, Kathleen. 2018. Bring the War Home: The White Power Movement and Paramilitary America. Cambridge, MA: Harvard University Press.

Blee, Kathleen. 2002. *Inside Organized Racism: Women in the Hate Movement*. Berkeley, CA: University of California Press.

Berbrier, Mitch. 1998. "'Half the Battle': Cultural Resonance, Framing Processes and Ethnic Affectations in Contemporary White Separatist Rhetoric." *Social Problems* 45: 431–450.

Berbrier, Mitch. 1999. "Impression Management for the Thinking Racist: A Case Study of Intellectualization as Stigma Transformation in Contemporary White Supremacist Discourse." *The Sociological Quarterly*, 40: 3, 411–433.

Berbrier, Mitch. 2000. "The Victim Ideology of White Supremacists and White Separatists in the United States." *Sociological Focus* 33, 2: 175–191.

Bergen, Peter and David Sterman. 2014. "U.S. Right Wing Extremists More Deadly than Jihadists," available at: http://us.cnn.com/2014/04/14/opinion/bergen-sterman-kansas-shooting/ (accessed December 1, 2014).

Berger, J.M. 2016. "How White Nationalists Learned to Love Donald Trump," available at: https://www.politico.com/magazine/story/2016/10/donald-trump-2016-white-nationalists-alt-right-214388 (accessed October 10, 2017).

Blumenthal, Paul and J.M. Rieger. 2017. "This Stunningly Racist French Novel Is How Steve Bannon Explains the World," available at: https://www.huffingtonpost.com/entry/steve-bannon-camp-of-the-saints-immigration_us_58b75206e4b0284854b3dc03 (accessed September 9, 2018).

Burris, Val, Emory Smith, and Ann Strahm. 2000. "White Supremacist Networks on the Internet." *Sociological Focus* 33: 215–234.

Center for the Study of Hate & Extremism. 2018. Final U.S. Status Report Hate Crime Analysis & Forecast for 2016/2017. California State University, San Bernardino.

Conti, Alice. 2017. "Neo-Nazi to Troll Army: 'We Have to Be Sexy' at the Big Alt-Right Rally," available at: https://www.vice.com/en_us/article/599zmx/neo-nazi-to-troll-army-we-have-to-be-sexy-at-the-big-alt-right-rally (accessed August 9, 2017).

Couto, Richard A. 1993. "Narrative, Free Space, and Political Leadership in Social Movements." *Journal of Politics* 55: 57–79.

Crothers, Lane. 2003. *Rage on the Right: The American Militia Movement from Ruby Ridge to Homeland Security.* Boulder, CO: Rowman & Littlefield.

Daniels, Jessie. 2009. *Cyber Racism: White Supremacy Online and the New Attack on Civil Rights.* Boulder, CO: Rowman & Littlefield.

Dobratz, B.A. and S.L. Shanks-Meile. 1997. *White Power, White Pride!: The White Separatist Movement in the United States.* New York: Twayne Publishers.

Easley, Jason. 2016. "His Racism Is No Accident: Trump Has Retweeted White Supremacists 75 Times," available at: https://www.politicususa.com/2016/07/03/proof-racism-accidenttrump-retweeted-white-supremacists-75-times.html (accessed October 10, 2017).

Eisinger, P. 1973. "The Conditions of Protest Behavior in American Cities." *American Political Science Review* 81: 11–28.

Emirbayer, Mustafa. 1997. "Manifesto for a Relational Sociology." *American Journal of Sociology 103*: 281–317.

Evans, Sarah M. and Harry C. Boyte. 1992. *Free Spaces.* Chicago: University of Chicago Press.

Freeman, Jo. 1983. "A Model for Analyzing the Strategic Options of Social Movements," in *Social Movements of the Sixties and Seventies*, ed. by Jo Freeman, 193–210. New York: Longman.

Futrell, Robert and Pete Simi. 2004. "Free Spaces, Collective Identity, and the Persistence of U.S. White Power Activism." *Social Problems* 51: 16–42.

Futrell, Robert, Pete Simi, and Simon Gottschalk. 2006. "Understanding Music in Movements: The White Power Music Scene." *The Sociological Quarterly* 47: 275–304.

Goldstein, Joseph. 2016. "Alt-Right Gathering Exults in Trump Election with Nazi-Era Salute," available at: https://www.nytimes.com/2016/11/21/us/alt-right-salutes-donald-trump.html (accessed October 10, 2017).

Graham, David A. 2018. "Trump Says Democrats Want Immigrants to 'Infest' the U.S.," available at: https://www.theatlantic.com/politics/archive/2018/06/trump-immigrants-infest/563159/ (accessed June 20, 2018).

Graham, Roderick. 2016. "Interideological Mingling: White Extremist Ideology Entering the Mainstream on Twitter." *Sociological Spectrum*, 36, 1: 24–36.

Hirsch, Eric. 1990. *Urban Revolt: Ethnic Politics in the Nineteenth Century Labor Movement.* Berkeley, CA: University of California Press.

Hoffman, David S. 1996. *The Web of Hate: Extremists Exploit the Internet.* New York: Anti-Defamation League.

Holland, Laurel L. and Sherry Cable (2002) "Reconceptualizing Social Movement Abeyance: The Role of Internal Processes and Culture in Cycles of Movement Abeyance and Resurgence." *Sociological Focus*, 35: 3, 297–314.

Jacobson, Louis. 2017. "Are There White Nationalists in the White House?" available at: https://www.politifact.com/truth-o-meter/article/2017/aug/15/are-there-white-nationalists-white-house/ (accessed September 9, 2018).

Johnson, Daryl. 2012. *Right-Wing Resurgence: How a Domestic Terrorist Threat is Being Ignored.* Boulder, CO: Rowman & Littlefield.

Johnston, Hank. 1991. *Tales of Nationalism.* New Brunswick, NJ: Rutgers University Press.

Kelley, Brendan Joel. 2018. "Post-Charlottesville, White Nationalists Double Down on Flash Demonstrations over Public Rallies," available at: https://www.splcenter.org/hatewatch/2018/08/23/post-charlottesville-white-nationalists-double-down-flash-demonstrations-over-public (accessed August 23, 2018).

Kendrick, Richard. 2000. "Swimming against the Tide: Peace Movement Recruitment in an Abeyance Environment," in *Social Conflicts and Collective Identities,* ed. Patrick G. Coy and Lynn M. Woehrle, 189–204. Boulder, CO: Rowman & Littlefield.

Kharakh, Ben and Dan Primack. 2016. "Donald Trump's Social Media Ties to White Supremacists," available at: http://fortune.com/donald-trump-white-supremacist-genocide/ (accessed October 10, 2017).

Klandermans, P.G. 2010. "Legacies from the Past: Eight Cycles of Peace Protest," in *The World Says No to War: Demonstrations against the War in Iraq,* ed. S. Walgrave and D. Rucht, 61–77. Minneapolis, MN: University of Minnesota Press.

Levin, Brian, James J. Nolan, and John David Reitzel. 2018. "New Data Shows US Hate Crimes Continued to Rise in 2017," available at: https://theconversation.com/new-data-shows-us-hate-crimes-continued-to-rise-in-2017-97989 (December 12, 2018).

Marullo, Sam, Ron Pagnucco, Jackie Smith. 1996. "Frame Changes and Social Movement Contraction: U.S. Peace Movement Framing After the Cold War." *Sociological Inquiry,* 66, 1: 1–28.

McAdam, Doug. 1986. "Recruitment to High-Risk Activism: The Case of Freedom Summer." *American Journal of Sociology,* 92: 64–90.

McAdam, Doug. 1988. *Freedom Summer.* Chicago: University of Chicago Press.

McAdam, Doug. 1989. "The Biographical Consequences of Activism." *American Sociological Review,* 54: 744–760.

McAdam, Doug. 1999 [1982]. *Political Process and the Development of Black Insurgency.* Chicago: University of Chicago Press.

McVeigh, Rory. 2009. *The Rise of the Ku Klux Klan: Right-Wing Movements and National Politics.* Minneapolis, MN: University of Minnesota Press.

Melucci, Alberto. 1989. *Nomads of the Present: Social Movements and Individual Needs in Contemporary Society.* Philadelphia: University of Temple Press.

Melucci, Alberto. 1996. *Challenging Codes: Collective Action in the Information Age.* Cambridge: Cambridge University Press.

Meyer, David. 2004. "Protest and Political Opportunities." *Annual Review of Sociology,* 30: 125–145.

Mooney, Patrick H. and Scott A. Hunt. 1996. "Repertoire of Interpretations: Master Frames and Ideological Continuity in U.S. Agrarian Mobilization." *The Sociological Quarterly,* 37: 177–197.

Mutz, Diana. C. 2018. "Status Threat, Not Economic Hardship, Explains the 2016 Presidential Vote." *PNAS* 119, 19: 4330–4339.

Nelson, Libby. 2017. "'Why We Voted for Donald Trump': David Duke Explains the White Supremacist Charlottesville Protests," available at: https://www.vox.com/2017/8/12/16138358/charlottesville-protests-david-duke-kkk (accessed August 20, 2017).

Newkirk, Vann R. 2018. "The End of Civil Rights," available at: https://www.theatlantic.com/politics/archive/2018/06/sessions/563006/ (accessed June 19, 2018).

Perliger, Arie. 2012. "Challengers from the Sidelines: Understanding America's Violent Far- Right," The Combating Terrorism Center at West Point, available at: https://

www.ctc.usma.edu/v2/wp-content/uploads/2013/01/ChallengersFromtheSidelines.pdf (accessed July 6, 2014).

Philips, Amber. 2016. "'They're rapists.' President Trump's campaign launch speech two years later, annotated," available at: https://www.washingtonpost.com/news/the-fix/wp/2017/06/16/theyre-rapists-presidents-trump-campaign-launch-speech-two-years-later-annotated/?noredirect=on&utm_term=.d6ce790fce5f (accessed March 3, 2018).

Pierce, William (as Andrew Macdonald.) 1989. *Hunter*. Hillsboro, VA: National Vanguard Books.

Pizzorno, Alessandro. 1986. "Decision or Interactions? Microanalysis of Social Change." *Rassegna Italiana di Sociologia*, 37: 107–132.

Polletta, Francesca. 1999. "'Free Spaces' in Collective Action." *Theory and Society*, 28:1–38.

Polletta, Francesca and James Jasper. 2001. "Collective Identity and Social Movements." *Annual Review of Sociology*, 27: 283–305.

Posner, Sarah. 2016. "How Donald Trump's New Campaign Chief Created an Online Haven for White Nationalists," available at: https://www.motherjones.com/politics/2016/08/stephen-bannon-donald-trump-alt-right-breitbart-news/ (accessed October 10, 2017).

Raspail, Jean. 1973 (1994). *Camp of the Saints*. Petoskey, MI: Social Contract Press.

Rojas, Fabio. 2007. *From Black Power to Black Studies: How a Radical Social Movement Became an Academic Discipline*. Baltimore, MD: Johns Hopkins University Press.

Rupp, Leila. 2011. "The Persistence of Transnational Organizing: The Case of the Homophile Movement." *American Historical Review*, 116: 1014–1039.

Rupp, Leila and Verta Taylor. 1987. *Survival in the Doldrums: The American Women's Rights Movement, 1945–1960s*. New York: Oxford University Press.

Sawyers, Traci M. and David S. Meyer. 1999. "Missed Opportunities: Social Movement Abeyance and Public Policy." *Social Problems*, 46: 187–206.

Schroer, Todd. 2001. "Issue and Identity Framing within the White Racialist Movement: Internet Dynamics," in *The Politics of Social Inequality: Research in Political Sociology*, Volume 9, ed. A. Dobratz, L.K. Waldner, and T. Buzzell, 27–231. London: Elsevier.

Scott, James C. 1985. *Weapons of the Weak: Everyday Forms of Peasant Resistance*. New Haven, CT: Yale University Press.

Scott, James C. 1990. *Domination and the Arts of Resistance: Hidden Transcripts*. New Haven, CT: Yale University Press.

Simi, Pete, Robert Futrell, and Bryan F. Bubolz. 2016. ">Parenting as Activism: Identity Alignment and Activist Persistence in the White Power Movement." *The Sociological Quarterly*, 57: 491–519.

Simi, Pete and Robert Futrell. 2009. "Negotiating White Power Activist Stigma." *Social Problems*, 56: 89–110.

Simi, Pete and Robert Futrell. 2015. *American Swastika: Inside the White Power Movement's Hidden Spaces of Hate*. Second edition. Lanham, MD: Rowman & Littlefield.

Sonmez, Felicia. 2018. "Trump: I'm a Nationalist and I'm Proud of It," available at: https://www.washingtonpost.com/politics/trump-im-a-nationalist-and-im-proud-of-it/2018/10/23/d9adaae6-d711-711e8-a10f-b51546b10756_story.html?noredirect=on&utm_ term=.6dcee5d229c5 (accessed October 25, 2018).

Southern Poverty Law Center. 2018. "Stephen Miller: A Driving Force behind the Muslim Ban and Family Separation Policy," available at: https://www.splcenter.org/ha

tewatch/2018/06/21/stephen-miller-driving-force-behind-muslim-ban-and-family-separation-policy (accessed June 21, 2018).

Speri, Alice. 2016. "Career Racist Jeff Sessions Is Donald Trump's Pick for Attorney General," available at: https://theintercept.com/2016/11/18/career-racist-jeff-sessions-is-donald-trumps-pick-for-attorney-general/ (accessed October 10, 2017).

Sutton. Joe. 2017. "Godaddy Boots Neo-Nazi Site after a Derogatory Story on the Charlottesville Victim," available at: https://www.cnn.com/2017/08/14/us/godaddy-daily-stormer-website-trnd/index.html (accessed August 20, 2017).

Tarrow, Sidney. 1998 [1994]. *Power in Movement*. Second Edition. Cambridge: Cambridge University Press.

Taylor, Verta. 1989. "Social Movement Continuity." *American Sociological Review*, 54: 761–775.

Taylor, Verta and Alison D. Crossley, 2013. "Abeyance," in *The Wiley-Blackwell Encyclopedia of Social and Political Movements*, ed. David A. Snow, Donatella Della Porta, Bert Klandermans, and Doug McAdam. Hoboken, NJ: Wiley-Blackwell.

Taylor, Verta and Nicole Raeburn. 1995. "Identity Politics as High-Risk Activism: Career Consequences for Lesbian, Gay, and Bi-sexual Sociologists." *Social Problems*, 42: 252–273.

Thrush, Glenn and Maggie Haberman. 2017. "Trump Gives White Supremacists and Unequivocal Boost," available at: https://www.nytimes.com/2017/08/15/us/politics/trump-charlottesville-white-nationalists.html (accessed August 20, 2017).

Tilly, Charles. 1978. *From Mobilization to Revolution*. Reading, MA: Addison-Wesley.

Tilly, Charles. 1984. "Social Movements and National Politics," in *State-Making and Social Movements: Essays in History and Theory*, ed. Charles Bright and Susan Harding, 297–317. Ann Arbor, MI: University of Michigan Press.

Trelease, Allen. 1971. *White Terror: The Ku Klux Klan Conspiracy and Southern Reconstructionism*. New York: HarperCollins.

U.S. Department of Homeland Security. 2009. "Rightwing Extremism: Current Economic and Political Climate Fueling Resurgence in Radicalization and Recruitment," available at: http://www.fas.org/irp/eprint/rightwing.pdf (accessed December 12, 2014).

Veugelers, Jack. 2011. "Dissenting Families and Social Movement Abeyance: The Transmission of Neo-Fascist Frames in Postwar Italy." *British Journal of Sociology*, 62: 241–261.

Veugelers, Jack. 2013. "Neo-Fascist or Revolutionary Leftist: Family Politics and Social Movement Choice in Postwar Italy." *International Sociology*, 28: 429–447.

Weigand, K. 2001. *Red Feminism: American Communism and the Making of Women's Liberation*. Baltimore, MD: Johns Hopkins University Press.

Whalen, Jack and Richard Flacks. 1989. *Beyond the Barricades: the Sixties Generation Grows Up*. Philadelphia: Temple University Press.

White, Jeremy B. 2018. "Jeff Sessions Accused of Fueling Racism after Speech Mentioning 'Anglo-American Heritage' of US Policing," available at: https://www.independent.co.uk/news/world/americas/us-politics/jeff-sessions-attorney-general-law-enforcement-racism- anglo-american-heritage-policing-a8207431.html (accessed September 9, 2018).

Whittier, Nancy. 1991. Feminists in the Post-Feminist Age: Collective Identity and the Persistence of the Women's Movement. Ph.D. Dissertation, Ohio State University.

Whittier, Nancy. 1995. *Feminist Generations: The Persistence of the Radical Women's Movement*. Philadelphia: Temple University Press.

Williams, Jennifer. 2018. "Trump's Tweet Echoing White Nationalist Propaganda about South African Farmers, Explained," available at: https://www.vox.com/policy-and-politics/2018/8/23/17772056/south-africa-trump-tweet-afriforum-white-farmers-violence (accessed September 9, 2018).

Zeskind, Leonard. 2009. *Blood and Politics: The History of the White Nationalist Movement from the Margins to the Mainstream*. New York: Farrar Straus Giroux.

Zidan, Karim. 2018. "Fascist Fight Clubs: How White Nationalists Use MMA as a Recruiting Tool," available at: https://www.theguardian.com/sport/2018/sep/11/far-right-fight-clubs-mma-white-nationalists (accessed September 11, 2018).

6 The biographical consequences of repression
Arab Americans in post-9/11 America

Wayne A. Santoro and Marian Azab

Social movement scholars are well aware that state and non-state repression ultimately targets people. Even when the state attacks a social movement organization, such as when police agents bombed or set fire to the headquarters of Chicano organizations in the sixties, it is always activists who endure the felt-consequences of such aggression. Despite this recognition, it is surprising how little work has documented the impact of repression on the lives of the people who experience it. Movement scholars know a great deal about the ways that repression can encourage or hinder subsequent activism—though, admittedly, the unit of analysis in such work is rarely the individual (Earl 2011). But the imprint of repression encompasses more than just whether it dissuades people from protesting. In this chapter, we extend the boundaries of repression research beyond protest by assessing its varied behavioral, cognitive, and emotional consequences on the lives of the people who are targeted—what we call the biographical consequences of repression. Specifically, we examine whether repression influences conventional political participation, the belief that laws and legal institutions are illegitimate, emotional well-being, and fear. We also assess the link between repression and protest participation to provide a baseline to compare to these results.

Using survey data, our empirical analysis focuses on whether repression pushes people into some behavioral, cognitive, and emotional domains more than other domains. Two issues strike us as interesting. First, we want to know if repression leads people into conventional political activity as frequently as it does protest participation. When repression inspires political engagement, it is reasonable to think that it principally motivates protest rather than conventional political activity like voting because repression undercuts regime legitimacy and hence provides incentives to break from routine behaviors. While that argument makes sense, most people avoid risk when given a choice. This latter observation suggests that repression will prompt people more commonly to pursue conventional political actions because in Western democracies such behaviors are inherently safer than protest. Our analysis is designed to adjudicate between these possibilities.

Second, we are curious if the deleterious consequences of repression, in our case being cynical about legal institutions, emotionally distressed, and fearful, more commonly occur than politically integrative outcomes, namely protest and conventional political participation.

Certainly, no one ever sees repression as manifestly positive. Yet movement scholars often tell stories of noble resistance by emphasizing how activists courageously rebel in oppressive contexts (McAdam 1986; Einwohner 2003; O'Hearn 2009). Indeed, the lion's share of research on the repression–mobilization nexus documents that repression spurs on mobilization, at least conditionally (White 1989; Koopmans 1997; Jenkins and Schock 2004; Santoro and Azab 2015). Under some circumstances, in fact, scholars even argue that movements are more successful if their adherents are repressed (Barkan 1984; Santoro 2008). But we suspect that the story less told is more typical: for most, abuse generates not political engagement but only outcomes like depression, paranoia, and emotional stress. Issues like these can be addressed only when researchers broaden their lens to capture a greater array of biographical consequence that repression may foster.

Our case study centers on Arab Americans shortly after 9/11. Our empirical and theoretical investigation takes seriously the fact that Arab Americans are a racialized population. Largely because of racial dynamics discussed shortly, the immediate post-9/11 context marked the apex of anti-Arab repression in the U.S. (Cainkar 2009; Santoro and Azab 2015; Azab and Santoro 2017). There were 700 incidents of violence against Arab Americans, a 1,600 percent surge in hate crimes, and 19 deaths. The federal government enacted 25 security initiatives that singled out Arabs in the U.S., especially Arab Muslims, resulting in authorities placing 7,000 email addresses under warrantless surveillance, 13,500 deportations, the mandatory registration of 83,000 individuals, and forced FBI interviews of perhaps as many as 200,000 people. While in many state–dissident conflicts authorities target only protestors, the harassment of Arab Americans was not limited to activists. State and non-state actors saw Arab Americans as threatening because of the person's (presumed) ethnic heritage or (supposed) religious creed.

One of the goals of this chapter is to re-think repression to make it better fit the experiences of racial minority populations. In other words, we want to take race seriously. In particular, we highlight that for racial minority populations repression is a common experience not limited to activists, that repression and racial discrimination are one and the same, and that non-state actors are key repressive agents whose actions are closely linked to the state.

Re-conceptualizing repression: Taking race seriously

Three assumptions underlie conventional understandings of repression. First, scholars agree with Tilly (1978) that repression is an action that "raise(s) the contender's cost of collective action" (p. 100). This means that what makes an action repressive is that it targets activists and/or the process that leads people to become activists. Cunningham (2003), for instance, writes that repression is an action that affects protest activities or the capacity of challengers to engage in dissent. Earl (2011) views repression as actions that prevent, control, or constrain protest. Even Ferree (2004: 88–89), who critiques traditional views by offering the concept of "soft" repression, defines such actions as the use of nonviolent power directed at collective identities and the ideas that support collective challenges. Second, because scholars assume that people are exposed to repression only when they protest, repression is seen as uncommon. After all, the vast majority of activists engage in protest only occasionally. Repression is thus viewed as more episodic than a daily lived experience. Third, traditional scholarship sees the state as the principal repressive actor. This is often done empirically with scholars measuring repression as actions carried out by police, government agencies like the FBI, or the military (Tilly 1978; Barkan 1984; White 1989; Koopmans 1997; Cunningham 2003, Einwohner 2003; O'Hearn 2009). Others go further and view state actions as a defining feature of what makes an action repressive. Davenport (1995: fn. 1), for example, thinks of repression as government regulatory action that targets challengers to existing power relationships. Our concern is that these conventional understandings of repression do not align with its experience by racialized populations like Arab Americans. For racial minority populations, in contrast, people are typically targeted for who they are rather than what they did; repression for many is a daily lived experience; and that non-state actors are the most common repressive agent.

We view repression as controlling actions—actions that control what the target feels, thinks, does, and experiences. This definition borrows from Pierce (1989), the scholar who coined the term microaggression, who writes that an oppressor "curbs and controls" the victim's "space, time, energy, and mobility" (p. 308). Repression controls cognitions and feelings. Its manifest intention is to strike fear, to make people feel dehumanized, and among those who would resist it seeks to make people feel that change is inappropriate or impossible. But its latent cognitive and emotional effects are more varied, including constructive and potentially useful outcomes like inspiring in-group solidarity and politicizing orientations; harmful consequences include making people angry, depressed, humiliated, paranoid, and stressed. Repression controls what people do and experience. Its manifest intention is to incapacitate and to dissuade lines of action. For movement scholars, this often means state actions that raise the cost of mobilization. But we see no reason why repression's effects have to be limited to mobilization outcomes. No doubt there are a wide array of latent consequences, some of which may be empowering, like shaping career choices to be in line with politicized identities. Other experiential consequences are detrimental, including undermining physical health, circumscribing everyday routines, and limiting social mobility.

Our approach to understanding repression is influenced by McAdam's (1992) insight that scholars need to more fully take into consideration the social locations of the actors we study. For us, paying attention to social location means that the experiences and consequences of repression differ for racial minority populations compared to Whites. People who are White and middle class may experience repression if they choose to protest against the state, but whether racial minority populations are exposed to repression is not a matter of choice (Morris and Braine 2001). Populations like Arab Americans, African Americans, and Mexican Americans are repressed *because* they are Arab, Black, or Mexican. Police repress Blacks, for instance, if they are "protesting while Black" (Davenport, Soule, and Armstrong 2011) or "driving while Black." Arab Americans are repressed if they advocate for Palestinian rights (Naber 2012) or for "flying while Arab." In both of these examples, calling the former repression but not the latter is an artificial and unhelpful distinction. Our approach is meant to capture experiences that race scholars label police abuse, microaggressions, chronic or everyday racism, acute discrimination, and direct institutional discrimination. Too often movement scholars either ignore these actions or do not label them as repression. For instance, Shultziner (2013) argues that the escalation of "contentious interactions" between White bus drivers and Black passengers helped spark the 1955 Montgomery bus boycott while Santoro and Broidy (2014) find that "police mistreatment" motivated Black riot participation in the late sixties. These studies do not use the "repression" nomenclature but what they discuss and measure, we believe, is repression. Racial discrimination *is* repression and to think otherwise is to be ignorant of race in America.

Movement scholarship has been slow to take race seriously. It is true that sociologists have devoted considerable attention to the modern civil rights movement. But other eras of Black resistance, including contemporary activism and slave resistance, have been understudied or ignored. With a few noteworthy exceptions (e.g., 1960s farm workers movement) sociologists have devoted even less attention to other racial minority populations. More challenging, there are deeper ways to think about what it means to take race seriously. Liu (2018), for instance, notes that researchers in the field often ignore theoretical tools developed by race scholars, such as intersectionality and critical race theory. Another way to take race seriously is to theorize how racial/ethnic minority movements differ from majority-White movements. A rare exception is Oliver (2017) who writes that minority movements have greater exposure to repression, are more dependent on allies, and are more likely to use community-based networks for mobilization.

Related, we think that movement scholars underappreciate how movement processes can be racially variant—what leads Whites to protest, for instance, does not necessarily parallel the process for people of color. For example, the construction of collective identity is different for racially oppressed populations who, unlike White majority movements, are rarely unaware of injustice (Morris and Braine 2001).

Not everyone would agree with the merits of our attempt to rethink repression. One point of contention concerns who scholars see as the social control agent. As noted earlier, most scholars focus on the state, an approach that is buttressed given the vast resources, coercive capacity, and public legitimacy accorded to state action. Our approach gives more attention to non-state actors in that acts of repression like verbal abuse, which we note shortly is the most common type of repression experienced by Arab Americans, is typically instigated by non-state actors. We do not deny the importance of the state; half of African Americans surveyed in 2017, for instance, report experiencing discrimination when interacting with the police (Victor 2018). Yet keep in mind that most people can avoid interacting with state actors on a daily basis but almost no one can avoid interacting with non-state actors. These are the people who are our neighbors, acquaintances, and co-workers. These are the people we interact with when we buy groceries, purchase gasoline for our car, or stand in line for a morning cup of coffee. These are the people who determine if we get hired, receive a bank loan, or obtain appropriate medical advice. Being repressed by non-state actors means that the locations where people are repressed are ubiquitous, making it especially pertinent to a person's lived experiences (Johnston 1991).

A focus on the state also ignores the fact that for stigmatized populations there are blurred boundaries between state and non-state actions. The state, for instance, often inspires non-state repression. To illustrate, within ten days of Donald J. Trump's election there were 844 hate incidents by non-state actors targeting immigrants, Blacks, Muslims, women, Jews, and LGBT people (Southern Poverty Law Center [SPLC] 2016). Many assailants, in fact, invoked Trump's name during their attack, as when a man verbally accosted a Muslim woman in an elevator by saying "Fuckin' sand-nigger. Thank God Trump is now president. He's gonna deport your terrorist ass" (SPLC 2016: 10; see also Council on American–Islamic Relations [CAIR] 2018). Additionally, the boundaries between state and non-state actions are muddled because non-state actors can call on the resources of the state when they repress. It is not uncommon for Whites to request police intervention when they feel threatened by racial minorities who are simply trying to go about their everyday lives. To illustrate, Whites recently found the following situations involving African Americans threatening enough to call the police: a group of women playing golf too slowly, a Yale graduate student asleep in the lounge of her student dorm, two men grilling out by the shore of an Oakland lake, and two people waiting for a business companion to arrive at a Philadelphia Starbucks (Victor 2018). Such enmity is not reserved for Blacks. In April of 2018, a White parent on a tour of Colorado State University called the police on two Native American high-school students on the same tour because she thought the students were, among other transgressions, suspiciously quiet.

Another potential concern with our approach is that some may see verbal insults and other actions akin to microaggressions as not severe enough to warrant the label of repression. The flaw to that reasoning is to assume that microaggressions are not serious. As race scholars point out, everyday experiences with discrimination undermine mental health and physical well-being. Among other outcomes, it causes psychological distress, feelings of powerlessness, paranoia, anxiety disorder, self-hared, psychosis, depression, anger, and elevated mortality risks; it undercuts self-esteem and psychological well-being such as happiness and life satisfaction; and it leads to negative coping strategies like cigarette smoking, alcohol use, and early initiation into substance use (Williams et al. 1997; Brown 2003; Williams et al. 2003; Sue, Capodilupo, and Holder 2008).

In sum, we have tried to take race seriously by aligning the concept of repression with its experience by racial minority populations. This leads us to highlight how common repression is for racial minority populations given its overlap with everyday forms of racial mistreatment, to emphasize that non-state actors are key repressive agents even though their actions are intertwined with the state, and to underscore that repression is directed at activists and non-activists alike given that racialized populations are targeted most typically because of who they are rather than what they did.

The racialization and repression of Arab Americans

Our theoretical approach to repression is grounded in the fact that, like other racial minority populations in the U.S., Arab Americans are racialized. We turn now to a brief discussion of the causes and consequences of their racialized experiences. The popular account is that the terrorists' attacks on the World Trade Center and the Pentagon motivated the state and its citizens to repress Arab Americans. That narrative is wrong. The genesis of anti-Arab repression lies not with acts of domestic terrorism but rather with the pre-9/11 racialization of the population (Cainkar 2009; Azab and Santoro 2017). State and non-state actors, as well as the mass media, socially construct Arab Americans to be a "race" that is distinct and innately inferior to Whites. Outsiders presume, at times inaccurately, that someone is of Arab ancestry based on markers like phenotype, mode of dress, and language. This Arab American otherness is expressed in beliefs that the population is religiously extremist, unreceptive to democratic institutions, exploitive of women if they are men or hopelessly submissive if they are women, and that their presumed rage against Western civilization fuels their terrorist proclivities. As Cainkar (2009) points out, the repressive situation that Arab Americans confronted after 9/11 paralleled what Japanese Americans encountered after the attack on Pearl Harbor in 1941. The U.S. government interned around 77,000 Japanese American citizens, rather than citizens of Italian or German heritage, because unlike these latter populations only the Japanese were viewed as an inferior, alien, and threatening race.

Another flaw to the "9/11 caused repression" narrative is that it obscures the fact that anti-Arab repression pre-dates 2001. After the 1967 Arab–Israeli war, domestic Zionist organizations pushed the federal government to see Arabs living in the U.S. as a domestic threat to U.S. interests in the Middle East (Fischbach 1985). This was especially the case for Arab Americans advocating for a more balanced U.S. positon toward Palestine. In response to the 1972 attack on the Israeli Olympic team in Munich, the Nixon administration instituted a coordinated effort among federal agencies, codenamed Operation Boulder, which targeted people of Arab heritage (Stork and Theberge 1973; Hagopian 1975/1976). The INS made it difficult for people from the Arab world to acquire U.S. visas and deported non-citizen Arabs, often college students, for minor visa violations. The FBI led a campaign of surveillance and intimidation. A typical tactic was for agents to show up in the early morning hours of a person's home, illegally search it, and then begin their interview by falsely accusing the person of belonging to a terrorist organization (Fischbach 1985). Agents singled out political activists, illustrated with the government's twenty-one-year attempt to deport eight individuals accused of providing aid to a Palestinian political organization (MacFarquhar 2007). Operation Boulder existed from 1972 to 1975, but aspects of it survived, especially the monitoring and harassment of individuals engaged in activities critical of U.S. Middle Eastern policies (Naber 2012). Throughout the pre-9/11 period, Arab Americans were victims of violent attacks. For instance, three offices of the American-Arab Anti-Discrimination Committee were bombed in 1985, resulting in the still unsolved murder of regional director Alex Odeh. Three days after the 1995 bombing of the federal building in Oklahoma City, there were 222 incidents of anti-Arab/Muslim harassment and seven attacks on mosques in the mistaken belief that Arab Americans were responsible (Suleiman 1999).

While repression predates 9/11, it peaked in 2001. State actors played a key role. For space considerations, we draw on Apuzzo and Goldman (2014) and focus our attention on the less well-known actions of the New York Police Department (NYPD). More Arab Americans live in New York City than any other city. The "Intel" division of the NYPD, in operation from 2002 to 2014, spearheaded the surveillance of Arab/Muslims within and outside of the city's jurisdiction. With a staggering annual budget of three billion dollars, Intel recruited undercover agents, including Middle Eastern and Muslim police officers, imams, local residents, as well as people with criminal records because such prior transgressions could be used as leverage to compel their participation. Intel particularly targeted mosques. Outside of mosques, agents recorded license plate numbers of cars in parking lots and placed hidden cameras on nearby light poles to monitor the area's activities. Within mosques, agents copied phone numbers and e-mail addresses of people who signed up for study groups, tape recorded conversations, noted who led prayers, and kept tabs on those who donated money to Muslim charities. The program aspired to have an informant in every mosque within 250 miles of New York City. In local restaurants, *halal* delis, coffee shops, and travel agencies, informants monitored people's conversations, noted the ethnicity of owners and customers, and recorded who watched Arabic-language television programs such as Al Jazeera. Informants infiltrated community meetings and rallies as well as private religious ceremonies like weddings and funerals. In institutions of higher education, agents infiltrated Muslim college associations, kept records on who attended the lectures of Muslim scholars, and noted what topics were discussed. Intel's "X Team" pulled over Arab American drivers at random to record the driver's name and to photograph their identification papers. Law enforcement interviewed Arabic-surname individuals who Americanized their name as well as individuals who did the reverse. Agents also nefariously acted as agent provocateurs by offering to sell bombs and weapons to Muslim Americans.

State actions and rhetoric encouraged non-state actors to target the population. When Arab Americans experience repression, non-state actors most often perpetrate it (Santoro and Azab 2015: Figure 3). Common sites for mistreatment include interactions with strangers in public places, like on sidewalks, at gas stations, or in grocery stores; mistreatment by classmates in schools; and hostility by employers, co-workers, and customers in workplaces. Using data from the Detroit Arab American Study (Baker et al. 2003), Figure 6.1 shows the share who experienced repressive incidents within two years of 9/11. The most common repressive experience is verbal insults and among respondents one-quarter report some form of abuse. Based on a smaller but national sample taken in early October of 2001, Zogby (2001) finds that 20 percent of Arab Americans experienced discrimination because of their ethnicity since 9/11. Both sources suggest that most did not directly encounter mistreatment, but if we extrapolate these findings to the entire Arab-ancestry population in 2000 it implies that a staggering 500,000 to 700,000 Arab Americans endured post-9/11 backlash.

Anti-Arab/Muslim repression has resurged. Figure 6.2 traces the number of victims of anti- Muslim hate crimes from 1995 to 2016 and shows a noticeable spike in the last two years. In 2016, there also was a 197 percent increase in the number of anti-Muslim hate organizations compared to the previous year (SPLC 2017). In 2017, there were 2,599 reports of anti-Muslim/Arab bias incidents, an 84 percent increase in the last two years (CAIR 2018). There were more attacks on mosques in 2016 and 2017 than any previous year

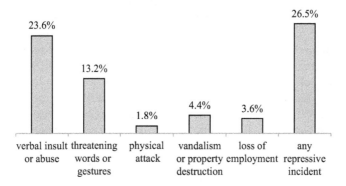

Figure 6.1 Percentage of Arab Americans who report repression two years after 9/11.
Source: Detroit Arab American Study.

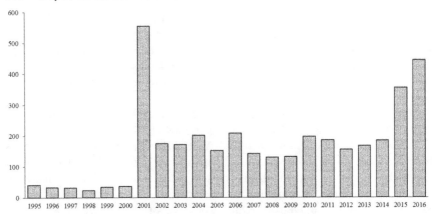

Figure 6.2 Number of victims of anti-Islamic hate crimes, 1995 to 2016.
Note: The FBI began collecting data on anti-Arab American hate crimes in 2015 and these data are included in the total for 2015 (n = 48) and 2016 (n = 57).
Source: FBI Uniform Crime Reports.

(Fadel 2018). As noted above, the presidential campaign and election of Trump inspired much of this outpouring of hate. CAIR (2018: 35) summarizes it well: "The 45th president's brazen display of animosity and prejudice has emboldened individuals seeking to express their bias and made the very word 'Trump' an encapsulating and potent symbol of wide-ranging racial and religious animus." The hostility of the contemporary climate renders our analysis of repression effects shortly after 9/11 relevant today and highlights that 9/11 was not merely a temporary setback for Arab Americans but part of the long-term trend (Alimahomed 2011).

The biographical consequences of repression

The post-9/11 repression of Arab Americans neither is reserved for protestors nor is its manifest intention directed at hindering subsequent activism. These circumstances provide an opportunity to ask what happens to people—activists and nonactivists alike—who personally experience repression. Analogous to research on the biographical consequences of activism, we refer to an investigation of this sort as the biographical consequences of repression. Experiencing repression likely leaves an indelible mark on a variety of personal and political cognitions, emotions, and behaviors but we are hard pressed to identify movement scholarship, besides work accounting for protest, that has done so in a systematic manner. Research on the biographical consequences of activism demonstrates how protest participation can impact marital status, career choices, earnings, political orientation, party identification, policy views, civic participation, organizational involvement, and of course ensuing activism (Fendrich 1974; McAdam 1989, 1992; Taylor and

Raeburn 1995; Sherkat and Blocker 1997; Van Dyke, McAdam, and Wilhelm 2000). Protest participation shapes a person's subsequent life because it can be an intense experience that alters attitudes, values, and schematic orientations. In this regard, protest involvement is a learning experience, an agent of re-socialization. Activism also matters because it further embeds people into an activist social network, deepening a person's emersion in the network's subculture (McAdam 1989).

These causal relationships stemming from activism should parallel those of repression given that, like activism, it is an intense, stressful, and at times a life-threatening experience. Moreover, repression based on group membership is a shared grievance that can build social bonds and a sense of linked fate. No doubt there are strong emotional imprints stemming from repression as well. Interestingly, scholars note that high-risk activism is a powerful experience in part because many activists are repressed during protest campaigns, leaving open the possibility that some of what scholars identify as the consequences of activism may in fact be the consequences of repression (Taylor and Raeburn 1995).

Figure 6.3 presents a visual depiction of the type of research we are advocating. The top arrow connecting repression to protest is well covered in the movement literature, especially at the macro-level. The left-hand-side arrows

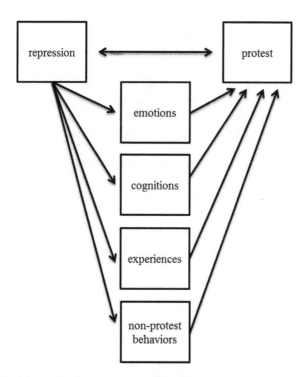

Figure 6.3 The biographical consequences of repression.

linking repression to cognitions, emotions, experiences, and (non-protest) behaviors illustrate the neglected types of biographical consequences of repression. We advocate that scholars who study repression pay greater attention to uncovering the breadth of lived experiences of stigmatization. It behooves researchers who want to understand repression to investigate the multidimensional and holistic ways that repression matters. But for those who remain wedded to the repression–mobilization nexus, Figure 6.3 makes clear another payoff for investigating the biographical consequences of repression. The right-hand-side arrows connecting the biographical consequences of repression to protest illustrate *indirect* ways that repression can shape protest.

Indirect effects are likely because the related literature on the consequences of activism find both direct and indirect effects (Fendrich 1974; McAdam 1989). If scholars wish to direct greater attention to the mechanisms by which repression affects mobilization, a good place to start is to focus on the causal sequence: repression → biographical outcomes → protest.

Living in the post-9/11 context shaped the biographies of many Arab Americans, although research in this area rarely compares people who experienced repression to those who did not. Some suffered economically. In the Detroit area, 4 percent of Arab American respondents reported losing a job because of post-9/11 backlash (Figure 6.1). The earnings of men from Arab and Muslim-majority countries fell by about 10 percent following 9/11, especially in states with elevated levels of hate crime (Kaushal, Kaestner, and Reimers 2007). Arab American physical and mental health declined, as Naber's (2006) ethnographic research in the San Francisco area found. Many of her respondents experienced an "internment of the psyche, or the general sense that one is always being watched and could at any time be attacked, deported, or disappeared" (p. 255). Lauderdale (2006) documents in California a spike in preterm births and low birth weights for Arabic-named women who were already pregnant on 9/11. Alimahomed's (2011) research suggests identity effects. She interviewed young Arab American Muslims in Los Angeles who came of age in post-9/11 America and found that the climate of hostility led to a heightened awareness of race such that they dis-identified with Whiteness. Others find quotidian disruptions, such as people avoiding public spaces, not riding on city buses, or eschewing commercial airline flights (Beitin and Allen 2005; Cainkar 2009).

Investigating the biographical consequences of repression

Repression can have wide-ranging biographical affects, but the data repository we draw on renders our empirical reach more modest. The survey we use allows us to investigate the short- term consequences of repression as there is only about a two-year time lag between 9/11 and the outcomes we examine. Moreover, our investigation is narrowed to outcomes that we can identify as having taken place after the peak of repression in 2001 so that we can better establish temporal order. These considerations lead us to limit our analysis to five outcomes.

We begin by establishing how repression influences post-9/11 protest participation so as to establish a baseline to compare to other results.[1] We then turn to the association between repression and post-9/11 conventional political participation. Movement scholars sometime underplay participation in routine political activities, even though most movements in Western democracies use institutional strategies to promote social change. We expect repression to motivate routine civic engagement because mistreatment politicizes attitudes and identities. Being treated unfairly is a grievance that can be framed as unjust and potentially malleable, brings about emotions like moral outrage and anger, and generates a sense of collective identity and linked fate. In democracies, politicized ways of thinking and feeling should prompt political behaviors directed at conventional or institutional activity. But does repression push people into conventional political activity as frequently as it does protest participation? Koopmans (1993) writes that repression can encourage conventional activity because it is a safer political act than protesting. Assuming that people will often take the less risky path when afforded the option, this suggests that repression will lead more people to participate conventionally than non-institutionally. Tarrow (1993), in fact, argues that this is one reason why conventional political actions far outnumber confrontational actions during protest cycles. Alternatively, mistreatment may push more people to protest than to engage in conventional politics. The state may lose legitimacy when repression is either carried out by the state or is inspired by state actions and rhetoric. People may see little reason to act in routine, state-sanctioned ways when the state itself is acting illegitimately. Such conditions can lead people to break with conventional behaviors (Piven and Cloward 1979). Our investigation can assess if repression is more likely to stimulate protest or conventional political activity.

Next, we investigate three detrimental outcomes, with an eye to assessing whether repression pushes people into these outcomes more commonly than the politically integrative outcomes noted above. We first look to legal cynicism, which means viewing the law as unresponsive and illegitimate. Criminologists, political scientists, and race scholars use the term when discussing how enduring hostile encounters with the criminal justice system renders American Blacks skeptical of the legal system. Studies have shown that African Americans, especially those living in areas of aggressive policing or acute poverty, doubt that police and the courts will treat them fairly. Legal cynicism, in turn, can lead to a variety of other negative outcomes, such as enhancing neighborhood levels of homicide and undermining positive involvement with actors in the criminal justice system (Bobo and Thompson 2006; Kirk and Papachristos 2011). We hypothesize that repression will make Arab Americans legally cynical. This is because *state* anti-Arab/Islamophobic rhetoric and actions fuels non-state actors to repress Arab Americans. President Bush's speeches, for instance, constructed an image of the new American enemy as Muslim and Arab. President Trump's venomous actions and words have taken hatred to a new level. Emblematic of his actions were his legal efforts to ban citizens from sixteen Muslim-majority countries from traveling to the U.S. as well as his attempts to block refugees who are Muslim from entering the country.[2]

Our last two hypothesized outcomes focus on emotional well-being, namely fear and psychological distress. Movement scholars are largely silent on mental health outcomes, perhaps because past generations of researchers held the discredited belief that activists have abnormal psychological profiles. But it is reasonable to think that repression undermines mental health because stressful events are a key predictor of negative emotional states (Williams et al. 1997; Williams, Neighbors, and Jackson 2003). Repression is stressful, often frightening, and at times traumatic. In a recent article, we have linked repression to fear among Arab Americans (Azab and Santoro 2017) and we present those findings in this study, slightly re-analyzed, so that that relationship can be placed within the context of this study. Psychological distress refers to feeling sad, anxious, hopeless, and experiencing unpleasant behavioral symptoms like being nervous as well as having malaise and depressed moods. We have already reviewed research on how everyday experiences of discrimination leads to psychological distress among African Americans, and we expect repression to affect Arab Americans similarly.

Data and methods

We use the Detroit Arab American Study (DAAS) (Baker et al. 2003), a face-to-face representative sample of 1,016 adults who self-identified as Arab or Chaldean (Christian Iraqis) living in the Detroit three-county metropolitan area. The survey, often conducted in Arabic, was administered between July and December of 2003. The response rate was 74 percent. Greater details on the probability sampling procedures can be found in the online documentation of the dataset in the ICPSR archives (https://www.icpsr.umich.edu/icpsrweb/ICPSR/studies/04413). We think the survey is ideal as it was designed to capture 9/11 impacts. Moreover, the principal investigators consulted more than twenty organizations that serve the local Arab population and their input helped generate culturally sensitive questions.

Such organizations made people feel safe in participating in the study because they publicized and endorsed the survey. It also is ideal that the survey was administered in the Detroit area given the locations long-standing, large, and geographically concentrated Arab community.

Before detailing operationalizations, we point out that it is not possible to unequivocally establish temporal order between repression and the outcomes we investigate. We do not know precisely when a repressive incident occurred, and for chronic forms of mistreatment respondents are not likely to remember the exact dates of events. Moreover, about half of the people who recalled a repressive incident in our sample report more than one hostile encounter, making pinpointing the timing of repression problematic. In general, no clear methodological procedure exists to fully take into consideration the temporal and cumulative aspects of mistreatment. The logic of our approach is to make the plausible assumption that repression first occurred close to September 2001 (see Figure 6.2). This assumption is buttressed by the Human Rights

Watch as well as the American-Arab Anti-Discrimination Committee which noted that the spike in anti-Arab repression after 9/11 returned to "normal" levels by December of 2001 (Lauderdale 2006). We then selected outcomes that took place as close as possible to the administration of the survey roughly two years later. In most cases we selected dependent variables that the respondent reported occurred "in the past 12 months." Thus, depending on when a given respondent was interviewed, the outcomes we investigate took place between ten to fifteen months after the likely date of the (first) repressive incident. In addition, the causal logic of our temporal-order assumptions is buttressed by the fact that there is no clear substantive argument concerning why outcomes like psychological distress would cause repression.

Dependent variables

Post-9/11 protest refers to whether the respondent in the past 12 months took part in a protest, march, or demonstration (1 = yes, 0 = no). Post-9/11 civic participation means the respondent in the past 12 months attended a public meeting where there was a discussion of civic affairs and/or contacted a government official to express an opinion on a political issue (1 = yes, 0 = no). The DAAS includes other likeminded political behaviors, such as making campaign donations and voting, but only the two indicators we select can be linked definitively to post- 9/11 actions. Legal cynicism compares respondents who had no confidence, or not very much confidence, in the U.S. legal system (= 1) to those with a great deal or a lot of confidence in the legal system (= 0). Legal cynicism is not benchmarked to post 2001 feelings but it is entirely plausible that respondents would be answering the question in reference to current circumstances. Psychological distress is coded 1 if in the past 12 months the respondent felt tired for no good reason, nervous, hopeless, restless and fidgety, depressed, worthless, and/or that everything was an effort. People without any of those seven distresses were coded 0. To capture fear of repression, respondents were asked how much, if any, the events of 9/11 shook their own personal sense of safety and security. We coded people as afraid if they felt "a good amount" or a "great deal" of fear (= 1), 0 otherwise.[3]

Independent and control variables

Non-state repression means that the respondent, because of his or her race, ethnicity, or religion, experienced in the last two years any of the following: verbal insults, threats, assaults, property destruction, and/or lost a job. As a robustness check, we re-operationalized repression into three dummy variables separating verbal insults (akin to Ferree's [2004] soft repression), severe repression (threats, assaults, property destruction, and/or job loss), and no repression (omitted category), but multivariate results from these analyses show similar findings as those we report. In bivariate analysis discussed shortly, we show the similarity of effects between soft and severe repression. For models predicting conventional civic participation, we include whether the respondent voted in the 2000 presidential election to purge our estimation for the respondents' propensity to have been engaged in pre-9/11 conventional political activity. All models control for organizational membership, socioeconomic status (SES), age, gender, nativity, religion, race, and national origin. In analysis not shown, we find repression is greater for those who are young, U.S.-born, higher SES, and do not self-identify as White. Muslims are also more likely to be repressed than Christians, but only when job loss is considered. The inclusion of these variables in our models helps isolate the effect of repression from factors that predict being repressed.

Method of analysis

We analyze our dichotomous dependent variables using logistic regression. We exclude cases with missing data on a given dependent variable, resulting in sample sizes that range from 1,012 for post-9/11 protest to 985 for legal cynicism. Using Stata 15.1, all data are weighted to correct for the unequal probability of household selection.

Findings

Table 6.1 presents the bivariate relationships between repression and the five dependent variables. The first column shows means for the entire sample, the second column selects people who were not repressed, and the remaining columns look at those who report any repression (column 3), soft repression (verbal insults, column 4), or severe repression (column 5). Table 6.1 highlights the biographical consequences of repression. Regardless of the measure of repression, about 21 percent of those repressed joined a protest event while less than 8 percent did so without a repressive experience. Across all repression measures, about half of the sample participated in a conventional civic act while about one-third did so without a hostile encounter. Experiencing repression nearly doubled the share of the population who lacked confidence in the

Table 6.1 Biographical consequences of repression among Arab Americans after 9/11: bivariate results

	Total Sample	*Repression Experience*			
		None	Any Repression	Soft Repression	Severe Repression
Protested after 9/11 (%)	11.11	7.65	20.76**	21.05**	20.58**
Civic Participation after 9/11 (%)	41.07	37.00	52.43**	51.53**	52.98**
Legal Cynicism (%)	33.73	27.64	50.19**	53.04**	48.47**
Psychological Distress (%)	35.15	30.60	47.44**	43.58**	49.75**
Fear (%)	48.16	45.21	56.28**	51.77	58.98**

U.S. legal system. Fear is significantly higher for people who experienced any or severe repression, although being afraid is the only outcome where soft repression does not matter. In sum, bivariate results highlight ways that repression has a controlling influence on emotions, cognitions, and behaviors.

Table 6.2 presents multivariate results. Adjusted for controls, model 1 reveals that experiencing repression prompted Arab Americans in metropolitan Detroit to protest, a finding Santoro and Azab (2015) uncovered earlier. As they argue, rather than withdrawing from public space, repression mobilizes Arab Americans because it undermines regime legitimacy, heightens activist commitment, generates emotions conducive to protest, and exacerbates discontent. Less well documented, model 2 shows that repression motivates people to participate in conventional political activity. We speculated that repression would have this effect because it politicizes ways of thinking and feeling and such energy can motivate not only protest but also routine political actions.

But does repression lead people to protest or participate in routine political activities more? To assess this issue, we calculated how much more likely people were to protest who had experienced repression compared to those who did not experience repression, averaged across the sample values of the predictors in the model (i.e., average marginal effects). We find that the predicated probability of protest was 8.8 percent for people without a repressive experience and 15.8 percent for people who were repressed. The first bar in Figure 6.4 displays the *difference* between these predicted probabilities. The resulting percent means that among people who are repressed, 7 percent more are predicated to have protested. We followed this procedure for the routine forms of civic engagement and found that among people who were repressed, about 11 percent more became civically engaged because of repression. Repression, in other words, prods more people to engage in conventional than unconventional political activity.

Given our interest in the consequences of repression for *people*, Figure 6.4 also shows the number of people who repression likely pushed into experiencing a given outcome. To calculate this number, we multiplied the proportion of Arab Americans who reported repression in the DAAS survey (.265) times the number of Arab American adults (18+) living in the metropolitan Detroit three-county area in 2000 (84,238 people out of a total Arab-ancestry population of 130,865) times the difference between the predicted probability people protested who were repressed minus the probability of protest for those not repressed (.07). Our models suggest that repression increased the number of protestors by 1,563 people but civic engagement by 2,411 people. While there is considerable attention in the movement literature to the effect of repression on non-institutional activity, such studies miss the even larger effect that mistreatment has on encouraging people to join more low-risk and conventional political activities. The state may lose legitimacy when people are repressed, but this apparently does not mean that individuals necessarily break away from state-sanctioned political behaviors. We suspect our findings are driven by the fact that our analysis takes place in a contemporary Western

Table 6.2 Weighted logistic regressions of impact of repression on biographical outcomes among Arab Americans after 9/11

	Post-9/11 Protest Model 1		Post-9/11 Civic Participation Model 2		Post-9/11 Legal Cynicism Model 3		Psychological Distress Model 4		Psychological Fear Model 5	
	b	SE	b	SE	b	SE	b	SE	b	SE
Post-9/11 Repression										
Experienced Repression	0.737 **	0.257	0.493 **	0.180	0.828 **	0.175	0.676 **	0.176	0.575 **	0.167
Controls										
Organizational Member	0.976 **	0.294	0.477 **	0.168	0.451 **	0.175	0.023	0.179	−0.081	0.161
Socioeconomic Status	0.168 *	0.083	0.164 **	0.050	0.078	0.048	−0.161 **	0.051	−0.109 *	0.046
Young Age	0.294 *	0.121	0.047	0.076	−0.006	0.072	0.181 *	0.071	−0.074	0.069
Female	−0.106	0.249	0.473 **	0.154	0.118	0.159	0.259	0.158	0.283	0.146
US Born	0.405	0.286	0.180	0.198	0.572 **	0.190	−0.009	0.194	−0.320	0.186
Muslim[1]	1.373 **	0.375	0.056	0.211	0.279	0.200	0.019	0.205	0.203	0.190
White	−0.100	0.256	−0.399 *	0.170	−0.037	0.172	−0.204	0.167	−0.216	0.156
Iraqi[2]	0.207	0.427	−0.149	0.227	−0.049	0.221	0.333	0.219	−0.250	0.207
Palestinian[2]	0.716	0.479	−0.615	0.320	0.106	0.339	−0.083	0.342	0.159	0.310

The biographical repression consequences 157

Other Arab[2]	0.288	0.321	−0.018	0.197	−0.191	0.199	0.058	0.199	0.138	0.187
Voted in 2000	–	–	0.750 **	0.173	–	–	–	–	–	–
Constant	−4.515 **	0.594	−1.108 **	0.330	−1.339 **	0.325	−1.435 **	0.311	−0.006 **	0.289
F-Statistic	5.47 **		7.48 **		4.81 **		4.33 **		3.47 **	
Number of Observations	1,012		1,006		985		989		1,007	

Notes: [1] reference category Christian; [2] reference category Syrian/Lebanese; * p ≤.05, ** p ≤.01 (two-tailed test)

158 *Wayne A. Santoro and Marian Azab*

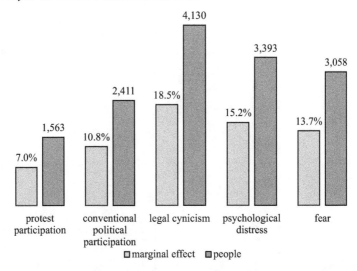

Figure 6.4 Comparing the biographical consequences of repression across outcomes.

democracy, contexts where conventional participation is inherently safer than protesting (Santoro and Segura 2011).

There also is reason to believe that most Arab Americans viewed the *local* political system as being receptive to their grievances. For instance, Dearborn police patrolled Arab neighborhoods and mosques by the early afternoon of September 11 to dissuade retaliation and that actions like these made the community feel safer in Dearborn than outside it (Human Rights Watch 2002; Santoro and Azab 2015). Within the first week of the attacks the local government released six statements warning its citizens about backlash against Arab Americans. The Arab Community Center for Economic and Social Services received $5 million in corporate and private donations to fund its cultural programs, including sensitivity training for law enforcement who dealt with Arab Americans (Howell and Shryock 2003). If all politics are indeed local, the perceived receptivity of the local political system may have made participating in routine political activities seem worthwhile.

We have demonstrated thus far that repression can have politically integrative consequences. Our concern is that such a focus obscures what we suspect is the much more common negative consequences that repression has on the lives of people who endure the mistreatment. The remaining findings in Table 6.2 and Figure 6.4 demonstrate this. Table 6.2 shows that repression generates legal cynicism (model 3), psychological distress (model 4), and fear (model 5). While movement scholars often focus solely on the politically integrative features of repression, Figure 6.4 reveals that the detrimental consequences more commonly occur. Among those repressed, 18% more became legally cynical, 15% more became psychologically distressed, and 14%

more became afraid. All of these percentages are higher, and sometimes considerably higher, than the repression effects for the politically integrative outcomes. To translate these percentages into counts of people, our models imply that repression made 4,130 people legally cynical, 3,393 people psychologically distressed, and 3,058 people fearful. In other words, compared with the numbers we estimated on the previous page, the one outcome most highlighted by movement scholars (protest) is the *least* likely outcome to result from repression. This observation underscores our apprehension that the movement literature has a decidedly optimist tilt as it is much more replete with stories of bold resistance in high-risk contexts than it is with what we think are more common stories of hardship and despair flowing from repression.

Conclusion

We are surprised that social movement scholars have paid so little systematic attention to how repression alters outcomes outside of making people more or less likely to protest. We hope our work encourages researchers who study repression to cast their net more broadly by investigating a greater range of biographical consequences of repression, including its impact on cognitions, emotions, experiences, and behaviors not limited to protest. One of the advantages of doing so is that it better connects the social movement field to other academic areas, including health researchers who study psychological distress, criminologists who investigate legal cynicism, and political scientists who focus on conventional political activity.

We take a step in that direction by looking at the short-term effects of repression on Arab Americans in the immediate post-9/11 context. While our findings are grounded in the aftermath of the terrorists' attacks in 2001, the resurgence of hate directed at Arab Americans and other stigmatized populations suggest the contemporary relevance of our results. We find that repression makes people civically engaged but also legally cynical, psychologically distressed, and fearful. It also stimulates protest participation. Experiencing repression first-hand is personally transforming and we are not surprised that it has wide-ranging consequences. While repression matters across all outcomes, it leads greater shares to engage in conventional political activity than protest. Moreover, the detrimental consequences of repression more commonly occur than the politically integrative outcomes. Perhaps this latter finding is not surprising, although it is an observation that is obscured by the tendency of movement research about the effects of repression to spotlight tales of noble resistance in high-risk contexts. Our focus on one population, in one historical moment, and in one Western democracy highlight the need for additional research.

Another goal of our study was to re-think repression. We find it helpful to think about repression as controlling actions and we have tried to spotlight ways that repression experienced by racial minority populations differs from that of Whites. Specifically, we have emphasized the role of non-state actors in repressing people, acknowledged the strong link between the repressive actions of non-state actors and the racial state, and emphasized the overlap between repression and forms of mistreatment that race scholars label microaggressions, chronic discrimination, and the like. We recognize that as conceptualizations broaden they run the risk of losing usefulness. For movement scholars who study constituencies who are ill-treated only because of what they do rather than who they are, such an expansion of the concept of repression may prove less helpful. Thus, researchers who study largely White middle-class movements, like activists for the student movement in the seventies, the nuclear freeze movement in the eighties, and the Resistance movement today, may find traditional definitions of repression adequate. But we hope our approach proves useful for scholars who want to understand how repression shapes outcomes, including protest, among populations who are repressed for traits they are born with. Scholars who study racial inequality have produced a rich literature on the consequences of mistreatment on the lives of minority populations and we hope our work makes clearer the connections between this literature and the social movement field. More broadly, we hope our chapter makes clearer ways that the movement field can take race more seriously.

Notes

1 A more elaborate discussion of how repression affects Arab American protest-participation can be found in Santoro and Azab (2015).
2 In June 2018, the Supreme Court upheld the Trump administration's ban on travel to the U.S. from six predominantly Muslim countries. Currently, the ban on refugees from Muslim-majority countries is lifted but new vetting policies have been enacted that have severely curtailed the number of refugees being resettled.
3 Our motivation to code civic participation, legal cynicism, psychological distress, and fear as dichotomous variables is that it allows us to compare repression effects across different outcomes because all models, including protest participation, use the same estimation technique.

References

Alimahomed, Sabrina. 2011. "Generation Islam." *Race/Ethnicity* 4 (3): 381–397.

Apuzzo, Matt, and Adam Goldman. 2014. *Enemies Within*. New York: Simon & Schuster.

Azab, Marian, and Wayne A. Santoro. 2017. "Rethinking Fear and Protest." *Mobilization* 22 (4): 417–436.

Baker, Wayne, Ronald Stockton, Sally Howell, Amaney Jamal, Ann Chih Lin, Andrew Shryock, and Mark Tessler. *Detroit Arab American Study (DAAS), 2003*. ICPSR04413-v2. Ann Arbor, MI: Inter-university Consortium for Political and Social Research [distributor], 2006-2010-25. doi:10.3886/ICPSR04413.v2.

Barkan, Steven E. 1984. "Legal Control of the Southern Civil Rights Movement." *American Sociological Review* 49 (4): 552–565.

Beitin, Ben K., and Katherine R. Allen. 2005. "Resilience in Arab American Couples after September 11, 2001." *Journal of Marital and Family Therapy* 31: 251–267.

Bobo, Lawrence D., and Victor Thompson. 2006. "Unfair by Design." *Social Research* 73: 445–472.

Brown, Tony N. 2003. "Critical Race Theory Speaks to the Sociology of Mental Health." *Journal of Health and Social Behavior* 44: 292–301.

Cainkar, Louise A. 2009. *Homeland Insecurity.* New York: Russell Sage Foundation.

Council on American–Islamic Relations. 2018. *Targeted: 2018 Civil Rights Report.* CAIR. Retrieved November 28, 2018 (https://d3n8a8pro7vhmx.cloudfront.net/cairhq/pages/15480/attachments/original/1526629741/CAIR_2018_Civil_Rights_Report.pdf?1526629741).

Cunningham, David. 2003. "The Patterning of Repression." *Social Forces* 82 (1): 209–240.

Davenport, Christian. 1995. "Multi-Dimensional Threat Perception and State Repression." *American Journal of Political Science* 39 (3): 683–713.

Davenport, Christian, Sarah A. Soule, and David A. Armstrong II. 2011. "Protesting While Black?" *American Sociological Review* 76 (1): 152–178.

Earl, Jennifer. 2011. "Political Repression." *Annual Review of Sociology* 37: 261–284.

Einwohner, Rachel L. 2003. "Opportunity, Honor, and Action in the Warsaw Ghetto Uprising of 1943." *American Journal of Sociology* 109 (33): 650–675.

Fadel, Leila. 2018. "How Muslims, Often Misunderstood, Are Thriving in America." *National Geographic.* Retrieved April 8, 2020 (https://www.nationalgeographic.com/magazine/2018/05/being-muslim-in-america/).

Fendrich, James M. 1974. "Activists Ten Years Later." *Journal of Social Issues* 30 (3): 95–118.

Ferree, Myra Marx. 2004. "Soft Repression." *Research in Social Movements, Conflicts and Change* 25: 85–101.

Fischbach, Michael R. 1985. "Government Pressures against Arabs in the United States." *Journal of Palestine Studies* 14 (3): 87–100.

Hagopian, Elaine. 1975/1976. "Minority Rights in a Nation-State." *Journal of Palestine Studies* 5 (1/2): 97–114.

Hess, David, and Brian Martin. 2006. "Repression, Backfire, and the Theory of Transformative Events." *Mobilization* 11: 249–267.

Howell, Sally, and Andrew Shryock. 2003. "Cracking Down on Diaspora: Arab Detroit and America's 'War on Terror." *Anthropological Quarterly* 76(3) 443–462.

Human Rights Watch. 2002. "We are Not the Enemy" Human Rights Watch. Retrieved April 8, 2020 (https://www.hrw.org/reports/2002/usahate/usa1102.pdf).

Jenkins, J. Craig and Kurt Schock. 2004. "Political Process, International Dependence, and Mass Political Conflict." *International Journal of Sociology* 33: 41–63.

Johnston, Hank. 1991. *Tales of Nationalism.* New Brunswick, NJ: Rutgers University Press.

Kaushal, Neeraj, Robert Kaestner, and Cordelia Reimers. 2007. "Labor Market Effects of September 11th on Arab and Muslim Residents of the United States." *Journal of Human Resources* 42: 275–308.

Kirk, David S., and Andrew V. Papachristos, 2011. "Cultural Mechanisms and the Persistence of Neighborhood Violence." *American Journal of Sociology* 116 (4): 1190–1233.

Koopmans, Ruud. 1993. "The Dynamics of Protest Waves." *American Sociological Review* 58: 637–658.

Koopmans, Ruud. 1997. "The Dynamics of Repression and Mobilization." *Mobilization* 2: 149–165.

Lauderdale, Diane S. 2006. "Birth Outcomes for Arabic-Named Women in California before and After September 11." *Demography* 43: 185–201.

Liu, Callie Watkins. 2018. "The Anti-oppressive Value of Critical Race Theory and Intersectionality in Social Movement Study." *Sociology of Race and Ethnicity* 4 (3): 306–321.

MacFarquhar, Neil. 2007. "U.S., Stymied 21 Years, Drops Bid to Deport 2 Palestinians." *New York Times*. Retrieved February 2, 2018 (http://www.nytimes.com/2007/11/01/us/01settle.html).

McAdam, Doug. 1986. "Recruitment to High-Risk Activism: The Case of Freedom Summer." *American Journal of Sociology* 92 (1): 64–90.

McAdam, Doug. 1989. "The Biographical Consequences of Activism." *American Sociological Review* 54 (5): 744–760.

McAdam, Doug. 1992. "Gender as a Mediator of the Activist Experience." *American Journal of Sociology* 97 (5): 1211–1240.

Morris, Aldon, and Naomi Braine. 2001. "Social Movements and Oppositional Consciousness." Pp. 20–37 in *Oppositional Consciousness*, edited by Jane Mansbridge and Aldon Morris. Chicago: University of Chicago Press.

Naber, Nadine. 2006. "The Rules of Forced Engagement." *Cultural Dynamics* 18: 235–267.

Naber, Nadine. 2012. *Arab America*. New York: New York University Press.

O'Hearn, Denis. 2009. "Repression and Solidarity Cultures of Resistance." *American Journal of Sociology* 115: 491–526.

Oliver, Pamela. 2017. "The Ethnic Dimensions in Social Movements." *Mobilization* 22 (4): 395–416.

Pierce, Chester M. 1989. "Unity in Diversity." Pp. 296–312 in *Black Students*, edited by Gordon LaVern Berry and Joy Keiko Asamen. Newbury Park, CA: Sage Publications.

Piven, Frances Fox, and Richard A. Cloward. 1979. *Poor People's Movements*. New York: Vintage Books.

Santoro, Wayne A. 2008. "The Civil Rights Movement and the Right to Vote." *Social Forces* 86 (4): 1391–1414.

Santoro, Wayne A., and Marian Azab. 2015. "Arab American Protest in the Terror Decade." *Social Problems* 62 (2): 219–240.

Santoro, Wayne A., and Lisa Broidy. 2014. "Gendered Rioting." *Social Forces* 93 (1): 329–354.

Santoro, Wayne A., and Gary M. Segura. 2011. "Generational Status and Mexican American Political-Participation." *Political Research Quarterly* 64 (1): 172–184.

Sherkat, Darren E., and T. Jean Blocker. 1997. "Explaining the Political and Personal Consequences of Protest." *Social Forces* 75 (3): 1049–1070.

Shultziner, Doron. 2013. "The Social-Psychological Origins of the Montgomery Bus Boycott." *Mobilization* 18 (2): 117–142.

Southern Poverty Law Center (SPLC). 2016. *Ten Days After*. SPLC. Retrieved February 1, 2018 (https://www.splcenter.org/sites/default/files/com_hate_incidents_report_2017_update.pdf).

Southern Poverty Law Center (SPLC). 2017. *Anti-Muslim*. SPLC. Retrieved November 11, 2017 (https://www.splcenter.org/fighting-hate/extremist-files/ideology/anti-muslim).

Sue, Derald Wing, Christina M. Capodilupo, and Aisha M.B. Holder. 2008. "Racial Microaggressions in the Life Experience of Black Americans." *Professional Psychology* 39 (3): 329–336.

Suleiman, Michael W. 1999. "Islam, Muslims and Arabs in America." *Journal of Muslim Minority Affairs* 19(1): 33–47.

Tarrow, Sidney. 1993. "Cycles of Collective Action." *Social Science History* 17 (2): 281–307.

Taylor, Verta, and Nicole C. Raeburn. 1995. "Identity Politics as High-Risk Activism." *Social Problems* 42(2): 252–273.

Tilly, Charles. 1978. *From Mobilization to Revolution*. New York: McGraw-Hill Publishing Company.

Nella Van Dyke, Doug McAdam, and Brenda Wilhelm. 2000. "Gendered Outcomes." *Mobilization* 5 (2): 161–177.

Victor, Daniel. 2018. "When White People Call the Police on Black People." *New York Times*. Retrieved May 18, 2018 (https://www.nytimes.com/2018/05/11/us/black-white-police.html).

White, Robert W. 1989. "From Peaceful Protest to Guerilla War." *American Journal of Sociology* 94: 1277–1302.

Williams, David R., Yan Yu, James S. Jackson, and Norman B. Anderson. 1997. "Racial Differences in Physical and Mental Health." *Journal of Health Psychology* 2 (3): 335–351.

Williams, David R., Harold W. Neighbors, and James S. Jackson. 2003. "Racial/Ethnic Discrimination and Health." *American Journal of Public Health* 93 (2): 200–208.

Zogby, John. 2001. A Poll of Arab-Americans since the Terrorist Attacks on the United States. Arab American Institute. Retrieved January 1, 2014 (http://www.aaiusa.org/index_ee.php/reports/arab-american-attitudes-the-september-11-attacks).

7 Localized political contexts
Undocumented youth mobilization during hostile times

Edelina M. Burciaga and Lisa M. Martinez

The undocumented youth movement is one of the most vibrant contemporary social movements in the United States. Yet, while research on undocumented youth abounds, their activism has yet to receive full attention in social movements scholarship. The corpus of research that does exist has focused primarily on activism in traditional immigrant gateways, such as California and Illinois (Enriquez and Saguy 2016; Gonzales 2010; Nicholls 2013a; Pallares and Flores-Pallares 2014). Traditional immigrant gateways tend to be distinguished by established immigrant populations and their relatively accommodating policies and practices. In contrast, re-emergent and new immigrant destinations, which have struggled with the influx of undocumented immigrants, are characterized by ambivalent or hostile policies and practices (Cebulko and Silver 2016; Marrow 2011; Martinez 2014). These variegated landscapes raise two important questions: How do local contexts shape undocumented youth movements? And how does the current hostile climate at the national level inform youths' activism? In this chapter, we focus on how an increasingly anti-immigrant political climate at the national level is affecting undocumented youth mobilization locally and how youth activists are shaping mobilization at the national level.

Building on political opportunity theory in social movements (Jenkins and Perrow 1977; McAdam and Snow 1997; Meyer 1993; Tarrow 1988, 2011) and segmented assimilation theory in migration studies (Portes and Rumbaut 2014; Portes and Zhou 1993), we examine how localized political contexts—contexts of varying of levels of antagonism or accommodation (Burciaga and Martinez 2017)—shape the emergence and character of undocumented youth movements in Los Angeles, Denver, and Atlanta. In comparing these immigrant destinations, we add to the growing body of literature in this field (Bloemraad and Voss 2011; Nicholls 2013b; Terriquez 2015a; Zepeda-Millán 2017) by providing a framework for understanding undocumented youth activism as multipronged and dynamic, successfully mobilizing despite the hostile political context under the Trump administration.

Segmented assimilation theory

Research about undocumented young adults is rooted in segmented assimilation theory, and specifically the concept of context of reception. Context of reception is broadly defined as the governmental, social, and institutional welcome immigrants face in their new country. Scholars have drawn on context of reception to theorize the precise role of an undocumented legal status in shaping immigrant integration, or immigrant illegality (De Genova 2002). As De Genova (2002) states, illegality is a "juridical status that entails a relationship to the state" (422). In practice, however, the experience of immigrant illegality is a sociopolitical process that is constantly constructed and reconstructed as undocumented immigrants navigate daily life. For undocumented youth, their experience of illegality is informed by the paradox of their social inclusion through high school and increasing legal exclusion as they transition to adulthood (Abrego 2006; Gonzales 2015; Martinez 2014). This process of legal exclusion may result in heightening a reactive or oppositional identity that encourages political mobilization (Gonzales 2011; Martinez and Salazar 2018; Negrón-Gonzales 2013; Rumbaut 2008). Undocumented young adults who become activists often engage in social spaces in college or in their communities that facilitate politicization. This finding is consistent with previous research that suggests that because of their early age at migration and contact with school, undocumented young adults are more likely to participate in activism compared to those who migrated as adults and whose primary institutional contact is through employment (Abrego 2011; Gleeson and Gonzales 2012). This highlights the fact that the undocumented immigrant experience is not monolithic but rather diverse and varied.

Further reflecting the heterogeneity of the undocumented immigrant experience, especially in relation to *where* undocumented immigrants are settling, immigration scholars also examine the role of subfederal policies in shaping immigrant inclusion and exclusion (Armenta 2017; Provine and Varsanyi 2012; Stuesse and Coleman 2014; Varsanyi 2010a). While immigration policy falls under the purview of the federal government, the past fifteen years have been characterized by a proliferation of state and local policies aimed at regulating undocumented immigrants (Varsanyi 2010b; Walker and Leitner 2011). As part of the devolution of immigration enforcement practices to states and localities, policing of undocumented immigrants by local law enforcement has also increased (Armenta 2017; Provine and Varsanyi 2012). Local immigration enforcement and regulation takes many different forms ranging from regulating the public spaces where immigrants look for work (Varsanyi 2010b) to holding them for ICE as a result of routine traffic stops or other minor violations (Armenta 2017; Stuesse and Coleman 2014). Even among undocumented youth and young adults previously protected from deportation through the Deferred Action for Childhood Arrivals (DACA) program, which was rescinded in September 2017, subfederal policy regimes significantly influence their everyday experiences of inclusion and exclusion (Gonzales 2015). Thus, the increase in state and local regulation and enforcement of undocumented immigrants has resulted in varied contexts for undocumented immigrant youth with ramifications for their incorporation and, as we argue in this chapter, for their political mobilization.

Political opportunity theory

Political opportunity theory complements segmented assimilation theory as both emphasize the relevance of political context. Political opportunity theory holds that endogenous and exogenous factors affect movement activists' ability to advance their claims and mobilize supporters (Meyer and Minkoff 2004: 126). Among the factors, claims making, the cultivation of alliances, and adoption of particular tactics and strategies all enhance or inhibit a movement's ability to mobilize (Meyer and Minkoff 2004). Furthermore, because movement activities are bound by the political arena in which they take place, political opportunity also posits that collective action is likely to occur only if participants believe they will succeed or that institutional channels are less effective (Meyer and Staggenborg 1996). Political opportunity theory also asserts that the political context affects whether a polity is receptive or vulnerable to collective action by a social movement (McAdam, McCarthy, and Zald 1988). For change to occur, the political structure must be favorable to particular grievances, which are then brought forward for remediation (Jenkins and Perrow 1977). In terms of immigrant mobilization, Nicholls's (2013b: 24) notion of niche-openings complements political opportunity theory and is useful for understanding the significance of varying contexts and undocumented youth activism:

> In the case of undocumented youth activists, they and their allies have responded to narrow openings by highlighting the qualities and attributes that make them into exceptionally good and deserving candidates of legal status. When effectively crafted and articulated, arguments about a group's exceptional qualities enhance public support for their cause and help provide a pathway to rights and recognition.

Nicholls (2013b: 31) further argues that, during times of political closure, immigrant rights activists may prioritize some immigrants (i.e., youth or asylum seekers) over others, looking for narrow niche-openings that provide avenues for small-scale activism, which can then be "scaled- up" to encompass others when bigger windows of opportunity present themselves.

Also important is the influence of claims (Koopmans and Statham 1999) and frames, which are a reflection of a movement's interests and ideology (McCammon, Muse, Newman, and Terrel 2007). Given that recent waves of Latin American immigrants are non-white, they are racialized and perceived as unassimilable (Portes and Zhou 1993), making them more likely to encounter a hostile context of reception (Portes and Rumbaut 2014; Portes and Zhou 1993). Their heightened visibility spawns demagoguery, which feeds public perceptions that immigrants are criminals, potentially limiting claims and frames employed by the movement. In the past, undocumented youths' claims tended to align with notions about meritocracy and deservingness and adopted similar frames as they were deemed more appealing to the public (Nicholls 2013b; Yukich 2013). In recent years, however, undocumented activists have increasingly rejected "deservingness" frames in favor of ones that are more inclusive of all immigrants, not only youth who migrated to the U.S. as children or "good" versus "bad" migrants (Dingeman-Cerda, Burciaga, and Martinez 2016; Andrews 2017).

Movement strategies and tactics also influence the targets of collective action (Meyer and Staggenborg 1996). In some cases, movements may opt to influence policy and maintain particular tactics and strategies unless other opportunities or threats suggest otherwise. When movements are experiencing defeat, for example, they are more likely to identify additional institutional venues for change and shifting to those that have a greater chance of success (Meyer and Staggenborg 1996). As we note below, undocumented youth activists in each of our three cities espoused different strategies and tactics not only across contexts but over time as well.

These strategies varied from targeting the policy arena (e.g., comprehensive immigration reform, state-level tuition bills) to campus activism to engaging in acts of civil disobedience and protest.

Finally, political opportunity theory accounts for how internal and external threats influence a movement's goals, tactics, and strategies. Internal threats include disagreements over framing, or frame disputes (Benford 1993), as movements may have to define their claims in response to their opposition rather than to their supporters. Such disagreements between moderate and more radical factions of a movement make it challenging to find frames that appeal to the public and elite supporters. Martinez (2008) finds, for example, that organizers of the 2006 immigrant rights marches were torn between what some considered radical frames and tactics versus moderate ones deemed more appealing to the public. Additionally, Gordon's (2009) work shows that youth movements are particularly susceptible to fractures over group aims, identity, and political visions, especially when trying to project these to adult publics.

External threats such as countermovements also play a significant role in a movement's ability to achieve its goals. Meyer and Staggenborg (1996: 1639) note, "When movement issues seem to symbolize a whole set of values and behaviors, they are likely to threaten a broader range of constituencies who will be attracted to countermovement action for different reasons." Moreover, political struggles are likely to ensue if a movement begins to symbolize broader rights and cultural values as in the case of the immigrant rights and undocumented youth movements. Thus, through the lens of political opportunity theory, undocumented youth have multiple opportunities or niche-openings (Nicholls 2013b) through which they can challenge the system—one institutional by affecting change through law and policy and the other extra- institutional via collective action. As we discuss below, the strategies and tactics undocumented you activists employed were a function of their localized political contexts.

Linking segmented assimilation theory and political opportunity theory, we apply the concept of localized political contexts to show how different environments influence the claims made by undocumented youth, the targets of their claims, and the strategies and tactics they employ. Further, we argue that the devolution of immigration law and policy to localities in recent years not only influences the incorporation of undocumented young adults, but also creates barriers and openings for change through mobilization (Nicholls 2013b). Before applying this framework to Los Angeles, Denver, and Atlanta, we situate our analysis in foundational work on the immigrant rights and undocumented youth movements.

The undocumented youth movement

Issues affecting undocumented youth have figured prominently in the immigrant rights movement agenda (Enriquez and Saguy 2016; Muñoz 2015; Negrón-Gonzales 2015; Nicholls 2013a), compelling young people to engage in high-risk activism (McAdam 1986) and challenge the marginalization they and others experience because of their liminal legal status (Abrego 2006; Gonzales 2007, 2009; Menjívar and Abrego 2012). In the last decade alone, undocumented youth have led efforts to reform the immigration system as during the 2006 mobilizations, opposing enhanced immigration enforcement during the Obama administration (Patler and Gonzales 2015), and advocating for access to higher education and state-level legislation such as tuition and driver's license bills (Gonzales 2008; Perez, Espinoza, and Ramos 2010; Rincon 2010). Others have taken an intersectional approach to collective action, advancing the rights of undocumented immigrants and LGBTQ+ youth (Terriquez 2015a), and forging other cross-movement alliances (Zepeda-Millán and Wallace 2018).

Despite the significance of the 2006 mobilizations and undocumented youth activism more recently, social movements scholars have been slow to embrace the immigrant rights movement as a topic of study. This may be due to its evolution outside the bounds of mainstream social movements and immigrant activists' undocumented status, which denies them traditional avenues for accessing political structures. As such, research merging the two areas remains underdeveloped, prompting calls to fill this gap (Menjívar 2010). In particular, Menjívar (2010: 18) argues the 2006 mobilizations provided a prime opportunity to wed these literatures:

> These unprecedented political demonstrations represented much more than simply millions of immigrants and their advocates marching in the streets asking for just immigration reform; they came to demonstrate that, contrary to previous assumptions about immigrants'

political inactivity and apathy based on their sociodemographic profile, immigrants, and their supporters could muster political action and clout.

Although social movements scholars have taken steps in this direction, much of the work centers on international contexts (e.g., Koopmans and Statham 1999; Giugni and Passy 2004; Karapin 2011; Morales and Ramiro 2011; Eggert 2014; Rosenberger and Winkler 2014) or immigration serves as a backdrop of the research (e.g., King 2008). Thus, aside from some notable exceptions (e.g., Nicholls 2013a, 2013b; Steil and Vasi 2014; Terriquez 2015a, 2015b; Bloemraad, Silva, and Voss 2016; Coddou 2016; Heredia 2016; Zepeda-Millán 2017; see also Swerts Chapter 8 in this volume), studies merging social movements and migration in the U.S. context remain relatively few in number.

Some scholars have begun to move the fields of migration studies and social movements forward by addressing how growing up undocumented shapes claims making and mobilization by youth activists (Abrego 2011; Negrón-Gonzales 2013; Enriquez and Saguy 2016) and how this varies by context (Marrow 2011; Silver 2018). For example, Laura Enriquez and Abigail Saguy (2016), find that "coming out" as undocumented holds a unique meaning in California, as undocumented youth activists reserve the label for disclosing their legal status in public spaces. Similarly, Silver's (2018) study in rural North Carolina reveals the complex terrain of immigration policies at the local, state, and national levels and how undocumented youth are navigating them. These findings suggest that despite being a national movement, undocumented youth mobilization varies across localized political contexts.

Despite advances in scholarship, however, we still know relatively little about how varied political contexts shape undocumented youth mobilization. Following in the vein of work at the intersection of these two fields, we offer insights about youth activists who have called for comprehensive immigration reform and access to institutions of higher education while also opposing family separation, detention, and deportation. Their activism has informed policy changes at the local, state, and federal levels, challenged anti-immigrant laws, and, depending on the context, provided immigrant communities with greater access to resources and opportunities. We highlight below how different localized political contexts ranging from high to moderate to low in their receptivity informed undocumented youths in three cities: Los Angeles, Denver, and Atlanta. We also attend to undocumented youth activism in the current political climate, which has grown increasingly caustic since 2016, and how it has expanded to include opposition to DACA's rescission, the zero tolerance policy, asylum denials, and the deprioritization approach to immigration enforcement that renders everyone targets for deportation.

Data and methods

We analyzed data from studies conducted in three immigrant destinations: Los Angeles (traditional), Denver (re-emergent), and Atlanta (new). Burciaga draws from two qualitative studies. The first, conducted between 2009 and 2011, includes participant observation and 20 in-depth interviews with undocumented youth activists in Orange County and Los Angeles, California. The primary purpose of the study was to understand how this group was making sense of the emergence of high-risk activism, notably participation in acts of civil disobedience, as a movement strategy in the undocumented youth movement. The data also include participant observation at community and campus-based undocumented youth organization meetings, protest events, educational forums, and social gatherings between 2010 and 2014. In addition, from 2014 to 2015, she conducted 70 interviews with undocumented young adults in Los Angeles and Atlanta. While the primary purpose of this study was to understand how divergent college access laws impact the educational experiences of this group, participants in both sites were involved in campus and community-based activism.

Martinez draws on two qualitative studies in Denver, Colorado. The first centered on the 2006 immigrant rights mobilizations, exploring the role of social movement organizations in mobilizing Colorado's immigrant communities and allies. The data includes 57 interviews with movement leaders and community organizers, immigrant activists and advocates, elected officials, and religious leaders collected from 2006 to 2008. The data are supplemented with observations at protests, community meetings, and gatherings at organization headquarters during the immigrant rights campaign. The second study from 2012 to 2017 is animated by 62 in-depth interviews with undocumented, Latino youth and young adults, many of whom were involved in campus or community-based activism. While the focus of the second study is to show the effect of legal reforms on young immigrants' educational and occupational trajectories, social justice, civic engagement, and political activism were recurring themes in the data.

Our method of analysis entailed individually coding interviews from our respective studies. After identifying recurring themes with regard to the movement's claims, the intended audience of their claims, and their mobilization strategies, we compared and contrasted each case together along these three dimensions. This allowed us to discern how similarities and differences in each context accounted for undocumented youth mobilization.

Localized political contexts

In this section, we address how different political contexts shape undocumented youths' activism. These contexts are ideal for understanding how threats and opportunities shape activism because they represent points along a continuum to claims making by immigrant youth ranging from high (Los Angeles); to moderate (Denver); to low (Atlanta) in receptivity.

Los Angeles, California

California is currently home to the second-largest unauthorized immigrant population in the United States. An estimated 1 million undocumented immigrants live in the region (Pew Hispanic Center 2017). California is often painted as of the most welcoming contexts for undocumented immigrants in the nation. California was the second state to offer in-state tuition starting in 2001. The state has also offered state and institutional financial aid since 2013. Also, in 2013, state legislature passed AB 60, providing driver's licenses for undocumented immigrants. In 2016, legislators amended the professional code to allow undocumented immigrants to apply for professional licenses. While these recent legislative changes indicate an accommodating trend in California, during the 1990s a severe economic recession plagued the state and anti-undocumented immigrant sentiment rose, culminating in the passage of Proposition 187 (HoSang 2010; Durand, Massey, and Charvet 2000).

Proposition 187, passed by a two-to-one margin amongst California voters in 1994, prevented undocumented immigrants from accessing a variety of social services including healthcare and education, both K-12 and college (Varsanyi 2010b). Prop 187 was considered a precursor to Arizona's SB1070 and similar anti-immigrant laws that proliferated in the 2010s. While the U.S. District Court invalidated the law (HoSang 2010; Varsanyi 2010b), the furor surrounding Proposition 187 had lasting effects on California's undocumented immigrant community. During interviews conducted in 2010, Latino undocumented youth activists cited the Proposition 187 campaign as a particularly tumultuous time for Latino undocumented immigrants. As young children, they were painfully aware of the criminalization and scapegoating of the broader undocumented immigrant community that not only characterized the 1990s, but continued through the 2000s. As Sarai shared, "when I was little, that was the big thing. These Mexicans, illegal immigrants, they're smuggling drugs across the United States, and we must secure our borders." Likewise, Adan shared that part of his motivation to be involved in the undocumented youth movement, was "to put a face to the issue ... it does change people's opinions once they meet someone who is actually undocumented and *is not* a criminal."

The 1990s through the early 2000s were a crucial period in shaping the undocumented youth movement in Los Angeles and Orange County. The passage of AB 540, the in-state tuition law, in 2001, was a grassroots victory, as undocumented youth were at the forefront of the legislative campaign, challenging the assumption that they did not have political power because of their age and legal status (Seif 2004). The rhetoric that characterized the 1990s, in part, shaped the early framing and strategies of the undocumented youth movement in Southern California. Heightened anti-immigrant sentiment pushed undocumented youth and their allies to craft a movement frame that distinguished undocumented youth from the pervasive criminalization narrative. Following the AB540s passage in 2001, undocumented student organizations grew on college campuses across California (Abrego 2008;

Nicholls 2013a), and the frames and claims that characterized the movement in the mid-2000s were, in part, a remnant of undocumented youth and ally mobilization for AB540, including an emphasis on educational access

Beyond providing undocumented youth the opportunity to pay in-state tuition, the law gave undocumented youth a new socially acceptable identity, "AB540" student, which facilitated undocumented youth finding one another to form campus-based groups (Abrego 2008). As Sarai, who had been a leader and member of the undocumented youth movement since 2006, shared:

> I did a lot of work locally, but I also did statewide with the statewide network of AB 540 student clubs, this bigger coalition than the thing we had here (*in Orange County*). I remember that first retreat, we had people from Chico State all the way to San Marcos in San Diego … it was amazing to realize we had each other. Even though we were the only ones from our school, we had more people who were creating change.

The AB540 student network, which was a part of work based out of Coalition for Humane Rights Los Angeles (CHIRLA), eventually gave rise to community-based organizing in Los Angeles and Orange County. Sarai recalled that these community-based organizations became a site for undocumented youth activists who had been "displaced" because they had graduated from college and lost the opportunity for campus-based mobilization. Thus, AB540 was a key mechanism for facilitating undocumented youth mobilization both on and beyond college campuses in Los Angeles and Orange County.

The education frame, which emphasizes the importance of access to higher education for undocumented youth, featured prominently in 2010 as activists in the region were focused on passing the DREAM Act as a stand-alone bill. When asked why someone should support the 2010 DREAM Act, Dolores, an activist on her campus and in a community-based undocumented student organization, shared, "I would tell you first, please don't look at it as an immigration issue. Think of it as an educational issue." Jesse, who was new to the undocumented student movement at the time of our interview, echoed Dolores' education frame, and shared his understanding of the relationship between the broader immigrant rights movement and the youth movement, "As far as I know, the immigration movement is pretty much like the whole immigration issue. Whereas the student movement is just the youth, trying to get their voices out. And just trying to get an education." Both Dolores and Jesse, who were themselves college students, conveyed their understanding of the main claim of the undocumented youth movement at the time, which was about equity and access to higher education.

However, by 2011 there were signs that the frame and relatedly the claims undocumented youth activists were making were beginning to shift, partly as a result of a change in tactics and strategies by undocumented youth in key locales including Southern California. At a town hall event in conservative Orange County in January 2011, a coalition of immigrant rights organizations gathered to raise awareness about the experiences of undocumented youth. As the event started, undocumented youth stood at the front of the room wearing their high school caps and gowns, forming a brightly colored rainbow. The event also featured a prominent undocumented youth scholar who shared his research about the social, economic, and educational struggles of undocumented youth. I stood in the back of the room at a merchandise table for a community-based undocumented youth organization. As the speaker conveyed the stigma undocumented youth experience as they transition to adulthood, Yessica, a leader in the organization, whispered, "It's not like that anymore ... now it's all about undocumented and unafraid" (*Fieldnotes*, September 27, 2011). Yessica's observation reflected what had already become apparent during and immediately following the push to pass the 2010 DREAM Act, referred to as DREAM Act summer. Undocumented youth activists were shedding the stigma associated with their undocumented status and claiming an empowered identity.

Despite the Federal DREAM Act's failure, undocumented youth activists in Southern California were empowered by the shift in mobilization tactics, including acts of civil disobedience. As Marcelo, a leader in Orange County noted about the mobilization around the 2010 DREAM Act, "I think it's given us an opportunity to go back and do work in our communities." He went on to add:

> I think nationally, there's not going to be much we can do. I think the movement is going to go back to states. Here in California, it's not going to be so much fighting off anti- immigrant legislation but making sure that we have enough support to pass healthy legislation. As opposed to states like Arizona, Georgia, or other states. Twenty-three other states have introduced anti-immigrant legislation in their states. For them, it's going to be fighting law.

Throughout the 2000s, undocumented youth in Southern California built a dynamic movement that, along with other traditional immigrant destinations, moved the undocumented youth movement to the forefront of the immigrant rights movement (Enriquez and Saguy 2016; Nicholls 2013a; Unzueta and Seif 2014). As Marcelo notes, the strategy in Southern California, and statewide, became proactive as opposed to reactive. Post-DREAM Act mobilization, shifted focus away from immigration reform to securing state financial aid *and* passing a driver's license law. Both became laws in 2013 (AB 130 & 131) and 2015 (AB 60). Some undocumented youth organizations in Southern California shifted their focus to ending detention and deportation.

These claims were a direct response to the record number of deportations under the Obama administration, but was also a rejection of the undocumented youth exceptionalism that was a key frame in the 2010 DREAM Act campaign. Undocumented youth activists turned their energy to rejecting programs like Secure Communities, passing the TRUST Act (limiting jail holds for Immigrations and Customs Enforcement), and expanding healthcare access. The evolution of California from a hostile climate in the 1990s to amongst the most welcoming in the nation has created a localized political context for undocumented youth activists to continue to push for positive state-level changes within a rapidly shifting and unstable federal context. In fact, in the wake of the 2016 presidential election, California has continued to be at the forefront of the resistance to the administration's hostile and exclusionary policy stance toward immigrants. This includes declaring the state a sanctuary state as well as being a part of several key lawsuits challenging the administration's executive orders, family separation policies, and the termination of DACA.

Denver, Colorado

Denver represents a moderate context of reception with a sizeable Latino-origin population. According to census data, Latinos comprise nearly a quarter (22.6 percent) of Denver's total population of which 27.4 percent are foreign-born and disproportionately Mexican-origin (Migration Policy Institute 2014; Passel, Cohn, and Rohal 2014). The city of Denver has a long and complex history of immigration. Waves of migrants have ebbed and flowed over time and, today, it is considered a re-emergent destination (Singer 2015).

Like Los Angeles, Denver was a hotbed of Chicano activism in the 1960s and 1970s with movement leaders such as the late Rodolfo "Corky" Gonzales who founded the Crusade for Justice. The Crusade, along with youth activists, called for ending police brutality, agitated for political representation, and worked to eradicate racial discrimination in Denver schools (Vigil 1999). Despite its history of Chicano activism, however, Denver has also served as ground-zero for vigilante groups, including the Colorado Minutemen, who took to patrolling the U.S.–Mexico border and staging counter-protests across the country in the early 2000s and is home to former Congressman Tom Tancredo who campaigned for president in 2012 on an immigration restrictionist platform.

Anti-immigrant sentiment as well as a desire to bring about comprehensive immigration reform in the face of failed attempts to get the DREAM Act[1] passed fueled the spring 2006 mass mobilizations. The movement employed a variety of tactics and strategies ranging from vigils, marches, public meetings with elected officials, student walkouts, and, on May 1, a citywide boycott and mass protest know across the country as "Day Without an Immigrant." Nearly 200,000 protestors participated in the Denver march, all part of a concerted effort between social movement and community-based organizations, civic and religious leaders, immigrants, activists, and allies. While many activists lauded the number of protestors as a major victory in the movement, that same day, Governor Bill Owens signed SB 90, one of the first "papers, please" laws in the country. Backed by immigration restrictionists, Defend Colorado Now, SB 90 gave local law enforcement the authority to stop persons suspected of being in the country without documents and running their information through federal databases. Not only did this mark the beginning of immigration federalism in Colorado where state and local authorities could enforce federal immigration law, it required activists to shift from pursuing comprehensive immigration reform to targeting policymakers and focusing on the new detention and deportation regime (De Genova 2010). Asked whether SB 90 was a major setback to the movement, one activist noted, "Denver is where L.A. was 30 years ago. We have to remind ourselves that change is slow."

Developments during the Obama Administration had significant implications for the undocumented youth movement as well. A few months prior to the 2012 election, Obama enacted Deferred Action for Childhood Arrivals (DACA). It fell short of providing a path to legalization or relief from deportation for recipients' parents and family members but provided some schooling and work opportunities for the nearly 700,000 young immigrants who qualified (Gonzales, Terriquez, and Ruszczyk 2014). Having been involved in the broader immigrant rights movement, many undocumented youth splintered off to form standalone organizations (Nicholls 2013b) such as United We Dream and campus DREAMer organizations, to challenge barriers to higher education.

Undocumented youth in Denver advocated for immigration reform in various ways, including walkouts, a hunger strike at the Democratic Party headquarters, and other forms of activism such as storytelling and counternarratives (Negrón-Gonzales 2015; see also Swerts Chapter 8 in this volume). Others took their activism national, participating in the Undocubus, a mobile "ride for justice" that traveled from Arizona to Washington, D.C. in support of immigration reform.

These forms of activism were a response to growing disillusionment that change could be achieved via institutional channels. Undocumented student, Viri, is a case in point. During college she played a pivotal role in an immigrant rights group that lobbied elected officials to support immigration reform. Having struggled to pay for college, the movement was important to her. After a few years, however, she became disenchanted with institutional approaches to reform and left the organization. She explained, "I want to really affect people ... in a more personal way, not just through politics because that doesn't help anyone at all. It's a fucking game, you know?"

While many youth activists focused on educational access, others worked on campaigns to repeal SB 90 by appealing to law-enforcement officials and the general public. Knowing young people's narratives would resonate (Yukich 2013), movement leaders made significant gains; however, nonstudent immigrants and those ineligible for relief through DACA continued to languish in legal limbo (Gonzales 2015). Some undocumented youth activists were critical of strategies that pitted immigrants against one another while others felt the focus on in-state tuition hurt the broader movement by diluting activists' demands. Another undocumented activist, Ismael, explained:

> It took me a while to reapply [for DACA]. I felt like even though it was helping me personally, I had this feeling like, "Maybe I don't want to." I feel like a lot of people in the movement, we got comfortable, that maybe

we could have asked for something more. We need something more permanent, not just the "good immigrants, the poster-child, educated, English-speaking, no-fault-of-their-own" messaging.

In 2013, almost a year after DACA was enacted, activists—in collaboration with elected officials, community organizers, and college administrators—achieved a significant victory when the Advancing Students for a Stronger Economy Tomorrow (ASSET) bill was signed into law after a ten-year political battle. The bill extended educational access to all students graduating from Colorado high schools, including those who came to the U.S. as children, to ensure that "students who have already benefited from Colorado schools can stay here and contribute to Colorado's economy, [offering] a higher return on our taxpayer investment" (Giron, Johnston, and Carroll n.d.).[2] With DACA's implementation in 2012 and ASSET in 2013, some undocumented youth activists shifted their claims-making revolved primarily around educational access. Others focused on ending detention and deportation through protests and vigils while still others continued to agitate for federal reform through traditional legislative channels. In terms of the latter, the targets were largely political elites, many of whom were key allies in passing ASSET.

Thus, the political context in Denver shifted from a hostile one with the passage of SB 90 in 2006 to a slightly more hospitable one with its repeal, the passage of ASSET, and a driver's license bill for undocumented drivers in 2013 (Cebulko and Silver 2016; Martinez 2014). While activists have not achieved large-scale relief for non-students or engaged in a widespread human rights agenda as in Los Angeles, modest legislative gains have provided some avenues for social mobility and integration for immigrant youth (Portes and Rumbaut 2014). Nonetheless, with DACA's rescission at the federal level and local elected officials' reluctance to declare Denver a sanctuary city, thousands of immigrants remain at risk. Moreover, given the Trump administration's focus on ramping up immigration enforcement, even those considered low priorities for deportation during the Obama administration are now at risk.

According to data from the Transactional Records Access Clearinghouse (TRAC), for example, deportations in Colorado are expected to increase 550 percent in 2019 relative to 2016. Immigrants are also being targeted via courthouse arrests despite sensitive locations policies designed to prevent ICE from interviewing, searching, or apprehending anyone in schools, hospitals, or places of worship. The state also failed to pass Virginia's Law in April 2019, which would have barred law-enforcement agencies from honoring detainer requests and giving immigration-related information to ICE in sensitive locations.[3] Thus, undocumented youth activists have made significant strides but continue to contend with a localized political context characterized by a mix of pro- and anti-immigrant policies and priorities.

Atlanta, Georgia

Georgia emerged as a "new immigrant destination" during the 1990s and 2000s, when the immigrant population growth rate in the metropolitan area increased from less than 10 percent to more than 25 percent (Singer 2015). During this time, labor economies in the South including manufacturing, poultry processing, and the service sector provided new and abundant opportunities for unauthorized immigrants (Lippard and Gallagher 2011; Odem and Lacy 2009; Weeks and Weeks 2011). Current estimates suggest that about 400,000 of the 10 million state residents are unauthorized immigrants, primarily from Mexico and Guatemala (Migration Policy Institute 2014), the seventh largest undocumented immigrant population in the country (Passel, Cohn and Rohal 2014). In Georgia the turn of the twenty-first century brought deteriorating economic conditions and a rapid growth in the Latino immigrant population, spurring public discourse that emphasized the social and economic costs of immigration (Odem and Lacy 2009).

Georgia was one of the first and most aggressive states in the South to seek to limit the rights of unauthorized immigrants. In 2010 the Georgia Board of Regents passed two related policies, 4.3.4. and 4.1.6. These policies banned undocumented immigrants from attending the top five public colleges in the state and required them to pay out-of-state tuition at any public college or university, including the state's community colleges. Then in 2011, the state passed HB87, The Georgia Illegal Immigration Reform and Enforcement Act, which required local law enforcement to ask for "papers" and criminalized everyday acts such as attending college or using emergency medical care services. Several provisions of the law were struck down by the United States Supreme Court's SB1070 decision.

In this same year, Jessica Colotl, a college student at Kennesaw State University, located in the metropolitan Atlanta area, was detained for driving without a license. Despite having immigrated when she was ten years old and spending half her life in Georgia, Jessica was detained and referred to Immigration and Customs Enforcement and sent to a Federal Immigration Detention Center in Alabama. She was held by local law enforcement for referral to ICE under the Secure Communities program. Her arrest and the deportation proceedings that followed were part of a larger firestorm in Georgia around issues related to undocumented immigrants. A key theme to emerge from the media coverage of her arrest was outrage that Jessica was paying in-state tuition at Kennesaw State, despite the passage of the Georgia Board of Regents' policies. The saga played out on local TV and there was significant coverage on the local Spanish television stations.

The Georgia immigrant rights community rallied around Jessica, and while she was eventually released from detention and returned to Kennesaw State as a student paying out-of-state tuition, this was a defining moment for undocumented youth activists in the state. For some, it was the first time they learned about the Board of Regents' policies and realized that they may not be able to attend college. As Mateo shared during our interview, "It was on the local news.

They found out she was going to Kennesaw State. That's where all these anti-immigrant folks started freaking out. They were like, 'These illegals are coming to our schools' and the politicians said, 'We got to do something about this.'" The media coverage of her fight to stay in the country but also to finish college, made the ban a reality for many undocumented young adults living in Georgia. As a result, "ending the ban" became a central organizing issue for undocumented youth activists in the state. Because the ban coincided with heightened activism nationally around passing the DREAM Act in 2010, undocumented young adults in Georgia were mobilizing and the ban provided a state-level focal point for their activism. Following the failure of the DREAM Act, this became the central mobilizing issue. Similar to California, community-based undocumented student organizations coalesced in major cities including Atlanta, Athens, and Savannah. Distinct from activism in California, however, undocumented youth in Georgia did not have the central organizing space that college campuses provided.

Instead, undocumented youth organized around an undocumented student frame. They also created dynamic community-based spaces for activism that fueled the growth of the undocumented student movement in the state. Among the key spaces for undocumented activism was Underground University, a grassroots non-profit organization based in the Atlanta area.

In response to the ban, faculty from the University of Georgia, located in Athens, GA about 90 miles outside of Atlanta, started an underground university modeled after Freedom Schools in the Deep South. Underground University (pseudonym) offers tuition-free, college-level classes and, while the primary purpose is to provide an educational space for undocumented students, it is a key organizing space for undocumented youth as well. Not all students who attend UU on a weekly basis are involved as activists, but UU along with the Georgia Undocumented Youth Alliance (GUYA) and uLEAD, community-based undocumented student organizations have been key sites for activism in the state. Despite a hostile context and fewer undocumented student organizations, the undocumented youth movement in Georgia is very active. Undocumented youth activists have taken a dual-purpose approach to increasing higher education in Georgia, focusing on increasing access to higher education in-state at both public and private institutions. Using similar tactics to the larger undocumented youth movement, since 2011 undocumented youth activists and citizen allies in Georgia have regularly participated in acts of civil disobedience. These have included disrupting the Board of Regents meetings, shutting down traffic in Atlanta, and occupying a classroom at the University of Georgia.

On January 9, 2015, over twenty undocumented youth and about thirty documented student allies attended a teach-in at the University of Georgia, one of the five universities in Georgia that undocumented youth are barred from attending because of their legal status. A sign posted on a classroom door read "Desegregation in Progress." At 5 p.m., when the University of Georgia police ordered participants to leave the classroom or face charges of criminal trespass, all but nine participants stayed in the classroom. Four of those who stayed behind in the classroom were undocumented, and knowingly risked arrest. Diana, one of the undocumented students who was arrested, explained during an interview at her home over a month later that she was motivated in part by her parents' sacrifice. Through tears, she said, "my parents sacrificed everything for me to have a better life ... and for Georgia to take that away, it's just something that I am not going to allow." Rodolfo, echoed this sentiment, "The original Dreamers are our parents. [...] They took the first step in bringing us here, and risking their life and ours. They knew it would give us a much better life, even though we have to struggle here." Thus, educational access remains a key claim in Georgia precisely because undocumented youth are motivated by their parents' sacrifices.

In addition to grassroots mobilization, undocumented youth in the state have also mobilized the law, bringing a lawsuit against the Georgia Board of Regents. GUYA members were named plaintiffs in a lawsuit challenging the BOR's interpretation of "lawful presence." In the wake of the DACA program, DACA recipients in Georgia claimed that they were lawfully present in the state for in-state tuition purposes. After a lengthy legal battle, in January 2017, a Superior Court judge held that DACA recipients had established lawful presence and were, therefore, eligible for in-state tuition. As the case of Georgia demonstrates, contrary to the intended impact of the state's hostile laws, undocumented young adults in Georgia are resisting anti-immigrant efforts through activist participation. One prime example of this is the 2018 Georgia Governor's race, where undocumented immigrant activists, including youth, campaigned for Stacey Abrams, the Democratic candidate.. Defying notions of undocumented immigrants being disengaged from the electoral process, undocumented immigrant activists in the state instead took a central role in canvassing for Abrams, highlighting the inherent understanding of localized political contexts.

Conclusion

In September 2017, then Attorney General Jeff Sessions announced the end of the DACA program. The announcement was just one in a series of virulently anti-immigrant initiatives under the Trump Administration including the Muslim Ban, the practice of family separation, and increasing focus on "merit-based" immigration policies. In the face of a relentless assault on immigrant communities in the United States, undocumented immigrant youth activists continue to be at the forefront of immigrant rights mobilization. The inability to get the DREAM Act and comprehensive immigration reform passed in 2006 compelled undocumented youth to direct their energies to local and state contexts, which have a more direct impact on migrants' everyday experiences than the abstract national context. Shaped by immigration discourse at the national level as well as the devolution of immigration enforcement and policymaking to states, counties, and municipalities, undocumented youth subsequently mobilized in the face of threats and opportunities (Cebulko and Silver 2016; Nicholls 2013b; Varsanyi 2010a; Walker and Leitner 2011).

The volatility of the national scene was mitigated by localized political contexts where activists and grassroots organizations determined they could exert more influence than at the federal level where grass-tops organizations and political elites largely excluded them (Martinez 2008b). The shift to local contexts also had important implications for undocumented youths' claims, targets, and tactics and strategies. In Los Angeles's accommodating context, the movement was issue-focused, centering on educational access and, once achieved, activists developed an agenda to advance immigrant rights as human rights (Cebulko and Silver 2016). In Denver's moderate context, the movement evolved from issue-focused (comprehensive immigration reform and SB 90) to student-focused (ASSET). And in Atlanta's antagonistic context, undocumented youth mobilized to oppose a ban barring them from accessing institutions of higher education; as such their efforts were primarily student-focused. Still, by respondents' own accounts, the undocumented youth movement is not a single-issue movement (Terriquez 2015a). Indeed, in 2010, when five undocumented youths were arrested after walking into Senator John McCain's Arizona office, and refused to leave until McCain agreed to sponsor the DREAM Act, it marked the first act of civil disobedience in the undocumented youth movement. It also heralded the beginning of extra-institutional tactics as a means for making their demands known. Since then, the chant "Undocumented and unafraid" has become a hallmark of the movement, serving as a major frame and signaling the manifestation of an agentic and empowered group consciousness among immigrant youth (Mansbridge and Morris 2001).Their goals are far-reaching, fueled by a desire to make their communities more hospitable (Cebulko and Silver 2016; Nicholls 2013b) while dismantling "papers, please" laws and local ordinances that curtail immigrant rights.

One thing is certain: The implementation of DACA and tuition-relief bills crystallized undocumented youths' collective identity (Polletta and Jasper 2001; Ramirez 2011), spurring mobilization to defend their interests through various institutional and extra-institutional strategies as political opportunity theory would predict (Meyer and Minkoff 2004). And, as segmented assimilation theory would predict (Portes and Zhou 1993), varying contexts influenced the claims they made, the target of their claims, and the strategies and tactics they employed in each city. Yet, even in hostile contexts, undocumented youth successfully advocated for social change and inclusion despite their liminally legal status (Menjivar 2006). They adopted frames that resonated with the general public (Yukich 2013), pushed back against negative characterizations about immigrants (Unzueta and Seif 2014), and took advantage of narrow niche-openings (Nicholls 2013b). The undocumented youth movement will need to rely on these tactics and strategies once again. As we are currently witnessing, anti-immigrant sentiment and elite opposition at the national level pose significant threats to all immigrant communities, including undocumented youth. Nonetheless, activists are once again recalibrating by focusing on growing local power, expanding their membership base, and developing long-term strategies to build a grassroots movement (Zepeda-Millán and Wallace 2018) informed by differences in localized political contexts.

Notes

1 The Development, Relief, and Education for Alien Minors Act would have provided a pathway to citizenship for undocumented youth who met eligibility criteria. Despite bipartisan efforts, it failed to pass.
2 Undocumented students are eligible to receive in-state tuition at Colorado's public colleges and universities provided they attended high school for three years before graduating, enroll within twelve months after graduating from high school, and sign an affidavit confirming they are not in the country legally, but are seeking or will seek legal status as soon as they are eligible.
3 Virginia's Law is named after Virginia Mancinas who called the police on her husband during a domestic violence dispute. Because she was undocumented, police arrested Mancinas and placed her in deportation proceedings.

References

Abrego, Leisy. 2006. "'I Can't Go to College Because I Don't Have Papers': Incorporation Patterns of Latino Undocumented Youth." *Latino Studies* 4 (3): 212–231.
Abrego, Leisy. 2008. "Legitimacy, Social Identity, and the Mobilization of Law: The Effects of Assembly Bill 540 on Undocumented Students in California." *Law & Social Inquiry* 33 (3): 709–734.
Abrego, Leisy. 2011. "Legal Consciousness of Undocumented Latinos: Fear and Stigma as Barriers to Claims-Making for First-and 1.5-Generation Immigrants." *Law & Society Review* 45 (2): 337–370.
Andrews, Abigail L. 2017. "Moralizing Regulation: The Implications of Policing 'Good' versus 'Bad' Immigrants." *Racial and Ethnic Studies* 41 (14): 2485–2503.
Armenta, Amada. 2017. *Protect, Serve, and Deport: The Rise of Policing as Immigration Enforcement*. Oakland, CA: University of California Press.
Benford, Robert D. 1993. "Frame Disputes within the Nuclear Disarmament Movement." *Social Forces* 71 (3): 677–701.
Bloemraad, Irene and Kim Voss. 2011. *Rallying for Immigrant Rights: The Fight for Inclusion in 21st Century America*. Oakland, CA: University of California Press.
Bloemraad, Irene, Fabiana Silva, and Kim Voss. 2016. "Rights, Economics, or Family? Frame Resonance, Political Ideology, and the Immigrant Rights Movement." *Social Forces* 94 (4): 1647–1674.
Burciaga, Edelina M. and Lisa M.Martinez. 2017. "How Do Political Contexts Shape Undocumented Youth Movements? Evidence from Three Immigrant Destinations." *Mobilization: An International Quarterly* 22 (4): 451–471.
Cebulko, Kara and Alexis Silver. 2016. "Navigating DACA in Hospitable and Hostile States: States Responses and Access to Membership in the Wake of Deferred Action for Childhood Arrivals." *American Behavioral Scientist*, 60 (13): 1553–1574.
Coddou, Marion. 2016. "An Institutional Approach to Collective Action: Evidence from Faith-Based Latino Mobilization in the 2006 Immigrant Rights Protests." *Social Problems* 63 (1): 127–150.
De Genova, Nicholas. 2010. "The Deportation Regime: Sovereignty, Space, and the Freedom of Movement." Pp. 33–65 in *The Deportation Regime*, edited by Nicholas De Genova and Nathalie Peutz. Durham, NC: Duke University Press.
De Genova, Nicholas. 2002. "Migrant Illegality and Deportability in Everyday Life." *Annual Review of Anthropology* 31: 419–477.

Dingeman-Cerda, Katie, Edelina M. Burciaga, and Lisa M. Martinez. 2016. "Neither Sinners Nor Saints: Complicating the Discourse of Non-Citizen Deservingness." *Association of Mexican American Educators Journal* 9 (3): 62–73.

Durand, Jorge, Douglas S. Massey, and Fernando Charvet. 2000. "The Changing Geography of Mexican Immigration to the United States: 1910–1996." *Social Science Quarterly* 81 (1): 1–15.

Eggert, Nina. 2014. "The Impact of Political Opportunities on Interorganizational Networks: A Comparison of Migrants' Organizational Fields." *Mobilization: An International Quarterly* 19 (4): 369–386.

Enriquez, Laura E and Abigail Saguy. 2016. "Coming Out of the Shadows: Harnessing a Cultural Schema to Advance the Undocumented Youth Movement." *American Journal of Cultural Sociology* 4 (1): 107–130.

Gleeson, Shannon and Roberto G. Gonzales. 2012. "When Do Papers Matter: An Institutional Analysis of Undocumented Life in the United States." *International Migration* 50 (4): 1–19.

Giron, Angela, Mike Johnston, and Morgan Carroll et al. n.d "Senate Bill 13–033." http://www.leg.state.co.us/clics/clics2013a/csl.nsf/fsbillcont/E083F0BE76DFD8F087257A8E0073BFC9?Open&file=033_enr.pdf.

Giugni, Marco and Florence Passy. 2004. "Migrant Mobilization between Political Institutions and Citizenship Regimes: A Comparison of France and Switzerland." *European Journal of Political Research* 43 (1): 51–82.

Gonzales, Roberto G. 2007. "Wasted Talent and Broken Dreams: The Lost Potential of Undocumented Students." *Immigration Policy in Focus* 5 (13): 1–11.

Gonzales, Roberto G. 2008. "Left Out But Not Shut Down: Political Activism and the Undocumented Student Movement." *Northwestern Journal of Law & Social Policy* 3: 219–239.

Gonzales, Roberto G. 2011. "Learning to Be Illegal Undocumented Youth and Shifting Legal Contexts in the Transition to Adulthood." *American Sociological Review* 76 (4): 602–619.

Gonzales, Roberto G. 2015. *Lives in Limbo*. Oakland, CA: University of California Press.

Gonzales, Roberto G., Veronica Terriquez, and Stephen P. Ruszczyk. 2014. "Becoming DACAmented: Assessing the Short-Term Benefits of Deferred Action for Childhood Arrivals (DACA)." *American Behavioral Scientist* 58 (14): 1852–1872.

Gordon, Hava Rachel. 2009. *We Fight to Win! Inequality and the Politics of Youth Activism*. New Brunswick, NJ: Rutgers University Press.

Heredia, Luisa L. 2016. "Of Radicals and DREAMers: Harnessing Exceptionality to Challenge Immigration Control." *Association of Mexican American Educators Journal* 9 (3): 74–85.

HoSang, Daniel. 2010. *Racial Propositions: Ballot Initiatives and the Making of Postwar California*. Oakland, CA: University of California Press.

Jenkins, J. Craig, and Charles Perrow. 1977. "Insurgency of the Powerless: Farm Worker Movements (1946–1972)." *American Sociological Review* 42 (2): 249–268.

Karapin, Roger. 2011. "Opportunity/Threat Spirals in the US Women's Suffrage and German Anti-Immigration Movements." *Mobilization: An International Quarterly* 16 (1): 65–80.

King, Leslie. 2008. "Ideology, Strategy and Conflict in a Social Movement Organization: The Sierra Club Immigration Wars." *Mobilization: An International Quarterly* 13 (1): 45–61.

Koopmans, Ruud and Paul Statham. 1999. "Political Claims Analysis: Integrating Protest Event and Political Discourse Approaches." *Mobilization: An International Quarterly* 4 (2): 203–221.

Lippard, Cameron D., and Charles A. Gallagher. 2011. *Being Brown in Dixie: Race, Ethnicity, and Latino Immigration in the New South*. Boulder, CO: First Forum Press.

Mansbridge, Jane and Aldon Morris. 2001. *Oppositional Consciousness: The Subjective Roots of Social Protest*. Chicago: University of Chicago Press.

Marrow, Helen. 2011. *New Destination Dreaming: Immigration, Race, and Legal Status in the Rural American South*. Palo Alto, CA: Stanford University Press.

Martinez, Lisa M. 2008. "Flowers from the Same Soil: Latino Solidarity in the Wake of the 2006 Immigrant Mobilizations." *American Behavioral Scientist* 52 (4): 557–579.

Martinez, Lisa M. 2014. "Dreams Deferred: The Impact of Legal Reforms on Undocumented Latina/o Youth." *American Behavioral Scientist* 58 (14): 1873–1890.

Martinez, Lisa M. and Maria del Carmen Salazar. 2018. "The Bright Lights: The Development of Oppositional Consciousness among DACAmented Latino Youth." *Ethnicities* 18 (2): 242–259.

McAdam, Doug, and David A. Snow. 1997. *Social Movements: Readings on Their Emergence, Mobilization, and Dynamics*. Los Angeles: Roxbury Publishing Company.

McAdam, Doug, John D. McCarthy, and Mayer N. Zald. 1988. "Social Movements." Pp. 695–737 in *Handbook of Sociology* by Neil J. Smelser (ed.). Thousand Oaks, CA: Sage Publications.

McAdam, Doug. 1986. "Recruitment to High-Risk Activism: The Case of Freedom Summer." *American Journal of Sociology* 92 (1): 64–90.

McCammon, Holly, Courtney Sanders Muse, Harmony D. Newman, and Teresa M. Terrell. 2007. "Movement Framing and Discursive Opportunity Structures: The Political Successes of the U.S. Women's Jury Movements." *American Sociological Review* 72: 725–749.

Menjívar, Cecilia. 2006. "Liminal Legality: Salvadoran and Guatemalan Immigrants' Lives in the United States." *American Journal of Sociology* 111 (4): 999–1037.

Menjívar, Cecilia. 2010. "Immigrants, Immigration, and Sociology: Reflecting on the State of the Discipline." *Sociological Inquiry* 80 (1): 3–27.

Menjivar, Cecilia, and Leisy J. Abrego. 2012. "Legal Violence: Immigration Law and the Lives of Central American Immigrants." *American Journal of Sociology* 117 (5): 1380–1421.

Meyer, David S. 1993. "Institutionalizing Dissent: The United States Structure of Political Opportunity and the End of the Nuclear Freeze Movement." *Sociological Forum* 8 (2): 157–179.

Meyer, David S., and Debra C. Minkoff. 2004. "Conceptualizing Political Opportunity." *Social Forces* 82 (4): 1457–1492.

Meyer, David S. and Suzanne Staggenborg. 1996. "Movements, Countermovements, and the Structure of Political Opportunity." *American Journal of Sociology* 101 (6): 1628–1660.

Migration Policy Institute. 2014. *State Immigration Data Profiles*. Washington, D.C.

Morales, Laura, and Luis Ramiro. 2011. "Gaining Political Capital through Social Capital: Policy-Making Inclusion and Network Embeddedness of Migrants' Associations in Spain." *Mobilization: An International Quarterly* 16 (2): 147–164.

Muñoz, Susana M. 2015. *Identity, Social Activism, and the Pursuit of Higher Education: The Journey Stories of Undocumented and Unafraid Community Activists*. New York: Peter Lang.

Negrón-Gonzales, Genevieve. 2013. "Navigating 'Illegality': Undocumented Youth and Oppositional Consciousness." *Children and Youth Services Review* 35 (8): 1284–1290.

Negrón-Gonzales, Genevieve. 2015. "Undocumented Youth Activism as Counter-Spectacle: Civil Disobedience and Testimonio in the Battle around Immigration Reform." *Aztlán: A Journal of Chicano Studies* 40 (1): 87–112.

Nicholls, Walter J. 2013a. *The DREAMers: How the Undocumented Youth Movement Transformed the Immigrant Rights Debate*. Stanford, CA: Stanford University Press.

Nicholls, Walter J. 2013b. "From Political Opportunities to Niche-Openings: The Dilemmas of Mobilizing for Immigrant Rights in Inhospitable Environments." *Theory and Society* 43 (1): 23–49.

Odem, Mary E. and Elaine Lacy. 2009. *Latino Immigrants and the Transformation of the U.S. South*. Athens, GA: University of Georgia.

Pallares, Amalia. 2014. *Family Activism: Immigrant Struggles and the Politics of Noncitizenship*. New Brunswick, NJ: Rutgers University Press.

Pallares, Amalia and Nilda Flores-Gonzales. 2010. *Marcha!: Latino Chicago and the Immigrant Rights Movement*. Urbana, IL: University of Illinois Press.

Passel, Jeffrey S., D'Vera Cohn, and Molly Rohal. 2014. "Unauthorized Immigrant Totals Rise in 7 States, Fall in 14." Washington, D.C.: Pew Research Center.

Patler, Caitlin, and Roberto G. Gonzales. 2015. "Framing Citizenship: Media Coverage of Anti- Deportation Cases Led by Undocumented Immigrant Youth Organisations." *Journal of Ethnic and Migration Studies* 41 (9): 1453–1474.

Perez, William, Roberta Espinoza, Karina Ramos, Heidi Coronado, and Richard Cortes. 2010. "Civic Engagement Patterns of Undocumented Mexican Students." *Journal of Hispanic Higher Education* 9 (3): 245–265.

Pew Hispanic Research Center. 2017. "20 U.S. Metropolitan Areas with the Largest Number of Unauthorized Immigrants." Washington, D.C.: Pew Research Center. Available at: http://pewrsr.ch/2vOkvHo.

Polletta, Francesca and James M. Jasper. 2001. "Collective Identity and Social Movements." *Annual Review of Sociology* 27: 283–305.

Portes, Alejandro and Rubén Rumbaut. 2014. *Immigrant America: A Portrait* (4th ed.). Oakland, CA: University of California Press.

Portes, Alejandro and Min Zhou. 1993. "The New Second Generation: Segmented Assimilation and Its Variants." *The Annals of the American Academy of Political and Social Sciences* 530 (1): 74–96.

Provine, Doris Marie, and Monica W. Varsanyi. 2012. "Scaled Down: Perspectives on State and Local Creation and Enforcement of Immigration Law Introduction the Special Issue of *Law and Policy*." *Law and Policy* 34 (2): 105–112.

Ramirez, Ricardo. 2011. *"Mobilization."* In *Rallying for Immigrant Right*, edited by Irene Bloemraad and Kim Voss. Oakland, CA: University of California Press.

Rincon, Alejandra. 2010. *Undocumented Immigrants and Higher Education: Si Se Puede!* New York: LFB Scholarly Publishing.

Rosenberger, Sieglinde, and Jakob Winkler. 2014. "Com/passionate Protests: Fighting the Deportation of Asylum Seekers." *Mobilization: An International Quarterly* 19 (2): 165–184.

Rumbaut, Rubén. 2008. "Reaping What You Sow: Immigration, Youth, and Reactive Ethnicity." *Applied Developmental Science*, 12 (2): 108–111.

Seif, Hinda. 2004. "'Wise Up!' Undocumented Latino Youth, Mexican-American Legislators, and the Struggle for Higher Education Access." *Latino Studies* 2 (2): 210–230.
Singer, Audrey. 2015. "Metropolitan Immigrant Gateways Revisited, 2014." Washington D.C.: The Brookings Institution.
Silver, Alexis. 2018. *Shifting Boundaries: Immigrant Youth Negotiating National, State, and Small-Town Politics*. Stanford, CA: Stanford University Press.
Steil, Justin Peter and Ion Bogdan Vasi. 2014. "The New Immigration Contestation: Social Movements and Local Immigration Policy Making in the United States, 2000–11." *American Journal of Sociology* 119 (4): 1104–1155.
Stuesse, Angela and Mathew Coleman. 2014. "Automobility, Immobility, Altermobility: Surviving and Resisting the Intensification of Immigrant Policing." *City & Society* 26 (1): 51–72.
Tarrow, Sidney. 1988. "National Politics and Collective Action: Recent Theory and Research in Western Europe and the United States." *Annual Review of Sociology* 14 (1): 421–440.
Tarrow, Sidney. 2011. *Power in Movement: Social Movements and Contentious Politics*. New York: Cambridge University Press.
Terriquez, Veronica. 2015a. "Intersectional Mobilization, Social Movement Spillover, and Queer Youth Leadership in the Immigrant Rights Movement." *Social Problems* 62 (3): 343–362.
Terriquez, Veronica. 2015b. "Training Young Activists: Grassroots Organizing and Youths' Civic and Political Trajectories." *Sociological Perspectives* 58 (2): 223–242.
Unzueta Carrasco, Tania A. and Hinda Seif. 2014. "Disrupting the Dream: Undocumented Youth Reframe Citizenship and Deportability through Anti-Deportation Activism." *Latino Studies* 12 (2): 279–299.
Varsanyi, Monica W. 2010a. *Taking Local Control: Immigration Policy Activism in U.S. Cities and States*. Stanford, CA: Stanford University Press.
Varsanyi, Monica W. 2010b. "City Ordinances as 'Immigration Policing': Local Governments and the Regulation of Undocumented Day Laborers." Pp. 135–154 in *Taking Local Control: Immigration Policy Activism in U.S. Cities and States*, edited by M.W. Varsanyi. Stanford, CA: Stanford University Press.
Vigil, Ernesto B. 1999. *The Crusade for Justice: Chicano Militancy and the Government's War on Dissent*. Madison, WI: University of Wisconsin Press.
Walker, Kyle E. and Helga Leitner. 2011. "The Variegated Landscape of Local Immigration Policies in the United States." *Urban Geography* 32 (2): 156–178.
Weeks, Gregory B., and John R. Weeks. 2011. *Irresistible Forces: Explaining Latin American Migration to the United States and its Effects on the South*. Albuquerque, NM: University of New Mexico Press.
Yukich, Grace. 2013. "Constructing the Model Immigrant: Movement Strategy and Immigrant Deservingness in the New Sanctuary Movement." *Social Problems* 60 (3): 302–320.
Zepeda-Millán, Chris. 2017. *Latino Mass Mobilization: Immigration, Racialization, and Activism*. New York: Cambridge University Press.
Zepeda-Millán, Chris and Sophia J. Wallace. 2018. "Mobilizing for Immigrant and Latino Rights Under Trump." Pp. 90–108 in *The Resistance: The Dawn of the Anti-Trump Opposition Movement*, edited by David S. Meyer and Sidney Tarrow. New York: Oxford University Press.

8 Gaining a voice

Storytelling and undocumented youth activism in Chicago

Thomas Swerts

At the 2012 Democratic National Convention, undocumented[1] youth activist Anita[2] shared the following story:

> My name is Anita, and I'm from San Antonio, Texas. Like so many Americans of all races and backgrounds, I was brought here as a child. I've been here ever since. I graduated as valedictorian of my class at the age of sixteen and earned a double major at the age of twenty. I know I have something to contribute to my economy and my country. I feel just as American as any of my friends or neighbors. But I've had to live almost my entire life knowing I could be deported just because of the way I came here.
>
> President Obama fought for the DREAM Act to help people like me. And when Congress refused to pass it, he didn't give up. Instead, he took action so that people like me can apply to stay in our country and contribute. We will keep fighting for reform, but while we do, we are able to work, study and pursue the American dream.

Anita's speech represents a growing trend in undocumented youth activism in the United States, namely the sharing of life stories as a political tool. In the struggle around the Development, Relief and Education for Alien Minors (DREAM) Act, the effectiveness of storytelling as a political tool comes to the fore. Introduced in 2001, the DREAM Act proposed to provide a path to citizenship for the estimated 1.8 million undocumented youth in the United States (Gonzales 2008). From the outset, immigrant rights advocates used undocumented youth's stories to legitimize their claims to rights. Yet, it was not until 2010, when undocumented youth activists started to organize their own actions, that storytelling became a central strategy within the movement. Supported by the slogan "undocumented, unafraid," undocumented youth have since shared their stories in public at coming-out rallies, civil disobedience actions, and mock graduations all over the country (see Seif 2011).

Previous research has demonstrated that undocumented youth's precarious legal status puts their mental, educational, social, and economic well-being in jeopardy (Abrego 2006; Gonzales 2008, 2011; Gonzales et al. 2014). Sociological theories of mobilization therefore lead us to expect that such marginalized actors would refrain from engaging in risky and emotionally stressful behavior like political participation. This raises the question of how we can understand the processes whereby undocumented youth become political. In this chapter, I present an ethnographic case study that investigates storytelling practices among undocumented youth organizers in Chicago.[3] Integrating insights from the social movement literature on narrative and emotions, I argue that storytelling is used as a means to incorporate undocumented youth into a community, mobilize support, and legitimize grievances. Furthermore, I will show that emotions play a key role in structuring the social transaction between storyteller and audience in each of these contexts. These findings indicate that scholars should pay greater attention to the power of personal narratives as a political tool for mobilizing marginalized populations.

This chapter is structured as follows. First, I outline how the case of undocumented youth activism speaks towards ongoing academic debates on narrative and emotions in social movements. Second, I explain the methods used in this study. Third, I focus on the different uses of storytelling as a social movement practice. Finally, I outline what this study teaches us about the theoretical linkages between storytelling and mobilization.

Narrative, emotions, and undocumented youth mobilization

In theoretical terms, this chapter deals with narratives[4] and their ability to "do political work" (Riessman 2007: 8). Indeed, stories can be used in order to mobilize people to take political action. The case of undocumented youth activism is an excellent lens through which we can further unravel the connection between narrative and mobilization. Excluded from citizenship, undocumented youth cannot rely on traditional forms of political participation. Due to their precarious legal status, they are barred from the opportunities, resources, and networks that traditional social movement scholars tend to highlight as drivers of mobilization. Against all odds, undocumented youth in the US have nevertheless been able to gain a voice in recent years. The role that storytelling plays in building and sustaining the undocumented youth movement has been relatively ignored (see Gonzales 2008; Galindo 2011). The aim of my research is to shed further light on the connection between narrative and mobilization by unraveling the processes whereby undocumented youth organize themselves politically.

Narrative made its entry into social movement scholarship in the mid-eighties. Framing scholars were among the first to pay explicit attention to the political functions of narrative, although indirectly (Snow et al. 1986; Benford and Snow 2000). These scholars argued that collective action frames, or action-oriented sets of beliefs and meanings, inspire and legitimate the activities and campaigns of social movement actors (Benford and Snow 2000: 614). Since then, critics have argued that framing scholars lack a deeper understanding of the emotional, moral, and cultural mechanisms that can explain the power of narrative to "inspire" and "legitimate" political action

(Polletta 1998; Davis 2002). In their view, framing theory has a tendency to overemphasize cognitive factors, logical persuasion, and consensus of belief (Davis 2002: 9). Instead, Polletta (1998, 2006) argued that the power of storytelling stems from its ambiguity and openness to interpretation. Furthermore, Ganz (2001) has argued that storytelling goes beyond framing because it allows actors to learn and exercise agency, supports individual and collective identity work, and provides emotional and moral motivations for political action. My analysis builds on these critiques to argue that the functionality of storytelling for social movements is much more fragmented and diverse than framing scholars lead us to believe. The case of undocumented activism illustrates that multiple storytellers tell stories in interaction with audiences in different contexts. The role that storytelling plays in social movements can thus only be grasped by developing an approach that studies "who is telling the story, with whom they are interacting, where and when stories are told" (Ganz 2001).

Existing empirical studies of storytelling in social movements have typically focused on a singular function that narrative performs at a specific moment in a movement's life course. For example, Polletta (1998) demonstrated the role that storytelling played in recruiting new members outside formal movement organizations during black students' sit-in protests in the 1960s. Similarly, Ganz's (2001) study of the 1960s farm workers' movement has indicated the influence of narrative at the early stages of movement emergence. Moreover, Plummer's study (1995) of the gay rights movement showed how telling sexual stories was an essential way in which gay rights activists built a sense of community. Finally, Gamson (2002) has argued that storytelling has encouraged the civic engagement of women in mediatized discussions on abortion. What is lacking, however, is a systematic consideration of the diverging uses and practices of storytelling at different stages in a movement's life course.

My goal is to advance the academic debate on narrative in social movements by mapping how the functionality of storytelling differs depending on the context and the audience. In this respect, I build on the work of Fine (2002), who has argued for an understanding of social movements as consisting of "bundles of narratives." Within group cultures, he argues, stories tend to become culturally central because they have functional group effects. The main analytical task then becomes to identify the different roles that storytelling plays in key social movement processes operating both in intra- and extra-movement contexts. In particular, this study outlines three main modalities of storytelling as a social movement practice, namely community building, mobilization, and claims making. It shows how storytelling is differentially employed throughout a movement's life course.

A systematic approach to storytelling in social movements simultaneously requires a more explicit theorization of the relationship between narrative and emotions. Stories are always collaborative productions that involve emotional transactions between the storyteller and the audience (Ewick and Silbey 2003: 1343). Narrative's ability to do political work is closely connected to the emotional work it does to persuade audiences. It is therefore all the more surprising that the theoretical connection between storytelling and emotions is underdeveloped. A largely detached literature on emotions and mobilization has emerged in the wake of the pioneering work of Jasper (1997, 1998). Jasper (2011: 286) argues that models and concepts of narrative in social movements are "misspecified if they do not include explicit emotional mechanisms," yet very few studies do so. I argue that we need to conceive of emotions as mechanisms that help to explain the political power of storytelling for marginalized populations.

The work on coming-out stories contains important insights with regards to studying the mobilization patterns of stigmatized groups. Coming out has a long history in the US that is heavily intertwined with the struggle for gay rights (see Epstein 1996). Most of the movements that deploy coming-out stories strategically use emotions to contest marginalized status. In this respect, studies on coming out allude to the fact that emotions are essentially related to the three modalities of storytelling advanced in this chapter: community building, mobilization, and claims making. For example, Bell's (1988, 2009) work on the women's health movement shows how women exposed to DES (diethylstilbestrol) become incorporated into the movement by collectively expressing emotions. Shrock, Holden, and Reid (2004) have shown how transgendered people create a sense of community and solidarity through interpersonal emotion work. Gould (2009) has argued that mobilization in response to the AIDS crisis can better be explained by referring to emotions than by standard political opportunity models. Finally, Whittier (2001) has demonstrated how the movement against child sexual abuse legitimized its claims to recognition by deploying oppositional emotions through coming out. Using the case of undocumented youth activism, I will argue that the political functionality of storytelling for marginalized groups in terms of community building, mobilization, and claims making is mediated by emotions.

Methods: ethnography, triangulation, and reflexivity

I employ a case study approach to investigate different uses of storytelling within the undocumented youth movement. Case study logic is most effective for asking questions about unknown processes before the start of the research (Small 2009). I selected the Immigrant Youth Justice League (IYJL) as my main research site because of its central position in the undocumented youth movement in the United States. IYJL is a "Chicago-based organization led by undocumented youth working towards full recognition of the rights and contributions of all immigrants through education, leadership development, policy advocacy, resource gathering, and mobilization" (IYJL 2011). IYJL organizers were the first to experiment with storytelling as a political strategy. Moreover, they spread this strategy through their participation in civil disobedience, rallies, and networking efforts in Alabama, Arizona, Georgia, California, New York, Washington, DC, and many other states. IYJL thus provides a compelling case to study the relationship between storytelling and undocumented youth mobilization.

Studying storytelling as an object of research involves methodological challenges (see Askham 1982; Gubrium and Holstein 1998; Polletta et al. 2011). As Atkinson and Delamont (2006) rightfully argue, there exists an "interview society culture" wherein social scientists are too ready to celebrate narratives without subjecting them to systematic scrutiny. I argue that we need to steer away from the methodological fallacy of reifying narratives by keeping our distance from the narrative data and by studying the context wherein stories are told. At the same time, one also needs to be cautious about how to use so-called metastories, or stories about storytelling (Riessman 1993). I address these issues, on the one hand, by triangulating complementary evidence about storytelling from different data sources, and, on the other, by being self-reflexive about the stories that I told during participant observation (see Bourdieu and Wacquant 1992).

I used a triangulation of qualitative research techniques (see Tashakkori and Teddlie 2003): ethnographic observation, in-depth interviewing, and content analysis. Doing an ethnography of IYJL allowed for observing how life stories are crafted, directed, and staged—in other words, how they are "brought to life." I participated at IYJL for two years between 2010 and 2012. I conducted about 70 observations during this period, corresponding to approximately 260 hours in the field. I participated in internal meetings, shout-it-out events, coming-out rallies, marches, press conferences, college fairs, and organizational retreats. In-depth interviewing was used to investigate how activists became involved and how they experienced being an IYJL member. I interviewed the fourteen core members of IYJL, twelve of whom were undocumented. Of these members, nine were female and five were male. All but two were from Mexican origin, and they were between nineteen and twenty-seven years old. Respondents were between one and ten years old when they migrated to the United States, corresponding with being undocumented for a period between ten and twenty-one years. The interviews lasted between about one hour and a half to two hours and were all done in English. English is the dominant language of expression for undocumented youth in the context of IYJL and all respondents spoke English fluently. All interviews were transcribed and analyzed with qualitative data analysis software.

Utterances such as "uhm" and "like" that were not crucial to understand the data were cleaned up for the sake of readability. All identifying information was edited out of the transcripts. The codebook for the interviews was comprised of 112 codes organized in sixteen groups. I focused on discovering overarching themes in youth's experiences (related to, for example, "being undocumented," "identity," "IYJL membership," and so on) that emerged in the interview interaction. I analyzed twenty-four coming-out narratives[5] from the 2010–2012 period in more detail in a separate analysis file. I contrasted and compared personal narratives across data sources. Besides participant observation and in-depth interviews, I undertook a content analysis of more than fifty minutes of meetings, eighteen personal blog posts, organizational pamphlets, reports, press releases, and website content.

In terms of reflexivity, I tried to be as conscious as possible about how researchers feed into processes of storytelling (see Andrews 2007: 3). My position as an "ally" in the organization had to be heavily negotiated. During this negotiation, I became aware of the importance of my self-presentation. The non-emotional version of my story as an academic doing research was rejected from the start. People questioned my intentions and wanted to know why I was doing this research. I quickly found out that I was being judged on my actions rather than on my qualifications. In order for me to be accepted, I had to demonstrate my intentions and earn my place in practice. I drove people around when I could. I helped build the stage for the coming-out rallies. I made posters and distributed flyers. I tried to do what was expected from other allies in the organization. I was often invited to check the privileges that I had due to my legal status. As an ally, I was at times excluded from activities that were reserved for people who were undocumented. Participating as an ally in IYJL's activities thus made me experience how boundaries were drawn and communities were defined first hand.

The social construction of life stories

I came across many life stories during my research at IYJL. At times, I listened to people's stories as a participant in a crowd. On other occasions, I sat next to journalists and actively took notes of stories during a press conference. Sometimes asking people how they got involved in the movement led them to recount their stories. I also read people's stories in press releases and blog posts or I watched people giving testimonies in video clips. Without exception, these stories were powerful, emotional accounts of how being undocumented had affected these youth's lives. At surface level, these stories seem to be deeply personal narratives, focusing on subjective experiences of exclusion. But in fact, storytelling has different meanings depending on the actors involved, the use that it fulfills as a practice, the context in which it is employed, and the type of interaction in which it is staged. In other words, undocumented youth activists carefully construct life stories in order to fit the intended purpose.

This is well illustrated by the following excerpt from my interview with IYJL organizer Raquel. Asked how she experienced sharing her story, Raquel replied,

> In IYJL we have guidelines for who you're talking to, who your audience is, so it depends how I tell my story or the things that I highlight. For example when I went to give a talk at a high school class today, it was a completely different experience than talking to a bunch of people at a rally or a shout-it-out event, so you have to know what to highlight so they can connect to you. And ... you kind of have to strategize all the time in terms of what you say.

As this example shows, undocumented youth organizers have institutionalized storytelling strategies that are supposed to "guide" storytellers to tell their story in the most effective way across diverging contexts. In each of these contexts, storytellers have different goals to achieve in interaction with the intended audience. It is exactly these processes of crafting, editing, and performing narrative within the undocumented youth movement that is the further subject of this chapter.

The social construction of life stories is a process that involves both rationality and emotions. While storytelling is always strategic, it nevertheless relies on the emotional impact that it has on the audience as to generate certain effects (see Ewick and Silbey 2003). Table 8.1 represents a typology of storytelling practices within the undocumented youth movement.

Table 8.1 shows that the functionality of storytelling depends on context and audience. First, storytelling is used within the organization to create a social environment of emotional support, belonging, and acceptance. It is this supportive environment that allows undocumented youth to overcome barriers to political participation. The audience here consists as much of organizational members as of new members who need to be incorporated into the organization. In this sense, storytelling is a *community-building* practice. Second, undocumented youth disclose their status in public interactions with their constituencies in order to encourage others to join the movement. These theatrical instances of storytelling tend to be staged at rallies, demonstrations, and other public gatherings. The audience here consists of people ranging from undocumented youth, who need to be further convinced to solidify their political involvement, to community leaders, who need to be urged to take action. Hence, in this context, storytelling is a *mobilizing practice*. Finally, undocumented youth collect, direct, and disseminate life stories in interactions with external actors like the media, politicians, and the general public in order to justify and legitimate their political grievances. In this way, storytelling is a *claims-making practice*. In what follows, I investigate these three dimensions of storytelling as a political tool in more detail.

Table 8.1 Storytelling as a social movement practice

Context	Audience	Type of Interaction	Purpose
Intra-organizational	Organization's members/Newcomers	Meetings, Shout-it-Outs, Retreats	Community building
Intra-movement	Movement constituency/ Community organizers	Coming-out rallies, Protests, Demonstrations	Mobilization
Extra-movement	Public/Media/ Politicians	Press Conferences, Lobbying	Claims making

Shout it out: storytelling as a community-building practice

Ilene initially took part in IYJL when the organization was not much more than an informal support group that was trying to prevent the deportation of a fellow student. When I asked her how she became involved, she referred to the emotional connection she felt to the stories of other undocumented youth.

> The other groups that I'd been, we never talked about being undocumented. When we were in IYJL, all sitting around that table and talking about our statuses and our stories, I was like, I've finally found a group where people know what frustrations I'm going through and can actually identify with them. And I don't have to explain what it feels like because they know. And they know how frustrating it is, and some of them have already dealt with it and can actually help, and some of them are just starting to go through it and so I think that when we met at the space and were able to come across some stories, that was beautiful and probably the best feeling I've ever had. And I fell in love with IYJL, and I think I fell in love with every single person in IYJL.

As this example illustrates, undocumented youth form and strengthen social ties by telling stories and sharing emotions. Storytelling is a social transaction that engages people in a communicative relationship (Davis 2002: 16). It is used to incorporate new members into the movement and to strengthen relationships between existing members (see Polletta 1998).

Through the act of listening to and sharing each other's stories, new members are able to identify themselves with undocumented youth as a community. Storytelling thus entails a collectivization of personal experiences and a personalization of collective experiences. Emotions play a key role in linking the "story of me" with the "story of us." The emotional transaction that takes place during storytelling fosters feelings of community and belonging, and creates and solidifies ties between community members. These feelings of community are in turn crucial for undocumented youth to experience a sense of agency.

Storytelling is heavily integrated into IYJL's internal organizational activities. In this context, coming out—which refers here to talking openly about one's legal status—is a central organizational strategy. My first encounter with coming out was at a meeting in August 2010. At the time, the DREAM Act debate was still ongoing and there was a general sense of urgency in the air. The meeting was called "Why we can't wait." IYJL members went around the circle introducing themselves to newcomers by saying, "My name is … and I'm undocumented." This organizational ritual of disclosing one's legal status was also an invitation for others to do the same as a display of personal strength. By disclosing their status in front of others, they indicate that IYJL is a "safe space" where you can openly do so (see Polletta 1999). During the weekly meetings that I would attend in the two years after this initiation, I experienced how this organizational ritual facilitated the incorporation of newcomers into the movement. Cynthia was one of the people who had just joined the movement when I started my research at IYJL. When I asked her how she joined the movement, she reflected on how this organizational ritual had affected her.

> I remember going to my first meeting .... IYJL ... came to campus and I went to their meeting. They said introductions, and they all said their names, and they said "I'm undocumented" and I was like "Why are they doing this?" ... And I remember there was a minibreak in between a meeting and someone came up to me and they were like, "Where are you from and why are you here?" and I'm like, "Oh, you know, this is where I'm from, and I'm undocumented," and so I was like ... "Why did I just say that?" ...
>
> And they were really open about their status, and that's what I think attracted me most about the group, cause, I've never ... been around people who were so open about something that you're not supposed to talk about. So I've been with IYJL for a little over a year now and at the beginning it might have been about you because you found someone you could talk to, you found a group of friends you were comfortable with, because you found people who are active. And eventually it becomes not so much about you, and you realize this is about everyone else.

While Cynthia came across as shy and insecure when I first met her, I witnessed how she transformed into a confident youth leader over time. In the beginning, she barely participated in the meetings. But when she slowly started to share her story with other members of the organization, her engagement in the movement solidified. In December 2010, I witnessed how she shared her personal struggles concerning mental health and suicide during a "die-in" in downtown Chicago. After that, Cynthia would become a central leader within IYJL who organized events, talked to the press, and came out in public numerous times.

Joining the undocumented youth community involves scrupulous self-examination, overcoming fear, and facing traumas. In this context, storytelling is a very emotional process for the storytellers and their audiences alike. Jobito recalls how he experienced hearing other people's stories:

> The first time I heard other people talk about being undocumented. I just cried for that whole day, I think, most of us did. It was just a big group of us who sat around the table and talked about being undocumented .... I think we cried because ... it was just so raw, the emotion, and good to be able to say it out loud, and have the group, like more than just one person, more than just you, knows how it feels to say you're undocumented.

As this example shows, it is through sharing stories and emotions that undocumented youth start to feel part of a community (see Plummer 1995). They tend to share their stories with others for the first time in the "safe space" of the organization. In this environment, they can share their story with an audience that is able to relate to their experiences. Sharing one's story is not only considered to be a prerequisite for personal growth but also, by extension, for membership of the undocumented youth community.

Just how storytelling fosters feelings of community became clear at the first shout-it-out I attended. IYJL member Claudia welcomed us. "First of all," she said, "We should all know that this is a safe space for people to come out and feel supported." Hence, everyone was told to respect the community agreements. "What is most important," she said, "is the [principle] that says what is said here stays here; what is learned here leaves here." Raquel started by telling her story to the group. While she was talking, it was quiet in the circle. At a certain point, she started crying. People passed around a box of tissues. Ulises shared how he had been lying in bed worrying all night about his legal status and the problems this was causing at school. Next up were some people who were coming out for the very first time. Miguel was a math student. He shared his experiences crossing the border and growing up undocumented. He was part of a mixed-status family, which meant that his younger siblings were American citizens. He became very emotional while he was talking and started to cry. The other youth who shared their stories that day cried as well. In an interview I did with Ulises afterwards, he talked about the emotional bond that storytelling creates:

> When you listen to others' stories, you feel a certain level of connection ... it's enlightening, and sometimes even emotional, but in a good way. I can talk to them and share my story and connect with them at an emotional level and they might be able to understand me, understand what I am going through.

When Ulises shared his worries related to his educational future that day, I noticed that this indeed changed my sense of personal connection with him. Whereas I had talked to him previously before or after meetings, hearing his personal story during the shout-it-out allowed me to get a better sense of what he had to go through emotionally on a daily basis. Seeing Raquel, another IYJL member who I had come to know as a confident youth leader, break down and cry in front of me moved me to the point that tears came into my eyes. When it was time for me to share my story, I highlighted my own migration to the US. Afterwards, I could not help but feel that what I was able to share as an "ally" with legal status was somehow not enough. This is because the act of sharing one's story has a distinctive power to it in the case of undocumented youth. Telling their stories to peers in the safe space of the organization is a first and necessary step towards political participation. In doing so, they break the circle of social isolation that governed their lives before and look for acceptance and recognition from their community of peers.

In an intra-organizational context, storytelling thus creates a sense of community among undocumented youth. Getting recognition for their personal experiences by their peers stimulates undocumented youth to regain feelings of self-worth and membership. Undocumented youth become gradually incorporated into the organization by engaging themselves in these emotional episodes of self-examination. As a narrative practice, storytelling allows individual youth to connect their "story of me" to the undocumented youth community's collective "story of us." The strength of the community then comes to depend on the continuous and recurring narrative mobilization of feelings of belonging and solidarity.

Coming out: storytelling as a mobilizing practice

In interactions with their constituencies, undocumented youth activists employ storytelling as a way to mobilize people. There is something about telling one's story in front of a crowd that can trigger strong emotional responses from the audience involved. When speakers share their stories with other supporters at public rallies, they stress those features of their own story that resonate with the shared grievances of their constituency—that is, other undocumented immigrants. In this sense, organizers do their best to ensure that individual stories resonate with the "story of us" that they have in mind. In other words, the movement's public testimonies are well-orchestrated performances that are partly directed by community organizers. Tamara explained how she strategically uses her life story as a political tool.

> Telling my story publicly, I have become very used to it. I feel like I try hard to be both entertaining and politically interesting, so I ... have told it so many times that I know which parts of my story shock people, and I know where the, like, "Oh" comes, and I also know which parts to highlight ... depending on the point that I am trying to make.

As one of the most experienced leaders, Tamara has trained several storytellers herself. She believes that there are several necessary characteristics of good public stories: narratives need to have entertainment value, they should be politically interesting, and they must cause moral shocks in people (see Jasper 1997).

The crafting of stories for mobilization purposes is best illustrated by the preparation of speakers for the coming-out rallies. In 2011, I investigated how Claudia, a new member at the time, was being trained to speak at a large coming-out event. Several IYJL members had gathered to make banners for the rally. Simultaneously, speakers for the rally were getting trained downstairs. When I entered the training room, people were practicing their speeches.

> They spoke loudly with powerful voices, and people had tears in their eyes. Claudia got interrupted during her speech by one of the organizers. "Less acting," she was told. "OK, you felt frustrated, but why?" A few

moments later, Claudia came into the room upstairs and sat down crying, and Ilene talked to her. "It is just so difficult to have to tell my story over and over again," she said. Ilene comforted her, and reassured her that coming out would be a great experience. Although coming out is a performance—a theatrical rendering of what undocumented youth go through in their lives—it cannot look or feel like a performance to the audience. Organizers strive to retain the authenticity of these stories in order to maximize each narrative's emotional resonance with the audience.

The subsequent year, I investigated how Xenia and Yolanda, two undocumented sisters who had been recently recruited by IYJL, experienced the training process for a large coming-out rally on March 10, 2012. They paired with Raquel and Jobito, who had spoken in previous years, to prepare their speeches. Tamara helped in the training too, saying, "With them [Raquel and Jobito], you should expect to share your story, cry, connect emotionally and practice your speech." Weeks after her coming out, Yolanda told me that she had gone through several stages before she was able to deliver her speech in the right way. First, she shared the unscripted version of her story, as she would tell it to a friend, in pairs. When she then had to share her story during a shout-it-out, she choked. Writing it down made her more comfortable the second time. By the last training, she felt ready to speak at the large rally. Xenia told me that she immediately knew that she would want to be one of the speakers for the rally. However, at the beginning, she did not fully understand what speaking at the March 10 event really meant, and who the audience was supposed to be:

> At the meetings we were discussing what was the target. Then I started learning that the target was undocumented [persons]. I thought that our personal stories were meant to be heard and that the target was going to be everybody ... but then they said that it was the undocumented ... so I had to think about how I would talk to another undocumented [person] in a way that, in my mind, I would have to convince them to get involved and active. So I think I went through a whole process of understanding ... what it meant to speak on March 10th .... That day we had a final training and ... that's when they were pushing me to be more expressive, more descriptive. I think that was the hardest part of the process, to be more open than I was expecting.

During the trainings, Xenia learned that undocumented youth were the target audience, the movement's primary constituency. She also learned that her speech had to be an emotional and expressive story in order to have the mobilizing effect that the organizers had in mind.

The coming-out events offer undocumented youth a public stage where they share stories with the others like themselves. These highly scripted narrative performances aim to evoke emotional identification with the audience to motivate them to join and/or support the movement. I witnessed my first coming-out rally on March 10, 2011. The eight undocumented youth who would be "coming out of the shadows" on Dailey Plaza in downtown Chicago were prepared one last time. A local theater group had agreed to lend their stage for the occasion. A crowd of youth, parents, allies, activists, scholars, journalists, and sympathizers greeted the eight speakers as they lined up on stage. When Claudia's turn came, this is what she had to say:

> As a helpless five-year-old, clutching the hands of my mother and father, I never dreamt of living a life entrenched in fear and shame. Neither did my parents when they uprooted my sisters and me from our quiet life in the Philippines to come to America—the land of plenty, the land of freedom. But for the greater part of the seventeen years I've lived in this country that I call home, I have been afraid. When I was eleven years old, a distant relative threatened to report my family to Immigration Services because we overstayed our visas and were now out of status. The thought of deportation prompted my family to flee our home and leave behind everything—my parents' jobs, my school, our friends—with little hope of ever coming back. We spent over a month and a half in hiding until we felt safe enough to return. From then on, my parents told me never to tell anyone about our status.
>
> I grew up feeling less than others, but my undocumented status only pushed me to work ten times harder to prove that I matter and deserve the life my parents sacrificed to give me. I did and continue to do what I think is right to make my parents proud and to persevere through all the obstacles in my education. And thus far, I have no regrets. But that's not to say I fully accept my situation. No, I still cry. I still cry for the dreams suspended in limbo as I reach with all my might yet remain constrained and stuck in place. ...
>
> To all the dreamers out there in my community, to all the young people hiding out in your bedrooms wishing with all your heart that something would change, that this country would finally recognize you as an American and allow you a chance at a real future, all I can say is you can't wish for change, nor can you go at it by yourself. The time is now to emerge from the shadows because you are not alone. Come out of the shadows and take action. Be honest with yourself and those around you. Reclaim your identity and accept yourself, regardless of discrimination and hate. Look at yourself in the mirror, in the eyes, and say, I am undocumented, but I am not ashamed. My name is Claudia. I am undocumented. I am unafraid. And I am unapologetic.

Standing in the crowd, I noted how many people cried or held hands while hearing Claudia speak. The emotional effect of the speeches on the audience was noticeable throughout the event. Whenever speakers paused or their voices trembled, the audience cheered or clapped to encourage storytellers to continue. Both the content and the theatrical staging of the speeches had been constructed as to amplify such effects. Indeed, Claudia's narrative was the outcome of intense coaching sessions with other organizers to craft a compelling story for mobilization purposes.

Emotions are hereby strategically invoked to invite an empathetic understanding of the audience. When we look at the narrative more closely, we can see how the emotions invoked change from fear, shame, feeling less than others and sadness to feeling proud, being honest, no longer feeling ashamed and being unafraid and unapologetic. The hardships Carla had to go through because of her status function as the personal pretext to launch a movement-wide call to action. Claudia's personal story (story of me) hereby becomes interwoven with the story of where the movement is going (story of us). The other five speeches made that day all evoked emotions like fear, shame, sadness, and hope. They also invariably ended with a standardized sentence that repeated the slogan of the rally, namely, "My name is X and I am undocumented, unafraid, and unapologetic."

Exactly one year later, I witnessed my second coming-out rally. Xenia spoke first that day. When Yolanda was up next, she gave the following speech:

> Hi, my name is Yolanda. When I was four I immigrated to the US along with my sister and my mom, not really knowing why we were leaving our home in Mexico. I just knew that I was probably going to be reunited with my dad. At that moment, all I wanted to do was remember the way he looked, I wanted him to carry me in his arms and, most importantly, I desperately wanted my family to be back together again.
>
> It did not take me long to consider Chicago as my new home. But as I got older, I began to realize that I was nine digits away from even beginning to consider a piece of the American Dream. The worst reminder came the night my dad called to tell me that my mom had been pulled over. Knowing that she did not have a driver's license, I tried to prepare myself mentally for how our lives would change. I felt helpless while I waited at the port steps of my school I couldn't even reach out to my teacher who was standing a few feet from me because he had no idea that I was undocumented. Every minute that went by, I felt myself becoming paralyzed with hopelessness. I will leave the home I have grown to love if my mom was forced to leave it. I should not have had to decide between my mom and my home. In fact, no child should have to decide between their parent and their home, yet thousands of kids have to feel the pain every single day because of racist, abusive, and dehumanizing laws.
>
> So I stand here today because I don't want anyone to feel like they don't have a voice. I know what that feels like. I will not let my struggles, my dreams, and my existence be pushed aside or used in the name of politics. My life is not a political token. As a human being I have a right to be happy, we all do. I invite you to stand up and fight with me for the justice we deserve. The government can attempt to take away our rights but it

cannot take away our will to fight. I am not backing down. I define myself. My name is Yolanda, I'm undocumented, unafraid, and unapologetic.

The remarkable commonalities between Claudia's speech and Yolanda's speech are immediately noticeable. These commonalities illustrate the institutionalized norms that "model stories" need to comply with for mobilization purposes. In a way similar to Claudia's speech, Yolanda starts off by recounting the story of how she migrated to the US as a child. The narrative then goes on by invoking emotions of fear and helplessness concerning the threat of deportation and the consequences of her legal status as in Claudia's case. Her speech ends with a call towards the audience to "stand up and fight" and a reiteration of the coming-out slogan.

While Yolanda gave her speech exactly one year later than Claudia, this example illustrates how stories are directed by youth organizers as to reflect a shared "story of us."

In communication with constituencies, storytelling is a vehicle to do outreach and mobilize undocumented youth. This section shows how individual stories are crafted, edited, directed, and performed in order to maximize outcomes in terms of mobilization. Organizers play an important role in aligning these "stories of me" with the movement's "story of us." Stories that are performed in the right way are meant to trigger emotional responses and moral shocks in the target audience as to motivate people to take political action. Hence, in this context, storytelling is a mobilizing social movement practice.

Unapologetic, unafraid: storytelling as claims-making practice

Life storytelling is not only important for community building and mobilization, but it is also an essential part of extra-movement communication with actors like the media, the broader public, and politicians (see Gamson 2002). What is at stake here is legitimizing grievances and making claims in the public realm. In the media, undocumented youth use their stories to "give a face" to the issue, and to connect with and make moral appeals to the general public. In the political arena, undocumented activists use their stories in order to encourage politicians to take action by appealing to their sense of humanity, morality, and empathy. Storytelling thus becomes a *claims-making practice*. Below, I demonstrate how undocumented youth legitimize their claims to recognition via interaction with the media, on the one hand, and with politicians, on the other hand.

Of all the settings where storytelling is employed, media interactions are among the most heavily controlled and managed. Community organizers play an important role in this respect as "directors" of these testimonies. As IYJL member Reyes declared in an interview, one of the major tasks of community leaders towards undocumented youth is to "teach them to speak with the media and to share their stories [because] despite being undocumented, they

Gaining a voice 201

have to be as visible as possible." Life stories are resources for undocumented activists because they can be used to legitimate organizational and/or movement claims. Community organizers act as brokers that connect the stories of the grassroots with the broader public and external actors like the media and politicians. At the same time, they act as gatekeepers who select particular life stories based on profiles that resonate with their more general narrative strategies.

The importance of collecting particular types of life stories was illustrated by an internal meeting I attended in preparation for a press conference around an immigrant rights march in Washington. When an organizer asked, "Should we organize a press conference?" an attendee answered, "Yes, but we need to have some stories for the media by then. There are some real horror stories of families being told. We have to collect them and bring them to the press." At the actual press conference, an undocumented pastor who was in deportation proceedings took the floor. The pastor cried intermittently while sharing the following story:

> Hello, I'm a pastor in Chicago and like everyone else today I'm tired seeing families being broken. Me, as a leader in Chicago, sixteen years ago, they took away my green card, and I'm facing deportation now. I have two kids, a wife, and I do not think it is fair, what is happening. I don't think that it is fair that families are being divided. Families are being separated just because they want to work. Please, please, please, listen to me.
>
> I'm not crying so that you would know me. I'm crying because I am feeling what thousands of families are feeling right now. Every day from Chicago, thousands of people are being deported. Stop deportation! Please reform immigration. President Obama, listen to me. Please do something. We believe in you. God bless you.

This type of story appeals to the public's sense of empathy because it stresses how this individual is "just like us." The narrative refers to his role as a father, man of God, and long-time community leader, in order to provide the moral grounds upon which the audience can develop a sympathetic and empathetic understanding of him and others like him. The emotions the pastor displayed during the narrative performance increase the ability of others to place themselves in his shoes. In this way, undocumented activists try to legitimize their demands and gain public support.

Storytelling provides politicians with the moral and emotional resources necessary to legitimate their support to undocumented youth as well. The case of the Illinois DREAM Act is revealing in this regard. After months of meetings, rallies in Springfield, faxes, emails, and phone calls, a local version of the Dream Act became law in Illinois on August 1, 2011, creating a private scholarship fund for undocumented youth. While this political outcome cannot be directly explained by storytelling, it did play an important role in steering the process whereby grievances and responses toward these grievances were legitimized. When I attended rallies at Springfield, I witnessed how undocumented youth personally approached politicians to tell them why they had to vote in favor. Rather than relying on rational, empirically verifiable discourses, these youth used their personal narratives of hardship, educational achievement, and community involvement to gain recognition. The following excerpt from my interview with Cynthia shows how she strategically uses her story while lobbying politicians:

> I think when they hear our stories, that's really when it starts to change things. With politicians, there's the supportive ones, there's the ones that sympathize, but won't vote in support of you, and there's the ones that don't, but, you know, you can change their minds if you talk to them. I've learned how to talk to them now ... and present our case, and make them sympathize and work in favor of us.

But the involvement of undocumented youth in the political process around the Illinois DREAM Act was not limited to lobbying efforts. In an unprecedented move, IYJL member Reyes was formally appointed as one of the members of the Illinois DREAM Act commission that helped draft the bill. At the official signing of the bill into law, Governor Pat Quinn addressed the crowd of undocumented youth, supporters, and activists. "This is what democracy is all about," he said, "when people band together and work together for a common goal, for a common good." Next, undocumented youth activist Amalia shared her personal experience participating in the Illinois DREAM act campaign.

> I remember sitting in the high school basement after school when I got a call from Maria. She asked me what I thought about and what I would like to see included in the Illinois DREAM Act. I thought about my junior and senior year, how I struggled to get information on how to continue with my higher education. My junior year in high school I walked into my counselor's office and I told her that I wanted to go to college but I was undocumented. She told me that going to college was going to be impossible since I don't qualify for financial aid. I felt frustrated. At the moment it seemed impossible that I would ever go to college, even though I had the same potential and dedication as my peers .... Shortly after the call, we decided to work and fight for the Illinois Dream Act. We, as undocumented students, were at the forefront. We were what made democracy happen, taking risks, and having the courage to share our stories, to go into our communities and inform them about the legislation, and to encourage students and others to take action, not stay quiet. Most importantly, we as undocumented students got to say what was included in this legislation. We used our voices to express what we believed in and ensured that we were heard.

Amalia's speech illustrates how stories are used to legitimize the participation of undocumented youth in the political process. Her narrative explains how their involvement is justified in view of the experiences of frustration that they went through in high school.

Furthermore, both the governor's introductory remarks and Amalia's speech refer to how undocumented youth "made democracy happen," thereby justifying their public recognition as political actors. The fact that her story was staged at the signing of the bill illustrates how personal narratives serve to moralize and depoliticize the support received from politicians.

This section shows that storytelling becomes a claims-making practice for social movement actors in an extra-organizational context. Especially for actors who do not have direct access to political institutions, personal narrative can be an effective way to legitimate grievances. The undocumented youth community's "stories of us" are hereby broadened to reflect a shared "story of us all." Strategic instances of storytelling in interactions with the media and politicians are meant to stress what we all have in common to evoke empathy and solidarity, and overcome political difference. The strategic mobilization of emotions through storytelling helps to explain narrative's ability to justify claims to public recognition.

Conclusion: narratives and the politics of recognition

This case study shows that personal narratives are used in three principal ways in the undocumented youth movement in Chicago. The modalities through which stories are brought to life differ depending on the audience, the type of interaction wherein they are staged, and the context. First, storytelling is used to create a social environment of support, belonging, and acceptance for undocumented youth. In this sense, storytelling is a *community-building* practice. Second, undocumented youth disclose their status in public in interactions with their constituencies in order to encourage others to join the movement. Hence, in this context, storytelling is a *mobilizing practice*. Third, undocumented youth collect, direct, and disseminate life stories in interactions with external actors in order to justify their political demands. In this way, storytelling is a *claims-making practice*. In short, my data show that storytelling strengthens collective bonds, mobilizes outsiders, and legitimizes political grievances. This study thus confirms the findings of social movement scholars who argue that storytelling is an essential social movement practice that helps to explain how social movements are built and sustained (Jasper 1997; Ganz 2001; Davis 2002; Fine 2002, 2006; Polletta 2006). At the same time, this chapter argues that a systematic approach to storytelling in social movements needs to take into account how storytelling is used at different stages in a movement's life course.

Moreover, this study's findings go beyond existing work on narrative and mobilization because they show that narratives are crucial for the ways in which marginalized actors like undocumented youth take part in the political process. In the absence of access to citizenship and the rights and privileges that come with it, undocumented youth rely on storytelling to gain a voice. In contrast to scholars who assume the "liberating" power of storytelling for marginalized actors in advance (see Atkinson and Delamont 2006), I demonstrate that highly organized, strategic elements need to be in play in order for personal narrative to be an effective political tool. More in particular, this study reveals that two dimensions of personal narrative help to explain its political functionality for marginalized actors: its ability to interweave the "story of me" with "the story of us," on the one hand, and the emotional transfer during story-telling interactions, on the other hand.

First, narrative is important for social movements because it interweaves "the story of me" with "the story of us." This study demonstrated how the incorporation of newcomers is driven by storytelling practices. Becoming a member of the undocumented youth community depends on people's willingness to share their personal stories to their peers. Through repeatedly engaging in storytelling in intra-organizational contexts, undocumented youth can experience a sense of belonging and membership that prepares them for public speaking engagements. The more public instances of storytelling become, the more experienced organizers direct these narratives' content and performance. While the stories that youth tell when they first come out in the confines of safe spaces are deeply personal, they have to be transformed into reflections of the "story of us" propagated by the movement. Storytelling operates across different contexts as a driver of the processes whereby undocumented youth become political. These insights thus stress the importance of narrative for personal and collective identity formation at different stages of a movement's life course. In other words, both the personal identities of activists and the collective identities of political communities are essentially constructed and shaped by narrative activities. This study simultaneously highlights that the connection between undocumented youth's "story of me" and "story of us" is bound together by emotions.

This brings me to the second insight, namely that the ability of narrative to do political work is mediated by emotions. This chapter reveals the need to construct theoretical linkages between the literatures on emotions (see Bell 1988; Whittier 2001; Gould 2009) and narrative (see Polletta 1998, 2006; Ganz 2001; Davis 2002) in social movements. I aim to bridge this theoretical gap by arguing that the emotional work performed by storytelling is not merely a by-product of but a necessary prerequisite for narrative's effectiveness as a political tool for marginalized actors. Undocumented youth cope through storytelling with mental challenges to political participation by expressing the fear and shame they experienced growing up. The emotional support they receive from peers in the safe spaces of organizations allows them to start believing in their own capacity to act politically. Movement constituencies are built and sustained by the narrative mobilization of emotions at community events, rallies and demonstrations. Personal narratives' openness to emotional identification enables the "moralization" of political claims and demands. Undocumented youth therefore strategically invoke emotions in order to gain acceptance by a wide range of actors in a society wherein their very existence is declared "illegal." In other words, emotions structure the community-building, mobilizing, and claims-making functions of storytelling.

To conclude, for marginalized populations with little access to resources like undocumented youth, life stories are powerful assets. Undocumented youth have struggled for many years to come up with a way to participate in a political process from which they are excluded because of their status. They have discovered the power of narrative as a way to gain a voice. Every day, undocumented youth share their stories to their families, counselors, teachers, employers, friends, and allies. Storytelling makes them believe in themselves again, it makes them feel part of a wider community and it allows them to reach out to members of that community to take political action. To the outside world, undocumented youth justify their claims to recognition by sharing their stories, as a way of saying, "I am from here, and thus I belong here." The stories that undocumented youth tell discuss where they came from, what their place is in society, what they stand for, and where they are going. They hold a mirror to society that reflects present social problems and relates them to those of the past. In this way, undocumented youth's stories echo stories we have heard many times before in history, just like the stories of Harvey Milk and Martin Luther King echoed the stories of those that preceded them.

Notes

1 I use the term "undocumented" instead of "illegal" or "clandestine" to avoid possible criminalizing/dehumanizing effects.
2 All undocumented research subjects' names were replaced by pseudonyms as per the Institutional Review Board's stipulations.
3 As a self-declared sanctuary city, Chicago has become a hotbed for undocumented activism (see Pallares and Flores-González 2010). In the methods section, I explain the rationale for this study's case selection in more detail.
4 A story or a narrative—used interchangeably—will be defined as a "method of recapitulating past experience by matching a verbal sequence of clauses to the sequence of events which actually occurred" (Labov 1972: 359–360).
5 The term "coming-out narratives" refers to the speeches given by undocumented youth at the annual Coming Out of the Shadows rallies organized by IYJL at Federal Plaza in Chicago. While these speeches typically recount the storytellers' life stories, I use this term to indicate that these are the public speeches given at these specific events. Each year, different speakers were recruited so each speech represents a different individual. I attended the coming-out rallies in 2011 and 2012 as a participant observer. Moreover, I collected the audio files of all twenty-four speeches (eight in 2010, six in 2011, and eight in 2012) and transcribed and analyzed them with qualitative analysis software.

References

Abrego, Janet L. 2006. "I Can't Go to College Because I Don't Have Papers: Incorporation Patterns of Latino Undocumented Youth." *Latino Studies* 4 (2): 212–231.

Andrews, Molly. 2007. *Shaping History: Narratives of Political Change*. New York: Cambridge University Press.

Askham, Janet. 1982. "Telling Stories." *The Sociological Review* 30 (4): 555–572.

Atkinson, Paul and Sara Delamont. 2006. "Rescuing Narrative from Qualitative Research." *Narrative Inquiry 16* (1): 164–172.

Bell, Susan. 1988. "Becoming a Political Woman: The Reconstruction and Interpretation of Experience through Stories." Pp. 97–123 in *Gender and Discourse: The Power of Talk*, edited by Alexandra Todd and Sue Fisher. Norwood, NJ: Ablex.

Bell, Susan. 2009. *DES Daughters: Embodied Knowledge and the Transformation of Women's Health Politics*. Philadelphia: Temple. University Press.

Benford, Robert D., and David A. Snow. 2000. "Framing Processes and Social Movements: An Overview and Assessment." *Annual Review of Sociology* 26: 611–639.

Bourdieu, Pierre and Loïc Wacquant. 1992. *An Invitation to Reflexive Sociology*. Chicago: University of Chicago Press.

Davis, Joseph E. 2002. "Narrative and Social Movements: The Power of Stories." Pp. 3–30 in *Stories of Change: Narrative and Social Movements*, edited by Joseph E. Davis. Albany, NY: State University of New York Press.

Epstein, Steven. 1996. *Impure Science: AIDS, Activism, and the Politics of Knowledge*. Berkeley, CA: University of California Press.

Ewick, Patricia, and Susan Silbey. 2003. "Narrating Social Structure: Stories of Resistance to Legal Authority." *American Journal of Sociology* 108 (6): 1328–1372.

Fox News Latino. 2012. "Undocumented Migrant Named to Illinois DREAM Commission, 18 February. Retrieved May 6, 2013.http://latino.foxnews.com/latino/politics/2012/02/18/undocumented-migrant-named-to-illinois-dream-commission/

Fine, Gary Alan. 2002. "The Storied Group: Social Movements as "Bundles of Narratives." Pp. 229–246 in *Stories of Change: Narrative and Social Movements*, edited by J. Davis. Albany, NY: SUNY Press.

Fine, Gary Alan. 2006. "Notorious Support: The America First Committee and the Narrative Personalization of Policy." *Mobilization*, 11 (4): 405–426.

Galindo, René. 2011. "Embodying the Gap between National Inclusion and Exclusion: The Testimonies of Three Undocumented Students at a 2007 Congressional Hearing." *Harvard Latino Law Review* 4: 377–391.

Ganz, Marshall. 2001. *"The Power of Story in Social Movements."* A paper presented at the Annual Meeting of the American Sociological Association, Anaheim, California.

Gamson, William A. 2002. "How Storytelling Can Be Empowering." Pp. 187–199 in *Culture in Mind: Toward a Sociology of Culture and Cognition*, edited by Karen Cerulo. New York: Routledge.

Gonzales, Roberto G. 2008. "Left Out But Not Shut Down: Political Activism and the Undocumented Latino Student Movement." *Northwestern Journal of Law and Social Policy* 3 (2): 1–22.

Gonzales, Roberto G. 2011. "Learning to be Illegal: Undocumented Youth and Shifting Legal Contexts in the Transition to Adulthood." *American Sociological Review* 76 (4): 602–619.

Gonzales, Roberto G., Carola Suárez-Orozco, and Maria Cecilia Dedidos-Sanguineti. 2014. "No Place to Belong: Contextualizing Concepts of Mental Health Among

Undocumented Immigrant Youth in the United States." *American Behavioral Scientist*, 58: 1852–1872.
Gould, Deborah B. 2009. *Moving Politics: Emotion and Act-Up's Fight against AIDS*. Chicago: University of Chicago Press.
Gubrium, Jaber F. and Holstein, James A. 1998. "Narrative Practice and the Coherence of Personal Stories." *Sociological Quarterly* 39 (2): 163–187.
Immigrant Youth Justice League. 2011. About Us. www.iyjl.org, retrieved November 8, 2011.
Jasper, James M. 1997. *The Art of Moral Protest: Culture, Biography, and Creativity in Social Movements*. Chicago: University of Chicago Press.
Jasper, James M. 1998. "The Emotions of Protest: Affective and Reactive Emotions In and Around Social Movements." *Sociological Forum*, 13 (3): 397–424.
Jasper, James M. 2011. "Emotions and Social Movements: Twenty Years of Theory and Research." *Annual Review of Sociology* 37: 285–303.
Labov, William. 1972. *The Transformation of Experience in Narrative Syntax*. Philadelphia: University of Pennsylvania Press.
Pallares, Amalia, and Nilda Flores-González, eds. 2010. *¡Marcha!: Latino Chicago and the Immigrant Rights Movement*. Chicago: University of Illinois Press.
Plummer, Ken. 1995. *Telling Sexual Stories: Power, Change, and Social Worlds*. London: Routledge.
Polletta, Francesca. 1998. "Contending Stories: Narrative in Social Movements." *Qualitative Sociology* 21 (4): 419–446.
Polletta, Francesca. 1999. "Free Spaces in Collective Action." *Theory and Society* 28 (1): 1–38.
Polletta, Francesca. 2006. *It Was Like a Fever: Storytelling in Protest and Politics*. Chicago: University of Chicago Press.
Polletta, Francesca, Pang C.B. Chen, Beth G. Gardner, and Alice Motes. 2011. "The Sociology of Storytelling." *Annual Review of Sociology* 37: 109–130.
Riessman, Catherine K. 1993. *Narrative Analysis*. Newbury Park, CA: Sage.
Riessman, Catherine K. 2007. *Narrative Methods for the Human Sciences*. Thousand Oaks, CA: Sage Publications.
Seif, Hinda. 2011. "'Unapologetic and Unafraid': Immigrant Youth Come out from the Shadows." Pp. 59–75 in *Youth Civic Development: Work at the Cutting Edge*, edited by Constance A. Flanagan and Brian D. Christens. San Francisco, CA: Jossey-Bass.
Shrock, Douglas, Daphne Holden, and Lori Reid. 2004. "Creating Emotional Resonance: Interpersonal Emotion Work and Motivational Framing in a Transgender Community." *Social Problems*, 51: 61–81.
Small, Mario L. 2009. "How Many Cases Do I Need? On Science and the Logic of Case Selection in Fieldbased Research." *Ethnography*, 10 (1): 5–38.
Snow, David A., E. Burke Rochford, Steven K. Worden, and Robert D. Benford. 1986. "Frame Alignment Processes, Micromobilization, and Movement Participation." *American Sociological Review* 51 (4): 464–481.
Tashakkori, Abas, and Charles Teddlie. 2003. *Handbook of Mixed Methods in Social and Behavioral Research*. Thousand Oaks, CA: Sage Publications.
Whittier, Nancy. 2001. "Emotional Strategies: The Collective Reconstruction and Display of Oppositional Emotions in the Movement against Child Sexual Abuse." Pp. 233–250 in *Passionate Politics. Emotions and Social Movements*, edited by Jeff Goodwin, James M. Jasper, and Francesca Polletta. Chicago: University of Chicago Press.

9 Racial, ethnic, and immigration protest during year one of the Trump presidency

Kenneth T. Andrews, Neal Caren and Todd Lu

Protest was a defining feature of Trump's first year in office. On January 21, one day following the inauguration, over four million people participated in the Women's March—one of the largest days of protest in U.S. history (Chenoweth and Pressman 2017). In the year that followed, over six thousand protest events were held with a cumulative attendance of more than 1,700,000 people.

Activists have mobilized around an incredibly diverse set of issues including immigration, health care, the environment, science and education, abortion rights, and racism. This diversity is reflected in the motivations of protest participants as well (Fisher, Dow, and Ray 2017). While some of the issues have clustered into distinct waves, others have been a continuing focus of activists since Trump's inauguration.

A central component of this diversity of issues was protests against racism and President Trump's immigration policies. One quarter of protest events and protesters during this period were concerned with these domains, from the nearly 180,000 people who protested Trump's proposed Muslim travel ban to almost 100,000 people who protested against the violence arising from the alt-right's Unite the Right rally in Charlottesville.

The targets and sites of protest have been diverse as well. Activists have staged protests at conventional sites like the national mall, state capitols, and college campuses and less common ones like airports and NFL stadiums. While the issues and targets of protest have been diverse, the tactical repertoire has been dominated by rallies, marches, and demonstrations. However, activists have employed innovative and more disruptive protest forms at times over the past year, including the airport protest. In addition, some of the most contentious protests have happened where demonstrators and counter-demonstrators face off such as the Confederate monuments protests.

We examine racial and ethnic protest during the first year of Trump's presidency. Our analysis has two goals: (1) to provide a comprehensive description of these protests including the scope and issues that have defined activism over this year and (2) to explore competing explanations for the movement's mobilization at the local level with a focus on protest concerning racial, ethnic and immigration issues. Specifically, we examine the ways that partisanship, movement infrastructure, and sociodemographic characteristics of communities shape the patterning of racial and immigration protest events.

Documenting protest

We use protest event data to estimate the count and size of protest against the Trump administration and its policies between January 20, 2017 and January 19, 2018. Our event data is primarily based on the Crowd Counting Consortium's (CCC) monthly crowd data (https://sites.google.com/view/crowdcountingconsortium). Spearheaded by Jeremy Pressman and Erica Chenoweth, the consortium collects "publicly available data on political crowds reported in the United States, including marches, protests, strikes, demonstrations, riots, and other actions" (n.d.). The data are produced through volunteer research assistants who review the results of a news crawl combined with user-submitted reports. The full dataset for each month is made available on the CCC website. While the CCC includes all political crowds, we restrict our analysis to events that oppose President Trump or his policies. This excludes a number of local events and pro-Trump events. Additionally, we exclude the LGBT Pride Parades that occurred in late March, as those annual events vary substantially in their political emphasis (Bruce 2016).

To fill in a temporal gap between January 21 and January 31 where CCC did not track events, we supplement these data with information from Count Love (https://countlove.org), a project led Tommy Leung and Nathan Perkins. Similar to CCC, Count Love data are based on a news crawl with additional human and machine learning coding (Leung and Perkins 2017).

CCC and Count Love datasets produce conservative estimates of crowd sizes by averaging multiple reports, discounting self-reports, and converting verbal descriptions of crowds to lowest plausible integers (e.g., "hundreds" is translated to 200). For 26 percent of events (n = 1,704), we were not able to establish reliable crowd estimates primarily because they were not reported in the source. In these cases, we imputed a size of 11, based on our understanding that these events often appeared to be small based on the tone of the article. Combined, we estimate that there were 1,962,457 protest participants. Our robustness check found similar coefficients and effect sizes for all models with and without the imputation.

Our team of research assistants reviewed each CCC and Count Love event. We coded each event on a variety of additional measures, including the topic and issue of the event, whether or not protest was part of a national wave of protests, among others. For example, we estimate that there were 310 protests against President Trump's proposed travel ban, part of 942 protests around a broader issue of immigration. Our coding of issues covers eleven major categories and over two dozen sub-categories, but our analysis in this chapter focuses on the two major issues of race and immigration. Admittedly, there is some overlap between these categories, and some events focus on multiple issues. Here, we have focused on the primary issues based on our coding of the event as described in media reports.

Patterning of protest: descriptive analysis

Nearly one-quarter of the protests in the first year of Trump's presidency were related to immigration or race. Of the eight thousand protest events we have counted, approximately 12 percent were immigration-related, and 12 percent were race-related. Their salience should not be surprising due to the Trump administration's rhetoric and policies that directly targeted racial and ethnic minorities, and his political support by, and connections to, overt White supremacists (Bobo 2017). In total, there were nearly 620,000 participants involved in 2,410 race or immigration-related protests during this period. Protests were also widespread, organized in 505 counties across all US states.

Although events were regularly sustained throughout the year, we identify two major protest waves and several smaller ones against the Trump administration. The first significant wave included protests around the immigration-related refugee and Muslim travel ban, occurring at the end of January and beginning February 2017. The second major wave included anti-racist protests organized in response to the far-right's "Unite the Right" rally and violence in Charlottesville in mid-August 2017. The monthly count of all protest events is shown in Figure 9.1. Next, we describe the patterning of protest related to race and immigration in greater detail.

Protests focused on immigrants and immigration

Among all immigration protests, we identified six major issues. These are the Travel Ban (39 percent of all immigration protests), Deferred Action on Childhood Arrivals (DACA) (23 percent), US Immigration and Customs Enforcement (ICE) raids (13 percent), Day without Immigrants (11 percent), May Day (8 percent), and Sanctuary Cities (5 percent). Furthermore, we identified four major protest clusters or waves throughout the first year of the Trump administration. The first wave emerged in late January and throughout February 2017. Activists first organized in late January against the Trump administration's refugee and Muslim travel ban and later organized protests in February for the Day without Immigrant demonstrations and against resurgent ICE raids. The second protest wave flared up in May 2017, mostly related to May Day protests around the country. The final two protest waves erupted in September 2017 and December 2017. These later protests were organized to advocate for the protection of DACA and DACA recipients. One wave was sparked in early September when the Trump administration announced plans to phase out the DACA program (Sacchetti and Stein 2017). Immigrant-rights groups organized the second protest wave in December to pressure US Congressional members to pass legislation protecting Dreamers and DACA before the end of the year (Siegel 2017). In total, we counted 1211 immigration-related events involving 368,000 protesters. These events were geographically widespread, occurring in 324 different counties in all 50 states.

Racial protest during the Trump presidency 211

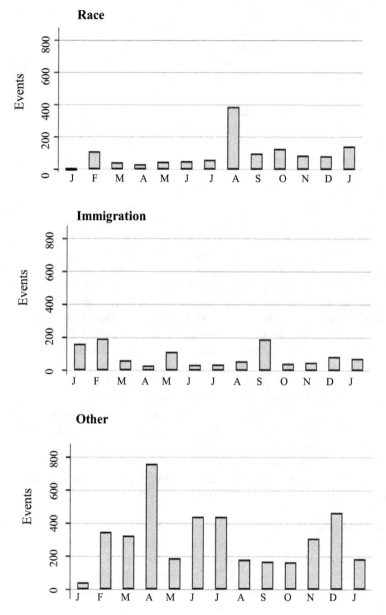

Figure 9.1 Monthly count of protest events by issue focus, 2017.

The average size of protests was 304 participants, with a median of 70. Protests were nearly all rallies and demonstrations (94%) and targeted the federal government (85%) and state or local governments (10%).

The first major immigration issue represented the refugee and Muslim travel ban. On January 27, 2017, the Trump administration signed into effect an executive order to temporarily suspend entry into the United States all refugees (indefinitely for Syrian refugees) and citizens from seven Muslim-majority countries. The nature and implementation of the order and initial reports that US airport security immediately detained affected peoples sparked widespread protests throughout the end of January and beginning of February (Bacon and Gomez 2017). Unlike the highly coordinated Women's Marches in the week before, the travel ban protests were notable for their spontaneity and non-traditional venues, with many participants converging at airports. In total, we identified 309 events involving nearly 180,000 protesters. Events were widespread across 101 counties and 39 states. Protests were generally large: an average of 581 protesters per event and a median of 200 protesters.

The second major immigration issue involved protests related to the DACA program. Implemented by President Obama on June 2012, DACA enabled undocumented people brought to the US as children to apply for and receive renewable two-year work permits and deferred action from deportations. Hundreds of thousands of undocumented youth applied for and received DACA status, benefiting from greater access to jobs, financial services, educational opportunities, and health care (Gonzales et al. 2014).

Nonetheless, the Trump administration announced to phase out DACA on September 5, 2017 (Shear and Davis 2017), sparking protests from thousands of DACA recipients and allies. The second wave of DACA protests erupted in the first week of December, right before the congressional recess. Thousands sought to pressure members of Congress to pass legislation to protect the DACA program and its recipients. In total, we identified 181 DACA-related events involving nearly 30,000 protesters. DACA protests were present in 106 counties in 35 states. Events featured an average of 162 protesters and a median of 24 protesters.

The third major immigration issue was ICE raids. Under President Obama, ICE deported millions of undocumented immigrants, directing ICE to prioritize those with serious criminal records (Law 2017). Through an executive order signed in early January 2017, President Trump expanded the powers of immigration officers to detain and deport undocumented immigrants and broadened the definition of groups prioritized for deportation to include most undocumented immigrants (Kopan 2017). Throughout the first year of the Trump presidency, ICE initiated numerous raids and arrests, leading to an uptick of arrests and deportations of undocumented peoples across the United States (Bialik 2018). Immigration-rights activists and community groups mobilized in response to ICE raids in their local communities. In total, we identified 98 events involving around 10,000 protesters. Unlike other issue-related protests, ICE raid protests were sustained throughout the year.

We identified four different peaks in February, March, and August of 2017 and January of 2018. ICE protests were much more geographically concentrated, occurring only in 57 counties across 30 states. Events had an average of 104 protesters and a median of 34 protesters.

The fourth major immigration issue was the Day Without Immigrant marches. On February 16, 2017, demonstrators called for nationwide rallies, strikes, and boycotts to protest against Trump's immigration policies and to showcase the importance of immigrants in the US economy (Robbins and Correal 2017). In total, we counted 87 events across 76 counties in 32 states, involving just over 30,000 protesters. Nearly all events were organized on February 16, with a few organized the next day. Some "Day Without Immigrant" events resurfaced months later during May 1 protests. Events on average had 352 protesters and a median of 50 protesters. Among events with tactics data available (38 events), half of the events involved strikes, walkouts, and lockouts while the other half involved rallies and demonstrations.

The fifth major immigration issue was May Day protests. While May Day events, occurring on the first day of May, historically celebrate the international labor movement, the 2017 May Day protests extensively took on immigrant rights in opposition to Trump's immigration policies (Francescani and Dobuzinskis 2017). In total, nearly 50,000 protesters came out to 64 events. May Day events were organized in 53 counties across 25 states, with events on average featuring 748 protesters and a median of 180 protesters.

The sixth major immigration issue was sanctuary city protests. Activists organized to pressure local municipalities to adopt sanctuary city statuses, which refer to municipalities that, by law or practice, prevent local law enforcement from questioning detained individuals about their immigration status or from notifying ICE federal agents of detained undocumented immigrants (Ridgley 2008). Although sanctuary cities predate the Trump administration, they have taken on a renewed importance as more undocumented immigrants and their allies seek local protections from federal deportations. Furthermore, the Trump administration publicly criticized cities that proclaimed sanctuary status, threatening to cut off federal funding or intentionally targeting sanctuary cities for ICE raids (Kaste 2017). Similar to the ICE-raids protests, sanctuary-city protests were sustained throughout the year, peaking in periods of other immigration protest waves in February and May 2017. In total, there were 39 events involving just over 4,000 protesters. Events featured on average 107 protesters and a median of 90 protesters and were dispersed in 25 counties across 13 states. As expected, the vast majority of these protests (82 percent) targeted state and local governments in support of sanctuary city policies, as we do not include pro-Trump rallies and protests in our data.

Protests focused on race and racial inequality

There were three major issues among race-related protests: Charlottesville/Confederate monuments (67 percent of all race-related protests), the national anthem (17 percent), and Black Lives Matter (9 percent). Events peaked three times during the year. First, demonstrations during August 2017 emerged in the wake of the violence at Charlottesville and against local Confederate monuments. Second, protests from September to December 2017 were national anthem related by NFL football players in the 2017 NFL season. Finally, January 2018 witnessed many rallies and demonstrations during the Martin Luther King Day weekend around racial equality and in commemoration of Dr. King's legacy. In total, we counted 1,197 race-related events, involving 247,600 protesters. Events were geographically widespread, occurring across 403 counties in all 50 states. The average event included 207 protesters, with a median of 34 protesters. Protests were mostly rallies and demonstrations (90 percent), with some vigils and other symbolic displays, 6 percent and 2 percent respectively. Protesters had a large variety of targets, but top ones were the general public (52 percent), local and state governments (26 percent), the federal government (5 percent), and other protesters (5 percent).

The first major issue revolved around the violence in Charlottesville and of Confederate monuments. These protests were organized in response to the "Unite the Right" rally in Charlottesville on August 12, 2017. A coalition of White supremacists, neo-Confederates, neo- Nazis, and far-right militias describing themselves as the "alt-right" rallied against the removal of a Confederate monument by the city of Charlottesville (Fausset and Feuer 2017). In response, anti-racist and anti-fascist protesters organized a counter-rally to confront the far-right demonstrators. National news reported the alt-right activists' attacks against the University of Virginia students during an evening march on campus the night before (Pearce 2017) and violent street clashes between the far-right demonstrators and anti-racist activists the next day. Most notably, a White supremacist protester rammed a car at high speed into a crowd of anti-racist demonstrators, injuring dozens and killing anti-racist activist Heather Heyer (Silverman and Laris 2017). Although mainstream politicians and civil rights organizations condemned the violence and events, President Trump's initial remarks on the rally failed to condemn the far right, claiming there were "very fine people on both sides" (Thrush and Haberman 2017). These events led to widespread protests around the country against the White supremacist violence in Charlottesville, against Trump's comments, and local Confederate monuments. We counted a total of 337 protest events, involving nearly 100,000 protesters. These peaked in the week after the Unite the Right rally and organized across 215 counties in 46 states. The average event had 295 protesters with a median of 63 protesters. Although most were rallies and demonstrations, a significant portion (17 percent) were vigils in commemoration of Heather Heyer. Protests targeted the general public (75 percent), but a significant minority of protests targeted parts of local and state government (15 percent) and other protesters (6 percent).

The second major issue was national anthem protests (Weffer et al. 2018). Many high-profile NFL football players participated in these events throughout the 2017 NFL season, between September and December 2017.

In total, we counted 88 national anthem events involving approximately 1600 total protesters. NFL players and allies were inspired by NFL player Colin Kaepernick's protests against police brutality of Blacks and US racism at the start of the 2016 NFL preseason. When the national anthem played at NFL games, Kaepernick consistently sat and knelt instead of standing. Explaining his actions, he stated to the media, "I am not going to stand up to show pride in a flag for a country that oppresses black people and people of color" (Wyche 2016). President Trump weighed in on national anthem protests in the next NFL season, tweeting on September 24, 2017 for NFL owners to fire players who refuse to pledge to the anthem (Phillip and Boren 2017). Many NFL players responded, protesting during the national anthem and issuing statements against Trump's comments and in opposition to US racism. These protests persisted throughout the 2017 NFL season across 48 counties in 28 states. Events were much smaller but still significant due to the high-profile involvement of NFL players. The average size of each event was 18, with a median of 5 protesters. In general, protests targeted the general public (84 percent).

The third major issue was Black Lives Matter protests. The Black Lives Matter movement received national attention in August 2014 when activists in Ferguson, Missouri demonstrated against the killing of Black teenager Michael Brown by White police officer Darren Wilson. In the years that followed, the movement has sustained repeated and widespread protests around Black victims who are brutalized and killed by police officers, drawing attention to more extensive systematic racism against Blacks in the US (Williamson et al. 2018). Throughout the Trump's first year, the Black Lives movement continued to sustain protests, with modest peaks in April, June, and July 2017. In total, we counted 45 events involving nearly 11,000 protesters spread across 32 counties in 19 states. We found that these protests mostly occurred in response to recent police killings of Black people. These include commemorative demonstrations that linked local Black victims of police violence to more well-known names like Michael Brown and Philando Castile, against local law-enforcement agencies and following local judicial proceedings. The average event size was 242 and a median of 55 protesters. Protesters mostly targeted officials and agencies in state and local governments (56 percent), but also targeted the general public in many cases (31 percent).

Why do communities protest about immigration and race?

The recent protest wave following Trump's election has raised important questions about the social bases for protest – who is participating and why – as well as questions about the persistence and potential impact of these mobilizations. We examine why some communities mobilized with higher intensity than others during the first year of Trump's presidency. We draw on prevailing theories and prior research in social movement studies to guide our analysis.

Partisanship and electoral mobilization

Scholars are paying increasing attention to the links between social movements, political parties, and elections. Although political process theorists included this as part of a larger political opportunity structure, most empirical analyses in this tradition only considered broad structural features of the political system such as the presence of elite allies or major electoral realignments. In recent years, scholars have looked more closely at the interactions and overlap between movements and parties (Almeida 2010, Heaney and Rojas 2015, McAdam and Tarrow 2010, Schlozman 2015). In the US context, this recent work has been motivated by efforts to understand the impact that movements have had on the party system and as a potential contributor to political polarization (Heaney 2017, McAdam and Kloos 2014).

Even before Trump won the election, the relationship between social movements and political parties had received substantial attention. Scholars had focused on the rise of the Tea Party, and its impact on the Republican Party (Almeida and Van Dyke 2014; Skocpol and Williamson 2012). Even Obama's first campaign borrowed heavily on organizing models developed by social movements and community organizers (McKenna and Han 2014). More recently, both Bernie Sanders and Donald Trump's primary campaigns in 2016 were built with connections to grassroots movements on the left and right, respectively.

With recent race and immigration protest, we ask how much this activism is a direct outgrowth of electoral mobilization. We consider the effect of partisan electoral support as well as the separate effects of relative support for establishment and insurgent candidates during the Democratic primary.

Movement infrastructure and spillover

Protest builds on the infrastructure from prior waves of activism (Meyer and Whittier 1994; Morris 1981; Terriquez 2015). By leveraging the leadership, communication networks, and prior experience of established organizations, activists can quickly mobilize large groups through bloc recruitment (Oberschall 1973) and drawing on the rituals and identities of the broader social movement community (Staggenborg 1998).

Protests in the Trump era were preceded by two major race and immigration movements. First, the Black Lives Matter movement rallied Black communities and allies to protest systematic racism and police brutality against Black people. As Oliver's Chapter 3 in this volume explains, the movement grew in the wake of protests against the 2013 acquittal of George Zimmerman, a White-passing Latino man who shot to death Black teenager Trayvon Martin and came to be identified with the hashtag and organization founded by three Black women (Garza 2014). In the years that followed, Black Lives Matter activists mobilized in hundreds of cities, bringing national media attention to not only police brutality against Blacks, but also the continued racism and economic neglect of Black communities in colorblind America (Taylor 2016). Activists later formed federated chapters of the Black Lives Matter Network and further organized themselves with other black advocacy organizations into the Movement for Black Lives (Morice 2015).

Second, the most prominent pre-Trump era immigration protest wave was the 2006 immigration reform protests. Millions of people mobilized in hundreds of cities to protest congressional legislation that sought to further criminalize undocumented immigrants and curtail unauthorized immigration. Civil society organizations and ethnic media played important roles in organizing Latino communities to marches and demonstrations (Rim 2009). The movement represented a potential turning point leading to greater Latino engagement in US politics (Zepeda-Millán 2017; Voss and Bloemraad 2011).

We expect that communities with a history of these events are more likely to see related anti-Trump protests focused on immigration and race, with established movement organizations and prior movement activity facilitating the upsurge of protest during the Trump presidency.

Threatened groups and movement constituencies

Social movement theory and research has long recognized that groups may mobilize in response to real or perceived threats (Almeida 2003, Andrews and Seguin 2015, Einwohner and Maher 2011, Maher 2010, Zepeda-Millán 2016), especially where groups see conventional politics as providing no viable support for their claims within the political system or where groups experience declines in economic, political, or social status (McVeigh 2009).

This recent work has led to a rethinking of conventional political opportunity structure arguments which hold that movements emerge in the presence of favorable political circumstances. While favorable or improving political conditions may spur some kinds of activism or movements (McAdam 1982), threats can create a greater sense of urgency, especially for groups that have the capacity to organize and carry out protests (Almeida 2018). The "suddenly imposed grievance" argument applies to the entire wave of protest after Trump's victory, but we may ask whether the places where more people are threatened have higher or lower levels of protest. Although our main expectation is that threatened groups will be more likely to mobilize, the relationship could go the other direction because groups targeted by political elites and authorities may be especially vulnerable to repression or face additional barriers to mobilization (Oliver 2017).

Trump's presidency presents an ideal case to assess this line of argument. Throughout the primaries and presidential campaign, Trump and his supporters targeted numerous groups, including minorities, immigrants, and women. In addition, Trump's attacks on science, environmentalism, and expert knowledge posed additional threats to universities and higher education.

Assessing whether threat drives protest is difficult. In rare cases, scholars have access to individual-level data, including information about perceptions of risk or harm. More often, scholars examine the relative size of threatened groups, which provides indirect evidence (Van Dyke et al. 2002). However, the relative size of a threatened group simultaneously indicates the potential efficacy of its constituency. Nevertheless, the central role of threat in the rhetoric of Trump and his supporters, as well as its perception among movement activists, suggest that threat may be an essential component of recent protest activity.

We focus on whether communities with a larger share of minority and foreign-born were more likely to mobilize, particular around issues relevant to those communities.

Country-level data

Since we are interested in the impact of local contextual factors on protest, our unit of analysis is US counties, which is a frequently used geospatial unit to analyze social movements and protest (e.g., McVeigh et al. 2014). In our analysis, we exclude Washington, DC, as its unique focus of presidential protest is likely influenced more by national than local contexts. Since all events in both datasets are coded with city and state, we used the geocod.io API to locate each protest event within a US county.

We include multiple measures of threat to capture characteristics of communities that would be especially vulnerable to policies proposed by the Trump administration. To measure racial groups that would be threatened, we include the proportion African American and proportion Latinx using the Census's American Community Survey (ACS) aggregated by Hamner (2016). We also include a measure of the proportion of residents foreign born in a county (also based on ACS data) because anti-immigrant ideas and policies have been central to Trump's campaign and presidency.

To measure local political beliefs, we include the share of votes in the 2016 presidential election who voted for Hillary Clinton, the Democratic nominee, aggregated by Hamner (2016). The second measure of local partisans is based on donation data. Here, we aggregate Federal Elections Committee reports to count the number of donors in 2016 to Hillary Clinton and Bernie Sanders, her most notable opponent in the Democratic primary. Our donation rates are the number of donors per 1,000 county residents.

We employ multiple measures of local social movement strength based on the past protest activity of progressive movements and local presence of advocacy organizations. We choose three movements to measure local movement strength: Occupy Wall Street, Black Lives Matter, and the 2006 Immigration Reform protests. These movements represent the most prominent US protests around progressive issues in the past decade. First, we measure Occupy Wall Street protests using the list of protest occupations aggregated by Simon Rogers at the *Guardian* newspaper (2011). Second, we measure Black Lives Matter protests from Alisa Robinson's repository of BLM protest events (https://elephrame.com/textbook/BLM/chart). We include all events that occurred prior to 2017. Third, we measure the 2006 immigration reform protests based on data on size and location of events collected by Xóchitl Bada, Jonathan Fox, Elvia Zazueta, and Ingrid García (2006). Finally, we measure the strength of existing organizations using the number of entities in the county in the "Civil Rights, Social Action, and Advocacy" category in the IRS's list of tax-exempt entities. These data are from the National Center for Charitable Statistics as constructed by McVeigh et al. (2014).

We include several county-level control variables: population size, median income, median commute time. Of note, we include commute time as protest events may be less likely to occur in sprawling suburbs with a geographic focus for events. The Gini measure is from McVeigh et al. (2014), and the other three controls are from the ACS.

Patterning of protest: regression analysis for country

We examine patterns in the geographic distribution of protests. Here our focus is on comparing the cumulative turnout in protests events, focusing on differences in the correlates of events with racial focus and immigration focus. The dependent variable is cumulative attendance at protests coded as either racial (Model 1 and 2) or Immigration (Model 3 and 4). Models 2 and 4 control for the attendance at the 2017 Women's March because these initial protests likely spurred subsequent mobilization. To control for the skew in the data, we use an inverse hyperbolic sine transformation, which can be interpreted as similar to log transformation but has the advantage of being defined when the dependent value is 0.

Table 9.1 reports the impact of political, movement, and threat factors on the size of protest attendance for racial and immigration protests. Partisanship is a critical factor for both type of events, with attendance positively correlated with Democratic voting patterns. Counties where Hillary Clinton, the Democratic nominee in 2016, did well had more protesters than counties where she fared poorly. However, the Democratic vote share is no longer significant after controlling for turnout in the prior Women's March.

Movement infrastructure also mattered for both types of protests. Notably, all three measures of previous protest activity, Occupations, BLM, and 2006 immigration protests, were each positively associated with attendance at both kinds of protest events. The impact of previous immigration protests spilled over to 2017 racial protests, and, likewise, earlier BLM protests positively impacted 2017 immigration protests. The presence of local advocacy organizations was positively related to attendance at racial protests (without controlling for Women's March turnout) but not immigration protests.

While there is no evidence of an impact of our threat measures on attendance at racial protests, the percentage foreign-born in a county was positively correlated with attendance at immigration protests. This relationship is likely because foreign-born populations were more directly threatened by proposed Trump

Table 9.1 Regression analysis of cumulative county anti-Trump protests attendance, 2017

	Race	Immigration
Partisan:		
% Dem Vote 2016	0.107**	0.132***
	(2.82)	(3.86)
Movement Infrastructure:		
OWS occupation	0.329***	0.485***
	(10.52)	(17.07)
BLM Protests	0.423***	0.336***
	(13.74)	(12.03)
2006 Immigration Protests	0.372***	0.407***
	(12.53)	(15.10)
Advocacy orgs, rate	0.072**	-0.000
	(2.63)	(-0.01)
Threat:		
Black, %	−0.031	−0.097**
	(−0.94)	(−3.25)
Latinx, %	−0.058	−0.042
	(−1.59)	(−1.27)
Foreign born, %	0.046	0.211***
	(1.11)	(5.65)
Controls:		
Median income, ln	−0.111**	−0.034
	(−3.01)	(−1.03)
College grad, %	0.259***	0.161***
	(6.21)	(4.26)
Population, ln	0.468***	0.312***
	(12.42)	(9.15)
Commute time	−0.085**	−0.013
	(−3.18)	(−0.53)
Constant	0.734***	0.620***
	(30.32)	(28.22)
Observations	3139	3139

Notes: All explanatory variables standardized. Dependent variable transformed using inverse hyperbolic sine to control for skew. * $p < 0.05$, ** $p < 0.01$, *** $p < 0.001$

administration policies and responded in those places with greater constituencies. The pattern related to race is more surprising because the initial wave of Black Lives Matter protest was shaped by the racial composition of localities (Williamson et al. 2018). However, those protests were spurred by local threats of lethal policing in Black communities. By contrast, many of the race-focused protests were mobilized as resistance to statements by Trump or in solidarity with protesters against the racial violence in Charlottesville. In other words, they had become nationalized. In contrast, Zepeda-Millán and Wallace (2018) find that immigrant rights activists have shifted their strategies downward as the national political opportunity structure has become more hostile. Thus, the specific form of threat is critical in determining whether local population characteristics shape protest.

Conclusion

Overall, we find that nonviolent racial and immigration protests were a central part of the Resistance protest events during 2017. Combined, they constituted a quarter of anti-Trump protests during this period. While events occurred frequently, there were several periods of high-intensity activism, in particular on the immigration ban and Charlottesville's Unite the Right event. In our regression analysis, we find that attendance at protests on racial and immigration issues was highest in Democratic counties with a prior history of activism. When the level of Women's March protests was controlled, the effect of Democratic voting went to zero, implying that partisanship promoted overall protests but not an especially high focus on Black issues or immigrants. We do find that the size of the immigrant population affected pro-immigrant protests, but there was no effect of Black population size on Black movement protests.

We also highlight relevant limitations of our data and analysis. Our reliance on media reports of protest for our primary dependent variables entails the usual limitations of potential reporting biases. Nevertheless, two characteristics of our data mitigate these concerns. First, we rely on a large number of sources overcoming the typical biases associated with using a small number of news agencies. Second, we focus on a period of heightened public attention to the protest that kept activism and resistance to the Trump administration as a central focus of reporters throughout the period of study.

In this chapter, we have focused on protest events, but it is important to note that activism has taken many other forms. For example, there has been ongoing litigation against Trump administration policies and opposition from employees in federal agencies. Several thousand local organizations affiliated with a national network, indivisible.org. Nevertheless, understanding the scope of protest and the forces driving it is important for multiple reasons.

First, protest spurs other forms of activism by drawing people into more sustained participation and organizing, by working in tandem with litigation and other tactics, and by inspiring different kinds of resistance. Second, although too early to gauge with precision, protest likely shapes broader attention to activist's grievances and claims and US politics. For example, Collingwood, Lajevardi, and Oskooii's (2018) analysis of the Muslim Ban indicates that protest helped shift public opinion against it. Protest may be shaping other political dynamics by expanding support for organizations opposed to the administration and its policies.

Our analyses document the centrality of immigration and race to emerging opposition to the Trump administration, and they motivate several questions for future scholarship.

Comparatively, it will be important to examine the way different constituencies respond to multiple threats. In this case, this includes racial groups and immigrants as we have done and other groups such as teachers, scientists, and LGBTQ communities. Looking forward, this case also presents opportunities for understanding the consequences of protest and movements include possible impacts on public opinion, political parties, and public policy.

References

Almeida, Paul D. 2003. "Opportunity Organizations and Threat-Induced Contention: Protest Waves in Authoritarian Settings." *American Journal of Sociology* 109 (2): 345–400.

Almeida, Paul. 2010. "Social Movement Partyism: Collective Action and Oppositional Political Parties." *Strategic Alliances: Coalition Building and Social Movements* 34: 170–196.

Almeida, Paul D. 2018. "The role of threat in collective action." Pp. 43–62 in *The Wiley Blackwell Companion to Social Movements*, edited by D. Snow, S. Soule, H. Kriesi, and H. McCammon. Chichester, UK: John Wiley & Sons.

Almeida, Paul and Nella Van Dyke. 2014. "Social Movement Partyism and the Tea Party's Rapid Mobilization." Pp. 55–71 in *Understanding the Tea Party Movement*, edited by N. Van Dyke and D. S. Meyer. Burlington, VT: Ashgate.

Andrews, Kenneth T. and Charles Seguin. 2015. "Group Threat and Policy Change: The Spatial Dynamics of Prohibition Politics, 1890–1919." *American Journal of Sociology* 121 (2): 475–510.

Bacon, John and Alan Gomez. 2017. "Protests Against Trump's Immigration Plan Rolling in More than 30 cities." USA Today. Retrieved November 5, 2018. https://www.usatoday.com/story/news/nation/2017/01/29/homeland-security-judges-stay-has-little-impact-travel-ban/97211720/.

Bada, Xóchitl, Jonathan Fox, Elvia Zazueta, and Ingrid García. 2006. "Immigrant Rights Marches, Spring 2006." http://www.wilsoncenter.org/sites/default/files/Data.pdf.

Bethea, Charles. 2016. "The Crowdsourced Guide to Fighting Trump's Agenda." *The New Yorker.* December 16. https://www.newyorker.com/news/news-desk/the-crowd-sourced-guide-to-fighting-trumps-agenda.

Bialik, Kristen. 2018. "ICE Arrests Went Up in 2017, with Biggest Increases in Florida, Northern Texas, Oklahoma." Pew Research Center. February 8. http://www.pewresearch.org/fact-tank/2018/02/08/ice-arrests-went-up-in-2017-with-biggest-increases-in-florida-northern-texas-oklahoma/.

Bobo, Lawrence D. 2017. The Empire Strikes Back: Fall of the Postracial Myth and Stirrings of Renewed White Supremacy. *Du Bois Review: Social Science Research on Race* 14 (1): 1–5.

Bruce, Katherine McFarland. 2016. *Pride Parades: How a Parade Change the World.* New York: New York University Press.

Chenoweth, Erica and Jeremy Pressman. 2017. "This is what we learned by counting the women's marches," *The Washington Post*, February 7, 2017. https://www.washingtonpost.com/news/monkey-cage/wp/2017/02/07/this-is-what-we-learned-by-counting-the-womens-marches/.

Collingwood, Loren, Nazita Lajevardi and Kassra A.R. Oskooii. 2018. "A Change of Heart? Why Individual-Level Public Opinion Shifted against Trump's "Muslim Ban"." *Political Behavior*. doi:10.1007/s11109-017-9439-z.

Crowd Counting Consortium. n.d. "Crowd Counting Consortium." Retrieved November 10, 2018. https://sites.google.com/view/crowdcountingconsortium.

Einwohner, Rachel and Thomas Maher. 2011. "Threat Assessment and Collective-Action Emergence: Death-Camp and Ghetto Resistance during the Holocaust." *Mobilization: An International Quarterly* 16 (2): 127–146.

Fausset, Richard and Alan Feuer. 2017. "Far-Right Groups Surge Into National View in Charlottesville." *The New York Times*. August 13. https://www.nytimes.com/2017/08/13/us/far-right-groups-blaze-into-national-view-in-cha rlottesville.html.

Fetner, Tina. 2008. *How the Religious Right Shaped Lesbian and Gay Activism.* Minneapolis, MN: University of Minnesota Press.

Fisher, Dana R., Dawn M. Dow and Rashawn Ray. 2017. "Intersectionality Takes It to the Streets: Mobilizing across Diverse Interests for the Women's March." *Science Advances* 3 (9): 1–8.

Francescani, Chris and Alex Dobuzinskis. 2017. "May Day Rallies across U.S. Target Trump Immigration Policy." Reuters. May 1. https://www.reuters.com/article/us-may-day-usa-protests-idUSKBN17X1H1.

Garza, Alicia. 2014. "A Herstory of the #BlackLivesMatter Movement by Alicia Garza." *The Feminist Wire*. October 7. http://www.thefeministwire.com/2014/10/blacklivesmatter-2/.

Gonzales, Roberto G., Veronica Terriquez, and Stephen P.Ruszczyk. "Becoming DACAmented: Assessing the Short-Term Benefits of Deferred Action for Childhood Arrivals (DACA)." *American Behavioral Scientist* 58 (14): 1852–1872.

Grammich, Clifford Anthony. 2012. "2010 Us Religion Census: Religious Congregations and Membership Study: An Enumeration by Nation, State, and County Based on Data Reported for 236 Religious Groups." Harvard University: Association of Statisticians of American Religious Bodies.

Hamner, Ben. 2016. "2016 Presidential Elections." Retrieved November 10, 2018. https://www.kaggle.com/benhamner/2016-us-election.

Heaney, Michael T and Fabio Rojas. 2015. *Party in the Street: The Antiwar Movement and the Democratic Party after 9/11*: New York: Cambridge University Press.

Heaney, Michael T. 2017. "Activism in an Era of Partisan Polarization." *PS: Political Science and Politics* 50 (4): 1000–1003.

Kaste, Martin. 2017. "Trump Threatens 'Sanctuary' Cities with Loss of Federal Funds." *NPR*. January 26. https://www.npr.org/sections/thetwo-way/2017/01/26/511899896/trumps-threatens-sanctuary-cities-with-loss-of-federal-funds.

Kopan, Tal. 2017. "Trump's Executive Orders Dramatically Expand Power of Immigration Officers." CNN. January 28. https://www.cnn.com/2017/01/28/politics/donald-trump-immigration-detention-deportations-enforcement/index.html.

Law, Anna O. 2017. "This Is How Trump's Deportations Differ from Obama's." *The Washington Post*. May 3, 2017. https://www.washingtonpost.com/news/monkey-cage/wp/2017/05/03/this-is-how-trumps-deportations-differ-from-obamas.

Leung, Tommy and Nathan Perkins, 2017. "Count Love: Aggregating protest data." Accessed November 10, 2018. http://datadrivenjournalism.net/featured_projects/count_love_aggregating_protest_data.

Maher, Thomas. 2010. "Threat, Resistance, and Collective Action: The Cases of Sobibor, Treblinka, and Auschwitz." *American Sociological Review* 75 (2): 252–272.

McAdam, Doug. 1982. *Political Process and the Development of Black Insurgency*. Chicago: University of Chicago Press.

McAdam, Doug and Sidney Tarrow. 2010. "Ballots and Barricades: On the Reciprocal Relationship between Elections and Social Movements." *Perspectives on Politics* 8 (02): 529–542.

McAdam, Doug and Karina Kloos. 2014. *Deeply Divided: Racial Politics and Social Movements in Post-War America*. Oxford: Oxford University Press.

McKenna, Elizabeth and Hahrie Han. 2014. *Groundbreakers: How Obama's 2.2 Million Volunteers Transformed Campaigning in America*. Oxford: Oxford University Press.

McVeigh, Rory. 2009. *The Rise of the Ku Klux Klan: Right-Wing Movements and National Politics*. Minneapolis, MN: University of Minnesota Press.

McVeigh, Rory, Kraig Beyerlein, Burrel Vann Jr., and Priyamvada Trivedi. 2014. "Educational Segregation, Tea Party Organizations, and Battles over Distributive Justice." *American Sociological Review* 79 (4): 630–652.

Meyer, David S. and Suzanne Staggenborg. 1998. "Countermovement Dynamics in Federal Systems: A Comparison of Abortion Politics in Canada and the United States." *Research in Political Sociology* 8: 209–240.

Meyer, David S. and Nancy Whittier. 1994. "Social Movement Spillover." *Social Problems* 41 (2): 277–298.

Morice, Jane. 2015. "Thousands of 'Freedom Fighters' in Cleveland for First National Black Lives Matter Conference." cleveland.com. July 25. https://www.cleveland.com/metro/index.ssf/2015/07/thousands_of_freedom_fighters.html.

Morris, Aldon. 1981. "Black Southern Student Sit-in Movement: An Analysis of Internal Organization." *American Sociological Review* 46: 744–767.

Oberschall, Anthony. 1973. *Social Conflict and Social Movements*. Englewood Cliffs, NJ: Prentice-Hall.

Oliver, Pamela. 2017. "The Ethnic Dimensions in Social Movements." *Mobilization: An International Quarterly* 22 (4): 395–416.

Pearce, Matt. 2017. "Chanting 'Blood and Soil!' White Nationalists with Torches March on University of Virginia." *Los Angeles Times*. August 11. http://www.latimes.com/nation/la-na-white-virginia-rally-20170811-story.html.

Phillip, Abby and Cindy Boren. 2017. "Players, Owners Unite as Trump Demands NFL 'Fire or Suspend' Players or Risk Fan Boycott." *The Washington Post*. September 24. https://www.washingtonpost.com/news/post-politics/wp/2017/09/24/trump-demands-nfl- teams-fire-or-suspend-players-or-risk-fan-boycott.

Ridgley, Jennifer. 2008. "Cities of Refuge: Immigration Enforcement, Police and the Insurgent Genealogies of Citizenship in U.S. Sanctuary Cities." *Urban Geography* 29 (1): 53–77.

Rim, Kathy H. 2009. "Latino and Asian American Mobilization in the 2006 Immigration Protests." *Social Science Quarterly* 90 (3): 703–721.

Robbins, Liz and Annie Correal. 2017. "On a 'Day Without Immigrants,' Workers Show Their Presence by Staying Home." *The New York Times*. February 16. https://www.nytimes.com/2017/02/16/nyregion/day-without-immigrants-boycott-trump-policy.html.

Rogers, Simon. 2011. "Occupy Protests around the World: Full List Visualised." *Guardian*. November 14. https://www.theguardian.com/news/datablog/2011/oct/17/occupy-protests-world-list-map #data.

Sacchetti, Maria and Perry Stein. 2017. "'We Are America': DACA Recipients, Supporters Say They Are Not Going Anywhere." *The Washington Post*. Retrieved November 5, 2018. https://www.washingtonpost.com/local/immigration/dacas-day-of-reckoning-white-house-protests-on-the-day-of-trumps-decision/2017/09/04/f5ca534a-9186-9111e7-89fa- bb822a46da5b_story.html.

Siegel, Rachel. 2017. "Thousands Rally Outside Capitol to Demand DACA Solution; Md. Lawmakers Arrested." *The Washington Post*. September 5. https://www.washingtonpost.com/local/immigration/thousands-rally-outside-capitol-to-demand-daca-solution-md-lawmakers-arrested/2017/12/06/4fcaa27e-dabf-11e7-b1a8–62589434a581_story.html.

Silverman, Ellie and Michael Laris. 2017. "Charlottesville Victim: 'She Was There Standing Up for What Was Right.'" *The Washington Post*. December 7. https://www.washingtonpost.com/local/public-safety/charlottesville-victim-she-was-there-standing-up-for-what-was-right/2017/08/13/00d6b034–8035–11e7-b359–315a3617c767b_story.html?utm_term=.fbb327cdfa93.

Schlozman, Daniel. 2015. *When Movements Anchor Parties: Electoral Alignments in American History*. Princeton, NJ: Princeton University Press.

Shear, Michael D. and Julie H. Davis. 2017. "Trump Moves to End DACA and Calls on Congress to Act." *The New York Times*. September 5. https://www.nytimes.com/2017/09/05/us/politics/trump-daca-dreamers-immigration.html.

Skocpol, Theda and Vanessa Williamson. 2012. *The Tea Party and the Remaking of Republican Conservatism*. Oxford: Oxford University Press.

Staggenborg, S. (1998). "Social Movement Communities and Cycles of Protest: The Emergence and Maintenance of a Local Women's Movement." *Social Problems* 45 (2): 180–204.

Taylor, Keeanga-Yamahtta. 2016. *From #BlackLivesMatter to Black Liberation*. Chicago: Haymarket Books.

Terriquez, Veronica. 2015. "Intersectional Mobilization, Social Movement Spillover, and Queer Youth Leadership in the Immigrant Rights Movement." *Social Problems* 62 (3): 343–362.

Thrush, Glenn and Maggie Haberman. 2017. "Trump Gives White Supremacists an Unequivocal Boost." *The New York Times*. August 15. https://www.nytimes.com/2017/08/15/us/politics/trump-charlottesville-white-nationalists.html.

Van Dyke, N. and S.A. Soule 2002. "Structural Social Change and the Mobilizing Effect of Threat: Explaining Levels of Patriot and Militia Organizing in the United States." *Social Problems* 49 (4): 497–520.

Voss, Kim, and Irene Bloemraad, eds. 2011. *Rallying for Immigrant Rights: The Fight for Inclusion in 21st Century America*. Berkeley, CA: University of California Press.

Walsh, Edward J. 1981. "Resource Mobilization and Citizen Protest in Communities around Three Mile Island." *Social Problems* 29: 1–21.

Weffer, Simon E., Rodrigo Dominguez-Martinez, and Raymond Jenkins. 2018. "Take a Knee." *Contexts* 17 (3): 66–68.

Williamson, Vanessa, Kris-Stella Trump and Katherine Levine Einstein. 2018. "Black Lives Matter: Evidence That Police-Caused Deaths Predict Protest Activity." *Perspectives on Politics* 16 (2): 400–415.

Wyche, Steve. 2016. "Colin Kaepernick Explains Why He Sat During National Anthem." NFL. August 27. http://www.nfl.com/news/story/0ap3000000691077/article/colin-kaepernick-explains-protest-of-national-anthem.

Zepeda-Millán, Chris. 2016. "Weapons of the (Not So) Weak: Immigrant Mass Mobilization in the U.S. South." *Critical Sociology* 42 (2): 269–287.

Zepeda-Millán, C., 2017. *Latino Mass Mobilization: Immigration, Racialization, and Activism*. New York: Cambridge University Press.

Zepeda-Millán, Chris and Sophia Wallace. 2018. "Mobilizing for Immigrant Rights under Trump." Pp. 90–108 in *The Resistance: The Dawn of the Anti-Trump Opposition Movement*, edited by David Meyer and Sidney Tarrow. New York: Oxford University Press.

Index

Note: **Bold** page numbers refer to tables and *italic* page numbers refer to figures; Page numbers followed by 'n' refer to notes.

AB540 171, 172
abeyance 18, 80, 112–16, 119, 131, 132
actions, non-state 144
active abeyance 18, 112–34; opportunities and reemergence 124–30; in WSM 117–18
activism 112–14, 118–21, 131, 148, 149, 164, 175, 178, 216, 221
actors, marginalized 187, 203, 204
Advancing Students for a Stronger Economy Tomorrow (ASSET) bill 176
affirmative action programs 42–5, 49, 58, 59
Affirmative Discrimination 37
Affordable Care Act 77
agents 9, 146, 147, 149
Alexander, Michelle 63, 68, 89
Alimahomed, Sabrina 150
American Indians 3, 4, 10
Americans 3, 32, 34, 44, 48, 66, 101, 113, 123, 186, 198
Anspach, Rachel 77
anti-Arab 141, 145, 153
anti-Arab/Muslim repression 147
Anti-Defamation League 126
Apuzzo, Matt 146
Arab Americans 18, 140–60; racialization and repression of 145–8
Arabs 18, 141, 143, 145, 151, 152
armored vehicles 91, 102, 103
Assata Daughters 72
Atkinson, Paul 190
attendance 66, 219, 221
Azab, Marian 155, 160n1

backward people 4, 5
Bada, Xóchitl 219

Bail, Christopher A. 92, 105
Baker, Kelly J. 129
Baltimore 71, 72, 75
beliefs 3, 28, 41–3, 91, 92, 140, 145, 146, 187, 188
Bell, Joyce M. 68
Bell, Susan 189
Benford, Robert D. 29, 93
Berbrier, Mitch 132
biases 2, 148, 221
Black Enterprise article 37
Black Guerrilla Family 65
Black leaders 37, 39, 43, 45, 47
Black Lives Matter 69–78; in Madison, Wisconsin 70–1
Black Lives movement 63–81; debates about funding 74–6; proactive agenda 73–4; White counter-revolt, surviving 76–8
Black mobilization 65
Black movement 11, 12, 17, 66, 78, 80, 94
Black organizations 11, 36, 39, 43, 47, 68, 78, 79
Black Organizing for Leadership and Dignity (BOLD) 69
Black Panther Party 65
Black Panthers 14, 63, 65
Black people 14, 15, 47, 48, 64, 67, 69, 74, 89, 91, 100, 102, 103, 215, 216
Black poverty 57
Black Power 65, 75, 78, 79; movement 65
Black protests 64, 67, 79
Black Twitter 69–70
Black urban rebellions 14
Black urban riots 16

228 *Index*

Black women 55, 57, 66, 67, 216
Black Youth Project 72
Blee, Kathleen 118
BLM protests 218, 219
Bobo, Lawrence 60n1
Bourdieu, Pierre 106n2
Boyte, Harry C. 133n4
Bracey, Glenn E. 10
Braz, Rose 66
Broidy, Lisa 143
Bush, George 49
busing 30, 31, 36, 43
Byfield, Natalie P. 63
BYP100 72

Cadora, Eric 68
Cainkar, Louise A. 145
California 76, 150, 164, 169–71, 173, 174, 178, 189
Camp, Jordan T. 66
Camp of the Saints 125
Carter, Jimmy 36, 38
Charlottesville 20, 127, 128, 208, 210, 213, 214, 221
chengguan 7
Chicago 63, 72, 75, 186–205
Chicago Tribune 46
Childs, John Brown 46–7
China 1, 4–13, 15
Civil Rights Act 59
Civil Rights Congress (CRC) 64
civil rights movement 4, 15, 17, 27, 29, 31, 33, 43, 63
claims-making practices 192, 200, 203
classic frame theory 91, 97
Cleveland coalition 72
coalition 46, 47, 51, 66, 71, 73, 77, 172, 214
Cohen, Cathy 72
Collingwood, Loren 222
Colored People 26, 38, 39, 55, 56
coming-out narratives 205n5
commitment 38, 40, 43, 53, 92, 116, 118, 122, 123, 132
comprehensive immigration reform 167, 169, 174, 175, 179, 180
conference 1, 49, 66, 72, 74
congruence 91–4, 97
consequences, biographical repression 141, 143, 145, 147, 149, 151, 153, 155, 159
contentious politics 115
control variables 153–4
Cordery, William 75, 76
countermovement dynamics 11–12
countermovements 16, 17, 30, 59, 167

counter-protesters 127, 128
country-level data 218–19
Couto, Richard A. 118
crime 12, 35, 45, 46, 55, 64, 71, 99, 100
criminal justice reform groups 67–9
Crisis magazine 30
Crossley, Alison D. 114
Crowd Counting Consortium (CCC) 209
cultural objects 92, 93, 102, 106
Cunningham, David 9, 141

Dafnos, Tia 8
Dagan, David 68
Dalai Lama 5, 12, 21n4
Davenport, Christian 14, 142
Davies, T.R. 29, 57
Davis, Angela 66
defensive adaptations 26–60;
   Black-organization coalitions 39–40;
   coalitions, expanding 51; corporate America, targeting 50–1; desperate measures and frame capitulation 48–57; direct action 51–2; hegemonic master frame 53–7; "new racism" recognition 48–9; to "post-racial" frame 34–5; programmatic and goal adaptations, post-racial frame 40–1; public opinion, molding 49–50; self-help 52–3; voiceless minorities 38–9; Whites and Blacks 32
Deferred Action for Childhood Arrivals (DACA) program 165, 169, 174–6, 179–80, 210, 212; protests 212
De Genova, Nicholas 165
Delamont, Sara 190
democracy 10–11
dependent variables 153–4, 219
deportations 16, 80, 141, 165, 169, 173, 175, 176, 193, 198, 200, 201, 212
detention 8, 16, 169, 173, 176, 177
Detroit Arab American Study (DAAS) 152
Development, Relief and Education for Alien Minors (DREAM) Act 172–3, 178, 180, 181n1, 186, 201, 202
discourse, countermovement 17
discrimination 2, 4, 17, 18, 26, 33–7, 41, 42, 44, 144, 152
Dream Defenders 72
Dreyfuss, Joel 37
DuBois, W.E.B. 74

Earl, Jennifer 142
educational access 172, 175, 176, 179, 180
Einstein, Katherine Levine 70

electoral mobilization 216
Ellingson, Stephen 93
emotions 148, 150, 151, 155, 187–9, 192–4, 199, 201, 203–5
Enriquez, Laura 169
Equal Educational Opportunities Act of 1972 30–1
Essence 74
ethnic conflict 11–12
ethnicity 1–16; China 4–6; United States of America 3–4
ethnic movements 16–20
ethnography 189–91
Evans, Sarah M. 133n4

fear 155
Ferguson, Karen 75
Ferguson, MO 89–107
Fernandes, Sujatha 76
Ferree, Myra Marx 142
Fine, Gary Alan 188
Fletcher, Bill Jr. 67
Fletcher, Will 66
formal movement organizations 90, 188
Fox, Jonathan 219
frames 30, 42, 49, 57, 89–95, 106, 166, 167, 172; alignment 89–107; theory 91, 92
framing 18, 31, 33, 41, 56, 89–91, 93–5, 99, 105, 106, 167, 188; contests 28–9
Francis, Megan 75
Frantz, Courtney 76
Freeman, Jo 131
free spaces 20, 114, 118, 123
Fullilove v. Klutznick 49

Gamson, William A. 188
Ganz, Marshall 188
García, Ingrid 219
gatherings 120, 121, 170; families and informal 118–21
Genova 165, 175
Georgia 19, 173, 177–9, 189
Georgia Undocumented Youth Alliance (GUYA) 178
Gilmore, Ruthie Wilson 66
Glazer, Nathan 37
Goldman, Adam 146
Goldstein, Robert Justin 14
Gordon, Hava Rachel 167
Gould, Deborah B. 189
Graham, Roderick 130
Gramsci, Antonio 106n2
Great Recession 123
Green, David B. 67

Griggs v. Duke Power Company 35
groups, threatened 217, 218
Guardian newspaper 218

Hamner, Ben 218
Hate Map 133n6
Heatherton, Christina 66
high-risk 131, 149, 168, 170
high school 16, 38, 67, 165, 176, 202, 203
Hill-Snowdon Foundation 75
Hoffman, David S. 122
Holden, Daphne 189
home schooling 119
Hooks, Benjamin L. 38, 50, 52, 54–6

immigrant rights 20, 80, 167, 168, 180, 186, 213; movement 20, 72, 168, 173
immigrants 15, 16, 19, 76, 79, 80, 125, 165–9, 174, 176, 210, 213; coercive exclusion and policing of 15–16
Immigrant Youth Justice League (IYJL) 189–90, 193, 194
Immigration and Customs Enforcement (ICE) 15, 16, 126, 165, 176, 177, 210, 212, 213
immigration issues 212, 213
immigration protests 208, 210, 216, 219, 221
independent variables 153–4
informal gatherings 117–20, 131
insurgency 90, 93, 95, 97
insurgent politics 92–4
insurgents 90, 91, 93–5, 97, 101, 105, 106
internet 121–3

Jasper, James M. 189
Jewish-liberal ideology 119
Jim Crow 63
Johnston, Hank 28, 92, 114
Jordan, Vernon 59
Jung, Moon-Kie 10
Justice Reinvestment initiative 68
Justified Anger 71

Kienscherf, Markus 9
King, Mike 15
Kohl-Arenas, Erica 76
Koopmans, Ruud 151
Krysan, Maria 60n1
Ku Klux Klan (KKK) 112–13, 126
Kwon, Yaejoon 10

laissez-faire liberalism 46–7
Lajevardi, Nazita 222

Lauderdale, Diane S. 150
Lee, Chungmei 59
legal cynicism 151, 153, 154, 158, 159
LGBTQ communities 222
Liberty Net 122
Liu, Callie Watkins 143
localized political contexts 164–81; Atlanta, Georgia 177–9; Denver, Colorado 174–6; Los Angeles, California 171–4
Los Angeles 19, 65, 78, 150, 164, 168–74, 176, 180
Los Angeles Times 30
lynching 12, 64

Marquez, Benjamin 75
Martinez, Lisa M. 167
Marx, Gary T. 14, 28
mass incarceration 14, 17, 63, 64, 67–9, 78, 80
Matthews, Katherine D. 14
McAdam, Doug 93, 142
McCammon, Holly J. 27
McDonnell, Terence E. 92, 105
McVeigh, Rory 219
Menjivar, Cecilia 168
Meyer, David S. 167
Meyers, Michael 49
Million Hoodies Movement for Justice 77
Million Man March 78
Mixed Martial Arts (MMA) 129
Montgomery bus boycott 143
Morris, Aldon D. 32, 75, 78
Moss, Dana M. 92
movement constituencies 217–18
movement-countermovement 17, 18
movement expansion 132
Movement for Black Lives (M4BL) 74, 76, 77
movement infrastructure 20, 209, 216–17, 219
movement organizations 17, 75, 217
The Movement Today 70, 77
music 121–3
MXGM (Malcolm X Grassroot Movement) 73

Naber, Nadine 150
narratives 19, 20, 118, 187, 196, 203–5
national anthem 214, 215
National Association for the Advancement of Colored People (NAACP) 26–60, 64; countermovement's rise 30–2; defensive adaptation, Whites and Blacks 32; expanding focus 34–5; organizational restructuring 35; post-racial America, framing 33–4; "post-racial" frame, defensive adaptation 34–5; racial project's "class not race" frame 36–7
national events 64, 70
National Research Council 68
The New Jim Crow 68, 89
New York 39, 40, 53, 55–7, 65–7, 69, 70, 73, 78, 79, 189
New York Times 30
Niagara Falls conference 74
Nicholls, Walter J. 166
9/11, attacks 145–7, 150
Noakes, John A. 9, 28
Non-Han minorities 4
non-state actors 11, 69, 141, 142, 144, 145, 147, 159–60
nonviolent resistance 1

Oliver, Pamela 14, 92, 143
Omi, Michael 10, 27
Operation Boulder 146
Orfield, Gary 59
Oskooii, Kassra A.R. 222
Our Madison Plan 71
Oyakawa, Michelle 76

pacification 8, 9, 12, 14, 17; policing in US 13–15; of populations 8–9; in Tibet and Xinjiang 12–13
Packnett, Ferguson Tweeter Brittany 78
participant observation 117, 170, 190
partisanship 216
Pena, A.M. 29, 57
Philly Coalition 72
Pierce, Chester M. 142
Plummer, Ken 188
police actions 95, 99, 102–4; assessing racism of 99–101; frame alignment process, repressive action 101–5; Twitter 95–7
police brutality 35, 64, 72, 174, 215, 216
police killings 65, 67, 70, 71, 73, 77, 79, 89, 98, 101, 102, 105
police violence 18, 64, 65, 67, 69, 71, 74, 78, 79, 215
political activities 151, 155, 158
political opportunities 18, 112–34, 166; theory 164, 166–8, 180
Politico 75

politics of recognition 203–5
Polletta, Francesca 133n4, 188
populations 1, 4, 5, 8, 9, 20, 63, 97, 143, 145, 147, 154, 159, 160
post-9/11 America 140–60
post-racial discourse 17, 34, 36, 37, 48, 58
practical concerns 97–9
practical resonance 89–107
private abeyance structures 118–21
protests 20, 79, 155, 159, 208–10, 212–17, 219, 221; communities, immigration and race 215–18; documenting 209; on immigrants and immigration 210–15; patterning, descriptive analysis 210; patterning, regression analysis for country 219–21, **220**; on race and racial inequality 213–15; racial, ethnic, and immigration 208–22
psychological distress 144, 152–4, 158, 159

race/racism 1–17, 26, 42, 45, 47, 52, 54, 55, 58, 99–101, 130, 132, 208; China 4–6; China and United States, racial construction comparing 6; China and United States, state capacity comparing 6–8; United States of America 3–4
racial disparities 70
racial equality 50
racial minority populations 141–3, 145, 159
racial movements 16–20
racial project 27–8; class not race frame amplification 45–6; code words 43; color-blind frame 43–5; reverse discrimination 41–2
racist policing 89–107; frame 18, 89, 90, 94, 105, 106, 106n1
Ransby, Barbara 67, 70, 72, 77
Reagan, Ronald 43, 44
reflexivity 189–91
Reid, Lori 189
repression 8, 14, 21n5, 115, 140, 141–5, 148–55, 158–60; biographical consequences of 140–60, *149,* **154,** *158*; Black movements against 64–7; criminal justice reform groups 67–9; re-conceptualizing 141–5; resisting 63–81; *see also individual entries*
repressive incidents 152, 153
research design 94–5
resistance: in Tibet and Xinjiang 12–13
reverse discrimination 41, 42, 48, 53
The Revolution Will Not Be Funded 76

Rios, Victor M. 14
Robinson, Alisa 69, 81n5
Rodriquez, Dylan 76
Roe v. Wade 29
Rogers, Jamala 66, 67
Rogers, Simon 218
rose-petal memorial 103–6

Sa'di, Ahmad H. 15
Saguy, Abigail 169
Santoro, Wayne A. 143, 155, 160n1
SB 90 174–6
Schroer, Todd 122
Schuman, Howard 60n1, 60n2
segmented assimilation theory 165–8
self-help 52, 54, 57, 65, 73
semi-publics spaces 121–3
Shrock, Douglas 189
Shultziner, Doron 143
Silver, Alexis 169
Sinyangwe, Samuel 78
situational dynamics 94
Smith, Andrea 76
Snow, David A. 29, 91, 92
social construction, life stories 191–2
social control 7–9
social media 90, 130
social movement: abeyance 113–16, 131; actors 27, 28, 115, 187, 203; field 159, 160; groups 8, 27; practice 187, 188, 192, 200, 203
social movement organization (SMO) 27, 28, 67, 89, 91, 92, 140, 170
social movements: contemporary 164; and protest 218
social movement theory 217
"soft" repression 142
Southern California 117, 171–3
Southern Poverty Law Center (SPLC) 123, 144, 147
Spencer, Richard 129
spillover 216–17
Staggenborg, Suzanne 29, 167
state actions 28, 142, 144, 147, 151
state actors 17, 18, 28, 144, 146
state organization 68, 69
state repression 14, 18, 114
state violence 64–6, 79
Steeh, Charlotte 60n1
Steinberg, Marc W. 92
Steinman, Erich 10
storytelling 186–205, **192,** 193, 195, 196, 200, 201, 203–5; claims-making practice 200–3; community-building

practice 193–6; mobilizing practice 196–200; unapologetic and unafraid 200–3
surveillance 7–9, 14, 16, 63, 146

Tarrow, Sidney 115, 151
Tavory, Iddo 92, 105
Taylor, Keeanga-Yamahtta 64, 67–70, 72, 73
Taylor, Verta 113, 114, 116, 118, 131, 132
technological opportunities 128–30
Teles, Steven M. 68
threatened groups 217–18
Tibetans 5, 7, 12, 13
Tilly, Charles 141
Transactional Records Access Clearinghouse (TRAC) 176
triangulation 189–91
Trump, Donald J. 124, 125, 127, 208–22
Trump, Kris-Stella 70
TRUST Act 173

undocumented immigrants 19, 126, 164–6, 168, 171, 177, 196, 212, 213, 217
undocumented youth 165, 168, 172, 173, 178–80, 186, 187, 192, 193, 196, 197, 202, 203–5; activism 19, 164, 166, 168, 169, 186–205; activists 166, 167, 170–8, 186, 191, 196; community 194–6, 203, 204; mobilization 19, 164–81, 187–90; movement 164, 167–73, 175, 178, 180, 187, 189, 192, 203
United States 1, 3, 4, 6–8, 10, 41, 48, 49, 171, 186, 189, 190, 212

"Unite the Right" (UTR) rally 127
U.S. post-racial project 26–60

verbal insults 144, 147, 153, 154
Virginia's Law 181n3
Vogel, Kenneth P. 75

Wacquant, Loic 14
Wallace, Sophia 221
Ward, Geoff 12
Washington Post 37
Weddington, George 70
Wheaton, Sara 75
white counter-movements 20
white movements 11, 17, 143
white supremacist activism 112–13, 117, 132
white supremacist movements (WSM) 12, 115, 117–18, 127
white supremacy 3, 11, 12, 17, 18, 76, 112–34
Whittier, Nancy 118, 189
Williamson, Vanessa 70
Winant, Howard 10, 27
Wisconsin reform network 68
women 29, 32, 33, 37, 38, 54–7, 66, 74, 79, 144, 145, 188, 189

Xinjiang 7

Young, Gifted and Black (YGB) Coalition 71

Zazueta, Elvia 219
Zepeda-Millán, Chris 221
Zogby, John 147

Printed in the USA
CPSIA information can be obtained
at www.ICGtesting.com
LVHW011136150324
774517LV00040B/1619